Advance Praise for *Head First iPhone Development*

"The great thing about this book is its simple, step-by-step approach. It doesn't try to teach everything—it just launches you right into building iPhone applications in a friendly, convers[...] book for people who already know how to write code and just want to get st[...] building iPhone applications."

— Eric Shephard, owner of Syndicomm

"*Head First iPhone Development* was clearly crafted to get you easily creating, using and learning iPhone technologies without needing a lot of background with Macintosh development tools."

— Joe Heck, Seattle Xcoders founder

"This book is infuriating! Some of us had to suffer and learn iPhone development 'the hard way,' and we're bitter that the jig is up."

— Mike Morrison, Stalefish Labs founder

"*Head First iPhone Development* continues the growing tradition of taking complex technical subjects and increasing their accessibility without reducing the depth and scope of the content. iPhone Development is a steep learning curve to climb by any measure, but with *Head First iPhone Development*, that curve is accompanied with pre-rigged ropes, a harness, and an experienced guide! I recommend this book for anyone who needs to rapidly improve their understanding of developing for this challenging and exciting platform."

— Chris Pelsor, snogboggin.com

"Another nice thing about *Head First Java, 2nd Edition* is that it whets the appetite for more. With later coverage of more advanced topics such as Swing and RMI, you just can't wait to dive into those APIs and code that flawless, 100000-line program on java.net that will bring you fame and venture-capital fortune. There's also a great deal of material, and even some best practices, on networking and threads—my own weak spot. In this case, I couldn't help but crack up a little when the authors use a 1950s telephone operator—yeah, you got it, that lady with a beehive hairdo that manually hooks in patch lines—as an analogy for TCP/IP ports... you really should go to the bookstore and thumb through *Head First Java, 2nd Edition*. Even if you already know Java, you may pick up a thing or two. And if not, just thumbing through the pages is a great deal of fun."

> **— Robert Eckstein, Java.sun.com, April 2005**

"Of course it's not the range of material that makes *Head First Java* stand out, it's the style and approach. This book is about as far removed from a computer science textbook or technical manual as you can get. The use of cartoons, quizzes, fridge magnets (yep, fridge magnets …). And, in place of the usual kind of reader exercises, you are asked to pretend to be the compiler and compile the code, or perhaps to piece some code together by filling in the blanks or … you get the picture... The first edition of this book was one of our recommended titles for those new to Java and objects. This new edition doesn't disappoint and rightfully steps into the shoes of its predecessor. If you are one of those people who falls asleep with a traditional computer book then this one is likely to keep you awake and learning."

> **— TechBookReport.com, June 2005**

"*Head First Web Design* is your ticket to mastering all of these complex topics, and understanding what's really going on in the world of web design...If you have not been baptized by fire in using something as involved as Dreamweaver, then this book will be a great way to learn good web design. "

> **— Robert Pritchett, MacCompanion, April 2009 Issue**

"Is it possible to learn real web design from a book format? *Head First Web Design* is the key to designing user-friendly sites, from customer requirements to hand-drawn storyboards to online sites that work well. What sets this apart from other 'how to build a web site' books is that it uses the latest research in cognitive science and learning to provide a visual learning experience rich in images and designed for how the brain works and learns best. The result is a powerful tribute to web design basics that any general-interest computer library will find an important key to success."

> **— Diane C. Donovan, California Bookwatch: The Computer Shelf**

"I definitely recommend *Head First Web Design* to all of my fellow programmers who want to get a grip on the more artistic side of the business. "

> **— Claron Twitchell, UJUG**

Other related books from O'Reilly

iPhone SDK Development

Programming the iPhone User Experience

iPhone Game Development

Best iPhone Apps

iPhone SDK Application Development

iPhone Open Application Development

Other books in O'Reilly's *Head First* series

Head First C#

Head First Java

Head First Object-Oriented Analysis and Design (OOA&D)

Head First HTML with CSS and XHTML

Head First Design Patterns

Head First Servlets and JSP

Head First EJB

Head First SQL

Head First Software Development

Head First JavaScript

Head First Physics

Head First Statistics

Head First Ajax

Head First Rails

Head First Algebra

Head First PHP & MySQL

Head First PMP

Head First Web Design

Head First Networking

Head First iPhone Development

Wouldn't it be dreamy if there was a book to help me learn how to develop iPhone apps that was more fun than going to the dentist? It's probably nothing but a fantasy...

Dan Pilone
Tracey Pilone

O'REILLY®

Beijing · Cambridge · Köln · Sebastopol · Taipei · Tokyo

Head First iPhone Development

by Dan Pilone and Tracey Pilone

Published by O'Reilly Media, Inc., 1005 Gravenstein Highway North, Sebastopol, CA 95472.

O'Reilly Media books may be purchased for educational, business, or sales promotional use. Online editions are also available for most titles (*http://my.safaribooksonline.com*). For more information, contact our corporate/institutional sales department: (800) 998-9938 or *corporate@oreilly.com*.

Series Creators:	Kathy Sierra, Bert Bates
Series Editor:	Brett D. McLaughlin
Editors:	Brett D. McLaughlin, Courtney Nash
Design Editor:	Mark Reese
Cover Designer:	Karen Montgomery
Production Editor:	Scott DeLugan
Indexer:	Angela Howard
Proofreader:	Colleen Toporek
Page Viewers:	Vinny and Nick

Printing History:

October 2009: First Edition.

Vinny

Nick

ISBN: 978-0-596-80354-4

To Dan, my best friend and husband, and Vinny and Nick, the best boys a mother could ask for.

—Tracey

This book is dedicated to my family: my parents who made all of this possible, my brothers who keep challenging me, and my wife and sons, who don't just put up with it—they help make it happen.

—Dan

Dan

Tracey

Dan Pilone is a Software Architect for Vangent, Inc., and has led software development teams for the Naval Research Laboratory, UPS, Hughes, and NASA. He's taught graduate and undergraduate Software Engineering at Catholic University in Washington, D.C.

Dan's previous Head First books are *Head First Software Development* and *Head First Algebra*, so he's used to them being a little out of the ordinary, but this is the first book to involve bounty hunters. Even scarier was watching Tracey shift to become a night owl and Apple fan-girl to get this book done.

Dan's degree is in Computer Science with a minor in Mathematics from Virginia Tech and he is one of the instructors for the O'Reilly iPhone Development Workshop.

Tracey Pilone would first like to thank her co-author and husband for sharing another book and being relentless in his willingness to stay up late to get things right.

She is a freelance technical writer who supports mission planning and RF analysis software for the Navy, and is the author of *Head First Algebra*.

Before becoming a writer, she spent several years working as a construction manager on large commercial construction sites around Washington, D.C. There she was part of a team responsible for coordinating the design and construction of office buildings, using engineering and management skills that somehow all came in handy writing Head First books.

She has a Civil Engineering degree from Virginia Tech, holds a Professional Engineer's License, and received a Masters of Education from the University of Virginia.

Table of Contents (Summary)

Table of Contents (the real thing)

Intro

Your brain on iPhone Development.
Here *you* are trying to *learn* something, while here your *brain* is doing you a favor by making sure the learning doesn't *stick*. Your brain's thinking, "Better leave room for more important things, like which wild animals to avoid and whether naked snowboarding is a bad idea." So how *do* you trick your brain into thinking that your life depends on knowing enough to develop your own iPhone apps?

getting started

Going mobile

The iPhone changed everything.

It's a **gaming** platform, a personal **organizer**, a full **web browser**, oh yeah, and a **phone**. The iPhone is one of the most exciting devices to come out in some time, and with the opening of the App Store, it's an opportunity for independent developers to compete worldwide with big named software companies. All you need to release your own app are a couple of **software tools**, some **knowledge**, and **enthusiasm**. Apple provides the software and we'll help you the knowledge; we're sure you've got the enthusiasm covered.

2

iPhone app patterns

Hello @twitter!

Apps have a lot of moving parts.

OK, actually, they don't have any real moving parts, but they do have lots of **UI controls**. A typical iPhone app has more going on than just a button, and now it's time to build one. Working with some of the **more complicated widgets** means you'll need to pay more attention than ever to how you **design** your app as well. In this chapter, you'll learn how to put together a bigger application and some of the **fundamental design patterns** used in the iPhone SDK.

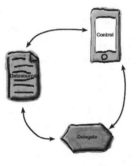

3

objective-c for the iPhone

Twitter needs variety

We did a lot in Chapter 2, but what language was that?

Parts of the code you've been writing might look familiar, but it's time you got a sense of what's really going on under the hood. The **iPhone SDK** comes with great tools that mean that you don't need to write code for everything, but you can't write entire apps without learning something about the underlying language, including **properties**, **message passing**, and **memory management**. Unless you work that out, all your apps will be just default widgets! And you want more than just widgets, right?

Messages going here between textField and the controller.

multiple views

A table with a view

Most iPhone apps have more than one view.

4

We've written a cool app with one view, but anyone who's used an iPhone knows that most apps aren't like that. Some of the more impressive iPhone apps out there do a great job of moving through complex information by using multiple views. We're going to start with navigation controllers and table views, like the kind you see in your Mail and Contact apps. Only we're going to do it with a twist...

Look, I don't have time for posting to Twitter. I need to know a ton of drink recipes every night. Is there an app for that?

plists and modal views

Refining your app

So you have this almost-working app...

That's the story of every app! You get some functionality working, decide to add something else, need to do some **refactoring**, and respond to some **feedback** from the App Store. Developing an app isn't ~~always~~ ever a linear process, but there's a lot to be learned in that process.

Anatomy of a crash

saving, editing, and sorting data

Everyone's an editor...

6

Displaying data is nice, but adding and editing information is what makes an iPhone app really rock. DrinkMixer is great—it uses some **cell customization**, and works with **plist dictionaries** to display data. It's a handy reference application, and you've got a good start on adding new drinks. Now, it's time to give the user the ability to modify the data—**saving, editing, and sorting**—to make it more useful for everyone. In this chapter we'll take a look at **editing patterns** in iPhone apps and how to guide users with the nav controller.

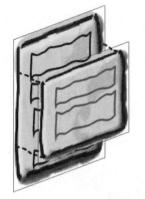

NSNotification object

Red-Headed School Girl

Canadian Whiskey

Cream Soda

Add the whiskey, then the cream soda to a shot glass and drink.

tab bars and core data
Enterprise apps

Enterprise apps mean managing more data in different

ways. Companies large and small are a significant market for iPhone apps. A small handheld device with a **custom app** can be huge for companies that have **staff on the go**. Most of these apps are going to manage **lots of data**, and iPhone 3.x has built in Core Data support. Working with that and another new controller, the **tab bar controller**, we're going to build an app for justice!

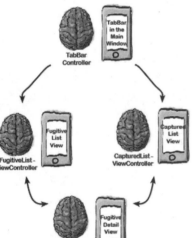

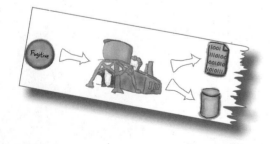

migrating and optimizing with core data

Things are changing

8

We have a great app in the works. iBountyHunter successfully loads the

data that Bob needs and lets him view the fugitives in an easy way. But what about when
the data has to change? Bob wants some **new functionality**, and what does that do to
the **data model**? In this chapter you'll learn how to handle **changes** to your data model
and how to take advantage of more Core Data features.

camera, map kit, and core location

9 Proof in the real world

The iPhone knows where it is and what it sees. As any iPhone user

knows, the iPhone goes way beyond just **managing data**: it can also take **pictures**, figure out your **location**, and put that information together for use in your app. The beauty about incorporating these features is that just by tapping into the tools that iPhone gives you, suddenly you can import pictures, locations, and **maps** without much coding at all.

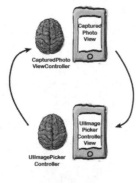

appendix i, leftovers

The top 6 things (we didn't cover)

Ever feel like something's missing? We know what you mean... Just when you thought you were done, there's more. We couldn't leave you without a few extra details, things we just couldn't fit into the rest of the book. At least, not if you want to be able to carry this book around without a metallic case and castor wheels on the bottom. So take a peek and see what you (still) might be missing out on.

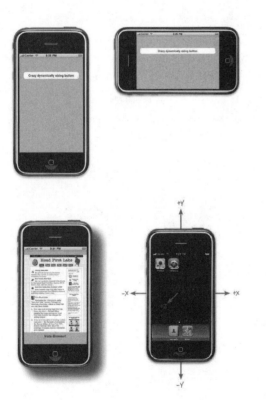

appendix ii, preparing your app for distribution

Get ready for the App Store

You want to get your app in the App Store, right? So

far, we've basically worked with apps in the simulator, which is fine. But
to get things to the next level, you'll need to **install an app** on an actual
iPhone or iPod Touch before applying to get it in the App Store. And the
only way to do that is to **register** with Apple as a developer. Even then,
it's not just a matter of clicking a button in Xcode to get an app you wrote
on your personal device. To do that, it's time to **talk with Apple**.

how to use this book

Intro

In this section, we answer the burning question:
"So why <u>DID</u> they put that in an iPhone development book?"

Who is this book for?

If you can answer "yes" to all of these:

 Do you have previous development experience?

 Do you want to **learn**, **understand**, **remember**, and *apply* important iPhone design and development concepts so that you can write your own iPhone apps, and start selling them in the App Store?

It definitely helps if you've already got some object–oriented chops, too. Experience with Mac development is helpful, but definitely not required.

 Do you prefer **stimulating dinner party conversation** to **dry**, **dull**, **academic lectures**?

this book is for you.

Who should probably back away from this book?

If you can answer "yes" to any of these:

Check out Head First Java for an excellent introduction to object–oriented development, and then come back and join us in iPhoneville.

 Are you **completely new** to software development?

 Are you already developing iPhone apps and looking for a *reference* book on Objective-C?

 Are you **afraid to try something different**? Would you rather have a root canal than mix stripes with plaid? Do you believe that a technical book can't be serious if there's a bounty hunter in it?

this book is not for you.

[Note from marketing: this book is for anyone with a credit card. Or cash. Cash is nice, too — Ed]

We know what you're thinking.

"How can *this* be a serious iPhone development book?"

"What's with all the graphics?"

"Can I actually *learn* it this way?"

And we know what your *brain* is thinking.

Your brain craves novelty. It's always searching, scanning, *waiting* for something unusual. It was built that way, and it helps you stay alive.

So what does your brain do with all the routine, ordinary, normal things you encounter? Everything it *can* to stop them from interfering with the brain's *real* job—recording things that *matter*. It doesn't bother saving the boring things; they never make it past the "this is obviously not important" filter.

How does your brain *know* what's important? Suppose you're out for a day hike and a tiger jumps in front of you. What happens inside your head and body?

Neurons fire. Emotions crank up. *Chemicals surge.*

And that's how your brain knows...

This must be important! Don't forget it!

But imagine you're at home, or in a library. It's a safe, warm, tiger-free zone. You're studying. Getting ready for an exam. Or trying to learn some tough technical topic your boss thinks will take a week, ten days at the most.

Just one problem. Your brain's trying to do you a big favor. It's trying to make sure that this *obviously* non-important content doesn't clutter up scarce resources. Resources that are better spent storing the really *big* things. Like tigers. Like the danger of fire. Like how you should never again snowboard in shorts.

And there's no simple way to tell your brain, "Hey brain, thank you very much, but no matter how dull this book is, and how little I'm registering on the emotional Richter scale right now, I really *do* want you to keep this stuff around."

Your brain thinks THIS is important.

Your brain thinks THIS isn't worth saving.

Great. Only 540 more dull, dry, boring pages.

We think of a "Head First" reader as a learner.

So what does it take to *learn* something? First, you have to *get* it, then make sure you don't *forget* it. It's not about pushing facts into your head. Based on the latest research in cognitive science, neurobiology, and educational psychology, *learning* takes a lot more than text on a page. We know what turns your brain on.

Some of the Head First learning principles:

Make it visual. Images are far more memorable than words alone, and make learning much more effective (up to 89% improvement in recall and transfer studies). It also makes things more understandable.

Put the words within or near the graphics they relate to, rather than on the bottom or on another page, and learners will be up to *twice* as likely to solve problems related to the content.

> This sucks. Can't we just import the list from Sam somehow?

Use a conversational and personalized style. In recent studies, students performed up to 40% better on post-learning tests if the content spoke directly to the reader, using a first-person, conversational style rather than taking a formal tone. Tell stories instead of lecturing. Use casual language. Don't take yourself too seriously. Which would *you* pay more attention to: a stimulating dinner party companion, or a lecture?

Get the learner to think more deeply. In other words, unless you actively flex your neurons, nothing much happens in your head. A reader has to be motivated, engaged, curious, and inspired to solve problems, draw conclusions, and generate new knowledge. And for that, you need challenges, exercises, and thought-provoking questions, and activities that involve both sides of the brain and multiple senses.

Get—and keep—the reader's attention. We've all had the "I really want to learn this but I can't stay awake past page one" experience. Your brain pays attention to things that are out of the ordinary, interesting, strange, eye-catching, unexpected. Learning a new, tough, technical topic doesn't have to be boring. Your brain will learn much more quickly if it's not.

> It's so great that Mike and I are communicating now! But I've noticed that Mike's starting to sound like he's in a rut, like saying the same thing over and over again! Is there something we need to talk about?

Touch their emotions. We now know that your ability to remember something is largely dependent on its emotional content. You remember what you care about. You remember when you *feel* something. No, we're not talking heart-wrenching stories about a boy and his dog. We're talking emotions like surprise, curiosity, fun, "what the...?" , and the feeling of "I Rule!" that comes when you solve a puzzle, learn something everybody else thinks is hard, or realize you know something that "I'm more technical than thou" Bob from engineering *doesn't*.

Metacognition: thinking about thinking

If you really want to learn, and you want to learn more quickly and more deeply, pay attention to how you pay attention. Think about how you think. Learn how you learn.

Most of us did not take courses on metacognition or learning theory when we were growing up. We were *expected* to learn, but rarely *taught* to learn.

But we assume that if you're holding this book, you really want to learn about iPhone development. And you probably don't want to spend a lot of time. And since you're going to build more apps in the future, you need to *remember* what you read. And for that, you've got to *understand* it. To get the most from this book, or *any* book or learning experience, take responsibility for your brain. Your brain on *this* content.

I wonder how I can trick my brain into remembering this stuff...

The trick is to get your brain to see the new material you're learning as Really Important. Crucial to your well-being. As important as a tiger. Otherwise, you're in for a constant battle, with your brain doing its best to keep the new content from sticking.

So just how *DO* you get your brain to think that iPhone development is a hungry tiger?

There's the slow, tedious way, or the faster, more effective way. The slow way is about sheer repetition. You obviously know that you *are* able to learn and remember even the dullest of topics if you keep pounding the same thing into your brain. With enough repetition, your brain says, "This doesn't *feel* important to him, but he keeps looking at the same thing *over* and *over* and *over*, so I suppose it must be."

The faster way is to do **anything that increases brain activity,** especially different *types* of brain activity. The things on the previous page are a big part of the solution, and they're all things that have been proven to help your brain work in your favor. For example, studies show that putting words *within* the pictures they describe (as opposed to somewhere else in the page, like a caption or in the body text) causes your brain to try to makes sense of how the words and picture relate, and this causes more neurons to fire. More neurons firing = more chances for your brain to *get* that this is something worth paying attention to, and possibly recording.

A conversational style helps because people tend to pay more attention when they perceive that they're in a conversation, since they're expected to follow along and hold up their end. The amazing thing is, your brain doesn't necessarily *care* that the "conversation" is between you and a book! On the other hand, if the writing style is formal and dry, your brain perceives it the same way you experience being lectured to while sitting in a roomful of passive attendees. No need to stay awake.

But pictures and conversational style are just the beginning.

Here's what WE did:

We used **pictures**, because your brain is tuned for visuals, not text. As far as your brain's concerned, a picture really *is* worth a thousand words. And when text and pictures work together, we embedded the text *in* the pictures because your brain works more effectively when the text is *within* the thing the text refers to, as opposed to in a caption or buried in the text somewhere.

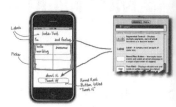

We used **redundancy**, saying the same thing in *different* ways and with different media types, and *multiple senses*, to increase the chance that the content gets coded into more than one area of your brain.

We used concepts and pictures in **unexpected** ways because your brain is tuned for novelty, and we used pictures and ideas with at least *some* **emotional** *content*, because your brain is tuned to pay attention to the biochemistry of emotions. That which causes you to *feel* something is more likely to be remembered, even if that feeling is nothing more than a little **humor**, **surprise**, or **interest.**

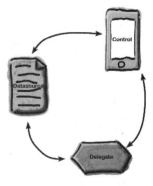

We used a personalized, **conversational style**, because your brain is tuned to pay more attention when it believes you're in a conversation than if it thinks you're passively listening to a presentation. Your brain does this even when you're *reading*.

We included loads of **activities**, because your brain is tuned to learn and remember more when you **do** things than when you *read* about things. And we made the exercises challenging-yet-do-able, because that's what most people prefer.

We used **multiple learning styles**, because *you* might prefer step-by-step procedures, while someone else wants to understand the big picture first, and someone else just wants to see an example. But regardless of your own learning preference, *everyone* benefits from seeing the same content represented in multiple ways.

BULLET POINTS

We include content for **both sides of your brain**, because the more of your brain you engage, the more likely you are to learn and remember, and the longer you can stay focused. Since working one side of the brain often means giving the other side a chance to rest, you can be more productive at learning for a longer period of time.

And we included **stories** and exercises that present **more than one point of view,** because your brain is tuned to learn more deeply when it's forced to make evaluations and judgments.

Fireside Chats

We included **challenges**, with exercises, and by asking **questions** that don't always have a straight answer, because your brain is tuned to learn and remember when it has to *work* at something. Think about it—you can't get your *body* in shape just by *watching* people at the gym. But we did our best to make sure that when you're working hard, it's on the *right* things. That **you're not spending one extra dendrite** processing a hard-to-understand example, or parsing difficult, jargon-laden, or overly terse text.

We used **people**. In stories, examples, pictures, etc., because, well, because *you're* a person. And your brain pays more attention to *people* than it does to *things*.

Here's what YOU can do to bend your brain into submission

So, we did our part. The rest is up to you. These tips are a starting point; listen to your brain and figure out what works for you and what doesn't. Try new things.

Cut this out and stick it on your refrigerator.

---

(1) Slow down. The more you understand, the less you have to memorize.

Don't just *read*. Stop and think. When the book asks you a question, don't just skip to the answer. Imagine that someone really *is* asking the question. The more deeply you force your brain to think, the better chance you have of learning and remembering.

(2) Do the exercises. Write your own notes.

We put them in, but if we did them for you, that would be like having someone else do your workouts for you. And don't just *look* at the exercises. **Use a pencil.** There's plenty of evidence that physical activity *while* learning can increase the learning.

(3) Read the "There are No Dumb Questions"

That means all of them. They're not optional sidebars—*they're part of the core content!* Don't skip them.

(4) Make this the last thing you read before bed. Or at least the last challenging thing.

Part of the learning (especially the transfer to long-term memory) happens *after* you put the book down. Your brain needs time on its own, to do more processing. If you put in something new during that processing time, some of what you just learned will be lost.

(5) Drink water. Lots of it.

Your brain works best in a nice bath of fluid. Dehydration (which can happen before you ever feel thirsty) decreases cognitive function.

(6) Talk about it. Out loud.

Speaking activates a different part of the brain. If you're trying to understand something, or increase your chance of remembering it later, say it out loud. Better still, try to explain it out loud to someone else. You'll learn more quickly, and you might uncover ideas you hadn't known were there when you were reading about it.

(7) Listen to your brain.

Pay attention to whether your brain is getting overloaded. If you find yourself starting to skim the surface or forget what you just read, it's time for a break. Once you go past a certain point, you won't learn faster by trying to shove more in, and you might even hurt the process.

(8) Feel something!

Your brain needs to know that this *matters*. Get involved with the stories. Make up your own captions for the photos. Groaning over a bad joke is *still* better than feeling nothing at all.

(9) Create something!

Apply this to your daily work; use what you are learning to make decisions on your projects. Just do something to get some experience beyond the exercises and activities in this book. All you need is a pencil and a problem to solve... a problem that might benefit from using the tools and techniques you're studying for the exam.

Read me

This is a learning experience, not a reference book. We deliberately stripped out everything that might get in the way of learning whatever it is we're working on at that point in the book. And the first time through, you need to begin at the beginning, because the book makes assumptions about what you've already seen and learned.

We start off by building an app in the very first chapter.

Believe it or not, even if you've never developed for the iPhone before, you can jump right in and starting building apps. You'll also learn your way around the tools used for iPhone development.

We don't worry about preparing your app to submit to the App Store until the end of book.

In this book, you can get on with the business of learning how to create iPhone apps without stressing over the packaging and distribution of your app out of the gate. But, we know that's what everyone who wants to build an iPhone app ultimately wants to do, so we cover that process (and all it's glorious gotchas) in an Appendix at the end.

We focus on what you can build and test on the simulator.

The iPhone SDK comes with a great (and free!) tool for testing your apps on your computer. The simulator lets you try out your code without having to worry about getting it in the app store or on a real device. But, it also has its limits. There's some cool iPhone stuff you just can't test on the simulator, like the accelerometer and compass. So we don't cover those kinds of things in very much detail in this book since we want to make sure you're creating and testing apps quickly and easily.

The activities are NOT optional.

The exercises and activities are not add-ons; they're part of the core content of the book. Some of them are to help with memory, some are for understanding, and some will help you apply what you've learned. ***Don't skip the exercises.*** Even crossword puzzles are important—they'll help get concepts into your brain the way you'll see them on the PMP exam. But more importantly, they're good for giving your brain a chance to think about the words and terms you've been learning in a different context.

The redundancy is intentional and important.

One distinct difference in a Head First book is that we want you to *really* get it. And we want you to finish the book remembering what you've learned. Most reference books don't have retention and recall as a goal, but this book is about *learning*, so you'll see some of the same concepts come up more than once.

The Brain Power exercises don't have answers.

For some of them, there is no right answer, and for others, part of the learning experience of the Brain Power activities is for you to decide if and when your answers are right. In some of the Brain Power exercises, you will find hints to point you in the right direction.

System requirements

To develop for the iPhone, you need an Intel-based Mac, period. We wrote this book using Snow Leopard and Xcode 3.2. If you are running Leopard with an older version of Xcode, we tried to point out where there were places that would trip you up. For some of the more advanced capabilities, like the accelerometer and the camera, you'll need an actual iPhone or iPod Touch and to be a registered developer. In Chapter 1, we point you in the direction to get the SDK and Apple documentation, so don't worry about that for now.

The technical review team

Michael Morrison

Joe Heck

Eric Shepherd

Technical Reviewers:

For this book we had an amazing, elite group of tech reviewers. They did a fantastic job, and we're really grateful for their incredible contribution.

Joe Heck is a software developer, technology manager, author, and instructor who's been involved with computing for 25 years, and developing for the iPhone platform since the first beta release. Employed at the Walt Disney Interactive Media Group, Joe is involved in various technologies and development platforms, and assisted the development team for Disney's iPhone game "Fairies Fly." He's the founder of the Seattle Xcoders developer group, which supports Macintosh and iPhone development in the Seattle area, and the author of SeattleBus, an iPhone app that provides real-time arrival and departure times of Seattle public transportation (available at the iPhone App Store). He also knows a ton about iPhones, and made sure that we were technically solid in every facet of the book. His attention to detail means that all of our nitty gritty answers are complete and correct.

Eric Shepherd got started programming at age nine and never looked back. He's been a technical writer, writing developer documentation since 1997, and is currently the developer documentation lead at Mozilla. In his spare time, he writes software for old Apple II computers—because his day job just isn't geeky enough—and spends time with his daughter. Eric's review feedback was hugely helpful. His input meant that any typos or bugs we left in the code were caught and fixed. His thorough review means that no one else has to go through the problems he had in actually making the code work.

Michael Morrison is a writer, developer, and author of *Head First JavaScript*, *Head First PHP & MySQL*, and even a few books that don't have squiggly arrows, stick figures, and magnets. Michael is the founder of Stalefish Labs (`www.stalefishlabs.com`), an edutainment company specializing in games, toys, and interactive media, including a few iPhone apps. Michael spends a lot of time wearing helmets, be it for skateboarding, hockey, or iPhone debugging. Since he has iPhone Head First experience, Mike was a great combo to have helping us. Reviewing in both capacities, he was nice enough to always propose a solution for us when he found a layout problem, which makes those comments easier to take!

All three of these guys did a tremendous amount of review at the end in a short period of time and we really appreciate it! Thanks so much!

Acknowledgments

Our editors:

Thanks to **Courtney Nash**, who was there from the beginning and took us through to production, which normally is a long time, but not for us! She pushed us to make sure that every step of the way the book stayed true to its Head First title, even when it would've been WAY easier not to. She knows the chapter we're talking about.

Courtney Nash

And to **Brett McLaughlin**, who started us off on this book by responding to an IM that said "What do you think about Head First iPhone?" and got it turned into a book. He also played the learner (complete with the occasional complaining) for us throughout the book and was a big help in pacing the initial chapters.

Brett McLaughlin

Mark Reese

The O'Reilly team:

To **Karen Shaner**, who handled the tech review process, which got a little—ahem—accelerated there at the end. And also to **Laurie Petrycki**, who trusted us to do another Head First book less than a year after the last one. Finally, to our design editor **Mark Reese** for his graphics and layout help.

Our friends and family:

To all of the **Pilones** and the **Chadwicks**, who put up with a lot being pushed until October while we worked on the book and gave us the support we needed to become grown ups who can write this stuff. To Dan's brother, **Paul**, whose relentless "Seriously, Macs are *awesome*" mantra convinced Dan to get one and find out what all this OS X development stuff is about.

To **Vinny** and **Nick**, who put up with a good bit of shuffling around the past couple of months so we could get this done, and are totally going to get some major Mommy and Daddy time now. They both want iPhones.

To our **friends** who listened to the whining about getting this thing done and who took the kids for a couple hours here and there so we could get finished and encouraged us when we needed it!

Finally, to **Apple**, as silly as it sounds, because without the iPhone being such a unique and game-changing device, there would be no book!

Safari® Books Online

Safari® Books Online is an on-demand digital library that lets you easily search over 7,500 technology and creative reference books and videos to find the answers you need quickly.

With a subscription, you can read any page and watch any video from our library online. Read books on your cell phone and mobile devices. Access new titles before they are available for print, and get exclusive access to manuscripts in development and post feedback for the authors. Copy and paste code samples, organize your favorites, download chapters, bookmark key sections, create notes, print out pages, and benefit from tons of other time-saving features.

O'Reilly Media has uploaded this book to the Safari Books Online service. To have full digital access to this book and others on similar topics from O'Reilly and other publishers, sign up for free at *http://my.safaribooksonline.com*.

1 getting started

Going mobile

I just don't see what all this iPhone fuss is about. My phone works just fine...

The iPhone changed everything. It's a gaming platform, a personal organizer, a full web-browser, oh yeah, and a phone. The iPhone is one of the most exciting devices to come out in some time, and with the opening of the App Store, it's an opportunity for independent developers to compete worldwide with big-name software companies. All you need to release your own app are a couple of software tools, some knowledge, and enthusiasm. Apple provides the software, and we'll help you with the knowledge; we're sure you've got the enthusiasm covered.

There's a lot of buzz and a lot of money tied up in the App Store...

The App Store is a HUGE success!

Developers have been submitting apps to the Apple App Store for the iPhone and the iPod Touch in record numbers, and making significant income.

Apple's App Store celebrates 1st birthday

Apple launched its acclaimed App Store one year ago and since has become the focus of trends, controversy, and lots and lots of money. While many apps up for sale are free, many are not, and the price for iPhone apps continues to rise.

Developers have been leveraging the capabilities of the iPhone in unexpected ways to bring fun and added utility to the device that you buy from the store.

Even users of the iPod Touch can also download the apps to their devices.

Many people try several new apps a day, and you can install enough apps on your phone to fill several screens....

Mobile applications aren't just ported desktop apps

There are about a billion good reasons to get into the App Store, and now it's time for you to jump in. To get there from here, you'll learn about designing and implementing an iPhone app, but it's not the same as developing for the desktop, or writing a web application.

It's important to think an iPhone application through from the beginning. You need to constantly ask yourself "What is it the user is trying to do?" Get rid of everything else, minimize the input they have to provide, and keep it focused.

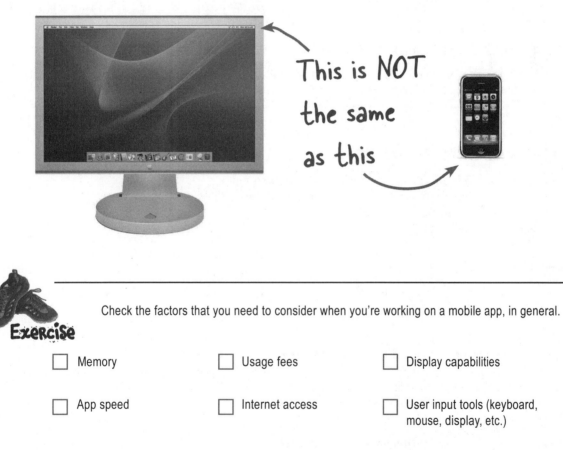

This is NOT the same as this

Exercise

Check the factors that you need to consider when you're working on a mobile app, in general.

☐ Memory   ☐ Usage fees   ☐ Display capabilities

☐ App speed   ☐ Internet access   ☐ User input tools (keyboard, mouse, display, etc.)

Which of these factors are different for the iPhone? ....

....

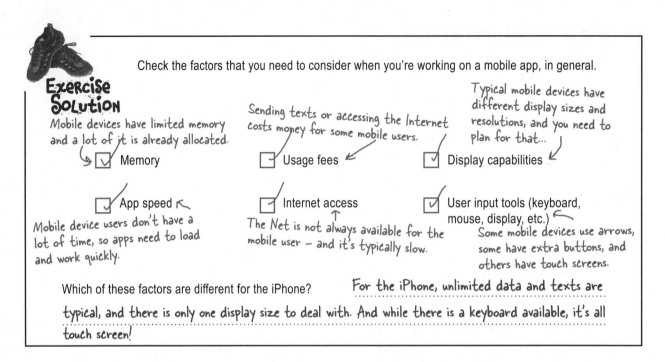

Exercise Solution

Check the factors that you need to consider when you're working on a mobile app, in general.

Mobile devices have limited memory and a lot of it is already allocated.
↳ ☑ Memory

Sending texts or accessing the Internet costs money for some mobile users.
☐ Usage fees

Typical mobile devices have different display sizes and resolutions, and you need to plan for that...
☑ Display capabilities

☑ App speed
Mobile device users don't have a lot of time, so apps need to load and work quickly.

☑ Internet access
The Net is not always available for the mobile user – and it's typically slow.

☑ User input tools (keyboard, mouse, display, etc.)
Some mobile devices use arrows, some have extra buttons, and others have touch screens.

Which of these factors are different for the iPhone? For the iPhone, unlimited data and texts are typical, and there is only one display size to deal with. And while there is a keyboard available, it's all touch screen!

iPhone apps are not small desktop apps

There's a lot of talk about how the iPhone is a small computer that people carry with them. That's definitely true, but it doesn't mean iPhone apps are just small desktop apps. Some of the most important issues that you'll encounter designing an app for the iPhone:

iPhones have a small screen and are task-focused
Even with the iPhone's fantastic screen, it's still relatively small (320x480). You need to put real thought into every screen and keep it focused on the specific task the user is doing.

iPhones have limited CPU and memory
On top of that, there's no virtual memory and every bit of CPU oomph you use means more battery drain. iPhone OS monitors the system closely and if you go crazy with memory usage, it'll just **kill** your app. And no one wants that.

Only one application can run at a time
If it's your application running, why should you care? Because if anything else happens, like the phone rings, a text message comes in, the user clicks on a link, etc., your app gets shut down and the user moves on to another application. You need to be able to gracefully exit at any time and be able to put users back into a reasonable spot when they return.

Anatomy of an iPhone app

Before we dive into creating our first app, let's take a look at what makes up a typical iPhone app.

First we have one or more views...

iPhone apps are made up of one or more **views**—in a normal app, these views have GUI components on them like text fields, buttons, labels, etc. Games have views too, but typically don't use the normal GUI components. Games generally require their own custom interfaces that are created with things like OpenGL or Quartz.

Views can be built using code, graphically using Interface Builder, or some combination of both. Most apps use a mix.

...then the code that makes the views work...

iPhone apps have a clean separation between the GUI (the view) and the actual code that provides the application logic. In general, each view has a **View Controller** behind it that reacts to button presses, table row selection, tilting the phone, etc. This code is almost always written in Objective-C using Apple's IDE (integrated development environment), Xcode.

Xcode is the IDE of choice for writing iPhone apps. It includes a number of application templates to get you started.

...and any other resources, all packaged into your application.

If you're new to developing for OS X you might be surprised to find out that applications (iPhone and full desktop apps) are really just directories. Any app directory contains the actual binary executable, some **metadata** about the application (the author, the icon filename, code signatures, etc.) and any other **application resources** like images, application data, help files, etc. iPhone applications behave the same way, so when you tell Xcode about other resources your application needs, it will bundle them up for you when you build the application.

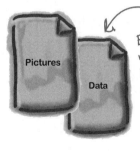

Every iPhone app has some resources associated with it. At a minimum, your application will have an icon file, an Info.plist that has information about the application itself, and the actual binary. Other common resources are interface files, called nibs.

Now let's get started on your first iPhone App...

Mike can't make a decision

Mike's a great guy, but he never knows what he wants to do. Help him save time waffling about what to do, and give him a straightforward answer.

The way I see it is I already made the decision to buy an iPhone... I shouldn't have to think again!

We'll write Mike an app.

Mike has an iPhone, so let's write him an app that requires a simple button push to tell him what to do when he needs to make a decision.

Mike

Make a good first impression

When users start up your application, the first thing they see is your view. It needs to be usable and focused on what your application is supposed to do. Throughout this book, whenever we start a new application, we're going to take a little time to sketch up what we want it to look like.

Our first application is pretty straightforward: it is going to be a single view with a button that Mike can press to get a decision. To keep things simple, we'll change the label of the button to show what he should do after he pushes it.

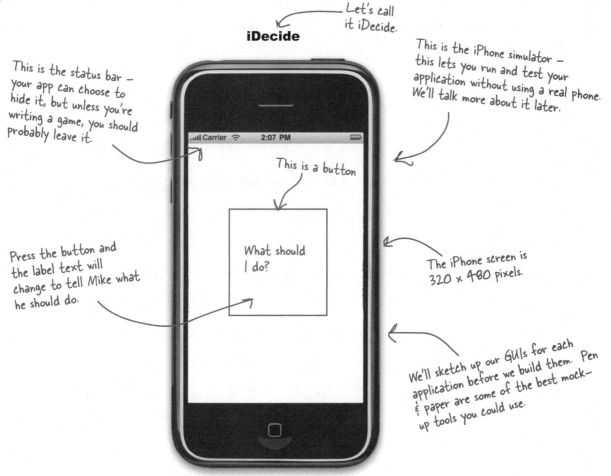

Let's call it iDecide.

iDecide

This is the status bar – your app can choose to hide it, but unless you're writing a game, you should probably leave it.

This is the iPhone simulator – this lets you run and test your application without using a real phone. We'll talk more about it later.

This is a button

What should I do?

Press the button and the label text will change to tell Mike what he should do.

The iPhone screen is 320 x 480 pixels.

We'll sketch up our GUIs for each application before we build them. Pen & paper are some of the best mock-up tools you could use.

Now that we know what to build, let's get into the tools.

It all starts with the iPhone SDK

It's time to go get some tools. Head over to http://developer.apple.com/iphone. You can download the SDK (and other useful Apple development resources) for free with the basic registration, but to distribute a completed app on the App Store or install your app on the iPhone for testing you need to become a paid Standard or Enterprise Developer. The SDK comes with a simulator for testing directly on your Mac, so free registration is all you'll need for now.

The SDK comes with Xcode, Instruments, Interface Builder, and the iPhone Simulator. Code for the iPhone is written in Xcode using Objective-C. Interface Builder is used for graphically editing GUIs, Instruments helps you assess memory usage and performance for your app, and the Simulator is used for testing.

☐ Register as a developer at http://developer.apple.com/iphone.

☐ Download the latest SDK; this book is based on the 3.1 SDK. Just look for the **Download** button at the top of the page.

☐ Install the SDK. Once the Installation completes, you can find Xcode.app in /Developer/Applications. Just double-click it to start it up.

You will probably want to drag it onto your Dock—we're going to be using it a lot.

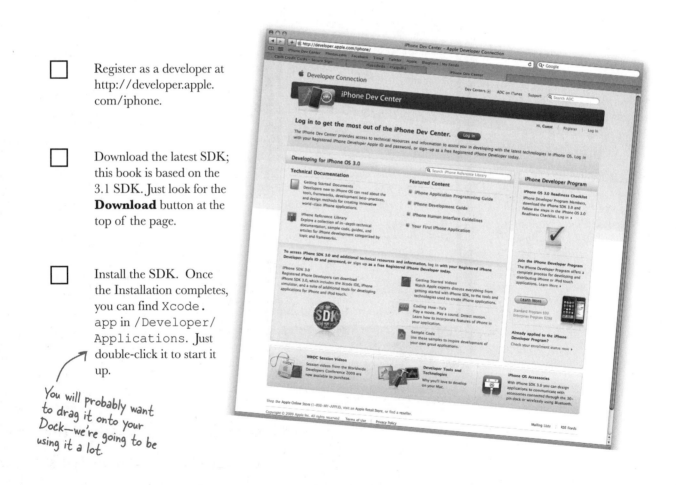

Q: What are the most important things to consider when developing a mobile app?

A: There are two key things to keep in mind when developing a mobile application. First, the device has limited resources: memory, CPU, storage, Net access speed (if they have access at all), etc. Second, usage patterns are different for mobile applications. Mobile apps are generally convenience applications—users want to fire up your application, quickly accomplish their goal, and go back to what they were doing in the real world.

Q: I've developed for mobile platforms before, and it was a mess. Nothing worked the same between different devices, you couldn't count on the screen size, they didn't even have the same number of buttons on different devices! Is this any better?

A: YES! For the most part, developing for iPhone avoids these problems. iPhones all have a 320x480 screen, an accelerometer, a single home key, etc. However...

Q: There are several different models of the iPhone out there. Are they all the same? What about the iPod Touch?

A: Not all iPhone and iPod Touch devices are the same. For example, not all devices have a camera or GPS. Net access speeds vary by device as well depending on whether

they're connected to EDGE, 3G, or Wifi. To make matters more complicated, the iPhone 3GS has a faster processor and better video card than previous iPhone models. If you take advantage of any features that might not be present on all devices you must make sure your code can handle not having that feature available. Apple will test for this (for example, trying to use the camera on a first generation iPod Touch) and reject your application if it doesn't accomodate a device properly.

Q: What language does the iPhone use?

A: iPhone apps are generally written in Objective-C, an object-oriented language that is also used for Mac development. However, you can use C and even C++ on the iPhone. Since the GUI and Core Framework libraries for the iPhone are written in Objective-C, most developers use Objective-C for their application; however, it's not uncommon to see support libraries written in C.

Q: Do I have to use an IDE? I'm really a command-line kinda developer.

A: Technically speaking, no, you don't have to use the Xcode IDE for straight development. However, the IDE makes iPhone development so much easier that you really should ask yourself if you have a good reason for avoiding it, especially since to deploy onto an actual iPhone or the simulator for testing, it's mandatory. This book uses the Xcode IDE as well as other

Apple development tools like Interface Builder, and we encourage you to at least try them out before you abandon them.

Q: Can I give applications I write out to friends?

A: Yes and no. First, if you want to put an application on anyone's actual device (including your own) you'll need to become a registered Apple iPhone Developer. Once you've done that, you can register a device and install your application on it. However, that's not really a great way to get your application out there, and Apple limits how many devices you can register this way. It's great for testing your application, but not how you want to go about passing it around.

A better way is to submit your application to the iTunes App Store. You can choose to distribute your application for free or charge for it, but by distributing it through the iTunes App Store, you make your application available to the world (and maybe make some money, too!). We'll talk more about distributing apps later in the book.

Q: Can I develop an app for the iPhone then rebuild it for other phones like Windows Mobile, Android, or Blackberries?

A: In a word, no. When you develop for iPhone, you use Apple's iPhone frameworks, like Cocoa Touch, as well as Objective-C. Neither of these are available on other devices.

**Now let's get started.
Launch Xcode...**

Xcode includes app templates to help you get started

When you start Xcode, you'll get a welcome screen where you can select **Create a New Project**. You'll get this dialog:

This is the very same Xcode that you'd use to develop for the Mac. Since we're working with the iPhone, make sure iPhone OS Application is selected..

These are the basic App templates. Based on your selection, different code and files are populated for you.

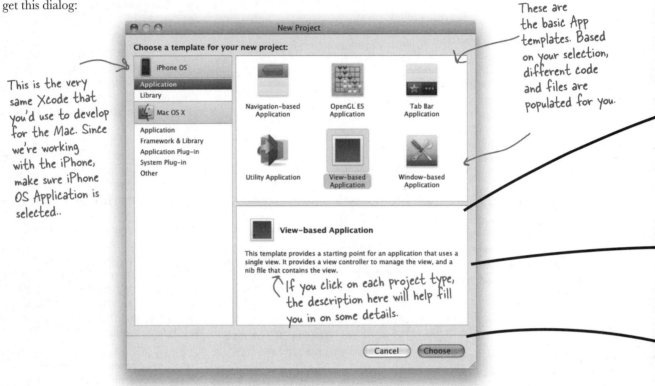

If you click on each project type, the description here will help fill you in on some details.

As we go through the book, we'll use different types of projects and discuss why you'd choose one over another for each app. For iDecide, we have one screen (or view) that we're not going to be flipping or anything, so start with the **View-based Application** and name it iDecide.

The Xcode template includes more than just source code.

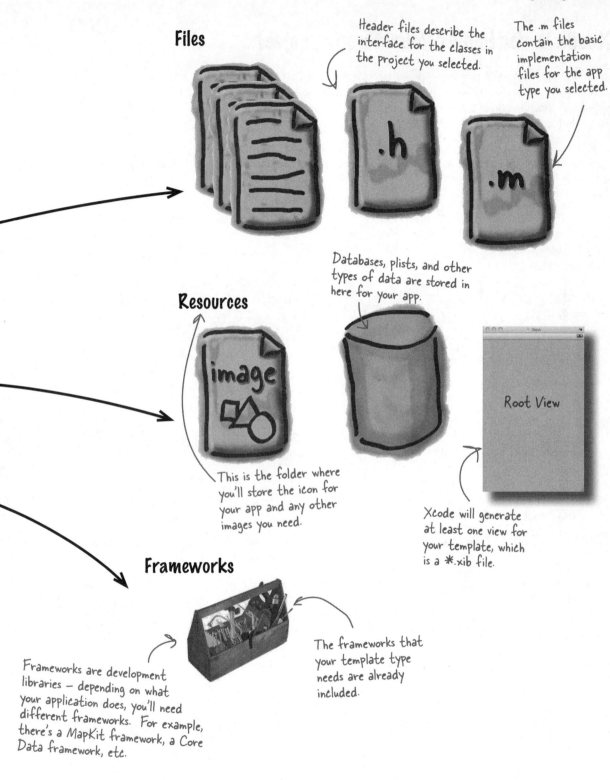

Files

Header files describe the interface for the classes in the project you selected.

The .m files contain the basic implementation files for the app type you selected.

.h

.m

Databases, plists, and other types of data are stored in here for your app.

Resources

image

Root View

This is the folder where you'll store the icon for your app and any other images you need.

Xcode will generate at least one view for your template, which is a *.xib file.

Frameworks

The frameworks that your template type needs are already included.

Frameworks are development libraries — depending on what your application does, you'll need different frameworks. For example, there's a MapKit framework, a Core Data framework, etc.

Xcode is the hub of your iPhone project...

When Xcode opens with your new View-based project, it will be populated with all of the files that you see below. We'll be using some of the other tools that came with the SDK (especially Interface Builder and the Simulator), but they are all working with the files that are included here.

The files and frameworks shown were stubbed out based on our selection of a View-based application. As we go forward, we'll use different types of apps and that will lead to different defaults.

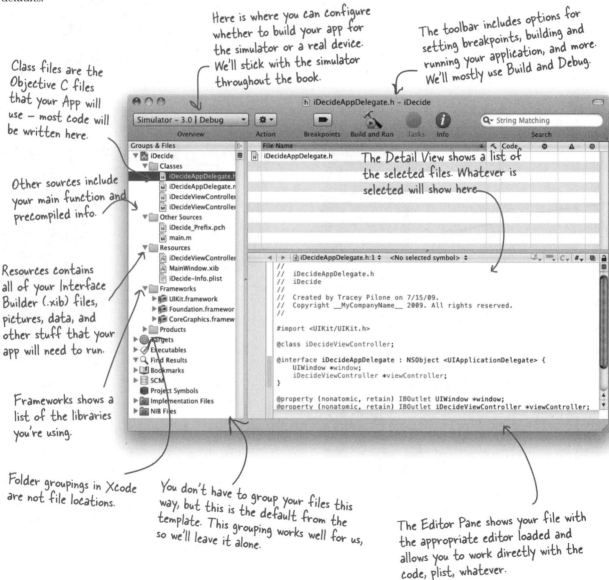

Here is where you can configure whether to build your app for the simulator or a real device. We'll stick with the simulator throughout the book.

The toolbar includes options for setting breakpoints, building and running your application, and more. We'll mostly use Build and Debug.

Class files are the Objective C files that your App will use — most code will be written here.

Other sources include your main function and precompiled info.

Resources contains all of your Interface Builder (.xib) files, pictures, data, and other stuff that your app will need to run.

Frameworks shows a list of the libraries you're using.

The Detail View shows a list of the selected files. Whatever is selected will show here.

Folder groupings in Xcode are not file locations.

You don't have to group your files this way, but this is the default from the template. This grouping works well for us, so we'll leave it alone.

The Editor Pane shows your file with the appropriate editor loaded and allows you to work directly with the code, plist, whatever.

...and plays a role in every part of writing your app

Xcode is much more than just a text editor. As you've already seen, Xcode includes the templates to get you started developing an application. Depending on your application, you may use all of a template or just parts of it, but you'll almost always start with one of them. Once you get your basic app template in place, you'll use Xcode for a lot more:

Maintaining your project resources

Xcode will create a new directory for your project and sort the various files into subdirectories. You don't have to stick with the default layout, but if you decide to reorganize, do it from within Xcode. Xcode also has built-in support for version control tools like Subversion and can be used to checkout and commit your project changes.

Editing your code and resources

You'll use Xcode to edit your application code, and it supports a variety of languages beyond just Objective-C. Xcode also has a number of built-in editors for resource files like plists (we'll talk more about them later on). For resources Xcode doesn't handle natively, like UI definition (.xib) files, double-clicking on one of those files in Xcode will launch the appropriate editor, in this case Interface Builder. Some file types Xcode can only view, like pictures, or it will merely list, like sound files.

Building and testing your application

Xcode comes with all of the compilers necessary to build your code and generate a working application. Once your application is compiled, Xcode can install it on the iPhone Simulator or a real device. Xcode includes a top-notch debugger with both graphical and command-line interfaces to let you debug your application. You can launch profiling tools like Instruments to check for memory or performance issues.

Prepare your application for sale

Once you get your application thoroughly tested and you're ready to sell it, Xcode manages your provisioning profiles and code signing certificates that let you put your application on real devices or upload it to the iTunes App Store for sale.

OK, enough talking about Xcode: double-click on iDecideViewController.xib and we'll start with the view.

Build your interface using... Interface Builder

When you open any *.xib file in Interface Builder, it will automatically show the Main window, your view, and a library of UI elements. Interface Builder allows you to drag and drop any of the basic library elements into your view, edit them, and work with the connections between the code and these elements. All of these elements come from the Cocoa Touch framework, a custom UI framework for the iPhone and the iPod Touch.

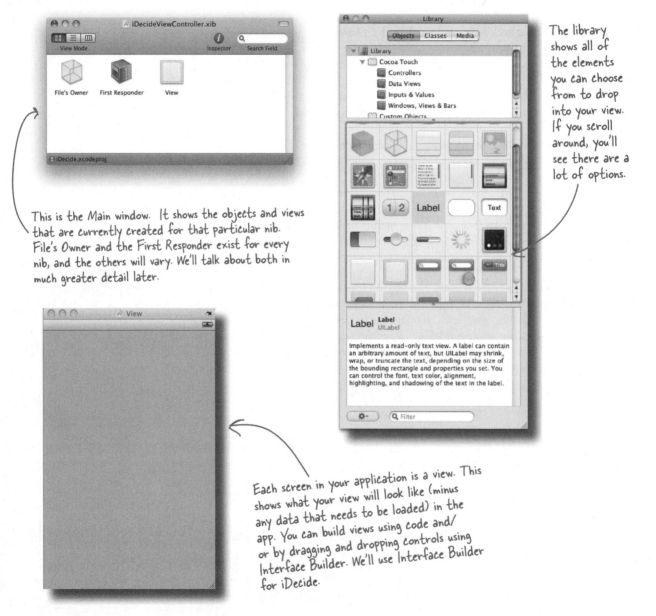

The library shows all of the elements you can choose from to drop into your view. If you scroll around, you'll see there are a lot of options.

This is the Main window. It shows the objects and views that are currently created for that particular nib. File's Owner and the First Responder exist for every nib, and the others will vary. We'll talk about both in much greater detail later.

Each screen in your application is a view. This shows what your view will look like (minus any data that needs to be loaded) in the app. You can build views using code and/ or by dragging and dropping controls using Interface Builder. We'll use Interface Builder for iDecide.

A GUI builder sure sounds easier. I guess it just spits out Objective-C code into my files?

No—Interface Builder creates nibs.

Nibs (which have .xib extensions) are XML documents that are loaded by the framework when the app starts up. We'll talk a lot more about this in the next chapter, but for now it's just important to understand that Interface Builder is not creating Objective-C code. It's creating an XML description of the GUI you're building, and the Cocoa Touch framework uses that to actually create the buttons and whatnot for your application at runtime. Everything we do in Interface Builder *could* be done in pure Objective-C code, but as you'll see, there are some things that are really just easier to lay out with a GUI builder.

...then the Cocoa Touch framework built into our app uses the description in the .xib file to create the actual Cocoa Touch objects in our view.

iDecideViewController.xib

We create the XML description using Interface Builder...

What should I do?

And that view is what the user sees when they run our app.

Views for iPhone Apps are called nibs, and have an .xib extension.

Add the button to your view

To add elements to the view, all you need to do is drag and drop the elements you want onto your view. For our app, we just need a button with a label on it.

 Drag the rectangular button onto the view.
The initial size of the button will be small, so resize it to be a bit bigger. Just grab the corners of the button and pull.

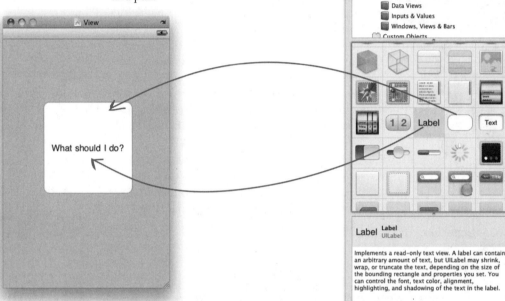

 Drag the label onto the button.
Edit the new label on the button to say "What should I do?" by double-clicking on the "label" and type the new text, then move the text around to center it on the button.

TesT DRive

Now, save in Interface Builder and return to Xcode and click Build and Run, either from the Build menu or from the button in the main Xcode window. That will launch the Simulator.

The iPhone Simulator lets you test your app on your Mac

The Simulator is a great tool for testing your apps quickly and for free. It doesn't come with all of the applications that a real phone does, but for the most part it behaves the same way. When you first start the simulator you see the Springboard, just like on a real iPhone, with iDecide installed (and a default icon that you can change later). Xcode then opens the app and your code is running.

There are some differences between using the Simulator and your iPhone. For starters, shaking and rotating your Mac won't accomplish anything. To approximate rotation and check landscape and portrait views, there are some commands under the **Hardware** menu.

Watch it!

The Simulator has limitations.

*Memory, performance, camera, GPS, and other characteristics **cannot** be reliably tested using the Simulator. We'll talk more about these later, but memory usage and performance are tough to test on the simulator simply because your Mac has so many more resources than the iPhone. To test these things, you need to install on an actual iPhone (which means joining one of the paid development programs).*

there are no Dumb Questions

Q: Are there other things that don't work on the Simulator?

A: The Simulator can only work with some gestures, network accessibility and core location are limited, and it doesn't have an accelerometer or camera. For more information, reference Apple's iPhone OS 3.0 Library documentation, via the **Help** menu in the **Simulator**.

The Simulator is great for getting started with your application, but at some point you have to move over to a real device. Also, be aware

that the iPod Touch and the iPhone are two different devices with different capabilities. You really should test on both, which means you'll need to join one of the paid programs.

Q: What's with this whole nibs have a xib extension thing?

A: That's an odd artifact showing the roots of OS X. Nibs date back to the NeXTStep days, before NeXT was acquired by Apple. In OS X Leopard, Apple released a new format for nib files based on an XML Schema and changed the extension to xib. So, while the format is XML and they have

a .xib extension, people still refer to them as nibs. You'll see more NeXTStep heritage in library class names too—almost everything starts with "NS", short for NeXTStep.

Q: Why didn't anything happen when I clicked on the button in the Simulator?

A: It's temping to expect that button to just work out of the gate, given how much XCode sets up for you. However, if you think about what we've done, there has been some XML created to load a framework and draw a button, but we didn't tell it to do anything with that button yet...

OK, so Interface Builder created XML, but we still need to write code to implement the button press, right?

UI behavior is implemented in Objective-C.

Interface Builder creates your button, but to make that button actually do something, you'll need to code what it should do.

Controls trigger events in Objective-C when things happen to them, like the button being pressed or text changing in a text field. For events like button presses, Interface Builder has to connect the view controls with code in your controller class for action methods, tagged with IBAction (for Interface Builder Action). We'll talk more about the Objective-C syntax later, but for now, you'll need to declare a method in your header (.h) file and the implementation in the .m.

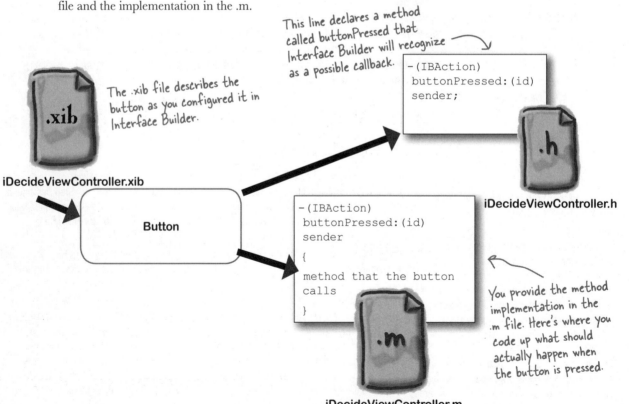

This line declares a method called buttonPressed that Interface Builder will recognize as a possible callback.

The .xib file describes the button as you configured it in Interface Builder.

iDecideViewController.xib

Button

```
-(IBAction)
buttonPressed:(id)
sender;
```

iDecideViewController.h

```
-(IBAction)
buttonPressed:(id)
sender

{

method that the button
calls

}
```

You provide the method implementation in the .m file. Here's where you code up what should actually happen when the button is pressed.

iDecideViewController.m

Sharpen your pencil

Below is the code for when the button gets tapped. Add the bolded
code to the iDecideViewController.h and iDecideViewController.m files.

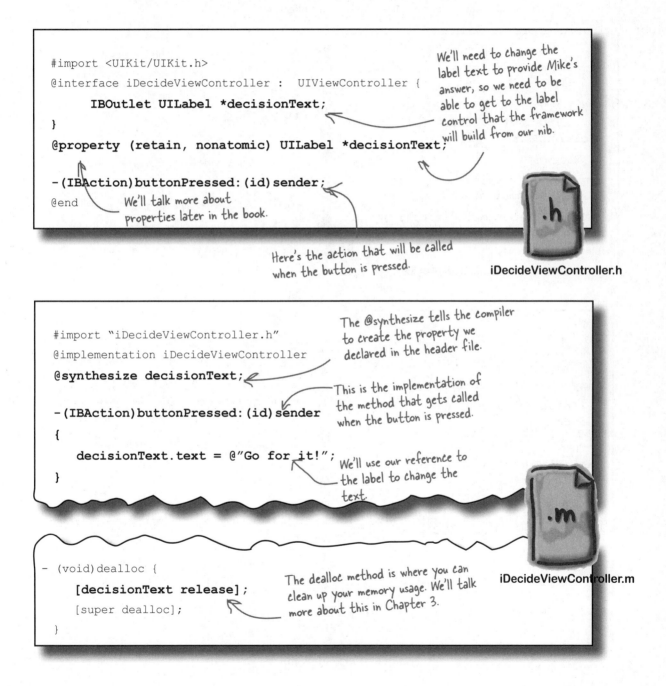

```
#import <UIKit/UIKit.h>
@interface iDecideViewController :  UIViewController {
    IBOutlet UILabel *decisionText;
}
@property (retain, nonatomic) UILabel *decisionText;

-(IBAction)buttonPressed:(id)sender;
@end
```

We'll need to change the
label text to provide Mike's
answer, so we need to be
able to get to the label
control that the framework
will build from our nib.

We'll talk more about
properties later in the book.

Here's the action that will be called
when the button is pressed.

iDecideViewController.h

```
#import "iDecideViewController.h"
@implementation iDecideViewController
@synthesize decisionText;

-(IBAction)buttonPressed:(id)sender
{
    decisionText.text = @"Go for it!";
}
```

The @synthesize tells the compiler
to create the property we
declared in the header file.

This is the implementation of
the method that gets called
when the button is pressed.

We'll use our reference to
the label to change the
text.

```
- (void)dealloc {
    [decisionText release];
    [super dealloc];
}
```

The dealloc method is where you can
clean up your memory usage. We'll talk
more about this in Chapter 3.

iDecideViewController.m

Sharpen your pencil
Solution

Here's the code from before in the context of the full files for iDecideViewController.h and iDecideViewController.m.

```objc
#import <UIKit/UIKit.h>
@interface iDecideViewController :
UIViewController {
        IBOutlet UILabel
*decisionText;
}
@property (retain, nonatomic)
UILabel *decisionText;
-(IBAction)buttonPressed:(id)
sender;
@end
```
.h

iDecideViewController.h

This code is typical of what you'll see in a header file. There's a declaration of the new IBOutlet and IBAction, and a property for our UILabel.

The IBAction is dealing with what happens when the button is pressed, and the IBOutlet is a reference to the label we'll use for output text for the button. We'll look at both of these in more detail later.

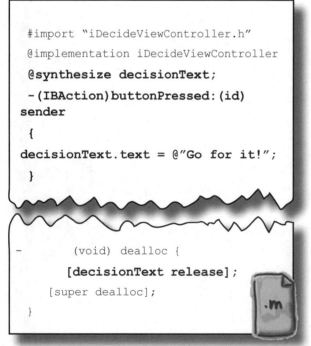

```objc
#import "iDecideViewController.h"
@implementation iDecideViewController
@synthesize decisionText;
-(IBAction)buttonPressed:(id)
sender
{
decisionText.text = @"Go for it!";
}
```

```objc
-       (void) dealloc {
        [decisionText release];
    [super dealloc];
}
```
.m

iDecideViewController.m

This is implementation code. Here, we're defining the method that is called when the button is pressed. We use a constant string to change the text in the label. Remember, decisionText is a reference to the UILabel we created in Interface Builder.

The release call is for memory management. Objective-C uses reference counting for memory management (we'll talk more about this in a bit) and needs to be released to free up the memory.

Test Drive

Build and run the code again. Try clicking on the button and see if it works.

.ıll Carrier 🛜   9:58 PM

What should I do?

Nothing happens!

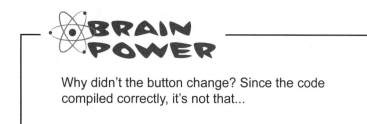

BRAIN POWER

Why didn't the button change? Since the code compiled correctly, it's not that...

What happened?

The Objective-C code is all set to handle it when the button is pressed, but Interface Builder has no idea it needs to connect the button to that code. We can use Interface Builder to hook up our button to the buttonPressed method we just wrote. Then, when the .xib file is loaded by the framework, it will connect the button object it creates with our code.

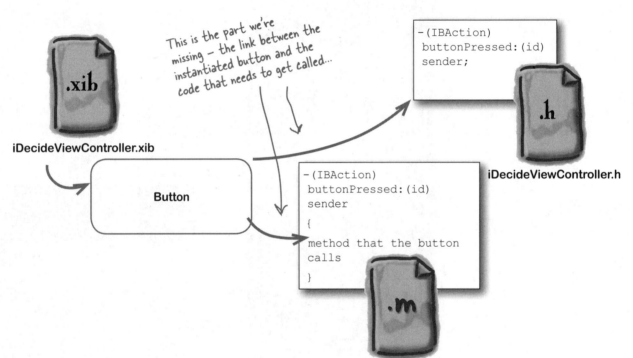

This is the part we're missing — the link between the instantiated button and the code that needs to get called...

.xib

iDecideViewController.xib

Button

```
-(IBAction)
buttonPressed:(id)
sender;
```

.h

iDecideViewController.h

```
-(IBAction)
buttonPressed:(id)
sender

{

method that the button
calls

}
```

.m

iDecideViewController.m

Unless the UI components are hooked up to the code, nothing is going to happen.

We need to connect the button's "Hey, I just got pressed" event to our buttonPressed action method. That will get our method called when the user taps on the button. We then need to get a reference to the UILabel that the framework is going to create for us when the nib is loaded—that's where the IBOutlet comes in. Let's start with the outlet so we can change the UILabel text when the button is pressed.

Use Interface Builder to connect UI controls to code

Jump back into Interface Builder for iDecideViewController.xib, and let's hook up the components to our new code.

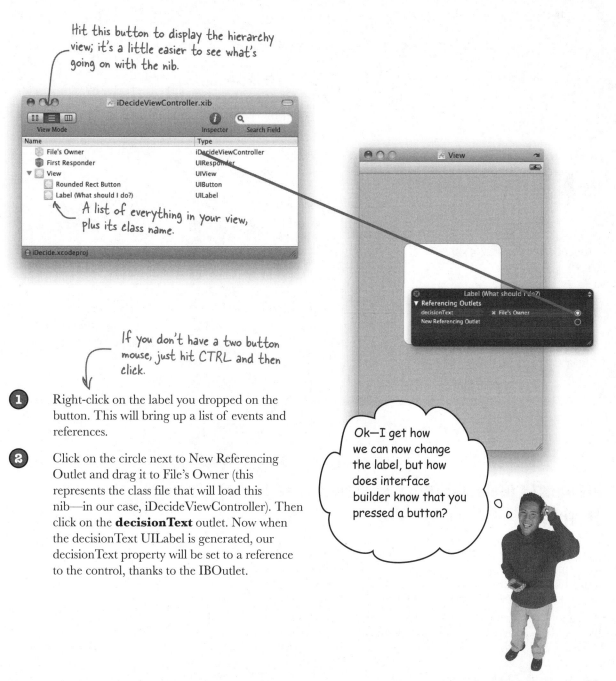

Hit this button to display the hierarchy view; it's a little easier to see what's going on with the nib.

A list of everything in your view, plus its class name.

If you don't have a two button mouse, just hit CTRL and then click.

1 Right-click on the label you dropped on the button. This will bring up a list of events and references.

2 Click on the circle next to New Referencing Outlet and drag it to File's Owner (this represents the class file that will load this nib—in our case, iDecideViewController). Then click on the **decisionText** outlet. Now when the decisionText UILabel is generated, our decisionText property will be set to a reference to the control, thanks to the IBOutlet.

Ok—I get how we can now change the label, but how does interface builder know that you pressed a button?

Interface Builder lists which events a component can trigger

We need to attach the right component event to the code. We wrote an action method earlier that we can connect the button to:

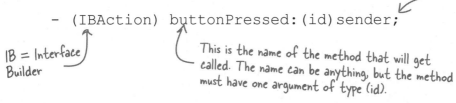

- (IBAction) buttonPressed:(id)sender;

IB = Interface Builder

This is the name of the method that will get called. The name can be anything, but the method must have one argument of type (id).

All IBAction messages take one argument: the sender of the message. This is the element that triggered the action.

Now we need to pick the event that should trigger this method. If you right-click on the button in Interface Builder, you'll see a list of events it could dispatch. We want the TouchUpInside event.

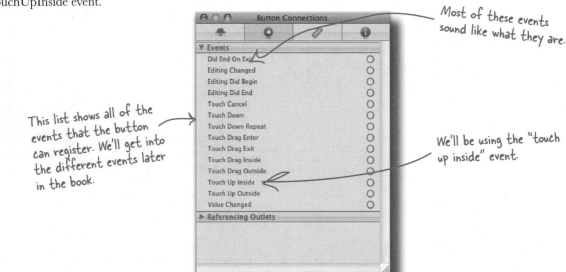

Most of these events sound like what they are.

This list shows all of the events that the button can register. We'll get into the different events later in the book.

We'll be using the "touch up inside" event.

Elements dispatch events when things happen to them

Whenever something happens to an element, for instance, a button gets tapped, the element dispatches one or more events. What we need to do is tell the button to notify us when that event gets raised. We'll be using the TouchUpInside event. If you think about how you click a button on the iPhone, the actual click inside the button isn't what matters: it's when you remove your finger (touch up) that the actual tap occurs. Connecting an event to a method is just like connecting an element to an outlet.

Connect your events to methods

Just like with outlets, you drag the connection from the
button event to File's Owner and select the action that
should be called.

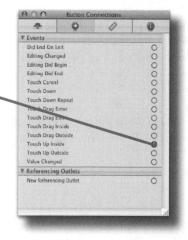

 Right-click on the button you dropped on the view. This
will bring up a list of events and references like it did with
the label.

Next click on the circle next to **Touch Up Inside** and
drag it to **File's Owner**. Click on the **buttonPressed**
action. Now when the button gets pressed, our
buttonPressed method will be called.

> So does it really matter whether I use an
> IBOutlet or an IBAction since Interface
> Builder can use both?

It matters a lot!

They're not the same. Use an IBOutlet when you need a
reference to something in the interface (e.g., so you can
change the label text). Use an IBAction when you want
a control to tell your code when something happens (like
the button gets pressed).

Fireside Chats

Tonight's talk: **IBActions speak louder than... a lot of things**

IBAction:	**IBOutlet:**
Hi, Outlet. What's it like to only be an enabler?	
	What are you talking about? I do stuff.
Uh—I'm an Action, all about doing. My job is to kick off a method when something happens—an event. That's getting something done. You just sit there and point to stuff going on.	
	Big deal. At least I'm aware of everything going on.
Yeah, but when the user does something, I make it happen! I do the saving, I do the actual clicking!	
	Listen, it's true that I'm just an instance variable that works with an object in a nib, but that doesn't mean I'm not important.
Really, because the compiler just ignores you!	
	It does, but I tell Interface Builder a lot. You're not very tight with IB, are you?
Well, for starters, the "IB" in IBAction stands for Interface Builder!	
	Big deal, I have "IB" in my name, too.
Well, we do have that in common. Anyway, Interface Builder knows when I'm around that some event in a nib can set me off and keep me informed.	
	Well, I guess that is pretty important.
Thanks. That's nice of you to admit.	

IBAction:

Care to explain?

Oh—I see. You know, there is one thing that you have that I've always wanted.

You can be anything! Stick IBOutlet in front of any variable name and you're good. I have more complicated syntax, because I need to have the idea of a sender in there.

Me too.

IBOutlet:

But I'm secure in my relationship with Interface Builder. Without me, the code couldn't change anything in the UI.

Sure. An IBOutlet variable can point to a specific object in the nib (like a text field or something), and code (yes, probably your code) can use me to change the UI, set a text field's content, change colors, etc.

What's that?

I do like the freedom! Glad we could work things out.

TEST DRIVE

Now that everything is hooked up, it's ready to run. Make sure that you save in Interface Builder and then go back into Xcode and build and run.

TEST DRIVE

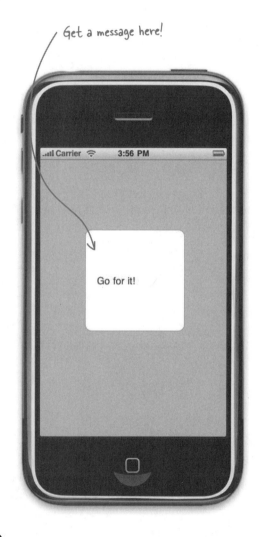

Get a message here!

Go for it!

What should I do?

Click here!

It works!

Phew. Now I know what to do!

Mike can make at least one decision.

Your app is working! All the pieces are fitting together: the *.xib file describes the interface, Interface Builder has connected it to the code, and Objective-C is making it all work together.

You're on your way to being #1 on the App Store.

How about a Twitter app?

there are no
Dumb Questions

Q: What is that File's Owner thing?

A: Interface Builder has an expectation of what class will be the nib's File's Owner. You can change what class Interface Builder thinks it will be, but by default a new project is set up so that the main View Controller created by Xcode is the File's Owner for the main view created by Xcode. That's why we didn't have to change anything. Since the File's Owner is set up to be our iDecideViewController, Interface Builder could look at the iDecideViewController header and see we had an IBOutlet named descriptionText and an IBAction named button pressed. When you connected the UILabel's referencing outlet to File's Owner descriptionText, Interface Builder

saved the information necessary so that when the nib is loaded by the application, the references are set correctly in our iDecideViewController. The same thing happened with the TouchUpInside event, except in this case instead of hooking up a component to a reference, it hooked up a component's event to a method that should be called.

Beware—Interface Builder's expectation of the class that will load the nib does not mean that other classes can't try—it just might not work well if that class doesn't have the necessary properties and methods.

Q: What's with the "Outlet" stuff?

A: Interface Builder has the idea of

Outlets and Actions, and we'll talk more about them in a bit. Basically an Outlet is a reference to something and an Action is a message (method) that gets sent (called) when something happens.

Q: Why does our new text string have an @ in front of it?

A: Cocoa Touch uses a string class named NSString for its text strings. Since it's so common, Objective-C has built in support for creating them from constants. You indicate a string constant should be an NSString by putting an @ symbol in front of it. Otherwise, it's just a normal char* like in C or C++.

BULLET POINTS

- Interface Builder creates nib files (with a .xib extension) that describe the GUI in XML

- Nib files are loaded by the Cocoa Touch framework and are turned into real instances of Cocoa Touch classes at runtime.

- In order to connect the components described in a nib to your code, you use IBOutlets and IBActions.

- Xcode is where your code and files are maintained for your application.

- Xcode is the hub for your project development and offers support for editing your code, building your application, and debugging it once it's running.

- The iPhone Simulator lets you test your application on your Mac without needing a real device.

Match each iPhone development item to its description.

Item	Description
IBOutlet	A typical iPhone plan that is different from most other mobile phones.
Functions of Xcode	Xcode, Instruments, Interface Builder, and the iPhone Simulator.
Unlimited data usage	Reference from the code to the interface.
IBAction	Images, databases, the icon file, etc.
Components of the SDK	Maintaining and editing code and resources, debugging code, and preparing an app for deployment.
Application resources	Indicates a method that can be called in response to an event.

WHO DOES WHAT?
SOLUTION

Match each iPhone development item to its description.

Item

Description

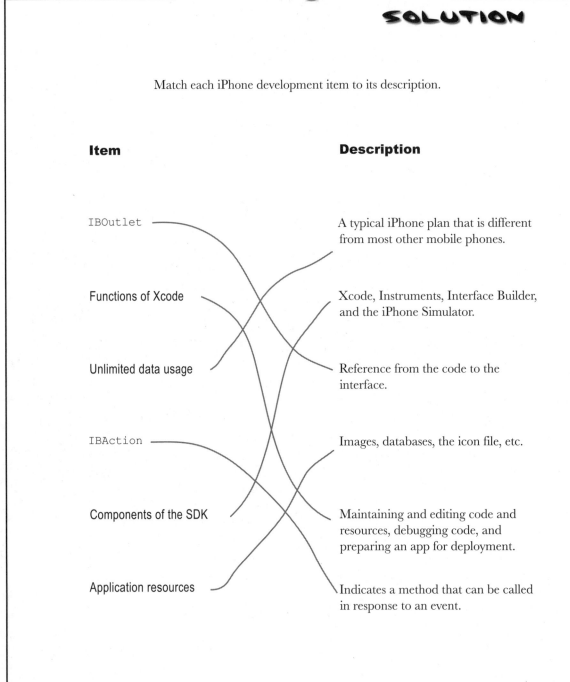

IBOutlet

A typical iPhone plan that is different from most other mobile phones.

Functions of Xcode

Xcode, Instruments, Interface Builder, and the iPhone Simulator.

Unlimited data usage

Reference from the code to the interface.

IBAction

Images, databases, the icon file, etc.

Components of the SDK

Maintaining and editing code and resources, debugging code, and preparing an app for deployment.

Application resources

Indicates a method that can be called in response to an event.

iPhonecross

Bend your brain around some of the new terminology we used in this chapter.

Across

4. Something that the simulator cannot reliably test.
5. This is used to set up an outgoing connection from the implementation code to the view.
7. The term to describe each screen of an iPhone app.
8. The framework used to write iPhone apps.
10. The folder used to organize the images for the app.
12. The name of the IDE for iPhone apps.
13. These are used in Xcode to provide classes to be accessed.

Down

1. The language used to write iPhone apps.
2. This is used on a desktop to test an app.
3. This is used to recieve an event in code and trigger something.
6. This is the name of the editor used for Objective-C.
9. The iPhone is this kind of device.
11. The name of a file used to create a view.

iPhonecross Solution

Bend your brain around some of the new terminology we used in this chapter.

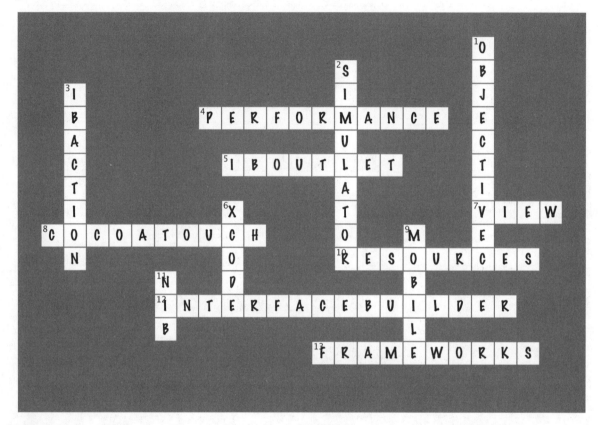

Across

4. Something that the simulator cannot reliably test. [PERFORMANCE]
5. This is used to set up an outgoing connection from the implementation code to the view. [IBOUTLET]
7. The term to describe each screen of an iPhone app. [VIEW]
8. The framework used to write iPhone apps. [COCOATOUCH]
10. The folder used to organize the images for the app. [RESOURCES]
12. The name of the IDE for iPhone apps. [INTERFACEBUILDER]
13. These are used in Xcode to provide classes to be accessed. [FRAMEWORKS]

Down

1. The language used to write iPhone apps. [OBJECTIVEC]
2. This is used on a desktop to test an app. [SIMULATOR]
3. This is used to recieve an event in code and trigger something. [IBACTION]
6. This is the name of the editor used for Objective-C. [XCODE]
9. The iPhone is this kind of device. [MOBILE]
11. The name of a file used to create a view. [NIB]

Your iPhone Toolbox

You've got Chapter 1 under your belt
and now you've added basic IPhone app
interactions to your tool box. For a complete
list of tooltips in the book, go to http://www.
headfirstlabs.com/iphonedev.

Views are constructed in Interface Builder

A view is made up of nib (*.xib) files and the GUIs are edited
with Interface Builder.

...then the code that makes the views work...

This code is almost always written in Objective-C using
Xcode.

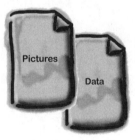

...and any other resources, all packaged into your application.

Images and other data are referenced together in Xcode so
that all of the files that you need can be easily dealt with.

2 iPhone app patterns

Hello @twitter!

@grandmom please bring me some soda. I'm so over the milk. #babyrants

Apps have a lot of moving parts. OK, actually, they don't have any real moving parts, but they do have lots of UI controls. A typical iPhone app has more going on than just a button, and it's time to build one. Working with some of the more complicated widgets means you'll need to pay more attention than ever to how you design your app, as well. In this chapter, you'll learn about some of the fundamental design patterns used in the iPhone SDK, and how to put together a bigger application.

Overheard at
Head First
Lounge

Author's note:
Head First does not take any responsibility for Mike's relationship problems.

Mike is back. He has a great girlfriend, Renee, but they've been having some problems. She thinks that he doesn't talk about his feelings enough.

A Twitter app is the way to go here. That would be perfect: I can just tweet about my feelings and then she'll be happy.

↑ Mike

There's (about to be) an app for that.

Using some solid design and the basic controls included in the Interface Builder library, you can have Mike posting to Twitter in no time. But first, what should his tweets say?

First we need to figure out what Mike (really) wants

Mike isn't a complex guy. He wants an easy interface to talk to Twitter and he really doesn't want to have to type much.

Here's what Mike handed you at the end of the night

Here's what I want:

– Not much typing

– Instant communication

– Easy to use

– My tweets like this: I'm _____ and feeling _____ about it."

App Magnets

Now that we know what Mike wants, what do we need to do? Take the magnets below and put them in order of the steps you'll follow to build his Twitter app.

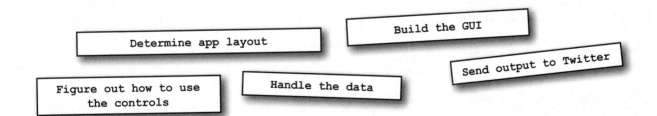

Determine app layout

Build the GUI

Send output to Twitter

Figure out how to use the controls

Handle the data

App Magnets Solution

Now that we know what Mike wants, what do we need to do? Take the magnets below and put them in order of the steps you'll follow to build his Twitter app.

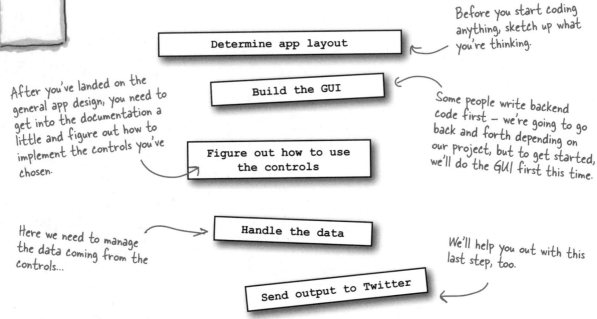

Before you start coding anything, sketch up what you're thinking.

Determine app layout

After you've landed on the general app design, you need to get into the documentation a little and figure out how to implement the controls you've chosen.

Build the GUI

Some people write backend code first — we're going to go back and forth depending on our project, but to get started, we'll do the GUI first this time.

Figure out how to use the controls

Here we need to manage the data coming from the controls...

Handle the data

We'll help you out with this last step, too.

Send output to Twitter

there are no Dumb Questions

Q: How do you figure out the app layout?

A: We're going to give you a couple to choose from to get started, but in general, it's important to think about what your app needs to do and focus on those features first.

Q: Are we always going to start with a sketch?

A: Yes! Good software design starts with knowing what you're building and how

the user is going to work with the app. The app for Mike is going to work with Twitter, and he's going to be able to make some selections for his feelings and thoughts. That's it!

Q: How do we talk to Twitter?

A: Don't worry, we'll give you some code to help you to work with that.

Just FYI, though, Twitter has a really well-documented API. We'll give you what you need, but feel free to add more features!

Q: Does every control work differently than the others?

A: For the most part, no—once you learn a few basic patterns, you'll be able to find your way through most of the SDK. Some of the controls have a few peculiarities here and there, but for the most part they should start to look familiar.

APP LAYOUT CONSTRUCTION

Here are two designs to evaluate. Based on aesthetics, usability, and standard iPhone app behavior, which one is better for Mike?

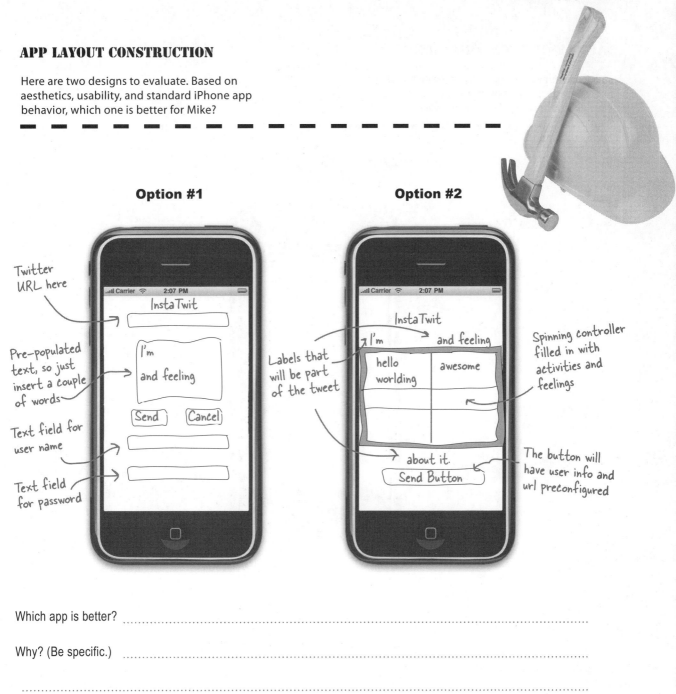

Option #1

Twitter URL here

InstaTwit

Pre-populated text, so just insert a couple of words

I'm
and feeling

Send   Cancel

Text field for user name

Text field for password

Option #2

InstaTwit

I'm   and feeling

Labels that will be part of the tweet

hello worlding   awesome

Spinning controller filled in with activities and feelings

about it.
Send Button

The button will have user info and url preconfigured

Which app is better? ....

Why? (Be specific.) ....

....

Why not the other? ....

APP LAYOUT CONSTRUCTION

We've given you two designs to evaluate. Based on aesthetics, usability, and standard iPhone app behavior, which one is better for Mike?

Bad Option #1

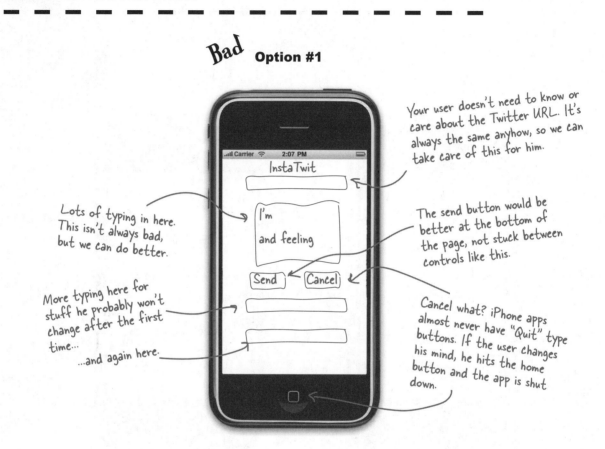

Your user doesn't need to know or care about the Twitter URL. It's always the same anyhow, so we can take care of this for him.

Lots of typing in here. This isn't always bad, but we can do better.

The send button would be better at the bottom of the page, not stuck between controls like this.

More typing here for stuff he probably won't change after the first time...

...and again here.

Cancel what? iPhone apps almost never have "Quit" type buttons. If the user changes his mind, he hits the home button and the app is shut down.

Which app is better?   #2.

Why? (Be specific.)   Option #2 has a lot less typing and fewer fields overall.
Since the user doesn't need to change his username or password often there's no reason to put it on the main view every time he runs the app.

Why not the other?   Option #1 has a lot of typing and settings to remember. The buttons are confusing.

Good! (Option #2)

App flows cleanly from top to bottom.

Common text is shown as a label — Mike doesn't have to try to move the cursor around it.

InstaTwit

I'm   and feeling

hello   awesome
worlding

about it.

Send Button

Instead of having Mike type in what he's doing and his feelings, we can give him a picker to select from. This means fewer options since they're predetermined, but is way easier to use and Mike's a simple guy after all, right?

Smart send button that keeps the user tweeting, not remembering passwords or URLs.

This is the one you're going to build for Mike.

there are no
Dumb Questions

Q: Do I really need to care about usability and aesthetics so much?

A: Usability and aesthetics are what made the iPhone a success, and Apple will defend them to the death. Even more importantly, you don't get to put anything on the App Store or on anyone else's iPhone without their approval. Apple has sold over a billion apps—if yours doesn't fit with the iPhone look and feel or is hard to use, people will find someone else's app and never look back.

Q: We got rid of the username, password, and URL fields. The URL one I understand, but what about the other two?

A: Anytime your app needs configuration information that the user doesn't need to change frequently, you should keep it out of the main task flow. Apple even provides a special place for these called a Settings bundle that fits in with the standard iPhone settings. We're not going to use that in this chapter (we'll just hardcode the values) but later we'll show you how to put stuff in the Settings page. That's usually the right place for things like login details.

Q: How am I supposed to know what Apple thinks is good design or aesthetically pleasing?

A: Funny you should ask... go ahead, turn the page.

App design rules—the iPhone HIG

The iPhone Human Interface Guide (HIG) is a document that Apple distributes for guidance in developing iPhone Apps for sale on the App Store. You can download it at http://developer.apple.com/iphone. This isn't just something nice they did to help you out; when you submit an app for approval, you agree that your app will conform to the HIG.

We can't overstate this: ***you have to follow the HIG,*** as Apple's review process is thorough and they will reject your application if it doesn't conform. Complain, blog with righteous anger, then conform. Now let's move on.

Apple also distributes a few other guides and tutorials, including the iPhone Application Programming Guide. This is another great source of information and explains how you should handle different devices, like the iPhone and the iPod Touch. Not paying attention to the iPod Touch is another great way to get your app rejected from the App Store.

Note: While the authors do not suggest testing these methods of being rejected from the App Store, we can speak with authority that they work.

Application types

The HIG details three main types of applications that are commonly developed for the iPhone. Each type has a different purpose and therefore offers a different kind of user experience. Figuring out what type of application you're building before you start working on the GUI helps get you started on the road to good interface design.

Immersive Apps

Games are a classic example, but like this simulated level, all immersive apps require a very custom interface that allows the user to interact with the device. As a result, HIG guidelines aren't as crucial in this case.

Productivity Apps

Help manage information and complete tasks. Info is hierarchical, and you navigate by drilling down into more levels of detail.

Utility Apps

Get a specific set of info to the user with as little interaction or settings configuration as possible.

Usually have more interface design than a productivity app, and are expected to stay very consistent with the HIG.

WHO DOES WHAT?

Below are a bunch of different application ideas. For each one, think about what kind of app it really is and match it to the app types on the right.

App Description

InstaTwit 1.0: Allows you to tweet with minimal typing.

News Reader: Gives you a list of the news categories and you can get the details on stories you choose.

Marble Game: A marble rolling game that uses the accelerometer to drive the controls.

Stopwatch Tool: Gives you a stopwatch that starts and stops by touching the screen

Recipe Manager: A meal listing that allows you to drill down and look at individual recipes.

Type of App

Immersive Application

Utility Application

Productivity Application

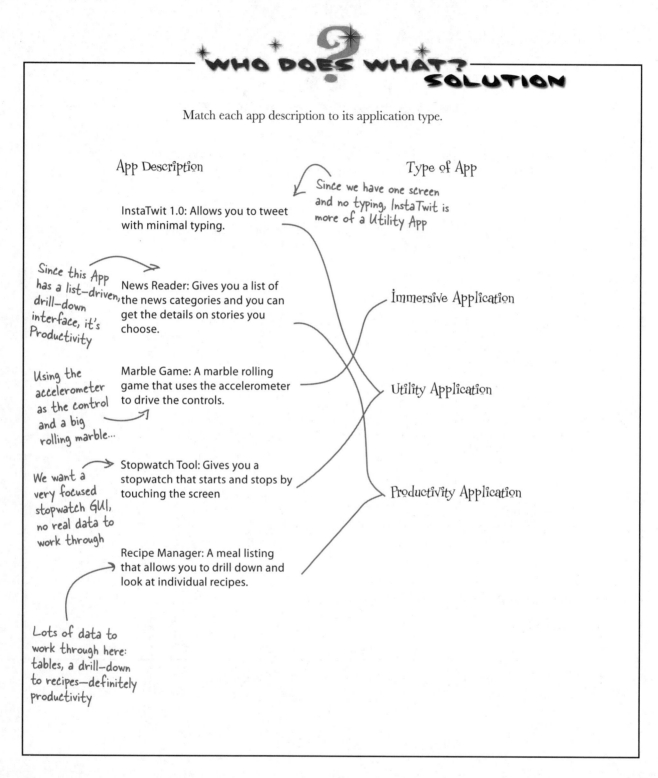

WHO DOES WHAT? SOLUTION

Match each app description to its application type.

App Description

Type of App

Since we have one screen and no typing, InstaTwit is more of a Utility App

InstaTwit 1.0: Allows you to tweet with minimal typing.

Since this App has a list-driven, drill-down interface, it's Productivity

News Reader: Gives you a list of the news categories and you can get the details on stories you choose.

Immersive Application

Using the accelerometer as the control and a big rolling marble...

Marble Game: A marble rolling game that uses the accelerometer to drive the controls.

Utility Application

We want a very focused stopwatch GUI, no real data to work through

Stopwatch Tool: Gives you a stopwatch that starts and stops by touching the screen

Productivity Application

Recipe Manager: A meal listing that allows you to drill down and look at individual recipes.

Lots of data to work through here: tables, a drill-down to recipes—definitely productivity

HIG guidelines for pickers and buttons

The HIG has a section on the proper use of all the standard controls, including the two that we've selected for InstaTwit. Before you build the view with your controls, it's a good idea to take a quick look at the recommendations from Apple. You'll find this information in Chapter 9, Application Controls, of the HIG.

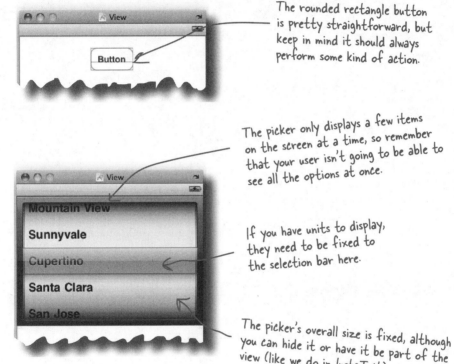

The rounded rectangle button is pretty straightforward, but keep in mind it should always perform some kind of action.

The picker only displays a few items on the screen at a time, so remember that your user isn't going to be able to see all the options at once.

If you have units to display, they need to be fixed to the selection bar here.

The picker's overall size is fixed, although you can hide it or have it be part of the view (like we do in InstaTwit).

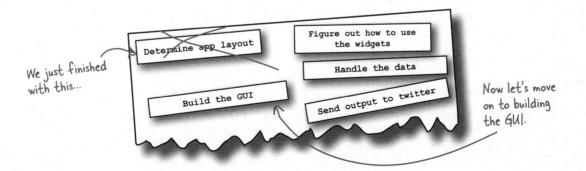

We just finished with this...

Determine app layout

Figure out how to use the widgets

Handle the data

Build the GUI

Send output to twitter

Now let's move on to building the GUI.

Create a new View-based project for InstaTwit

Once you've started Xcode, select **File** → **New Project.**
Just like iDecide, for InstaTwit we have one screen and we're
not going to be flipping it or anything fancy, so again choose
the **View-based Application** and name it Instatwit.

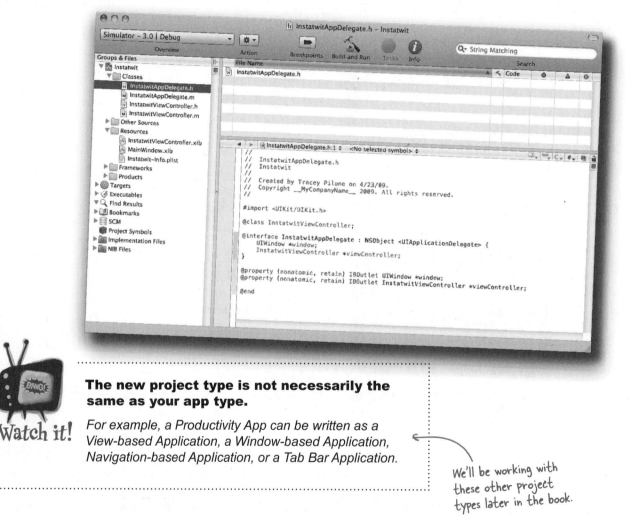

![Television icon with "BANG!" — **Watch it!**]

The new project type is not necessarily the same as your app type.

*For example, a Productivity App can be written as a
View-based Application, a Window-based Application,
Navigation-based Application, or a Tab Bar Application.*

We'll be working with
these other project
types later in the book.

Start with the view layout

Now that we have the autogenerated code, we're going to start working with
the interface. To do that, we'll be editing the nib (.xib) file. Double-click on
InstatwitViewController.xib in the Resources folder, and launch Interface Builder.

It's time to build the View. Using drag and drop, pull over the elements from the Interface Builder library that you need to build the view.

Exercise

1 Find each of the elements (we've given them the proper name for you) in the library and drag and drop them into the **View** window.

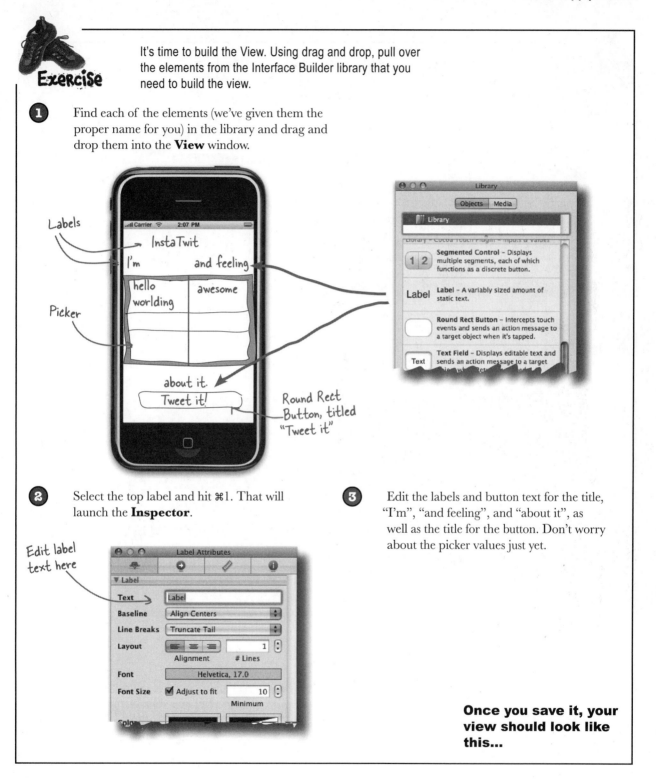

Labels

Picker

Round Rect Button, titled "Tweet it"

Library

Objects | Media

Library

Library · Cocoa Touch Plugin · Inputs & Values

1 2   **Segmented Control** – Displays multiple segments, each of which functions as a discrete button.

Label   **Label** – A variably sized amount of static text.

Round Rect Button – Intercepts touch events and sends an action message to a target object when it's tapped.

Text   **Text Field** – Displays editable text and sends an action message to a target

InstaTwit

I'm   and feeling

hello worlding | awesome

about it.

Tweet it!

2 Select the top label and hit ⌘1. That will launch the **Inspector**.

Edit label text here

Label Attributes

▼ Label

Text	Label
Baseline	Align Centers
Line Breaks	Truncate Tail
Layout	≡ ≡ ≡ 1 Alignment # Lines
Font	Helvetica, 17.0
Font Size	☑ Adjust to fit 10 Minimum
Color	

3 Edit the labels and button text for the title, "I'm", "and feeling", and "about it", as well as the title for the button. Don't worry about the picker values just yet.

Once you save it, your view should look like this...

Exercise Solution

The View is all built and ready to go. Here's what you should have on your screen now. Once you tweak everything to look just how you want it, we'll run InstaTwit.

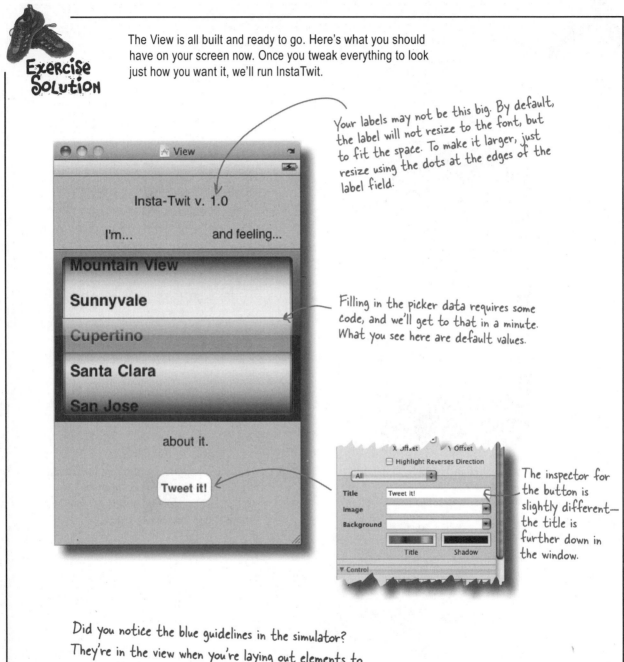

Your labels may not be this big. By default, the label will not resize to the font, but to fit the space. To make it larger, just resize using the dots at the edges of the label field.

Filling in the picker data requires some code, and we'll get to that in a minute. What you see here are default values.

The inspector for the button is slightly different— the title is further down in the window.

Did you notice the blue guidelines in the simulator? They're in the view when you're laying out elements to help you center things and keep them lined up with each other.

Test Drive

Now it's time to check out InstaTwit in the Simulator. Save in Interface Builder, go back into Xcode, and hit **Build and Debug** from the Build menu (or ⌘ return).

The picker isn't showing up because there isn't any data yet...

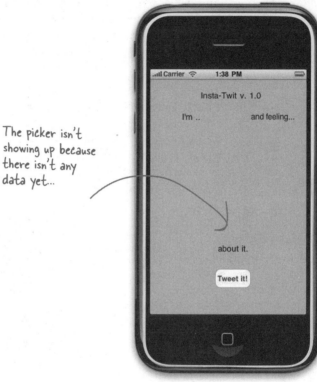

BRAIN POWER

To get the picker to show, it needs to have data to fill it. Where do you think that the code for the data should go?

The life of a root view

In Chapter 1 we touched on how Interface Builder creates XML descriptions of your view, called a nib, and that the Cocoa Touch framework turns that into a real view in your application. Now that you've built a couple apps, let's take a closer look at what's going on under the hood.

 Like in most other languages, main(...) gets called first.
When your application is launched by the user, the iPhone provides a quick animation of your app zooming into the screen (this is actually a PNG file you can include with your app), then calls your main method. Main is provided by the templates and you almost never need to touch it.

Main
Window

Main kicks off a Cocoa Touch Application.
The standard main(...) kicks off a Cocoa Touch UIApplicationMain, which uses the information in your application's Info.plist file to figure out what nib to load. With the View template we used, it's a nib called MainWindow.xib.

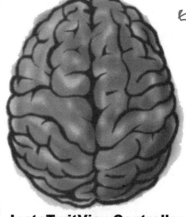

This is the View Controller. It subclasses UIViewController.

3 MainWindow.xib contains the connections for our application.
If you look in MainWindow.xib, you'll see it has an instance of our InstaTwitAppDelegate, for its UIApplicationDelegate and an instance of our InstaTwitViewController. When the Cocoa framework loads this nib, it will create an instance of our InstaTwitViewController and tell it to load our InstaTwitViewController.xib.

We'll talk more about delegates soon, too.

InstaTwitViewController
instantiated from
MainWindow.xib

When we built the nib, we used the generic proxy File's Owner for outlet and action connections. When the nib is actually loaded, there's a real object there to receive those connections. For us, it's the InstaTwitViewController.

4 **The Cocoa Touch framework creates our custom view from the InstaTwitViewController.xib.**
When we constructed the nib, we used the File's Owner proxy object to stand in for the object that owns the nib contents. At this point the framework is loading the nib on behalf of our InstaTwitViewController class so that instance is used for connections. As the framework creates instances of our components, they're connected up to the instance of InstaTwitViewController.

This is our view.

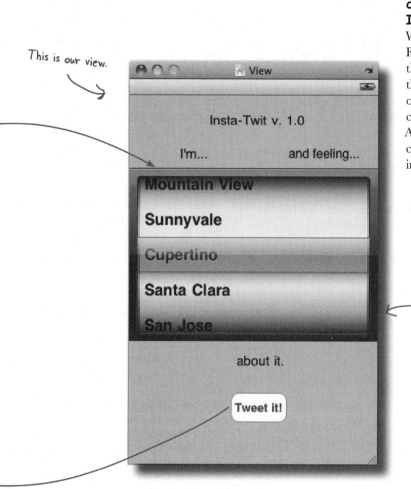

The nib file contains serialized instances of objects as we configured them. They are usually control objects like buttons or labels, but can be anything that can be serialized.

5 **When events occur with components, methods are invoked on our controller instance.**
The actions we associated between the controls and the File's Owner in the nib were translated into connections between the controls and our instance. Now when a control fires off an event, the framework calls a method on our InstaTwitViewController instance.

Now let's put this knowledge to use and add some data for the picker.

there are no
Dumb Questions

Q: Isn't good design vs. bad design a little subjective?

A: Yes and no. Obviously, different people will have differing opinions about what UI looks better. However, Apple has very specific guidelines about how certain controls should be used and best practices that should be followed. In general, if you're using a common iPhone control, make sure you're using it in a way that's consistent with existing applications.

Q: How can I run these apps on my iPhone?

A: To get an app you write installed on your iPhone you'll need to sign up for either the Standard or Enterprise Developer programs at http://developer.apple.com/iphone/. Everything in this book is designed to work with just the **Simulator**, so don't feel like you need to go do that just yet. We'll talk more about putting apps on an actual phone later in the book.

Q: The InstaTwit icon looks horrible. What can I do?

A: The icon for an application is just a PNG file in your project. We'll add and configure icons later, but for now, just know that you'll need a .png file in the resources directory for that purpose—we'll hook you up with some cool icons later.

Q: Do I have to use Interface Builder for the view?

A: No. Everything that you do in Interface Builder can be done in code. Interface Builder makes it a lot easier to get things started, but sometimes you'll need that code-level control of a view to do what you want. We'll be switching back and forth depending on the project and view.

Q: I'm still a little fuzzy on this nib thing. Do they hold our UI or regular objects?

A: They can hold both. When you assemble a view using Interface Builder, it keeps track of the controls you're using and the links to other classes. These controls are serialized into an XML document; when you save it out, this is your nib. Interface Builder is able to serialize non-control classes, too. That's how it saves out our InstaTwitViewController in MainWindow.xib. When the nib is restored from disk, objects in the nib are reinstantiated and populated with the values you gave them in Interface Builder.

Q: So does Interface Builder save out the File's Owner too?

A: No, File's Owner is a proxy. File's Owner represents whatever class is asking to have this nib loaded. So the File's Owner proxy isn't actually stored in the nib, but Interface Builder needs that proxy so you can make association with controls you used in your view. When the nib is restored (and the control objects are instantiated), the nib loading code will make the connections to the real owning object that asked to load the nib.

First, get the data from Mike

Mike likes what you have put together for the UI, so now we need a little more information before we fill the picker.

I like the interface. Here's my list of what I do and how I feel about it so you can fill in the rest. Can't wait until it's done because I'm soooo over talking about it...

Things I do:

sleeping

eating

working

thinking

crying

begging

leaving

shopping

Things I feel:

awesome

sad

happy

ambivalent

nauseous

psyched

confused

hopeful

anxious

Gotta add "hello worlding"

⚛ BRAIN POWER

This data will be used as part of the picker, but how do you implement that?

Use pickers when you want controlled input

In our case, the picker is the perfect element for our app. No typing at all, but it allows Mike to have some input over what gets selected. There's some terminology that you need to know about pickers before we get our data in there.

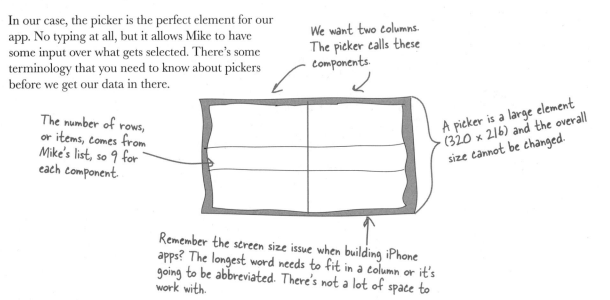

We want two columns. The picker calls these components.

The number of rows, or items, comes from Mike's list, so 9 for each component.

A picker is a large element (320 × 216) and the overall size cannot be changed.

Remember the screen size issue when building iPhone apps? The longest word needs to fit in a column or it's going to be abbreviated. There's not a lot of space to work with.

When in doubt, check out Apple's API documentation

By now you're already thinking about how to implement that picker. It's time to get into the API documentation. In Xcode, go to the **Help** menu and then the **Documentation** option.

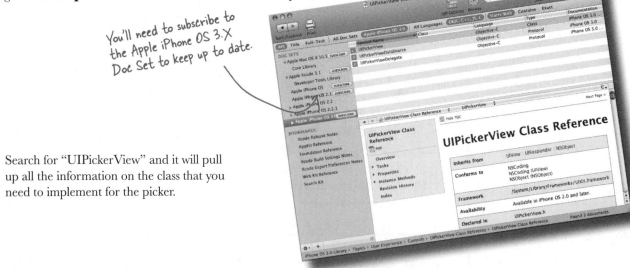

You'll need to subscribe to the Apple iPhone OS 3.X Doc Set to keep up to date.

Search for "UIPickerView" and it will pull up all the information on the class that you need to implement for the picker.

Fill the picker rows with Mike's data

The picker needs to know how many rows it needs and how many columns. And that information is tied to the words that Mike provided.

OK, so we can just set the picker rows with the values Mike gave us like we did with the button label, right?

The picker is different.

The picker doesn't want to be told what to do, it's going to **ask** when it wants your input. You're going to see this pattern show up with controls that could use a lot of data like pickers and later, table views. Let's take a closer look...

Pickers get their data from a datasource...

Most of the elements in the Cocoa Touch framework have the concept of datasources and delegates. Each UI control is responsible for how things look on the screen (the cool spinning dial look, the animation when the user spins a wheel, etc.), but it doesn't know anything about the data it needs to show or what to do when something is selected.

The **datasource** provides the bridge between the control and the data it needs to display. The control will ask the datasource for what it needs and the datasource is responsible for providing the information in a format the control expects. In our case, the datasource provides the number of components (or columns) for the picker and the total number of rows for the picker. Different controls need different kinds of datasources. For the picker, we need a **UIPickerViewDatasource**.

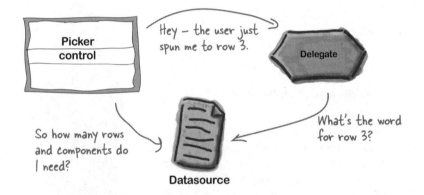

...and tell their delegates when something happens.

A **delegate** is responsible for the behavior of an element. When someone selects something—or in this case, scrolls the picker to a value—the control tells the delegate what happened and the delegate figures out what to do in response. Just like with datasources, different controls need different kinds of delegates. For the picker, we need a **UIPickerViewDelegate**.

there are no Dumb Questions

Q: Why is the delegate providing the content? That really seems like data.

A: That's something particular to a picker and it has to do with the fact that the picker delegate can change how the data is shown. In the simplest form, it can just return strings to the picker. If it wants to get fancy, it can return the entire view (yes, just like the view you built with Interface Builder, but smaller) to use images or special fonts, whatever.

There's a pattern for that

You're going to see this **Control-Datasource-Delegate** pattern show up throughout the rest of this book. Nearly all of the complex controls use it. If you squint a little, even the **View-View Controller** relationship we've been using follows this pattern (minus the datasource).

A control represents the GUI that your user will interact with. Generally, it will be assembled with Interface Builder, but it can be built in code, too. Each approach has benefits and drawbacks, and sometimes you'll use both on the same project.

A datasource works with the databases, plists, images, or general information that your app will need.

The delegate contains the logic that controls the flow of information. It saves and displays information and controls which view is seen when. Even our views follow this pattern — their delegate is the ViewController.

Control

Datasource

Delegate

Controls have their own specific datasources and delegates

Each control has specific needs for its datasource and delegate and we'll talk about how that's handled in Objective-C in a minute. However, it's important to realize that while the responsibilities are split between the datasource and the delegate in the pattern, *they don't necessarily have to be implemented in different classes*. The control wants a delegate and a datasource—it doesn't care whether they're provided by the same object or not: it's going to ask the datasource for datasource-related things and the delegate for delegate-related things.

Let's take a closer look at how the UIPicker uses its datasource and delegate to get an idea of how all of this fits together.

The Picker Exposed

**This week's interview:
How to avoid spinning out of control...**

Head First: Hello Picker, thanks for joining us.

Picker: My pleasure. I don't usually get to talk to anyone but my datasource and delegate so this is a real treat.

Head First: I'm glad you brought those up. So we've worked with controls like buttons and labels, but they just have properties. What's going on with this delegate and datasource business?

Picker: Well, to be clear, I have properties too— there just isn't too much exciting going on there. What makes me different is that I could be working with a lot of data. I might only have one row or I might have a hundred; it just depends on the application.

Head First: Ah, OK. A label only has one string in it, so there can be a property that holds that string. No problem.

Picker: Exactly! So, instead of trying to cram all of the data into me directly, it's cleaner to just let me ask for what I need when I need it.

Head First: But you need to ask for it in a specific way, right?

Picker: That's the beauty of my setup. I ask for what I need to know in a specific way—that's why there's a UIPickerDatasource—but I don't care where my datasource gets its information. For example, I need to know how many rows I need to show, so I ask my datasource. It could be using an array, a database, a plist, whatever—I don't care. All I need to know is how many rows.

Head First: That's really nice—so you could be showing data coming from just about anything, and

as long as your datasource knows how to answer your questions, you don't care how it stores the data internally.

Picker: You got it. Now the delegate is a little different. I can draw the wheels and all that, but I don't know what each application wants to do when someone selects a row, so I just pass the buck to my delegate.

Head First: So whichever one implements the delegate, it codes things so that when you tell it what happened, it performs the right action, like saving some value or setting a clock or whatever....

Picker: That's it. Now, I have to confess I have one little oddity going on...

Head First: Oh, I was waiting for this... this is where you ask the delegate for the value to show in a row, right?

Picker: Yeah—other controls ask their datasource. I could come up with a lot of excuses, but... well, we all have our little quirks, right?

Head First: I appreciate your honesty. It's not all bad, though; your delegate can do some neat things with each row, can't it?

Picker: Oh yeah! When I ask the delegate for a particular row, it can give me back a full view instead of just a string. Sometimes they have icons in them or pictures—really, anything you can cram in a view, I can display.

Head First: That's great. Well, we're out of time, but thanks again for stopping by.

Picker: My pleasure! Now I'm off to take my new datasource for a spin...

WHO DOES WHAT?

Match each picker characteristic to where it belongs—the delegate or the datasource. You'll need to go digging in the API to figure out where the three methods go.

Picker characteristic (or method)   Delegate or datasource?

Directions for drawing the view
for the items

The number of components   **Delegate**

`pickerView:numberOfRowsInComponent`

`pickerView:titleForRow:forComponent`   **Datasource**

The row values (strings or views)

`numberOfComponentsInPickerView`

Working together, the delegate and the datasource provide what is needed to render the picker.

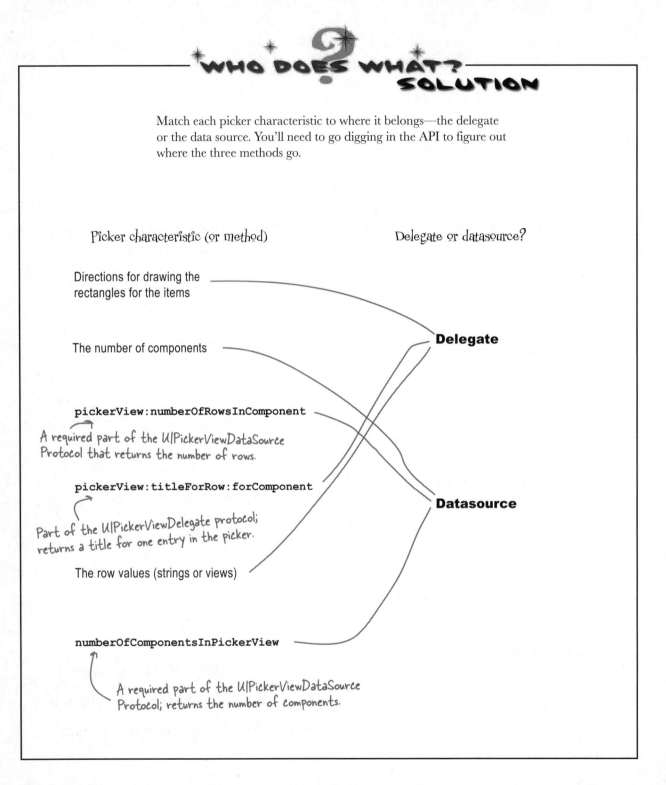

WHO DOES WHAT? SOLUTION

Match each picker characteristic to where it belongs—the delegate or the data source. You'll need to go digging in the API to figure out where the three methods go.

Picker characteristic (or method)

Delegate or datasource?

Directions for drawing the rectangles for the items

The number of components

Delegate

`pickerView:numberOfRowsInComponent`

A required part of the UIPickerViewDataSource Protocol that returns the number of rows.

`pickerView:titleForRow:forComponent`

Datasource

Part of the UIPickerViewDelegate protocol; returns a title for one entry in the picker.

The row values (strings or views)

`numberOfComponentsInPickerView`

A required part of the UIPickerViewDataSource Protocol; returns the number of components.

Hang on—there are protocols in both the datasource and the delegate?

Protocols define what messages the datasource and delegates need respond to.

Pickers (and other controls that use delegates and datasources) have specific messages to which their supporting classes need to respond. These messages are defined in *protocols*. Protocols are Objective-C's idea of a pure interface. When your class can speak a particular protocol, you're said to **conform to it**.

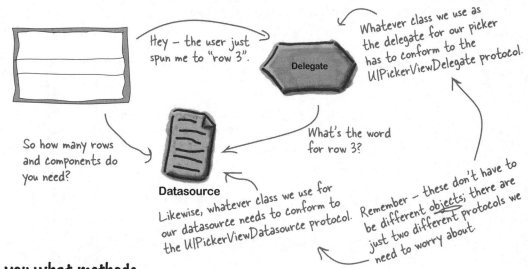

Hey — the user just spun me to "row 3".

Delegate

Whatever class we use as the delegate for our picker has to conform to the UIPickerViewDelegate protocol.

What's the word for row 3?

So how many rows and components do you need?

Datasource

Likewise, whatever class we use for our datasource needs to conform to the UIPickerViewDatasource protocol.

Remember — these don't have to be different objects; there are just two different protocols we need to worry about.

Protocols tell you what methods (messages) you need to implement

Protocols typically have some required methods to implement and others that are optional. For example, the UIPickerViewDatasource protocol has a required method named `pickerView:numberOfRowsInComponent`; it has to be in the datasource for the picker to work. However, UIPickerViewDelegate protocol has an optional method named `pickerView:titleForRow:forComponent`, so it doesn't need to be in the delegate unless you want it.

So how do you know what protocols you need to worry about? The documentation for an element will tell you what protocols it needs to talk to. For example, our UIPickerView needs a datasource that speaks the UIPickerDataSource protocol and a delegate that speaks the UIPickerDelegate protocol. Click on the protocol name and you'll see the documentation for which messages are optional and which are required for a protocol. We'll talk more about how to implement these in the next chapter; for now, we'll provide you the code to get started.

First, declare that the controller conforms to both protocols

Now that you know what you need to make the picker work, namely a delegate and a datasource, let's get back into Xcode and create them. Under **Classes** you have two files that need to be edited: InstatwitViewController.h and InstatwitViewController.m. Both files were created when you started the project.

The .h and .m files work together, with the header file (.h) declaring the class's interface, variable declarations, outlets, and actions, etc.; the implementation file (.m) holds the actual implementation code. We need to update the header file to state that our InstatwitViewController conforms to both the UIPickerViewDataSource and the UIPickerViewDelegate protocols.

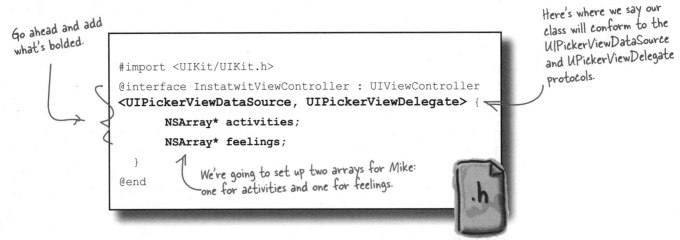

Go ahead and add what's bolded.

```
#import <UIKit/UIKit.h>

@interface InstatwitViewController : UIViewController
<UIPickerViewDataSource, UIPickerViewDelegate> {

    NSArray* activities;

    NSArray* feelings;

}
@end
```

Here's where we say our class will conform to the UIPickerViewDataSource and UIPickerViewDelegate protocols.

We're going to set up two arrays for Mike: one for activities and one for feelings.

InstatwitViewController.h

Next, add Mike's activities and feelings to the implementation file

Now we're into InstatwitViewController.m file, the actual implementation. We'll need to add some methods to implement the required methods from the protocols, but we'll get back to that in a second. First, let's add the list from Mike. We're going to use the two arrays we declared in the header to store the words that Mike gave us.

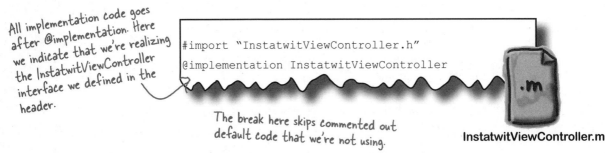

All implementation code goes after @implementation. Here we indicate that we're realizing the InstatwitViewController interface we defined in the header.

```
#import "InstatwitViewController.h"
@implementation InstatwitViewController
```

The break here skips commented out default code that we're not using.

InstatwitViewController.m

Remove the /* marks that were here and then add the code.
This method gets called on your view controller after the view
is loaded from the .xib file. This is where you can do some
initialization and setup for the view.

```
// Implement
viewDidLoad to do additional setup after loading the view,
typically from a nib.

 - (void)viewDidLoad {
    [super viewDidLoad];

        activities = [[NSArray alloc] initWithObjects:@"sleeping",
@"eating", @"working", @"thinking", @"crying", @"begging",
@"leaving", @"shopping", @"hello worlding", nil];

        feelings = [[NSArray alloc] initWithObjects:@"awesome",
@"sad", @"happy", @"ambivalent", @"nauseous", @"psyched",
@"confused", @"hopeful", @"anxious", nil];

}
```

Here we
establish the
arrays with
Mike's lists.
We'll call them
in a bit to fill
in the picker.

InstatwitViewController.m

The "@" before those strings tells the compiler to
make them NSStrings instead of char*. NSStrings
are real Objective-C classes, as opposed to a simple
C-style character pointer. Most Objective-C classes use
NSStrings instead of char*'s.

```
 -
(void)dealloc {
    [activities release];
    [feelings release];
    [super dealloc];

}
@end
```

You need to release all of these
objects to clean up the memory, as an
iPhone is small (so not much memory).
We'll talk about memory a lot more in
Chapter 3.

Now we just need the protocols...

The datasource protocol has two required methods

Let's focus on the datasource protocol methods first. We said in the header file that InstatwitViewController conforms to the `UIPickerViewDatasource` protocol. That protocol has two required methods, `numberOfComponentsInPickerView:pickerView` and `pickerView:numberOfRowsInComponent`. Since we know we want two wheels (components) in our view, we can start by putting that method in our implementation file:

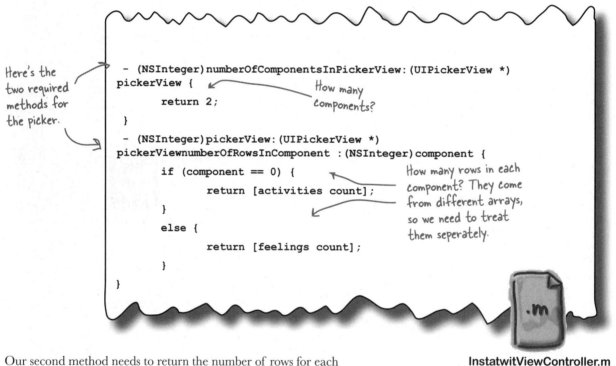

Here's the two required methods for the picker.

```
-  (NSInteger) numberOfComponentsInPickerView: (UIPickerView *)
pickerView {
        return 2;
}

-  (NSInteger) pickerView: (UIPickerView *)
pickerViewnumberOfRowsInComponent  : (NSInteger) component {
        if (component == 0) {
                return [activities count];
        }
        else {
                return [feelings count];
        }
}
```

How many components?

How many rows in each component? They come from different arrays, so we need to treat them seperately.

InstatwitViewController.m

Our second method needs to return the number of rows for each component. The `component` argument will tell us which component the picker is asking about, with the first component (the activities) being component 0. The number of rows in each component is the just the number of items in the appropriate array.

Now that we have the methods implemented, let's wire it up to the picker.

Connect the datasource just like actions and outlets

Now that the datasource protocol is implemented, the data is in place and it's just a matter of linking it to the picker. Hop back into Interface Builder to make that connection:

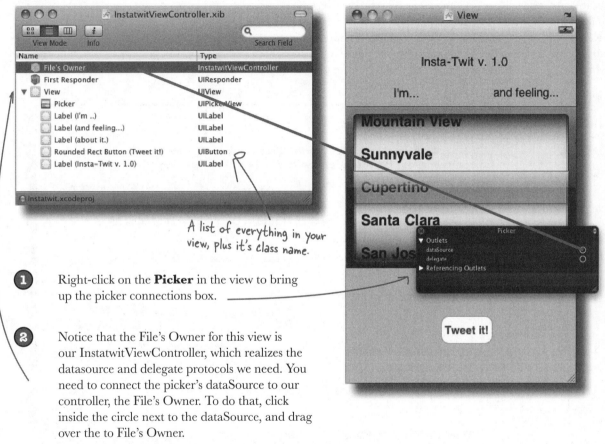

A list of everything in your view, plus it's class name.

1 Right-click on the **Picker** in the view to bring up the picker connections box.

2 Notice that the File's Owner for this view is our InstatwitViewController, which realizes the datasource and delegate protocols we need. You need to connect the picker's dataSource to our controller, the File's Owner. To do that, click inside the circle next to the dataSource, and drag over the to File's Owner.

If you don't save in Interface Builder, it won't work!

Xcode will run the last saved version, not anything else.

Watch it!

On to the delegate...

There's just one method for the delegate protocol

The UIPickerViewDelegate protocol only has one required method (well, technically there are two optional methods, and you have to implement one of them). We're going to use pickerView:titleForRow:forComponent. This method has to return an NSString with the title for the given row in the given component. Again, both of these values are indexed from 0, so we can use the component value to figure out which array to use, and then use the row value as an index.

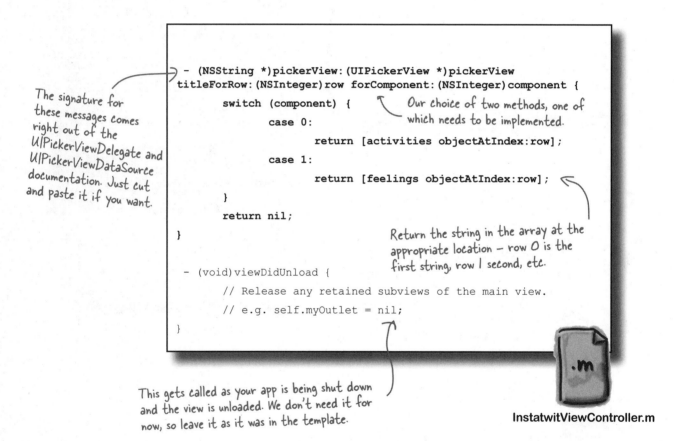

The signature for these messages comes right out of the UIPickerViewDelegate and UIPickerViewDataSource documentation. Just cut and paste it if you want.

```
- (NSString *)pickerView:(UIPickerView *)pickerView
titleForRow:(NSInteger)row forComponent:(NSInteger)component {
    switch (component) {
        case 0:
            return [activities objectAtIndex:row];
        case 1:
            return [feelings objectAtIndex:row];
    }
    return nil;
}

- (void)viewDidUnload {
    // Release any retained subviews of the main view.
    // e.g. self.myOutlet = nil;
}
```

Our choice of two methods, one of which needs to be implemented.

Return the string in the array at the appropriate location – row 0 is the first string, row 1 second, etc.

This gets called as your app is being shut down and the view is unloaded. We don't need it for now, so leave it as it was in the template.

InstatwitViewController.m

Now back to Interface Builder to wire up the delegate...

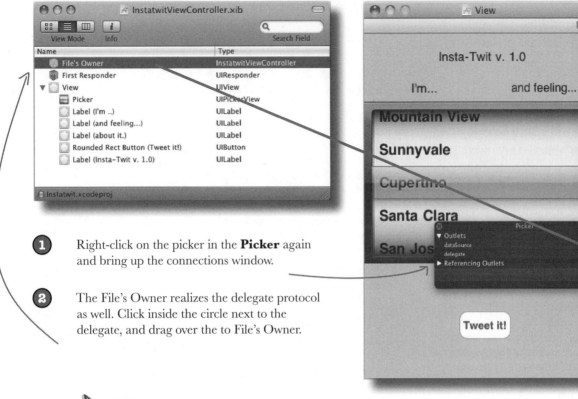

(1) Right-click on the picker in the **Picker** again and bring up the connections window.

(2) The File's Owner realizes the delegate protocol as well. Click inside the circle next to the delegate, and drag over the to File's Owner.

Test Drive

Save your work in Interface Builder, go back into Xcode and save that, and Build and Run (⌘ return). When the Simulator pops up, you should see everything working!

Spin those dials — they're all the things on Mike's list and they work great!

there are no Dumb Questions

Q: What happens if I don't implement a required method in a protocol?

A: Your project will compile, but you'll get a warning. If you try to run your application, it will almost certainly crash with an "unrecognized selector" exception when a component tries to send your class the missing required message.

Q: What if I don't implement an optional method in a protocol?

A: That's fine. But whatever functionality that it would provide isn't going to be there. You do need to be a little careful in that sometimes Apple marks a couple of methods as optional but you **have to implement at least one of them.** That's the case with the UIPickerViewDelegate. If you don't implement at least one of the methods specified in the docs, your app will crash with an error when you try to run it.

Q: Are there limits to the number of protocols a class can realize?

A: Nope. Now, the more you realize, the more code you're going to need to put in that class, so there's a point where you really need to split things off into different classes to keep the code manageable. But technically speaking, you can realize as many as you want.

Q: I'm still a little fuzzy, what's the difference between the interface we put in a header file and a protocol?

A: An interface in a header file is how Objective-C declares the properties, fields, and messages a class responds to. It's like a header file in C++ or the method declarations in a Java file. However, you have to provide implementation for everything in your class's interface. A protocol on the other hand is just a list of messages—there is no implementation. It's the class that realizes the protocol that has to provide implementation. These are equivalent to interfaces in Java and pure virtual methods in C++.

BULLET POINTS

- The picker needs a delegate and a data-source to work.

- In a picker, each dial is a component.

- In a picker, each item is a row.

- Protocols define the messages your class must realize—some of them might be optional.

> OK, that's great and all. It looks really nice. But the "Tweet it!" button doesn't do anything yet...

Now let's get that button talking to Twitter...

We got the picker working, but if you try out the "Tweet it!" button, nothing happens when something's selected. We still need to get the button responding to Mike and then get the whole thing to talk to Twitter.

Think about what we need to do to get the button working. What files will we use? What will the button actually do?

The button needs to be connected to an event

We need to wire up the button like we did in Chapter 1. Once Mike has selected what he's doing and feeling, he'll hit "**Tweet it!**" Then we need to get his selections out of the picker and send them to Twitter.

All that, in one little button...

So we just need to go back to IB and wire up the TouchUpInside event again, right?

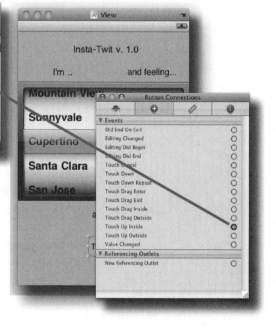

Yes, but what will we wire that event to?

Without an action, your button won't work!

We learned about actions in Chapter 1, and without one there won't be anything in the connections window to wire up in Interface Builder.

Here's the action we created for the button press in Chapter 1:

```
- (IBAction) buttonPressed:(id)sender;
```

All IBAction messages take one argument: the sender of the message. This is the element that triggered the action.

IB = Interface Builder

This is the name of the method that will get called. The name can be anything, but the method must have one argument of type (id).

Exercise

We need to change both the header and implementation files for the InstatwitViewController.

1 Start with the header and add an IBAction named sendButtonTapped.

2 Then provide an implementation for that method in our .m file, and write a message to the log so you know it worked before sending to Twitter

---

Exercise Solution

Declare your IBAction in the header file and provide the implementation in the .m file.

1

```objc
#import <UIKit/UIKit.h>

@interface InstatwitViewController : UIViewController
<UIPickerViewDataSource, UIPickerViewDelegate> {
        NSArray* activities;
        NSArray* feelings;
}
- (IBAction) sendButtonTapped: (id) sender;
```

The IBAction is what allows the code to respond to a user event, remember...

Declare your IBAction here so we can use it in the .m file and Interface Builder knows we have an action available.

InstatwitViewController.h

2

```objc
 - (void)didReceiveMemoryWarning {
     // Releases the view if it doesn't have a superview.
   [super didReceiveMemoryWarning];
     // Release any cached data, images, etc that aren't in use.
}

- (IBAction) sendButtonTapped: (id) sender {
     NSLog(@"Tweet button tapped!");
}
```

Same method declaration as the .h

This will give you the output on the console..

InstatwitViewController.m

Now go back and hook it up with Interface Builder...

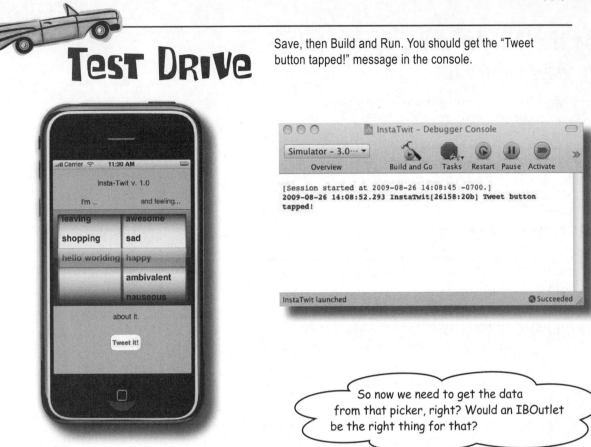

TEST DRIVE

Save, then Build and Run. You should get the "Tweet button tapped!" message in the console.

> So now we need to get the data from that picker, right? Would an IBOutlet be the right thing for that?

Yes! An IBOutlet provides a reference to the picker.

In Chapter 1, we used an outlet to access and change the text field value on the button. Now, to gather up the actual message to send to Twitter, we need to extract the values chosen from the picker, then create a string including the label text.

So far the picker has been calling us when it needed information; this time, when Mike hits the "Tweet it" button, we need to get data out of the picker. We'll use an IBOutlet to do that.

Add the IBOutlet and property to our view controller

In addition to declaring the IBOutlet, we'll declare a property with the same name. We'll talk more about properties in the next chapter, but in short, that will get us proper memory management and let the Cocoa Touch framework set our tweetPicker field when our nib loads.

Start with the header file...

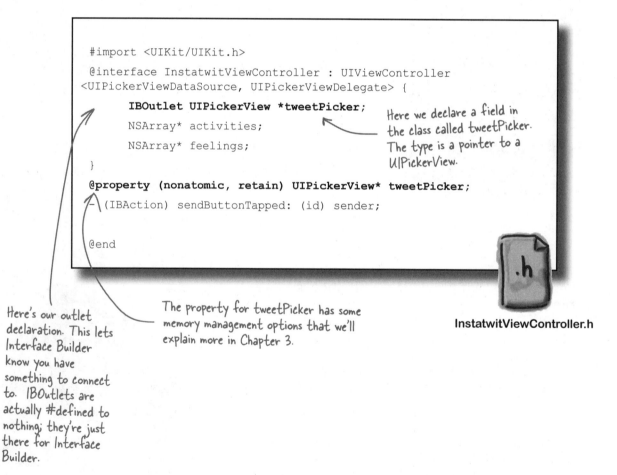

```objc
#import <UIKit/UIKit.h>

@interface InstatwitViewController : UIViewController
<UIPickerViewDataSource, UIPickerViewDelegate> {

    IBOutlet UIPickerView *tweetPicker;
    NSArray* activities;
    NSArray* feelings;

}

@property (nonatomic, retain) UIPickerView* tweetPicker;
- (IBAction) sendButtonTapped: (id) sender;


@end
```

Here we declare a field in the class called tweetPicker. The type is a pointer to a UIPickerView.

Here's our outlet declaration. This lets Interface Builder know you have something to connect to. IBOutlets are actually #defined to nothing; they're just there for Interface Builder.

The property for tweetPicker has some memory management options that we'll explain more in Chapter 3.

InstatwitViewController.h

...and then add the implementation.

```
#import "InstatwitViewController.h"
@implementation InstatwitViewController
@synthesize tweetPicker;
```

InstatwitViewController.m

@ synthesize goes along with the @property declaration in the .h file. See Chapter 3 for more info...

```
-  (void)dealloc {
        [tweetPicker release];
        [activities release];
        [feelings release];
     [super dealloc];
}

@end
```

The last thing you need to do with tweetPicker is release our reference to it — another memory thing. We'll come back to the memory management in Chapter 3, we promise.

What's next?

Connect the picker to our outlet

You're probably expecting this by now! Back into Interface Builder to make the connection from the UIPickerView to the IBOutlet in our view controller. Right-click on the UIPickerView, grab the circle next to the "New Referencing Outlet," and drop it on File's Owner—our InstatwitViewController sporting its new tweetPicker outlet.

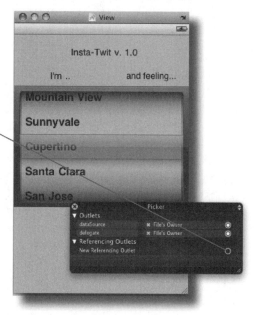

When you click and drag up to File's Owner, you will be able to connect it to the tweetPicker outlet you just created.

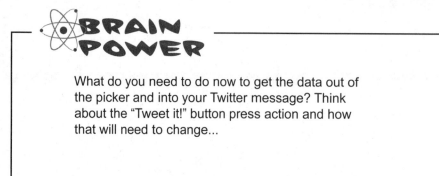

BRAIN POWER

What do you need to do now to get the data out of the picker and into your Twitter message? Think about the "Tweet it!" button press action and how that will need to change...

Use our picker reference to pull the selected values

Now all that's left is to use our reference to the picker to get the actual values Mike selects. We need to reimplement the `sendButtonTapped` method to pull the values from the picker. Looking at the `UIPickerView` documentation, the method we need is `selectedRowInComponent:`. That method returns a row value, which, just like before, we can use as an index into our arrays.

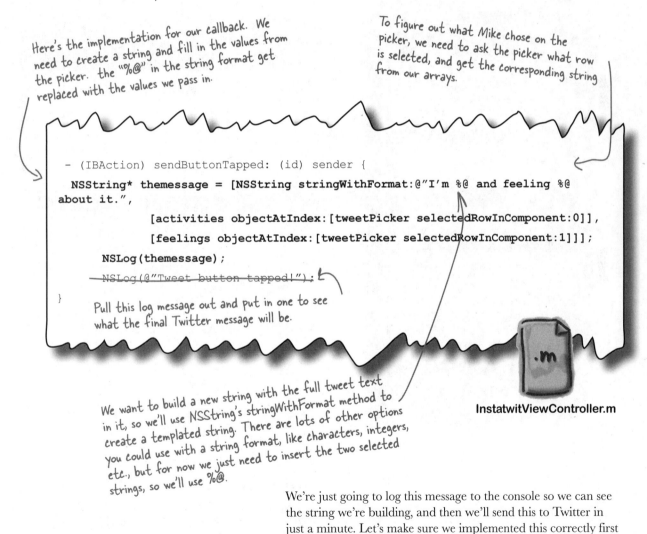

Here's the implementation for our callback. We need to create a string and fill in the values from the picker. The "%@" in the string format get replaced with the values we pass in.

To figure out what Mike chose on the picker, we need to ask the picker what row is selected, and get the corresponding string from our arrays.

```
- (IBAction) sendButtonTapped: (id) sender {
    NSString* themessage = [NSString stringWithFormat:@"I'm %@ and feeling %@ about it.",
            [activities objectAtIndex:[tweetPicker selectedRowInComponent:0]],
            [feelings objectAtIndex:[tweetPicker selectedRowInComponent:1]]];
    NSLog(themessage);
    NSLog(@"Tweet button tapped!");
}
```

Pull this log message out and put in one to see what the final Twitter message will be.

We want to build a new string with the full tweet text in it, so we'll use NSString's stringWithFormat method to create a templated string. There are lots of other options you could use with a string format, like characters, integers, etc., but for now we just need to insert the two selected strings, so we'll use %@.

InstatwitViewController.m

We're just going to log this message to the console so we can see the string we're building, and then we'll send this to Twitter in just a minute. Let's make sure we implemented this correctly first before tweeting to the whole world...

TEST DRIVE

OK, try it out. You should get a convincing tweet in the console:

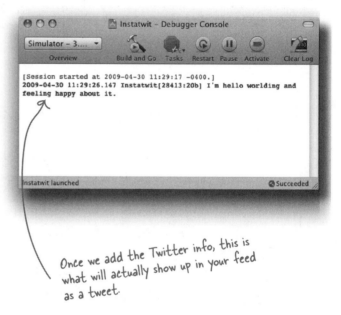

Once we add the Twitter info, this is what will actually show up in your feed as a tweet.

All that's left is to talk to Twitter—we'll help you with that.

Ready Bake Code

To post to Twitter, we're going to use their API. Rather than go into a Twitter API tutorial, we'll give you the code you need to tweet the string. Type the code you see below into the InstatwitViewController.m, just below the NSLog with the Twitter message in the sendButtonTapped method.

Your username and password need to go in here.

```
//TWITTER BLACK MAGIC
    NSMutableURLRequest *theRequest=[NSMutableURLRequest requestWithURL:[NSURL
URLWithString:@"http://YOUR_TWITTER_USERNAME:YOUR_TWITTER_PASSWORD@twitter.com/
statuses/update.xml"]
                cachePolicy:NSURLRequestUseProtocolCachePolicy
                timeoutInterval:60.0];
    [theRequest setHTTPMethod:@"POST"];
    [theRequest setHTTPBody:[[NSString stringWithFormat:@"status=%@",
themessage] dataUsingEncoding:NSASCIIStringEncoding]];
    NSURLResponse* response;
    NSError* error;
    NSData* result = [NSURLConnection sendSynchronousRequest:theRequest
returningResponse:&response error:&error];
    NSLog(@"%@", [[[NSString alloc] initWithData:result
encoding:NSASCIIStringEncoding] autorelease]);
//     END TWITTER BLACK MAGIC
```

InstatwitViewController.m

Relax

If you don't have a Twitter account, just go get one!

Just go to twitter.com and register. Once you do that, you can enter your username and password, and this will work like a charm.

After adding that code, you can just save, build and go. It will now show up on your Twitter feed. Go ahead, try it out!

iPhonecross

Flex your vocab skills with this crossword.

Across

3. This typically handles the information itself in the app.
6. This is the document Apple uses to evaluate apps for the App Store.
7. You see this listed in the view and it controls the view.
9. This component allows for controlled input from several selections.
10. This type of app is typically one screen, and gives you the basics with minimal interaction.
11. These define to which messages the datasource and delegate respond.

Down

1. This typically contains the logic that controls the flow of information in an app.
2. The best way to figure out what protocols you need to worry about is to check the _____.
4. This app type typically involves hierarchical data.
5. This app type is mostly custom controllers and graphics.
8. The other name for an *.xib file.

Exercise

We've listed a couple of descriptions of a some different apps. Using the app description, sketch out a rough view and answer the questions about each one.

1 Generic giant button app

There are several of these currently up for sale on the app store. This app consists of pushing a big button and getting some noise out of your iPhone.

What type of app is this?

....

What are the main concerns in the HIG about this app type?

....

....

....

2 Book inventory app

This app's mission is to keep a list of the books in your library, along with a quick blurb of what it's about and the author.

What type of app is this?

....

What are the main concerns in the HIG about this app type?

....

....

....

iPhonecross Solution

Flex your vocab skills with this crossword.

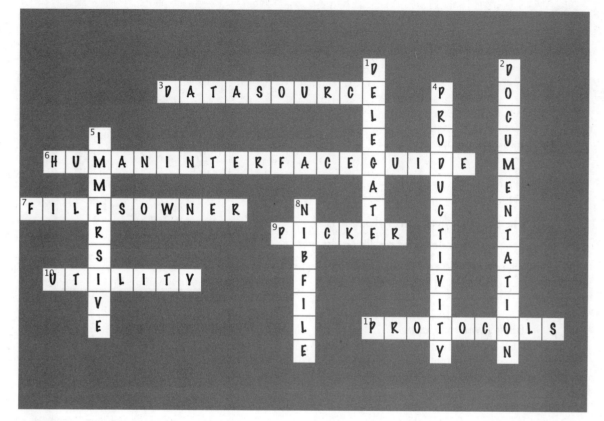

Across

3. This typically handles the information itself in the app. [DATASOURCE]
6. This is the document apple uses to evaluate apps for the App Store. [HUMANINTERFACEGUIDE]
7. You see this listed in the view and it controls the view. [FILESOWNER]
9. This component allows for controlled input from several selections. [PICKER]
10. This type of app is typically one screen, and gives you the basics with minimal interaction. [UTILITY]
11. These define to which messages the datasource and delegate respond. [PROTOCOLS]

Down

1. This typically contains the logic that controls the flow of information in an app. [DELEGATE]
2. The best way to figure out what protocols you need to worry about is to check the _____. [DOCUMENTATION]
4. This app type typically involves hierarchical data. [PRODUCTIVITY]
5. This app type is mostly custom controllers and graphics. [IMMERSIVE]
8. The other name for an *.xib file. [NIBFILE]

Exercise Solution

We've listed a couple of descriptions of a some different apps. Using the app description, sketch out a rough view and answer the questions about each one.

① Generic giant button app

There are several of these currently up for sale on the app store. This app consists of pushing a big button and getting some noise out of your iPhone.

What type of app is this?

An immersive app

What are the main concerns in the HIG about this app type?

The big thing Apple cares about is that controls "provide an internally consistent experience." So everything can be custom, it needs to focused and well organized.

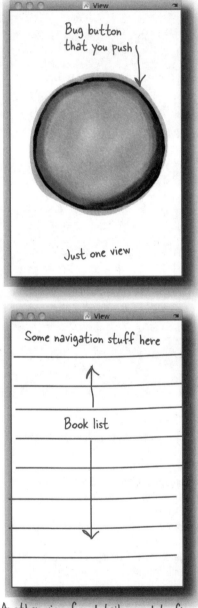

View

Bug button that you push

Just one view

② Book inventory app.

This app's mission is to keep a list of the books in your library, along with a quick blurb of what it's about and the author.

What type of app is this?

A productivity app

What are the main concerns in the HIG about this app type?

The HIG has many more specific rules about this app type, because you'll be using standard controls. EACH control needs to be checked out for proper usage.

View

Some navigation stuff here

Book list

Another view for details, need to figure out how to get to it...

Your iPhone Toolbox

You've got Chapter 2 under your belt and now you've added protocols, delegates, and datasources to your toolbox. For a complete list of tooltips in the book, go to http://www.headfirstlabs.com/iphonedev.

Delegate

Responsible for the behavior of a UI element.

Contains the logic that controls the flow of information, like saving or displaying data, and which view is seen when.

Can be in same object as the datasource, but has its own specific protocols.

Protocols

Define the messages your datasource and delegate must respond to.

Are declared in the header (.h) file.

Some of them might be optional.

Datasource

Provides the bridge between the control and the data it needs to show.

Works with databases, plists, images, and other general info that your app will need to display.

Can be the same object as a delegate, but has its own specific protocols.

BULLET POINTS

- The picker needs a delegate and data-source to work.
- In a picker, each dial is a component.
- In a picker, each item is a row.
- Protocols define the messages your class must realize—some of them might be optional.

This is Renee, Mike's girlfriend

It's so great that Mike and I are communicating now! But I've noticed that Mike's starting to sound like he's in a rut, saying the same thing over and over again! Is there something we need to talk about?

Sounds like Mike is going to need some modifications to InstaTwit to keep his relationship on solid ground...

3 objective-c for the iPhone

Twitter needs variety

I know these are letters and all, but I have no idea what you're saying...

We did a lot in chapter 2, but what language was that?

Parts of the code you've been writing might look familiar, but it's time you got a sense of what's really going on under the hood. The iPhone SDK comes with great tools that mean that you don't need to write code for everything, but you can't write entire apps without learning something about the underlying language, including properties, message passing, and memory management. Unless you work that out, all your apps will be just default widgets! And you want more than just widgets, right?

Renee is catching on....

Mike has been diligently using InstaTwit to communicate his feelings, but his girlfriend is starting to think something weird is going on. Even for Mike, who is a guy who likes his routines, his tweets are starting to sound suspicious.

InstaTwit was working great, and is so easy to use! But I think Renee is on to me. She said I sound like I'm in a rut. I need to be able to add to my tweets or this isn't going to work much longer.

We need to make some adjustments to our InstaTwit design.

Take a look at the various UI controls available in Interface Builder, and think about what would be a quick and easy way for Mike to add to his tweets.

Make room for custom input

It's nothing fancy, but Mike could add a little personal flavor to his tweets with a text field at the start. It means he'll need to do some typing, but in the end his tweets will be more unique.

Scoot this stuff down a little

We'll put the text field in here

Code Magnets

Using what you know from adding the picker and the button, match the magnet with the method or file that you'll need to edit to add the text field.

1 .... to InstatwitViewController.h.

2 .... to the top of InstatwitViewController.m.

3 .... to the `dealloc` in InstatwitViewController.m.

4 .... using Interface Builder.

5 .... to the property created in step #1, using Interface Builder.

```
Create a delegate and
datasource for the notesField
```

```
Add UITextField
to the view
```

```
Add an IBOutlet and @property
declaration for the UITextField
```

```
Add an IBAction for
the UITextField
```

```
Add
notesField to
@synthesize
```

```
Add [notesfield release]
```

```
Link the UITextField
to the IBOutlet
```

Design Magnets Solution

Using what you know from adding the picker and the button, match the
magnet with the method or file that you'll need to edit to add the text field.

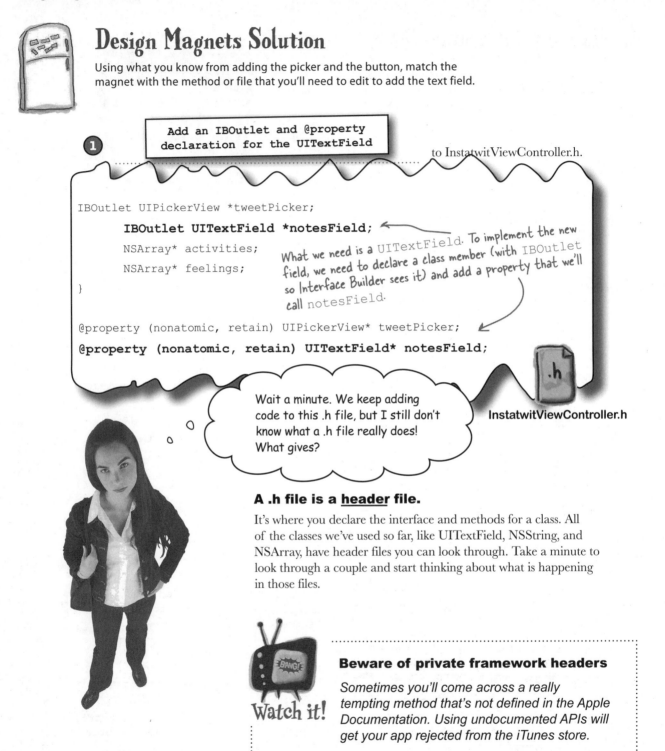

1 | Add an IBOutlet and @property
declaration for the UITextField | to InstatwitViewController.h.

```
IBOutlet UIPickerView *tweetPicker;
    IBOutlet UITextField *notesField;
    NSArray* activities;
    NSArray* feelings;
}

@property (nonatomic, retain) UIPickerView* tweetPicker;
@property (nonatomic, retain) UITextField* notesField;
```

What we need is a `UITextField`. To implement the new
field, we need to declare a class member (with `IBOutlet`
so Interface Builder sees it) and add a property that we'll
call `notesField`.

.h

InstatwitViewController.h

Wait a minute. We keep adding
code to this .h file, but I still don't
know what a .h file really does!
What gives?

A .h file is a <u>header</u> file.

It's where you declare the interface and methods for a class. All
of the classes we've used so far, like UITextField, NSString, and
NSArray, have header files you can look through. Take a minute to
look through a couple and start thinking about what is happening
in those files.

Beware of private framework headers

*Sometimes you'll come across a really
tempting method that's not defined in the Apple
Documentation. Using undocumented APIs will
get your app rejected from the iTunes store.*

Watch it!

Header files describe the interface to your class

In Objective-C, classes are defined with interfaces in the header file. It's where you declare if your class inherits from anything, as well as your class' fields, properties, and methods.

Interfaces, class fields, methods, and properties

InstatwitViewController.h

```
@interface InstatwitViewController :
            UIViewController

    IBOutlet UIPickerView *tweetPicker;
```

```
- (IBAction) sendButtonTapped: (id) sender;
```

InstatwitViewController.m

Sharpen your pencil

Here's our current **InstatwitViewController.h** file. Fill in the blanks and explain what each line does.

```
#import <UIKit/UIKit.h>

@interface InstatwitViewController : UIViewController
<UIPickerViewDataSource, UIPickerViewDelegate> {
    IBOutlet UIPickerView *tweetPicker;
    IBOutlet UITextField *notesField;
    NSArray* activities;
    NSArray* feelings;
}

@property (nonatomic, retain) UIPickerView* tweetPicker;
@property (nonatomic, retain) UITextField* notesField;

- (IBAction) sendButtonTapped: (id) sender;
- (IBAction) textFieldDoneEditing:(id) sender;

@end
```

InstatwitViewController.h

Sharpen your pencil
Solution

Here's our current InstatwitViewController.h file. Fill in the blanks and explain what each line does.

```
#import <UIKit/UIKit.h>
```

import incorporates another file (almost always a header file) into this file when it's compiled. It's used to pull in classes, constants, etc. from other files.

It's almost identical to C's #include, except that it automatically prevents including the same header multiple times (so no more #ifndef MY_HEADER).

@interface indicates you're going to declare a class.

Next comes the class name, and if it inherits from something then a colon and the super class's name.

Objective-C doesn't support multiple inheritance...

Here's our inheritances and interfaces.

```
@interface InstatwitViewController :
UIViewController <UIPickerViewDataSource,
UIPickerViewDelegate> {
```

Any protocols you implement go in angle brackets separated by commas. Protocols are like Java interfaces or pure virtual classes in C++, and a class can realize as many as you want.

IBOutlet allows Interface Builder to recognize fields that you can attach to controls (like our notes field in InstaTwit).

This is where we can declare fields of our class.

```
    IBOutlet UIPickerView *tweetPicker;
    IBOutlet UITextField *notesField;
    NSArray* activities;
    NSArray* feelings;
}
```

The syntax for fields is just like in C++: Basic types like int and float are used as is; pointer types use an asterisk. By default, all fields are given protected access, but you can change that with @private or @public sections similar to C++.

InstatwitViewController.h

Sharpen your pencil
Solution

Once you've closed the field section of your interface, you can declare properties. @property tells Objective-C to autogenerate getter and setter methods for you.

These are property attributes; we'll talk more about these shortly...

```
@property (nonatomic, retain) UIPickerView* tweetPicker;
```

The @property keyword tells the compiler this is a property that will be backed by getter and (maybe) setter methods.

Here's our type and property name, just like the field in the class.

```
@property (nonatomic, retain) UITextField* notesField;
```

The minus sign means it's an instance method (a + means it's static). All methods in Objective-C are public.

These are the method declarations.

```
- (IBAction) sendButtonTapped: (id) sender;
- (IBAction) textFieldDoneEditing:(id) sender;
```

IBAction lets Interface Builder identify methods that can be attached to events.

IBAction method signatures must take one argument of type id, which is like a void * in C++ or Object reference in Java.

```
@end
```

@end: ends your class interface declaration.

.h

InstatwitViewController.h

Design Magnets Solution (Continued)

Back in that design we were working on...

Using what you know from adding the picker and the button, match the magnet with the method or file that you'll need to edit to add the text field.

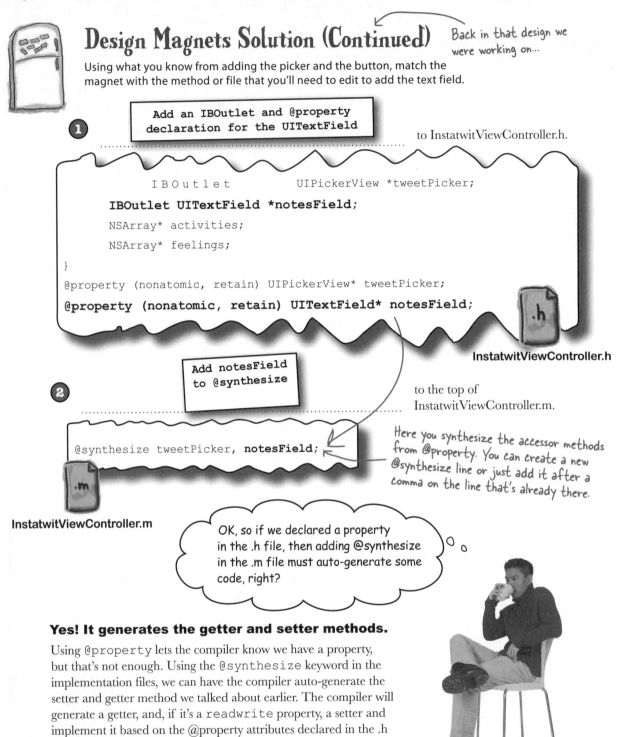

1 Add an IBOutlet and @property declaration for the UITextField

to InstatwitViewController.h.

```
    IBOutlet          UIPickerView *tweetPicker;
IBOutlet UITextField *notesField;
NSArray* activities;
NSArray* feelings;
}
@property (nonatomic, retain) UIPickerView* tweetPicker;
@property (nonatomic, retain) UITextField* notesField;
```

InstatwitViewController.h

2 Add notesField to @synthesize

to the top of InstatwitViewController.m.

```
@synthesize tweetPicker, notesField;
```

Here you synthesize the accessor methods from @property. You can create a new @synthesize line or just add it after a comma on the line that's already there.

InstatwitViewController.m

OK, so if we declared a property in the .h file, then adding @synthesize in the .m file must auto-generate some code, right?

Yes! It generates the getter and setter methods.

Using @property lets the compiler know we have a property, but that's not enough. Using the @synthesize keyword in the implementation files, we can have the compiler auto-generate the setter and getter method we talked about earlier. The compiler will generate a getter, and, if it's a readwrite property, a setter and implement it based on the @property attributes declared in the .h file. So what do the different @property attributes do...?

WHO DOES WHAT?

Below is a list of the most commonly used property attributes and definitions. Match each attribute with its definition.

readonly

When you want the property to be modifiable by people. The compiler will generate a getter and a setter for you. This is the default.

retain

When you're dealing with basic types, like ints, floats, etc. The compiler just creates a setter with a simple myField = value statement. This is the default, but not usually what you want.

readwrite

When you're dealing with object values. The compiler will retain the value you pass in (we'll talk more about retaining in a minute) and release the old value when a new one comes in.

copy

When you don't want people modifying the property. You can still change the field value backing the property, but the compiler won't generate a setter.

assign

When you want to hold onto a copy of some value instead of the value itself; for example, if you want to hold onto an array and don't want people to be able to change its contents after they set it. This sends a copy message to the value passed in then retains that.

WHO DOES WHAT? SOLUTION

Below is a list of the most commonly used property attributes and definitions. Match each attribute with its definition.

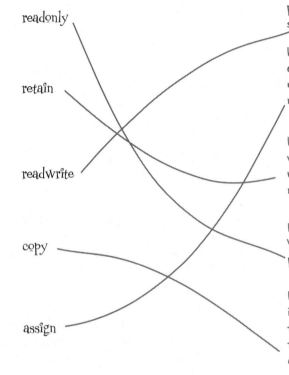

readonly

retain

readwrite

copy

assign

When you want the property to be modifiable by people. The compiler will generate a getter and a setter for you. This is the default.

When you're dealing with basic types, like ints, floats, etc. The compiler just creates a setter with a simple myField = value statement. This is the default, but not usually what you want.

When you're dealing with object values. The compiler will retain the value you pass in (we'll talk more about retaining in a minute) and release the old value when a new one comes in.

When you don't want people modifying the property. You can still change the field value backing the property, but the compiler won't generate a setter.

When you want to hold onto a copy of some value instead of the value itself; for example, if you want to hold onto an array and don't want people to be able to change its contents after they set it. This sends a copy message to the value passed in then retains that.

there are no Dumb Questions

Q: How does the compiler know what field to use to hold the property value?

A: By default, the compiler assumes the property name is the same as the field name. In reality, it doesn't have to be. You can specify the field to use to back a property when you @synthesize it like this: @synthesize secretString=_superSecretField;.

Q: What about that nonatomic keyword?

A: By default, generated accessors are multithread safe and use mutexes when changing a property value. These are considered atomic. However, if your class isn't being used by multiple threads, that's a waste. You can tell the compiler to skip the whole mutex thing by declaring your property as nonatomic.

Auto-generated accessors also handle memory management

Objective-C on the iPhone doesn't have a garbage collector, so you have to use *reference counting*. That involves keeping up with how many references there are to an object, and only freeing it up when the count drops to zero (it's no longer being used). When you use properties, the compiler handles it for us. The properties we've declared so far have all used the retain attribute. When the compiler generates a setter for that property, it will properly handle memory management for us, like this:

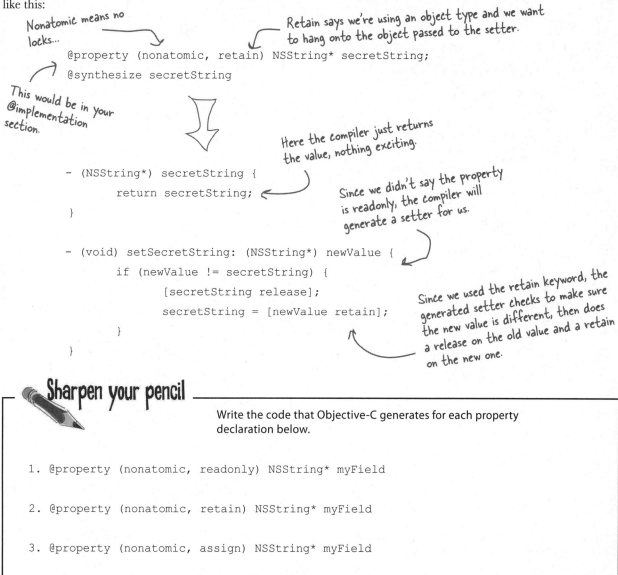

Nonatomic means no locks...

Retain says we're using an object type and we want to hang onto the object passed to the setter.

```objective-c
@property (nonatomic, retain) NSString* secretString;
@synthesize secretString
```

This would be in your @implementation section.

Here the compiler just returns the value, nothing exciting.

```objective-c
- (NSString*) secretString {
    return secretString;
}


- (void) setSecretString: (NSString*) newValue {
    if (newValue != secretString) {
        [secretString release];
        secretString = [newValue retain];
    }
}
```

Since we didn't say the property is readonly, the compiler will generate a setter for us.

Since we used the retain keyword, the generated setter checks to make sure the new value is different, then does a release on the old value and a retain on the new one.

Sharpen your pencil

Write the code that Objective-C generates for each property declaration below.

1. `@property (nonatomic, readonly) NSString* myField`

2. `@property (nonatomic, retain) NSString* myField`

3. `@property (nonatomic, assign) NSString* myField`

Sharpen your pencil
Solution

Below is the code that the compiler will generate for each property.

1. `@property (nonatomic, readonly) NSString* myField`

```
- (NSString*) myField {
  return myField;
}
```

2. `@property (nonatomic, retain) NSString* myField`

```
- (NSString*) myField {
   return myField;
}
- (void) setMyField: (NSString*)
newValue {
   if (newValue !=myField) {
     [myField release];
     myField = [newValue retain];
   }
}
```

3. `@property (nonatomic, assign) NSString* myField`

```
- (NSString*) myField {
   return myField;
}
 - (void) setMyField: (NSString*) newValue
 {
    myField = newValue;
}
```

Be careful with this one... NSStrings are reference counted objects, so while this will technically work, having an assign property for an NSString is probably a bad idea.

However, for basic types like booleans and floats, you can't do reference counting. Assignment is almost always what you want.

I bet that release just lets go of the memory that your properties use up, right?

Objective-C can automatically release references, too.

In addition to retain and release, Objective-C has the concept of an autorelease pool. This is basically an array of objects that the runtime will call release on after it's finished processing the current event. To put something in the autorelease pool, you simply send it the autorelease message:

```
[aString autorelease];
```

It will still have the same retain count, but after the current event loop finishes, it will be sent a release. You won't want to use this all the time because it's not nearly as efficient and has some performance overhead. It's not a bad thing to use, but it's better to explicitly retain and release when you can.

To keep your memory straight, you need to remember just two things

Get it? Memory, remember?

Memory management can get pretty hairy in larger apps, so Apple has a couple of rules established to keep track of who's in charge of releasing and retaining when.

1 **You must release objects you create with alloc, new, copy, or mutableCopy.**
If you create an object with alloc, new, copy, or mutableCopy, it will have a retain count of 1 and you're responsible for sending a release when you're done with the object. You can also put the object in the autorelease pool if you want the system to handle sending a release later.

2 **Consider everything else to have a retain count of 1 and in the autorelease pool.**
If you get an object by any other means (string formatters, array initializers, etc.) you should treat the object as having a retain count of 1 and put it in the autorelease pool. This means that if you want to hang onto that object outside of the method that got the object, you'll need to send it a retain (and a corresponding release later).

Memory Management Up Close

```
- (void)dealloc {
        [tweetPicker release];
        [activities release];
        [feelings release];
    [super dealloc];
}
```

This is some of the memory management code that YOU have already written!

Memory management is definitely important on iPhone, but that doesn't mean it's complicated. Once you get the hang of a few key principles, you'll be able to structure your app so that it doesn't leak memory and get you kicked out of the app store.

When you create an object, it starts with a count of 1, and different things you do can raise and lower the count. When the count reaches 0, the object is released and the memory is made available.

At first, there's no memory allocated....

```
NSString *aString = [[NSString alloc] init];
```

...when you alloc a class, the reference count is set to 1.

1

[aString retain];

Each retain call adds one to the count...

2

[aString release];

...and a release call subtracts one.

1

`[someArray addObject:aString];`

If another object (like this array) needs to hang onto your object, it will retain it....

2

`[someArray removeObject:aString];`

...and release its reference when it's done with it.

1

`[aString release];` *Once the count gets to 0, the object's dealloc is called and the memory is freed.*

Determine how many references are left at the end of the chunk of code and if we have to send it a release for each string.

Final Reference Count

```
NSString *first = [[NSString alloc] init];
```

```
NSString *second = [[NSString alloc] init];
[someStringArray addObject:second];
```

```
NSString *third = [[NSString alloc] init];
[third autorelease];
```

```
NSString *fourth = [NSString
stringWithFormat:@"Do not read %@", @"Swimming
with your iPhone by TuMuch Monee"];
```

```
NSMutableArray *newArray = [[NSMutableArray alloc] init];
    NSString *fifth = [[NSString alloc]
initWithFormat:@"Read this instead: %@", "Financing your
iPhone 4G by Cerius Savar"];
    [newArray addObject:fifth];
    [newArray release];
```

```
NSString *sixth = [NSString stringWithString:@"Toughie"];
    NSArray *anotherArray = [NSArray
arrayWithObjects:sixth count:1];
    NSDictionary *newDictionary = [NSDictionary
dictionaryWithObjects:sixth    forKeys:@"Toughie"
count:1];
    NSString *ignoreMe = [sixth retain];
```

Exercise

Determine how many references are left at the end of the chunk of code and if we have to send it a release for each string.

Final Count

```
NSString *first = [[NSString alloc] init];
```

1 — Reference count will be 1 because alloc automatically sets count to 1.

```
NSString *second = [[NSString alloc] init];
[someStringArray addObject:second];
```

2 — "second" will have a retain count of 2 after this block of code: 1 from the alloc, 1 from inserting it into the array. Arrays automatically retain items added to them.

```
NSString *third = [[NSString alloc] init];
[third autorelease];
```

1 — This still has a retain count of 1 because of the alloc, but is now in the autorelease pool, meaning it will be sent a release automatically after the current event loop has completed.

```
NSString *fourth = [NSString
stringWithFormat:@"Do not read %@", @"Swimming
with your iPhone by TuMuch Monee"];
```

1 — This will have a retain count of 1, but will be in the autorelease pool because we didn't get it via an alloc, new, copy, or mutableCopy.

Determine how many references are left at the end of the chunk of code and if we have to send it a release for each string.

<u>Final Count</u>

"fifth" will have a retain count of 1:

```
NSMutableArray *newArray = [[NSMutableArray
alloc] init];
    NSString *fifth = [[NSString alloc]
initWithFormat:@"Read this instead: %@",
"Financing your iPhone 4G by Cerius Savar"];
    [newArray addObject:fifth];
    [newArray release];
```

1

First it gets a retain count of 1 from the alloc.

Next it goes to 2 because it's inserted into the "newArray".

Then it goes back to 1 because an array will send a release to all of its items when the array is destroyed.

"sixth" starts out with an autoreleased retain count of 1 from the initial creation (note it wasn't from alloc, so it's autoreleased).

Next, another retain from inserting it into the array. Note the array wasn't alloc'ed either, so it will be autoreleased, too.

```
NSString *sixth = [NSString
stringWithString:@"Toughie"];
    NSArray *anotherArray = [NSArray
arrayWithObjects:sixth count:1];
    NSDictionary *newDictionary =
[NSDictionary dictionaryWithObjects:sixth
forKeys:@"Toughie" count:1];
    NSString *ignoreMe = [sixth retain];
```

4

Then one more retain from the dicionary, also not alloc'ed and will be autoreleased.

Finally, an explicit retain...
So, even though "sixth" has a retain count of 4, we, the developers, only need to send one release to "sixth" and let everything else clean up with the autorelease pool.

Hey, could we get back to my app please?

Design Magnets Solution (Continued)

Using what you know from adding the picker and the button, match the magnet with the method or file that you'll need to edit to add the text field.

①

> **Add an IBOutlet and @property declaration for the UITextField**

to InstatwitViewController.h.

```
        IBOutlet          UIPickerView *tweetPicker;
    IBOutlet UITextField *notesField;
    NSArray* activities;
    NSArray* feelings;
}
@property (nonatomic, retain) UIPickerView* tweetPicker;
@property (nonatomic, retain) UITextField* notesField;
```

InstatwitViewController.h

②

> **Add notesField to @synthesize**

to the top of InstatwitViewController.m.

```
@synthesize tweetPicker, notesField;
```

Here you synthesize the accessor methods from @property. You can create a new @synthesize line or just add it after a comma on the linthat's already there.

InstatwitViewController.m

③

> **Add [notesfield release]**

to the dealloc in InstatwitViewController.m.

The property will automatically retain a reference passed to it – we need to release that in dealloc.

```
- (void)dealloc {
    [tweetPicker release];
    [activities release];
    [feelings release];
    [notesField release];
    [super dealloc];
}
```

When we're being freed and our dealloc is called we need to release our reference to the text field.

We don't need an action or a datasource for the notes field.

> **Add an IBAction for the UITextField**

> **Create a delegate and datasource for the notesField**

InstatwitViewController.m

Add UITextField to the view .... using Interface Builder.

To get into this, you'll need to open up InstatwitViewController.xib and find the text field in the library. Then drag and drop the text field in between the "InstaTwit" label and the "I'm .... and feeling ..." labels. You'll also need to put a label that says "Notes" in front of the text field.

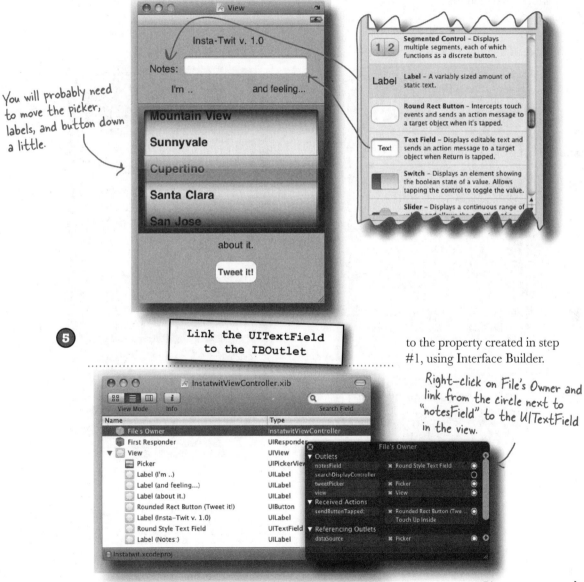

You will probably need to move the picker, labels, and button down a little.

Link the UITextField to the IBOutlet .... to the property created in step #1, using Interface Builder.

Right-click on File's Owner and link from the circle next to "notesField" to the UITextField in the view.

Save it and then...

TEST DRIVE

Now that everything is saved, go back into Xcode and build and run, and launch the simulator.

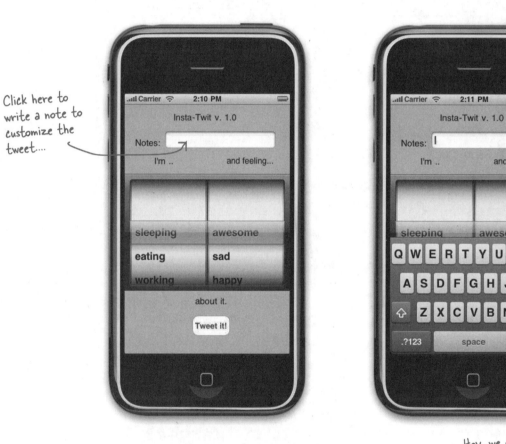

Click here to write a note to customize the tweet....

It works!

Hey, we didn't even have to do anything to make the keyboard show up for the text field. Cool!

Objective-C Exposed

**This week's interview:
Who are you anyway?**

Head First: Hello Objective-C! Thanks for coming.

Objective-C: Thanks! It's great to be here. I've been getting a lot of attention recently with this whole iPhone thing.

Head First: So you have a pretty strong lineage, right? Why don't you tell us a little about yourself?

Objective-C: Sure. I'm an Object Oriented language, so I have classes and objects, but I come from strong C roots. My OO concepts come from Smalltalk. Really, there's not much to me.

Head First: What do you mean you come from C roots?

Objective-C: Well, nearly all of my syntax is just like C syntax. For loops, types, pointers, etc. You can easily use other C libraries like SQLite with me. Things like that.

Head First: But you're more than just that, right?

Objective-C: Oh yeah, definitely. Most obviously, I am an OO language, so classes, abstract interfaces (which I call protocols), inheritance, etc. all work great.

Head First: So what about memory management? Malloc and free like C?

Objective-C: Well, malloc and free work just like they do in C, but I have a really nice memory management model for objects. I use reference counting.

Head First: Ah—so you keep track of who's using what?

Objective-C: Yup. If you want to keep an object around, you just tell me you want to retain a reference to it. Done with it? Just release your reference. When there aren't any references left I'll clean up the object and free up the memory for you.

Head First: Nice. Any other tricks?

Objective-C: Oh yeah. You know those getter and setter methods you need to write for other OO languages to wrap fields in a class? Not here. I can automatically generate them for you. Not only that, you can tell me how you want to handle the memory associated with them. Oh, and one of my favorites: I can graft new methods onto classes without a problem. They're called categories.

Head First: Oh, that's slick. We're about out of time, so just one more question. What's up with all those "NSs" all over the place, like NSString and NSInteger?

Objective-C: Ah—those are all part of the CocoaTouch framework. I mentioned my strong lineage earlier; most of the core classes that people use on iPhone come from CocoaTouch, which is a port of Cocoa which came from OpenStep, which came from NeXTStep, and that's where the NS comes from. The frameworks are written in Objective-C, but they're frameworks, not really language things. When you write for iPhone, you'll be using things like that all of the time. For example, instead of using char*s for strings, you usually use NSStrings or NSMutableStrings. We all kind of blur together.

Head First: This is great information! Thanks again for coming by, and best of luck with the iPhone!

Objective-C: No problem. Thanks for having me.

there are no
Dumb Questions

Q: What happens if I don't retain an object I'll need later?

A: Most likely the object's retain count will hit 0 and it will be cleaned up before you get to use it. This will crash your application. Now here's the sad part: it might not crash your object on the simulator every time. The simulator has a lot more memory to work with and behaves differently than a real iPhone or iPod Touch. Everything might look great until you put it on your phone to test it. Then sadness ensues.

Q: What if I release my object too many times?

A: Basically the same thing. When the reference count hits 0, the object will be released and memory will be freed. Sending that now-freed memory another release message will almost certainly crash your application.

Q: What if my project works on the simulator and dies on the real phone? Could that be a memory problem?

A: Absolutely. Memory on a real device is much tighter than on the simulator. We'll talk more about debugging these and using Instruments to track memory usage and leaks in a later chapter.

Q: How can I check if I'm managing my memory effectively?

A: The iPhone SDK comes with a great memory tool called Instruments that can show you how your memory is being used, peak memory usage, how fast your allocating and deallocating it, and possibly most importantly, if you're leaking memory. We'll talk about it in detail later in the book.

Q: What happens if I set things to nil?

A: Well, it depends on what you're setting to nil. If it's just a local variable, nothing. The variable is now nil, but the memory for the object it used to point to is still allocated and you've almost certainly leaked something. Now, if it's a property...

Q: Do I have to retain things I want to set on my properties?

A: No! Well, probably not. That's what the "retain" parameter is on the @property declaration. If you put retain there the property will automatically send values retains and releases when the property is set or cleared. Be careful about clearing properties in your dealloc, though. If you have a property with a retain parameter and it still has a value when your object is released, then whatever that property is set to hasn't been freed. You can either send the field an explict release in your dealloc or set the property to nil.

One more quick note: the automatic retain/release ability of properties only works if you use the "." notation. If you explicitly modify the field that backs the property, there's nothing the property can do about it and can't retain/release correctly.

Q: Doesn't Objective-C have garbage collection like Java or .NET?

A: Actually, on the Mac it does. Apple didn't provide garbage collection on iPhone OS however, so you need to fallback to reference counting with retain and release.

Q: What about malloc and free? Can I still use them?

A: Yes, but not for object types. Malloc and free work fine for basic blocks of memory as they do in C, but use alloc to instantiate classes.

Q: What's with that init call that you always put after the alloc?

A: Objective-C doesn't have constructors like other Object Oriented languages do. Instead, by convention, you can provide one or more init methods. You should always call init on any class you allocate, so you almost always see them together as [[SomeClass alloc] init].

Q: How do I know if something retains my object, like an array or something?

A: Basically you shouldn't care. Follow the memory rules that say if you got it from alloc, new, copy, or mutableCopy, you have to send it a release. Otherwise, retain/release it if you ant to use it later. Beyond that, let the other classes handle their own memory management.

Q: Can't we just append the message to the string?

A: NSStrings are immutable, but we could with NSMutableString.

But when Mike's finished typing...

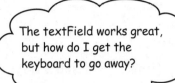

The textField works great, but how do I get the keyboard to go away?

The keyboard is permanent?

Go ahead, play with it and try to get the keyboard to go away. Return won't do it, and neither will clicking anywhere else on the screen. Not so cool.

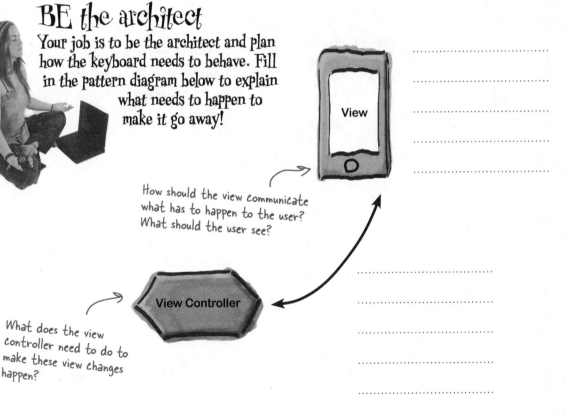

BE the architect

Your job is to be the architect and plan how the keyboard needs to behave. Fill in the pattern diagram below to explain what needs to happen to make it go away!

View

How should the view communicate what has to happen to the user? What should the user see?

View Controller

What does the view controller need to do to make these view changes happen?

BE the architect solution

Your job is to be architect and plan how the keyboard needs to behave. Fill in the pattern diagram below to explain what needs to happen to make it go away!

View

The user needs to understand what to do to make the keyboard go away, so change the "return" button to say "done".

Conventions like using "done" to let the user hide the keyboard are discussed in Apple's HIG. There are lots more; "done" is just one of them.

View Controller

The view controller needs to receive the "done" message and then make the keyboard go away.

This kind of back and forth between the view and view controller is common and is going to show up all over the place. A view controller provides the behavior for a view.

there are no Dumb Questions

Q: Why didn't we have to do anything to make the keyboard appear in the first place?

A: When the users indicate they want to interact with a specific control, iPhoneOS gives that control focus and sets it to be the "first responder" to events. When certain controls become the first responder, they trigger the keyboard to show automatically.

Let's start with the view.

Customize your UITextField

In Interface Builder, select Mike's custom field and ⌘ 1 to bring up the inspector. You can specify an initial value of the text in the field (**Text**), text that the field shows in grey if there's no other text to display (**Placeholder**), left, center, or right **Alignment**, the **Borders** can be different, etc. For now you don't need to add anything for field, so leave these blank.

Next change the label on the return key

Changing the name of the button in the keyboard (so it's "done" instead of the "return") is another option in the inspector. The big thing that changing the label on the button brings to the table is that it clearly communicates to the user what to do to make they keyboard go away.

Click on the **Return Key** popup menu and pick **Done**.

By default, Clear When Editing Begins is checked. That means whenever the users tap in the textfield, whatever value it previously had is cleared. It also means they couldn't edit that value if they wanted to.

Watch out for the HIG!

Beyond the Text and Placeholder fields, changing some of the other options may hurt your usability and make Apple unhappy, so be careful.

There are other options for the "return" button — some of them are obvious (like "Google") and others are little more subtle. Check out Apple's HIG for when to use some of the other ones.

Now, get the keyboard to talk to the view controller...

Components that use the keyboard ask it to appear...

When users click in the text field, iPhone OS gives that control focus and assigns it as "first responder" to that click event. A component can get focus a number of ways: the users explicitly tap on the control, the keyboard is set up so that the Return key moves to the next control they should fill out, the application sets some control to explicitly become first responder because of some event, etc. What a component does when it becomes the first responder varies by component, however; for a UITextField, it asks iPhoneOS to display the keyboard. All this chatter between the application and components is fundamental to writing an application, and it all happens through message passing.

...by passing messages to other objects

The idea is that whenever one object (whether that object is your ApplicationDelegate, another component, or the GPS in the iPhone) wants some other object to do something, it sends it a message.

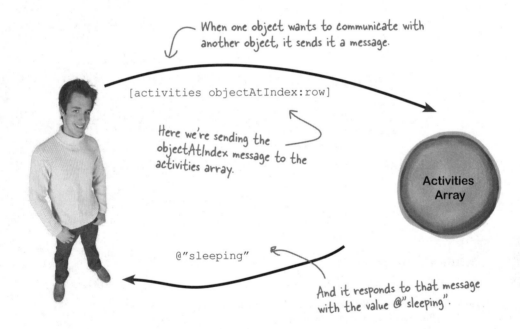

When one object wants to communicate with another object, it sends it a message.

`[activities objectAtIndex:row]`

Here we're sending the objectAtIndex message to the activities array.

Activities Array

`@"sleeping"`

And it responds to that message with the value @"sleeping".

In Objective-C you *send a message to an object* and it *responds to that message* (as opposed to returning a value from a method). The Objective-C runtime turns those messages into method calls on objects or classes (in the case of static methods), but get used to thinking about these as messages; you'll see things like "the receiver of this message will..." all over Apple's documentation. Now, let's use message passing to get rid of the keyboard when the user is done with it.

Ask the textField to give up focus

In order to get the keyboard to go away, we need to tell the text field that the user is done with it. We do this by asking the textfield to resign its first responder status.

Sending messages in Objective-C is easy: you list the receiver of the message, the message to send, and any arguments you need to pass along.

Surround message passing with square brackets.

This is a statement like any other—don't forget the semicolon.

```
[notesField resignFirstResponder];
```

This is the receiver for the message – in our case, the notesField.

This is where you put the actual message. In our case we have no arguments, so this is all we need. See the Apple documentation for details on what messages each component will respond to.

> Is that how the View is sending the View Controller information?

Yes! Our View Controller can respond to a number of messages like sendButtonTapped and viewDidLoad.

You've been responding to messages all this time. Now here's the trick: the textField can send a message when the user taps the Done button on they keyboard. We just need to tell it that our ViewController is interested in knowing when that happens.

You can pass messages to nil with no obvious problems.

Objective-C lets you send messages to nil without complaining. If you're used to NullPointerExceptions from other languages, this can make debugging tricky. Be careful of uninitialized variables or nil values coming back as other nil values when you debug.

Watch it!

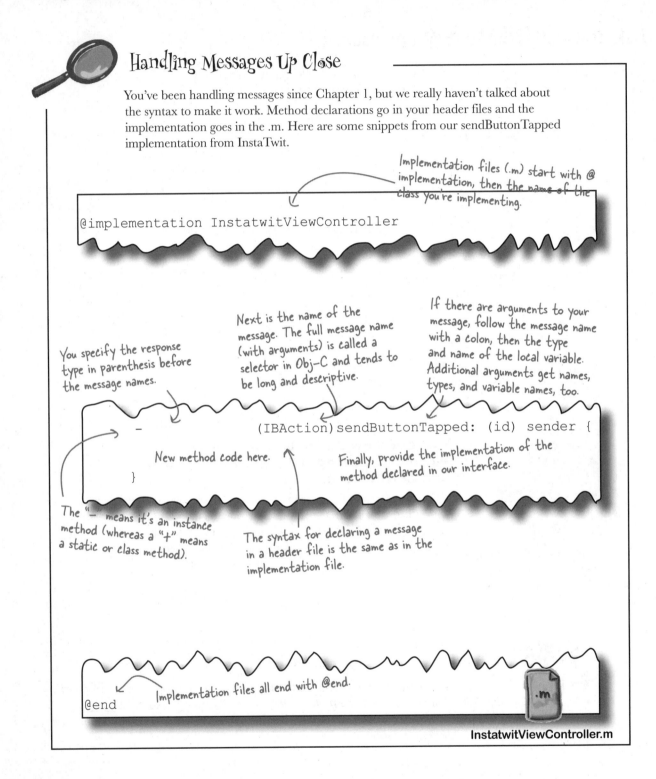

Handling Messages Up Close

You've been handling messages since Chapter 1, but we really haven't talked about the syntax to make it work. Method declarations go in your header files and the implementation goes in the .m. Here are some snippets from our sendButtonTapped implementation from InstaTwit.

Implementation files (.m) start with @ implementation, then the name of the class you're implementing.

```
@implementation InstatwitViewController
```

Next is the name of the message. The full message name (with arguments) is called a selector in Obj-C and tends to be long and descriptive.

If there are arguments to your message, follow the message name with a colon, then the type and name of the local variable. Additional arguments get names, types, and variable names, too.

You specify the response type in parenthesis before the message names.

```
-          (IBAction) sendButtonTapped: (id) sender {

          New method code here.

}
```

Finally, provide the implementation of the method declared in our interface.

The "-" means it's an instance method (whereas a "+" means a static or class method).

The syntax for declaring a message in a header file is the same as in the implementation file.

```
@end
```
Implementation files all end with @end.

InstatwitViewController.m

Messages in Objective-C use named arguments

In Objective-C, message names tend to be long and descriptive. This really starts to make sense when you see arguments tacked on. When you send a message with arguments, the message and argument names are all specified. Objective-C messages read more like sentences. Let's look at a method declaration from UIPickerViewDataSource. This method returns the number of rows for a given component in a picker view. It's declared like this:

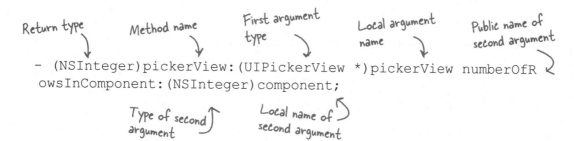

```
- (NSInteger)pickerView:(UIPickerView *)pickerView numberOfR
  owsInComponent:(NSInteger)component;
```

Methods can have internal and external names for arguments; the external name is used when sending the message to the receiver. So when iPhoneOS wants to send this message to our delegate, it creates a call like this:

```
[pickerDelegate pickerView:somePicker numberOfRowsInComponent:component];
```

there are no Dumb Questions

Q: You keep switching terms back and forth between methods and messages. Which is it?

A: Both are correct, depending on your context. In Objective-C, you send messages to objects and they respond. The Objective-C runtime turns your message into a method call, which returns a value. So, generally you talk about sending some receiver a message, but if you're implementing what it does in response, you're implementing a method.

Q: So about those arguments to methods ... what's the deal with the name before the colon and the one after the type?

A: In Objective-C you can have a public name and a local name for arguments. The public name becomes part of the selector when someone wants to send that message to your object. That's the name before the colon. The name after the type is the local variable; this is the name of the variable that holds the value. In Objective-C they don't have to be the same, so you can use a nice

friendly public name for people when they use your class and a convenient local name in your code.

One more interesting fact: the public name is optional. If you don't provide one, people just use a colon and the argument value when sending the message to your object. Obviously, the argument order is critical.

More on selectors in a minute.

Use message passing to tell our view controller when the Done button is pressed

The text field can tell our ViewController when the Done button was pressed on the keyboard; we just need to tell it what message to send. We can do this with Interface Builder. You'll need to declare an action in both the .h and and implement it in the .m file:

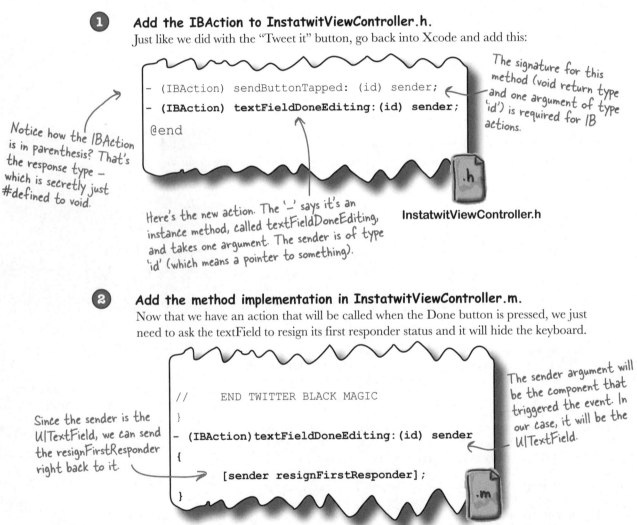

Messages going here between UITextField and the controller.

1   **Add the IBAction to InstatwitViewController.h.**
Just like we did with the "Tweet it" button, go back into Xcode and add this:

```
- (IBAction) sendButtonTapped: (id) sender;

- (IBAction) textFieldDoneEditing:(id) sender;

@end
```

The signature for this method (void return type and one argument of type 'id') is required for IB actions.

Notice how the IBAction is in parenthesis? That's the response type – which is secretly just #defined to void.

Here's the new action. The '–' says it's an instance method, called textFieldDoneEditing, and takes one argument. The sender is of type 'id' (which means a pointer to something).

InstatwitViewController.h

2   **Add the method implementation in InstatwitViewController.m.**
Now that we have an action that will be called when the Done button is pressed, we just need to ask the textField to resign its first responder status and it will hide the keyboard.

```
//      END TWITTER BLACK MAGIC
}
- (IBAction)textFieldDoneEditing:(id) sender
{
    [sender resignFirstResponder];
}
```

Since the sender is the UITextField, we can send the resignFirstResponder right back to it.

The sender argument will be the component that triggered the event. In our case, it will be the UITextField.

InstatwitViewController.m

Almost there, we just need to wire it up...

Connect the UITextField event in Interface Builder
Now the actions are declared, go back into Interface Builder by double clicking on InstatwitViewController.xib. If you right-click on the UITextField you'll bring up the connections.

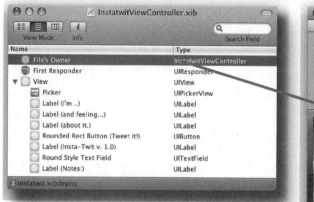

In the list of events that the UITextField can send, choose the "Did End on Exit" event and connect it to the File's Owner's "textFieldDoneEditing" action we just created.

 **Geek Bits**

The UITextField has a number of events that it can raise, just like the round rectangular button. Take a second and check out the list that's there. Along with the customizing that you can do in the Inspector with the field, you can wire up different (or even multiple!) responses to interaction with the field. Keep it in mind for your own apps.

there are no
Dumb Questions

Q: Why did we send the message back to the sender in our action and not to our notesField property?

A: Either one would work fine; they're both references to the same object. We used the sender argument because it would work regardless of whether we had a property that was a reference to our UITextField.

Q: You mentioned selectors, but I'm still fuzzy on what they are.

A: Selectors are unique names for methods when Objective-C translates a message into an actual method call. It's basically the method name and the names of the arguments separated by colons. For instance, the code on page 66 is using

the selector `pickerView:numberOfRowsInComponent`. You'll see them show up again in later chapters when we do more interface connecting in code. For now, Interface Builder is handling it for us.

Q: When we send the resignFirstResponder message to sender, the sender type is "id". How does that work?

A: "id" is an Objective-C type that can point to any Objective-C object. It's like a void* in C++. Since Objective-C is a dynamically typed language, it's perfectly ok with sending messages to an object of type "id". It will figure out at runtime whether or not the object can actually respond to the message.

Q: What happens if an object can't respond to a message?

A: You'll get an exception. This is the reason you should use strongly typed variables whenever possible. However, there are times when generic typing makes a lot of sense, such as callback methods when the sender could be any number of different objects.

Q: So seriously, brackets for message passing?

A: Yes. And indexing arrays. We all just have to deal with it.

BULLET POINTS

- In Objective-C you send messages to receivers. The runtime maps these to method calls.

- Method declarations go in the header (.h) file after the closing brace of an interface.

- Method implementations go in the implementation (.m) file between the @implementation and the @end.

- Method arguments are usually named, and those names are used when sending a message.

- Arguments can have an internal and external name.

- Use a "-" to indicate an instance method; use "+" to indicate a static method.

Test Drive

Do some typing, go ahead!

It works! The keyboard goes away and you can play around with the text field and add some notes now.

If you have your account info in the code, remember every time you tweet it actually will!

Tap the "done" button...

Something's still not right

Mike's ready to try out the custom field and see what happens, but when he puts in his custom message...

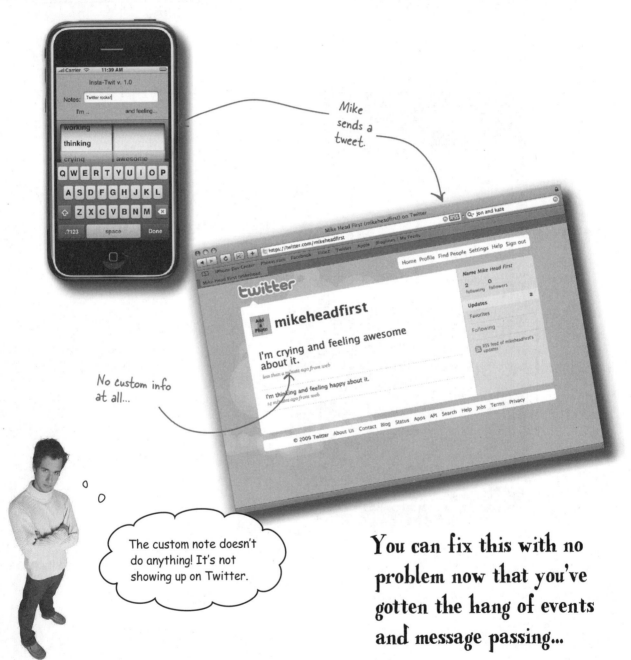

Mike sends a tweet.

No custom info at all...

The custom note doesn't do anything! It's not showing up on Twitter.

You can fix this with no problem now that you've gotten the hang of events and message passing...

BE the architect

Your job is to be architect and figure out how the UITextField and the Tweet button need to work together using the View - View Controller model.

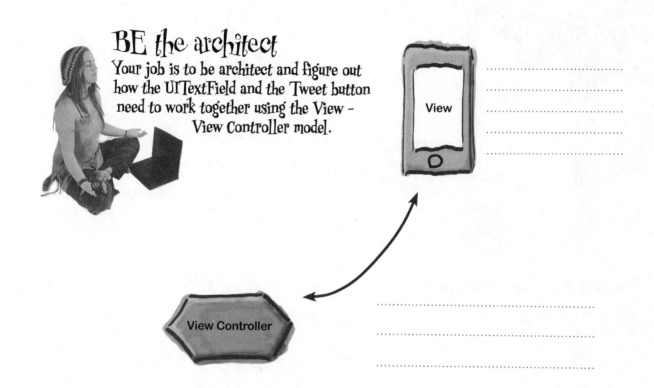

View

View Controller

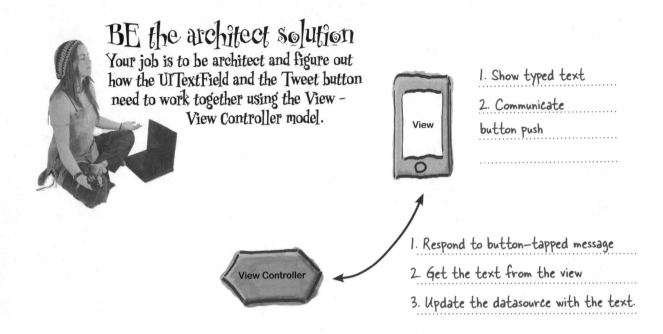

BE the architect solution
Your job is to be architect and figure out how the UITextField and the Tweet button need to work together using the View – View Controller model.

View

1. Show typed text
2. Communicate button push

View Controller

1. Respond to button-tapped message
2. Get the text from the view
3. Update the datasource with the text.

Build the tweet with strings

We need to incorporate the note text into our tweet. In order to do that, we're going to do a little string manipulation with the core string classes. You've already built a message to send to Twitter, but this time we have more text to include. Before you refactor the code to send the tweet with the new text in it, let's take a closer look at what you did in Chapter 2:

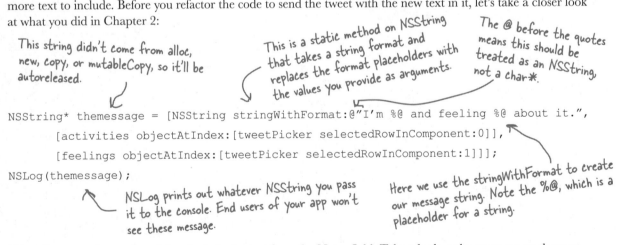

This string didn't come from alloc, new, copy, or mutableCopy, so it'll be autoreleased.

This is a static method on NSString that takes a string format and replaces the format placeholders with the values you provide as arguments.

The @ before the quotes means this should be treated as an NSString, not a char*.

```
NSString* themessage = [NSString stringWithFormat:@"I'm %@ and feeling %@ about it.",
        [activities objectAtIndex:[tweetPicker selectedRowInComponent:0]],
        [feelings objectAtIndex:[tweetPicker selectedRowInComponent:1]]];
NSLog(themessage);
```

NSLog prints out whatever NSString you pass it to the console. End users of your app won't see these message.

Here we use the stringWithFormat to create our message string. Note the %@, which is a placeholder for a string.

Now all you need to update this to include the text from the Notes field. Take a look at the magnets on the next page and get it working.

Xcode Magnets

You need to modify InstatwitViewController.m file to add the custom field to the message. Using the information you just learned and the magnets below, fill in the missing code.

```objective-c
- (IBAction) sendButtonTapped: (id) sender {
    NSString* themessage = [NSString stringWithFormat:@"
    I'm %@ and feeling %@ about it.",


    _____  ____  _____    _____  ____

    [activities objectAtIndex:[tweetPicker
selectedRowInComponent:0]],
    [feelings objectAtIndex:[tweetPicker selectedRowInComponent:1]]];
    NSLog(themessage);
```

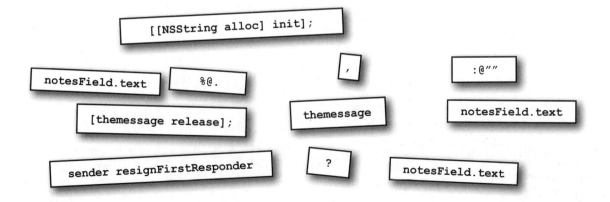

Xcode Magnets Solution

You need to modify InstatwitViewController.m file to add the custom field to the message. Using the information you just learned and the magnets below, fill in the missing code.

InstatwitViewController.m

Here's our new string placeholder for the notes text.

```objc
- (IBAction) sendButtonTapped: (id) sender {
    NSString* themessage = [NSString stringWithFormat:@"    %@.
    I'm %@ and feeling %@ about it.",
```

```
notesField.text        ?        notesField.text        :@""        ,
```

```objc
    [activities objectAtIndex:[tweetPicker
selectedRowInComponent:0]],
    [feelings objectAtIndex:[tweetPicker selectedRowInComponent:1]]];
    NSLog(themessage);
```

We have to handle the case where the user didn't enter any text. If the text field is empty, its text property will be nil. Here we use the C style ternary operator. If notesField.text isn't nil, it will use the value in notesField.text....

...and if it is nil, we'll send an empty string. Remember, it has to be an NSString, so we put the @ before the quotes.

The ? is a ternary operator, just like in Java or C++, where if the expression is true it returns the first value, otherwise, it returns the second.

```
[[NSString alloc] init];
```

```
[themessage release];
```

```
themessage
```

```
sender resignFirstResponder
```

```
notesField.text
```

Test Drive

Go ahead and build and run the app with the new text code in it.

Now it has custom text! wOOt!

It's so great that we can talk about our feelings...

Objective-Ccross

Practice some of your new Objective-C terminology.

Across

5. The control with focus has _____ status.
6. This incorporates another file.
7. Unique names for methods after Objective-C translation are

   _____.
8. Signals that the compiler will retain the object.
9. Automatic methods.
10. This tells the compiler to skip mutexes.

Down

1. An array of objects that will be released after the current event.
2. A "+" before a method declaration indicates that it's a

   _____.
3. This is sent between objects.
4. _____ management is important for iPhone apps.

Your Objective-C Toolbox

You've got Chapter 3 under your belt and now you've added Objective-C to your toolbox. For a complete list of tooltips in the book, go to http://www.headfirstlabs.com/ iphonedev.

Attribute	You want it...
readwrite	When you want the property to be modifiable by people. The compiler will generate a getter and a setter for you. This is the default.
readonly	When you don't want people modifying the property. You can still change the field value backing the property, but the compiler won't generate a setter.
assign	When you're dealing with basic types, like ints, floats, etc. The compiler just creates a setter with a simple myField = value statement. This is the default, but not usually what you want.
retain	When you're dealing with object values. The compiler will retain the value you pass in (we'll talk more about retaining in a minute) and release the old value when a new one comes in.
copy	When you want to hold onto a copy of some value instead of the value itself. For example, if you want to hold onto an array and don't want people to be able to change its contents after they set it. This sends a copy message to the value passed in then retains that.

Objective – C

- Is the language of iPhone apps
- Is an object oriented language
- Has advanced memory management
- Uses message passing and dynamic typing
- Has inheritance and interfaces

Memory Management

- You must release objects you create with alloc, new, copy or mutableCopy

- Everything else needs to have a retain count of 1 and in the autorelease pool

Objective-Ccross Solution

Practice some of your new Objective-C terminology.

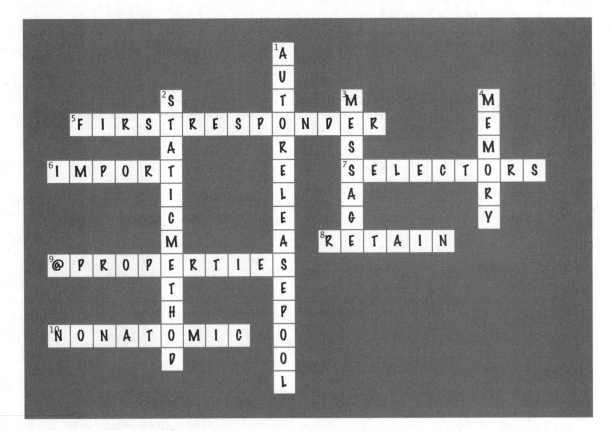

Across

5. The control with focus has _____ status. [FIRSTRESPONDER]
6. This incorporates another file. [IMPORT]
7. Unique names for methods after Objective-C translation are _____. [SELECTORS]
8. Signals that the compiler will retain the object. [RETAIN]
9. Automatic methods. [@PROPERTIES]
10. This tells the compiler to skip mutexes. [NONATOMIC]

Down

1. An array of objects that will be released after the current event. [AUTORELEASEPOOL]
2. A "+" before a method declaration indicates that it's a _____. [STATICMETHOD]
3. This is sent between objects. [MESSAGE]
4. _____ management is important for iPhone apps. [MEMORY]

4 multiple views

A table with a view

I like my coffee with two sugars, cream, a sprinkle of cinnamon, stirred twice, then ...

Most iPhone apps have more than one view.

We've written a cool app with one view, but anyone who's used an iPhone knows that most apps aren't like that. Some of the more impressive iPhone apps out there do a great job of moving through complex information by using multiple views. We're going to start with navigation controllers and table views, like the kind you see in your Mail and Contact apps. Only we're going to do it with a twist...

Overheard at
Head First
Lounge

Look, I don't have time for posting to Twitter. I need to know a ton of drink recipes every night. Is there an app for that?

Sam, bartender at the HF Lounge

BRAIN BARBELL

This chapter is about multiple-view apps. What views would you need to have for a bartending app?

....

....

....

iPhone UI Design Magnets

Using the components shown below, lay out the two
views we'll be using for the app.

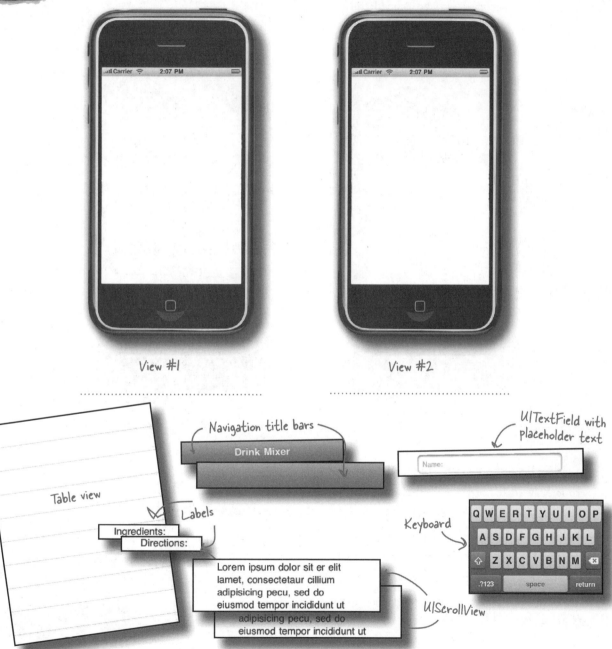

View #1

View #2

Navigation title bars

Drink Mixer

UITextField with
placeholder text

Name:

Table view

Labels

Ingredients:

Directions:

Keyboard

Lorem ipsum dolor sit er elit
lamet, consectetaur cillium
adipisicing pecu, sed do
eiusmod tempor incididunt ut

adipisicing pecu, sed do
eiusmod tempor incididunt ut

UIScrollView

Q W E R T Y U I O P
A S D F G H J K L
⇧ Z X C V B N M ⌫
.?123   space   return

iPhone UI Design Magnets Solution

Using the components shown below, lay out the two views we'll be using for the app.

This bar will have buttons, like the back and forward buttons in a web browser

We'll call it Drink Mixer

It will also show your app's title

UITextField with placeholder text

Labels

UIScrollView

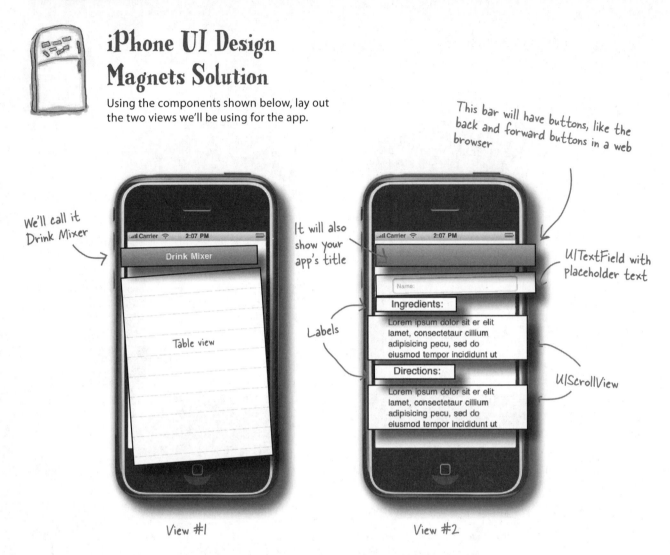

View #1

View #2

Sam needs a list of drink names and to be able to look up what's in them. He'll also want to know how much he needs of each ingredient, and any instructions — what's on the rocks, whether to shake or stir, when to light things on fire, etc. So for our two views, we'll put the drinks in a list (view #1), then when Sam taps on one we'll show the details (view #2).

We're not going to use the keyboard for now — it's a reference app, and Sam just needs to read stuff...

So, how do these views fit together?

Before you pick the template for our bartending app, take a minute to look at how you want the user to interact with the drink information. We're going to have a scrollable list of drink names, and when the user taps on a row, we'll show the detailed drink information using view #2, our detailed view. Once our user has seen enough, they're going to want to go back to the drink list.

Once our users are done with the detailed information, the Navigation bar gives them a way to get back to the list.

We're going to want some kind of transition between these views...

We need a list of items to work with...

We're going to be coming in and out of this view a lot — each time our user selects a drink.

BRAIN BARBELL

Below are the templates available for an app. Which do you think we should use for DrinkMixer?

☐ Window-based Application ☐ View-based Application ☐ Utility Application

☐ Tab Bar Application ☐ OpenGL ES Application ☐ Navigation-based Application

The navigation template pulls multiple views together

For this app, we're going to use a Navigation-based project. To get started, go into Xcode and choose the **File→New Project** option. Choose the Navigation-based application and save it as DrinkMixer.proj. Make sure that "Use Core Data for storage" is **not** checked.

The navigation template comes with a lot of functionality built in:

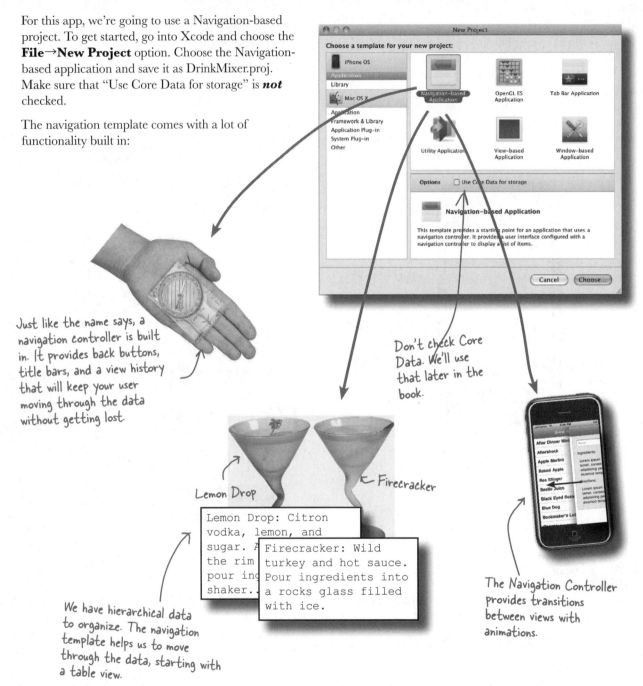

Just like the name says, a navigation controller is built in. It provides back buttons, title bars, and a view history that will keep your user moving through the data without getting lost.

Don't check Core Data. We'll use that later in the book.

Lemon Drop

Firecracker

Lemon Drop: Citron vodka, lemon, and sugar. A the rim pour inc shaker..

Firecracker: Wild turkey and hot sauce. Pour ingredients into a rocks glass filled with ice.

We have hierarchical data to organize. The navigation template helps us to move through the data, starting with a table view.

The Navigation Controller provides transitions between views with animations.

The navigation template starts with a table view

The navigation template comes with a navigation controller and a root view that the controller displays on startup. That root view is set up as a table view by default, and that works great for our app. A table view is typically used for listing items, one of which then can be selected for more details about that item.

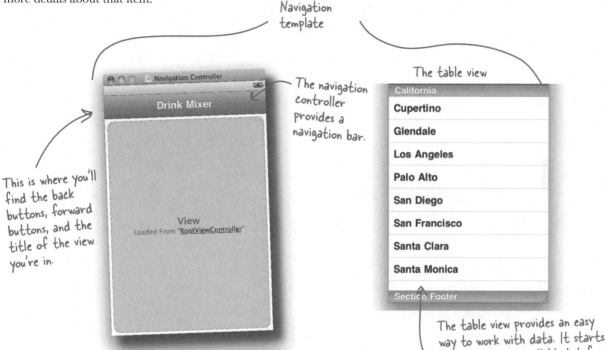

Navigation template

The navigation controller provides a navigation bar.

This is where you'll find the back buttons, forward buttons, and the title of the view you're in.

The table view

The table view provides an easy way to work with data. It starts with an empty, scrollable list for the main view of your application.

there are no Dumb Questions

Q: If the navigation template is about handing lots of views, why does it only come with one?

A: Most navigation-based applications start out with a table view and show detailed views from there. How many detailed views, what they look like, etc. are very application-specific, so you have to decide what views you want and add those views. The navigation template doesn't assume anything beyond the initial table view.

Q: What built in apps on iPhone use the Navigation control?

A: Contacts and Mail, which are both core iPhone apps, use this design. It's a good idea to get into those apps on your phone to see how the entire template is implemented. For a neat twist, take a look at the Messages (SMS) app. That one uses a navigation controller but frequently starts in the "detail" view, showing the last person you sent or received a message from.

Q: Do I have to use a table view for my root view?

A: No, it's just the most common, since it provides a natural way to show an overview of a lot of data and have the user drill down for more information. Table views are very customizable, too, so some apps that might not seem like table views really are, like Notes or the iTunes store, for example.

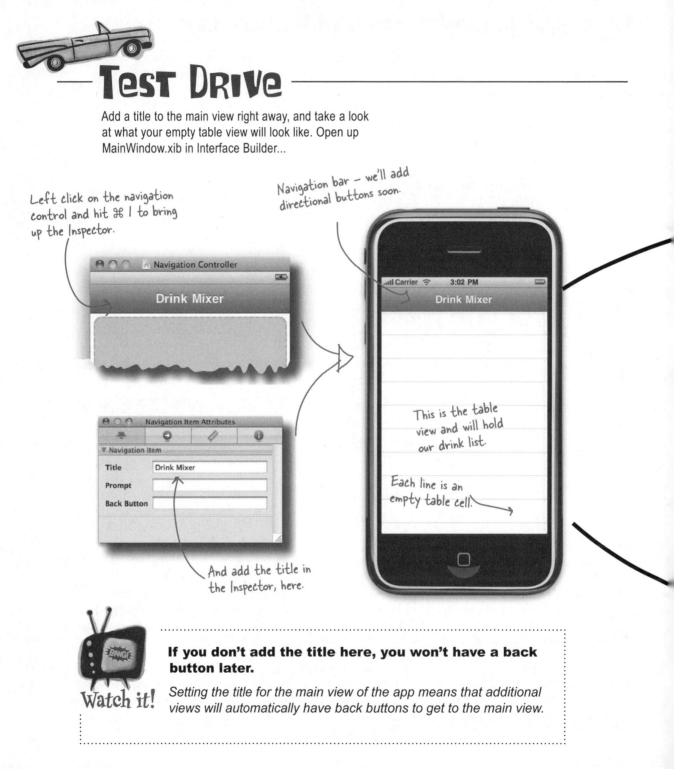

Test Drive

Add a title to the main view right away, and take a look
at what your empty table view will look like. Open up
MainWindow.xib in Interface Builder...

Left click on the navigation
control and hit ⌘ I to bring
up the Inspector.

Navigation bar — we'll add
directional buttons soon.

Navigation Controller

Drink Mixer

.ıll Carrier 🤶   3:02 PM   ▭

Drink Mixer

This is the table
view and will hold
our drink list.

Each line is an
empty table cell!

Navigation Item Attributes

▼ **Navigation Item**

Title   Drink Mixer

Prompt

Back Button

And add the title in
the Inspector, here.

**If you don't add the title here, you won't have a back
button later.**

*Setting the title for the main view of the app means that additional
views will automatically have back buttons to get to the main view.*

Watch it!

The Table View Up Close

Navigation controllers and table views are almost always used together. When you selected the navigation-based project as your template, Xcode created a different view setup than we've used in the past:

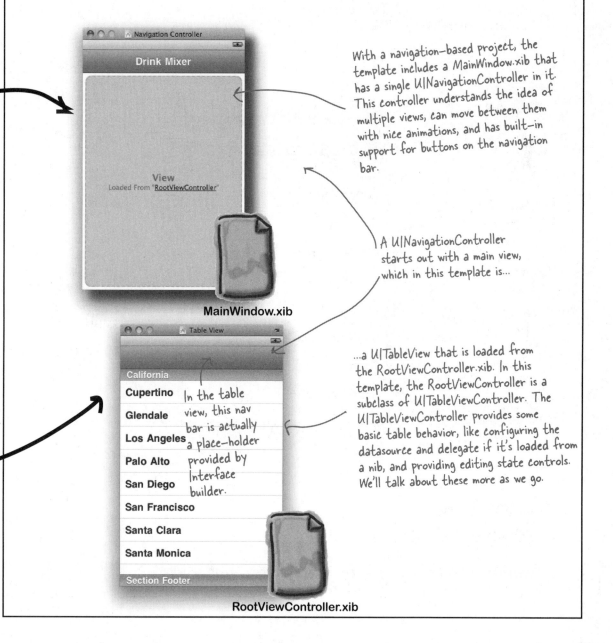

With a navigation-based project, the template includes a MainWindow.xib that has a single UINavigationController in it. This controller understands the idea of multiple views, can move between them with nice animations, and has built-in support for buttons on the navigation bar.

A UINavigationController starts out with a main view, which in this template is...

MainWindow.xib

...a UITableView that is loaded from the RootViewController.xib. In this template, the RootViewController is a subclass of UITableViewController. The UITableViewController provides some basic table behavior, like configuring the datasource and delegate if it's loaded from a nib, and providing editing state controls. We'll talk about these more as we go.

In the table view, this nav bar is actually a place-holder provided by Interface builder.

RootViewController.xib

A table is a collection of cells

The UITableView provides a lot of the functionality we need right away, but it still needs to know what data we're actually trying to show and what to do when the user interacts with that data. This is where the datasource and delegate come in. A table view is easy to customize and is set up by the template to talk to the datasource and delegate to see what it needs to show, how many rows, what table cells to use, etc.

The navigation controller, not the table view, provides the navigation bar. Since we're in interface builder, this is just a simulated one.

Table views have built-in support for editing their contents, including moving rows around, deleting rows, and adding new ones.

Table views can tell you when your user taps on a cell. It'll tell you the section and row that was tapped.

We're using the default table view cell, but you can create your own and lay them out any way you want.

Table views try to conserve memory by reusing cells when they scroll off the screen.

A table can only have one column, but you can put whatever you want in that column by customizing your table cells.

A table can have multiple sections, and each section can have a header and a footer. We only have one section, so we don't need either for DrinkMixer.

A table view is made up of multiple table cells. The table view will ask how many cells (or rows) are in each section.

Table View

California

Cupertino

Glendale

Los Angeles

Palo Alto

San Diego

San Francisco

Santa Clara

Santa Monica

Section Footer

BRAIN POWER

Look through some of the apps you have on your device. What are some of the most customized table views you can find? Are they using sections? Are they grouped? How did they layout their cells?

Table Cell Code Up Close

Below is an excerpt from our updated RootViewController.m file. This is where we create table cells and populate them with the drink list information.

The indexPath contains the section and row number for the needed cell.

This method is called when the table view needs a cell.

```objc
// Customize the appearance of table view cells.
- (UITableViewCell *)tableView:(UITableView *)tableView cellForRowAtIndexPath
:(NSIndexPath *)indexPath {

    static NSString *CellIdentifier = @"Cell";


    UITableViewCell *cell = [tableView dequeueReusableCellWithIdentifier:CellI
dentifier];
    if (cell == nil) {
        cell = [[[UITableViewCell alloc] initWithStyle:UITableViewCellStyleDe
fault reuseIdentifier:CellIdentifier] autorelease];
    }

        // Configure the cell.
    cell.textLabel.text = [self.drinks objectAtIndex:indexPath.row];
        return cell;
}


- (NSInteger)numberOfSectionsInTableView:(UITableView *)tableView {
    return 1;
}
// Customize the number of rows in the table view.
- (NSInteger)tableView:(UITableView *)tableView numberOfRowsInSection:(NSInte
ger)section {
    return [self.drinks count];
}
```

Table cells have identifiers so when you try to find a cell for reuse, you can be sure you're grabbing the right kind.

Here we check with the table view to see if there are any reusable cells with the given cell identifier available.

If there aren't any available for reuse, we'll create a new one.

Here we customize the text in the cell with the information for the specific drink we need to show.

These methods tell the table view how many sections we have and how many rows in each section.

there are no
Dumb Questions

Q: How do cells get into that reusable list to begin with?

A: The table view handles that. When cells scroll off the screen (either the top or the bottom,) the table view will queue up cells that are no longer needed. When it asks the datasource for a cell for a particular row, you can check that queue of cells to see if there are any available for use.

Q: I don't understand the cell identifier... does it have to be "Cell"?

A: No—that's just the default. When you do more complex table views, you can create custom cell types depending on what data you're trying to display. You use the cell identifier to make sure that when you ask for a reusable cell, the table view gives you back the type you expect. The identifier can be anything you want—just make sure you have a unique name for each unique cell type you use.

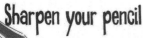

Sharpen your pencil

It's time to start displaying some drinks. You'll need to make some modifications to both the RootViewController.h and RootViewController.m files.

 Declare the drinks array.
Using syntax similar to what we used for the picker, declare an array called drinks in RootViewController.h with the necessary properties declaration.

 Implement and populate the array.
In RootViewController.m, uncomment and expand the viewDidLoad method to create the array with the drinks from the drink list here.

 Tell the table how many rows you have.
The auto-generated code needs to be modified to tell the table that it will have the same number of rows as there are drinks in the array. Modify the implementation file under this line: **// Customize the number of rows in the table view**.

 Populate the table cells.
Implement the code that we talked about on the previous page in **Table Cell Up Close** so that the table gets populated with the items from the array.

Drink List:
Firecracker
Lemon Drop
Mojito

> Wait, memory on the iPhone is a big deal, right? How can we put in all those drinks?

Like everything else on iPhone, the UITableView has to worry about memory.

So, how does it balance concerns about memory with an unknown amount of data to display? It breaks things up into cells.

Each drink gets its own cell... sorta

The UITableView only has to display enough data to fill an iPhone screen—it doesn't really matter how much data you might have in total. The UITableView does this by reusing cells that scrolled off the screen.

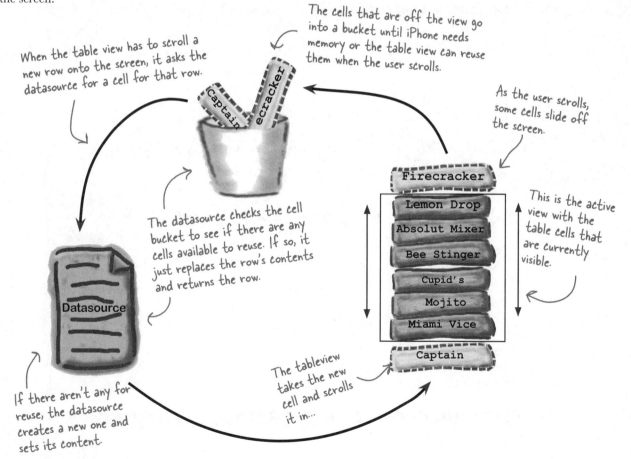

When the table view has to scroll a new row onto the screen, it asks the datasource for a cell for that row.

The cells that are off the view go into a bucket until iPhone needs memory or the table view can reuse them when the user scrolls.

As the user scrolls, some cells slide off the screen.

The datasource checks the cell bucket to see if there are any cells available to reuse. If so, it just replaces the row's contents and returns the row.

This is the active view with the table cells that are currently visible.

If there aren't any for reuse, the datasource creates a new one and sets its content.

The tableview takes the new cell and scrolls it in...

Firecracker

Lemon Drop

Absolut Mixer

Bee Stinger

Cupid's

Mojito

Miami Vice

Captain

Datasource

Sharpen your pencil
Solution

It's time to start displaying some drinks. You'll need to make some modifications to both the RootViewController.h and RootViewController.m files.

1 Declare the drinks array.

```
@interface RootViewController : UITableViewController {

    NSMutableArray* drinks;   Add the new drinks
                              array.
}
@property (nonatomic, retain) NSMutableArray* drinks;
@end
```

UITableViewController handles the datasource and delegate for you, so you don't need to declare them here.

Declare the properties for the drinks array.

RootViewController.h

```
@synthesize drinks;
```

```
-
(void)dealloc {
    [drinks release];
    [super dealloc];
}
@end
```

RootViewController.m

② **Implement and populate the array.**
In RootViewController.m, uncomment and expand the
ViewDidLoad methods.

This will initially be commented out.

RootViewController.m

```
- (void)viewDidLoad {
    [super viewDidLoad];


    NSMutableArray* tmpArray = [[NSMutableArray
alloc] initWithObjects:@"Firecracker", @"Lemon Drop",
@"Mojito",nil];
    self.drinks = tmpArray;
    [tmpArray release];


    // Uncomment the following line to display an Edit button in
the navigation bar for this view controller.
    // self.navigationItem.rightBarButtonItem = self.
editButtonItem;
}
```

Starter drinks we gave you.

③ **Tell the table how many rows you have.**

```
//Customize the number of rows in the table view.
 - (NSInteger)tableView:(UITableView *)tableView numberOfRowsInS
ection:(NSInteger)section {
    return [self.drinks count];
    }
```

This used to say return: 0.

Now it tells the table view that we have the same number of rows as the number of items in the drinks array

④ **Populate the table cells.**

```
// Configure the cell.
cell.textLabel.text = [self.drinks objectAtIndex:indexPath.row];
    return cell;
}
```

Here we customize the text in the cell with the information for the specific drink we need to show.

Test Drive

Now you're ready to go. Save it, build and run, and you'll see the three drinks in your app in the main view.

Try it out — the list will scroll, too!

Everything looks great. I'll just email over our complete list—it's 40 drinks...

Q: You mentioned the table view's datasource and delegate, but why didn't I have to declare anything like we did with UIPickerView?

A: Great catch. Normally you would, but the navigation-based template we used already set this up. To see what's happening, look at the RootViewController.h file. You'll see that it is a subclass of UITableViewController, and that class conforms to the UITableViewDataSourceProtocol and the UITableViewDelegateProtocol. If you look in RootViewController.xib, you'll see that the table view's datasource and delegate are both set to be our RootViewController. If we weren't using a template, you'd have to set these up yourself (we'll revisit this in Chapter 7).

Q: I noticed we used an NSMutableArray. Is that because we had to initialize it?

A: No—both NSMutableArray and NSArray can be initialized with values when you create them. We're using an NSMutableArray because we're going to manipulate the contents of this array later. We'll get there in a minute.

Q: What's the nil at the end of the drink names when we create the drink array?

A: NSMutableArray's initializer takes a variable number of arguments. It uses nil to know it's reached the end of the arguments. The last element in the array will be the value before the nil—nil won't be added to the array.

Q: Tell me again about that @ symbol before our drink names?

A: The @ symbol is shorthand for creating an NSString. NSArrays store arrays of objects, so we need to convert our text names (char*s) to NSStrings. We do that by putting an @ in front of the text constant.

Q: When we customized the table view cells, we used the cell.textLabel. Are there other labels? What's the difference between cell.textLabel and cell.text?

A: Before iPhone 3.0, there was just one label and set of disclosure indicators in the default cell, and it was all handled by the cell itself. You just sent the text you wanted on the cell.text property. Nearly everyone wanted a little more information on the table cells, so in iPhone 3.0, Apple added a few different styles with different label layouts. Once they did that, they introduced specific properties for the different text areas, like textLabel, detailLabel, etc., and deprecated the old cell.text property. You shouldn't use cell.text in your apps—Apple will likely remove it at some point in the future. We'll talk more about the other labels later in the chapter.

Q: You mention that we can use section headers and footers—how do you specify those?

A: The datasource is responsible for that information, too. There are optional methods you can provide that return the title for section headers and the title for section footers based on the section number. They work a lot like our cellForRowAtIndexPath, except they only return strings.

Q: What's the difference between a plain table view and a grouped table view?

A: The only difference is the appearance. In a plain table view, like the one we're using, all the sections touch each other and are separated by the section header and footer if you have them. In a grouped table view, the table view puts space between the sections and shows the section header in bigger letters. Take a look at your contact list, then select a contact. The first view, where all of your contacts are listed together and separated by letters is a plain table view. The detailed view, where the phone numbers are separated from email addresses, etc, is a grouped table view.

Just a few more drinks

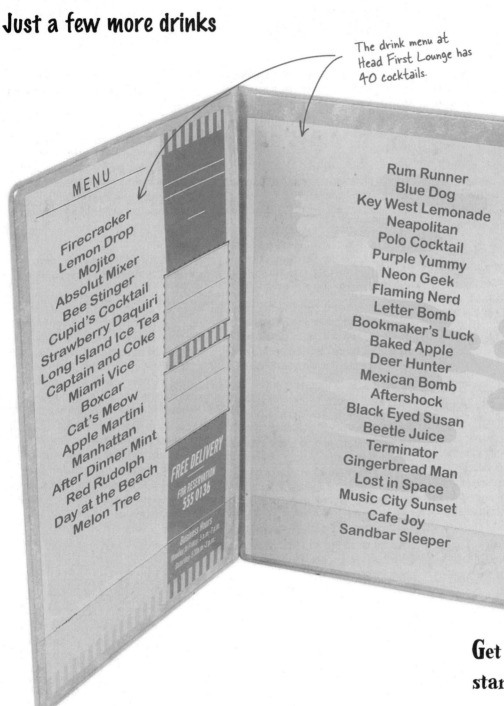

The drink menu at Head First Lounge has 40 cocktails.

MENU

Firecracker
Lemon Drop
Mojito
Absolut Mixer
Bee Stinger
Cupid's Cocktail
Strawberry Daquiri
Long Island Ice Tea
Captain and Coke
Miami Vice
Boxcar
Cat's Meow
Apple Martini
Manhattan
After Dinner Mint
Red Rudolph
Day at the Beach
Melon Tree

FREE DELIVERY
FOR RESERVATION
555 0136

Business Hours

Rum Runner
Blue Dog
Key West Lemonade
Neapolitan
Polo Cocktail
Purple Yummy
Neon Geek
Flaming Nerd
Letter Bomb
Bookmaker's Luck
Baked Apple
Deer Hunter
Mexican Bomb
Aftershock
Black Eyed Susan
Beetle Juice
Terminator
Gingerbread Man
Lost in Space
Music City Sunset
Cafe Joy
Sandbar Sleeper

Get ready to start typing...

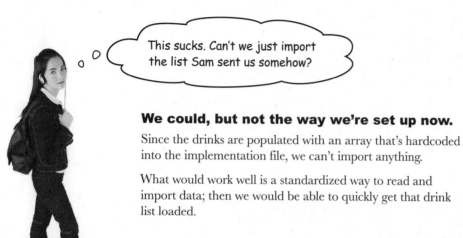

This sucks. Can't we just import the list Sam sent us somehow?

We could, but not the way we're set up now.

Since the drinks are populated with an array that's hardcoded into the implementation file, we can't import anything.

What would work well is a standardized way to read and import data; then we would be able to quickly get that drink list loaded.

BRAIN BARBELL

What can we do? There needs to be a way to speed up the process.

....

....

....

....

....

Plists are an easy way to save and load data

Plist stands for "property list" and it has been around for quite a while with OS X. In fact, there are a number of plists already in use in your application. We've already worked with the most important plist, DrinkMixer-Info.plist. This is created by Xcode when you first create your project, and besides the app icons, it stores things like the main nib file to load when the application starts, the application version, and more. Xcode can create and edit these plists like any other file. Click on DrinkMixer-Info.plist to take a look at what's inside.

Key	Value
▼ Information Property List	(12 items)
Localization native development re	English
Bundle display name	${PRODUCT_NAME}
Executable file	${EXECUTABLE_NAME}
Icon file	
Bundle identifier	com.yourcompany.${PRODUCT_NAME:rfc1034identifier}
InfoDictionary version	6.0
Bundle name	${PRODUCT_NAME}
Bundle OS Type code	APPL
Bundle creator OS Type code	????
Bundle version	1.0
Application requires iPhone enviror	☑
Main nib file base name	MainWindow

DrinkMixer-Info.plist

Simulator – 3.0 | Debug

Overview   Build and Go   Tasks   Ungrouped   Project

DrinkMixer–Info.plist

Some of these items are obvious, like the icon file and the main nib to load.

Others are less obvious, but we'll talk more about them in later chapters.

Built-in types can save and load from plists automatically

All of the built-in types we've been using, like NSArray and NSString, can be loaded or saved from plists automatically. We can take advantage of this and move our drink list out of our source code.

We'll move our drink list out of the source code here and into a plist instead...

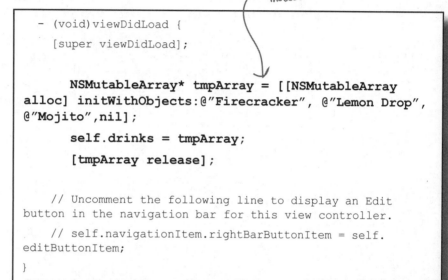

```objc
- (void)viewDidLoad {
    [super viewDidLoad];


    NSMutableArray* tmpArray = [[NSMutableArray
alloc] initWithObjects:@"Firecracker", @"Lemon Drop",
@"Mojito",nil];
    self.drinks = tmpArray;
    [tmpArray release];


    // Uncomment the following line to display an Edit
button in the navigation bar for this view controller.
    // self.navigationItem.rightBarButtonItem = self.
editButtonItem;

}
```

Exercise

Before you import Sam's list, let's create a sample plist that's the same format. We'll make sure we get that working properly, and then pull in Sam's list.

1 **Create the empty plist.**
Go back into Xcode and expand the **Resources** folder. Right-click on **Resources** and select **Add → New file**, **Mac OS X Resource**, and **Property List**. Call the new list **DrinkArray.plist**.

Make sure you pick "Resource" under Mac OS X—plists aren't listed under iPhone Resources.

2 **Format and populate the plist.**
Open up the file and change the root type to **Array** and the item types to **strings**. Then you can populate the names for the drinks.

Drink List
Firecracker
Lemon Drop
Mojito

Exercise Solution

With the sample list created, we can use it for testing before we get the big list.

1 **Create the empty plist.**

Go back into Xcode and expand the **Resources** folder. Right-click on **Resources** and select **Add → New file**, **Mac OS X Resource**, and **Property List**. Call the new list `DrinkArray.plist`.

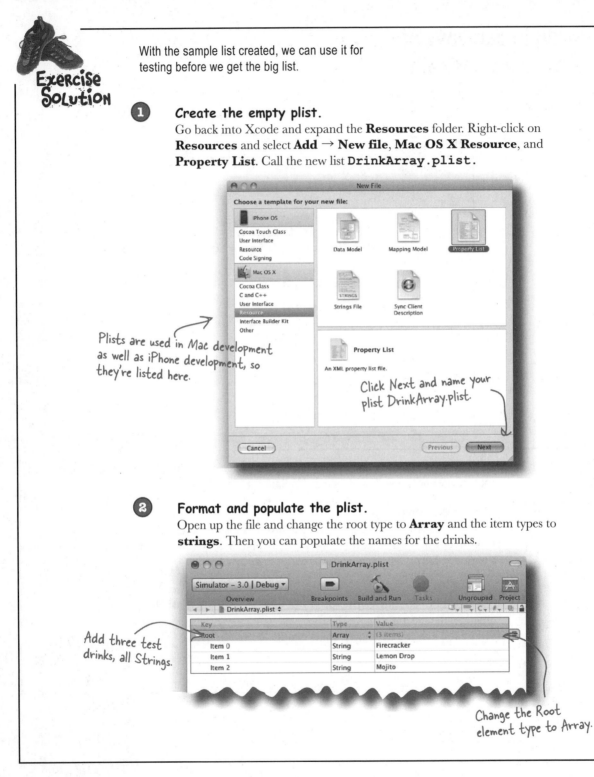

Plists are used in Mac development as well as iPhone development, so they're listed here.

Click Next and name your plist DrinkArray.plist.

2 **Format and populate the plist.**

Open up the file and change the root type to **Array** and the item types to **strings**. Then you can populate the names for the drinks.

Add three test drinks, all Strings.

Change the Root element type to Array.

Arrays (and more) have built-in support for plists

Changing the array initialization code to use the plist is remarkably easy. Most Cocoa collection types like NSArray ad NSDictionary have built-in support for serializing to and from a plist. As long as you're using built-in types (like other collections, NSStrings, etc.,) you can just ask an array to initialize itself from a plist.

The only piece missing is telling the array which plist to use. To do that, we'll use the project's resource bundle, which acts as a handle to application-specific information and files.

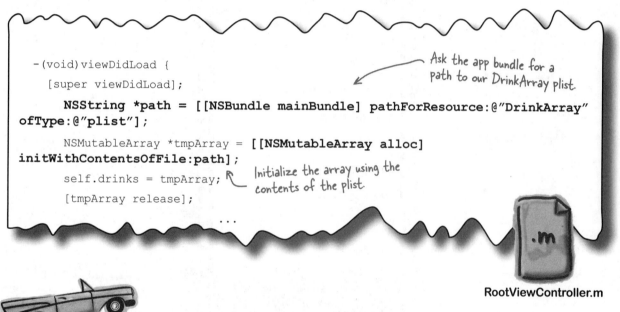

```objc
- (void)viewDidLoad {
    [super viewDidLoad];

    NSString *path = [[NSBundle mainBundle] pathForResource:@"DrinkArray"
ofType:@"plist"];

    NSMutableArray *tmpArray = [[NSMutableArray alloc]
initWithContentsOfFile:path];
    self.drinks = tmpArray;
    [tmpArray release];
    ...
```

Ask the app bundle for a path to our DrinkArray plist.

Initialize the array using the contents of the plist.

RootViewController.m

TEST DRIVE

After you've finished up these two things, go ahead and build and run. It should look the same, with just the three drinks.

Ready Bake Plist

Once this list works, head over to http://www.headfirstlabs/iphonedev and download the DrinkArray.plist file. It has the complete list of the drinks from the Head First Lounge. Drop this in on top of your test plist, rebuild DrinkMixer, and try it out!

Test Drive

The whole list is in there now!

By moving the drinks out of the code and into an external file, you can change the drink list without needing to touch a line of code.

PLists are just one way to save data on the iPhone – we'll talk about others later in the book.

PLists work great for built-in types. If you're going to be using custom types, you probably want to consider another option.

Drink Mixer

- Lemon Drop
- Letter Bomb
- Long Island Ice Tea
- Lost in Space
- Manhattan
- Melon Tree
- Mexican Bomb
- Miami Vice
- Mojito
- Music City Sunset

Now we just need to get that detail view all set up, right?

Creating your detail view will complete the app.

The entire list of drinks is great, but Sam still needs to know what goes in them and how to make them. That information is going to go in the detail view that we sketched up earlier.

BRAIN BARBELL

How are we going to get from the list to the detail view? And how are we going to display the details?

Use a detail view to drill down into data

Earlier, we classified DrinkMixer as a productivity app and we chose a navigation controller because we have hierarchical data. We have a great big list of drinks loaded, but what Sam needs now is the detailed information for each drink: what are the ingredients, how do you mix them, etc. Now we'll use that navigation controller to display a more detailed view of a drink from the list.

The standard pattern for table views is that you show more information about an item when a user taps on a table cell. We'll use that to let the user select a drink then show our detailed view. The detail view follows the same pattern as our other views:

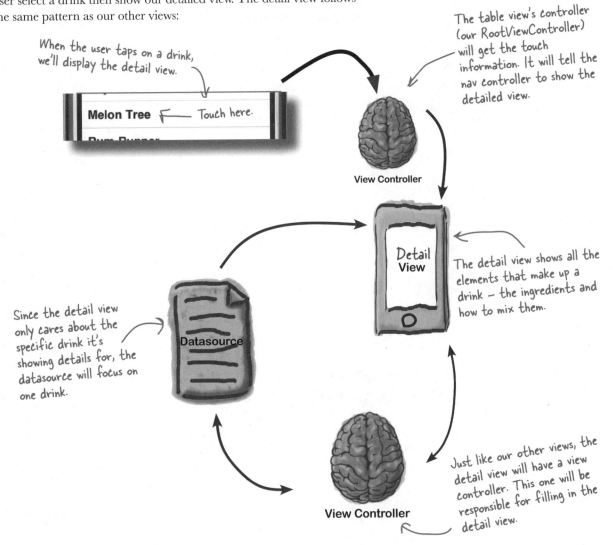

When the user taps on a drink, we'll display the detail view.

Melon Tree ← Touch here.

The table view's controller (our RootViewController) will get the touch information. It will tell the nav controller to show the detailed view.

View Controller

The detail view shows all the elements that make up a drink — the ingredients and how to mix them.

Detail View

Since the detail view only cares about the specific drink it's showing details for, the datasource will focus on one drink.

Datasource

Just like our other views, the detail view will have a view controller. This one will be responsible for filling in the detail view.

View Controller

A closer look at the detail view

We sketched out the detail view earlier—but we need to look more closely at what we're about to build.

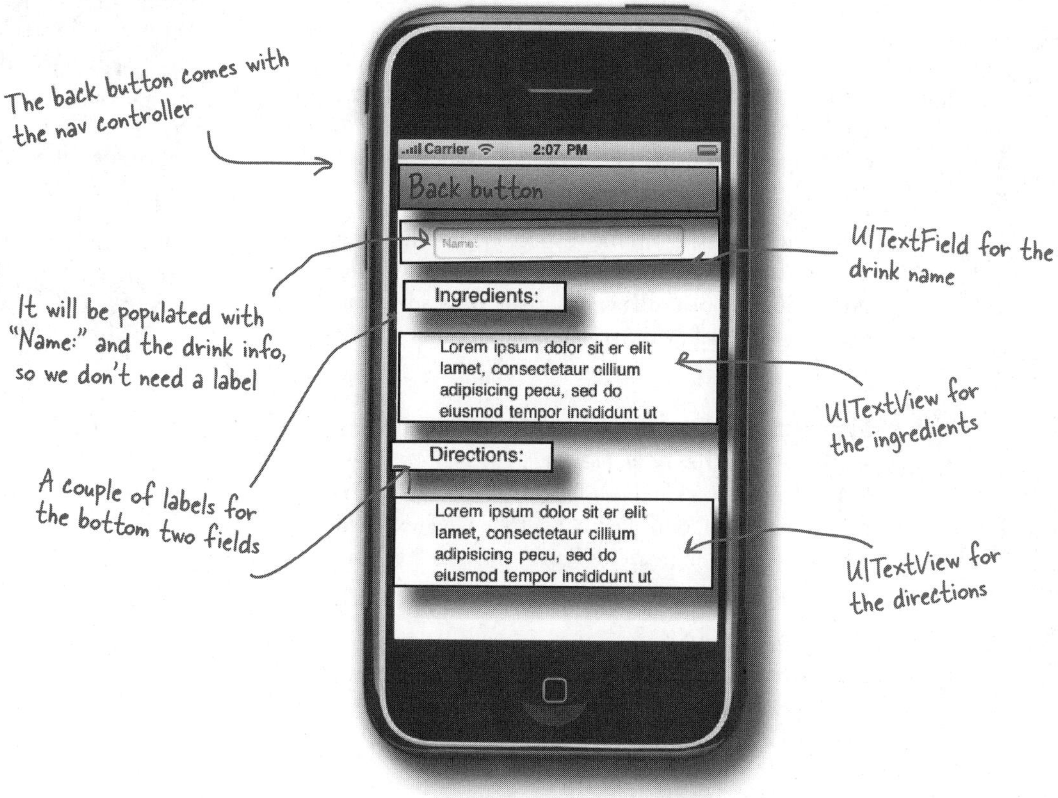

The back button comes with the nav controller

Back button

UITextField for the drink name

It will be populated with "Name:" and the drink info, so we don't need a label

Name:

Ingredients:

Lorem ipsum dolor sit er elit lamet, consectetaur cillium adipisicing pecu, sed do eiusmod tempor incididunt ut

UITextView for the ingredients

A couple of labels for the bottom two fields

Directions:

Lorem ipsum dolor sit er elit lamet, consectetaur cillium adipisicing pecu, sed do eiusmod tempor incididunt ut

UITextView for the directions

Let's start building...

Long Exercise

You've got the hang of this now. Start building your detail view by creating the files and code you'll need, then put it together in Interface Builder and wire it up. Get to it!

 Create the files you'll need.
To create the new view, you need a new *.xib file, as well as the supporting header and implementation files. The file type is a Cocoa Touch Class type, and it's a UIViewController subclass.

② **Lay out the new view in Interface Builder.**
Use the library to drag and drop the elements that you need and build the view we sketched out earlier.

Here's a hint: to reserve the space for the navigation controller, just bring up the Inspector, and under **Simulated Interface Elements**, **Top Bar**, select **Navigation Controller.** That will make sure that you lay out your view below the navigation bar.

 Write the code to handle the declarations and outlets for the new fields.
You'll need to work in both DetailViewController.h and DetailViewController.m. Call the new text fields nameTextField, ingredientsTextView, and directionsTextView.

④ **Connect the detail view to the new outlets.**
Just like we did for InstaTwit, use Interface Builder to make the new view work.

⑤ **Make the text fields uneditable.**
Using the inspector, find the checkbox that makes the fields uneditable.

Q: We keep drawing the datasource, view, and view controller as separate things, but then we stick them together into the same class. What's going on?

A: It's all about the pattern. In general, you'll have a few defined in a nib, a view controller backing it, and a set of data it needs to work on. Whether these are combined into one class or not really depends on the complexity of your application. If you're not using Interface Builder, you can go completely off the deep end and have your single class create the view programmatically. We'll show more of that later in the book. Conceptually, however, you still have a view that's calling into the view controller when things happen. Likewise, you usually have one or more datasource protocols being realized somewhere that are providing data to your view.

Q: Why do we have to move the *.xib file into the Resources group?

A: You don't *have* to, but we recommend it to help keep your code organized. Different developers use different groups, things like "User Interface", "Business Objects", "Data Objects", etc. Xcode really doesn't care; it's just important that you know how your code is organized and you can find what you're looking for. Reusing a structure that others will recognize is a good practice so people can pick up your code quickly and you can understand their code. We use the templated defaults in this book.

Q: What are other ways to save data?

A: There are quite a few of them. We'll cover the more common ones in this book in different projects. The one you're using now, plists, is the simplest, but it does limit what you can save and load. That doesn't make it bad; if it works for what you need, it's a fine solution—it's just too limited for everything. There's a serialization method called NSCoding that works well for custom objects, but can make version migration a challenge. iPhone supports saving and loading to a database using SQLite. This used to be the preferred way to go if you have a lot of data or need to search and access it without loading it all into memory. However, with iPhone 3.0, Apple introduced Core Data. Core Data is a very powerful framework that provides an OO wrapper on persistence and has nearly all of the benefits of using SQLite. It's definitely not trivial to get started, but it's really powerful. We'll build an app on it later.

Q: Why didn't you use a label for the name field?

A: UITextFields allow you to have placeholder text that appears in the field when it's empty. Rather than using up screen space with a Name label, we chose to use the placeholder. If the meaning of the text shown on the screen is obvious to the user, consider using placeholder text.

Q: So why didn't we use it for the ingredients and directions?

A: We could have, but since those contain multiple lines of text, we wanted to break them up with labels clearly showing what they were. Ultimately it's an aesthetic and usability decision, not a technical one.

BULLET POINTS

- Productivity apps work great with hierarchical data.

- Navigation controllers are a good way to manage multiple views.

- Table views usually go with navigation controllers.

- iPhone tables only have one column but can render custom cells.

- Tables need a datasource and a delegate.

- Multiple views usually mean multiple *.xib files.

Here's all the info for the new detail view. After this, you should have a working (but still empty) detail view.

Exercise Solution

1 **Create the files you'll need.**

We need a new .xib for the detail view. To create one from scratch, go back into Xcode and click on the **File→New File...** menu option

Make sure that you have the Cocoa Touch Class line selected under iPhone OS.

The new file dialog box has lots of options for making new files. In our case, we need both the nib and the supporting files, so we need to create a new Cocoa Touch Class with .m and .h files, and the .xib file.

Select the UIViewController subclass.

Enable this checkbox so the nib is created, too.

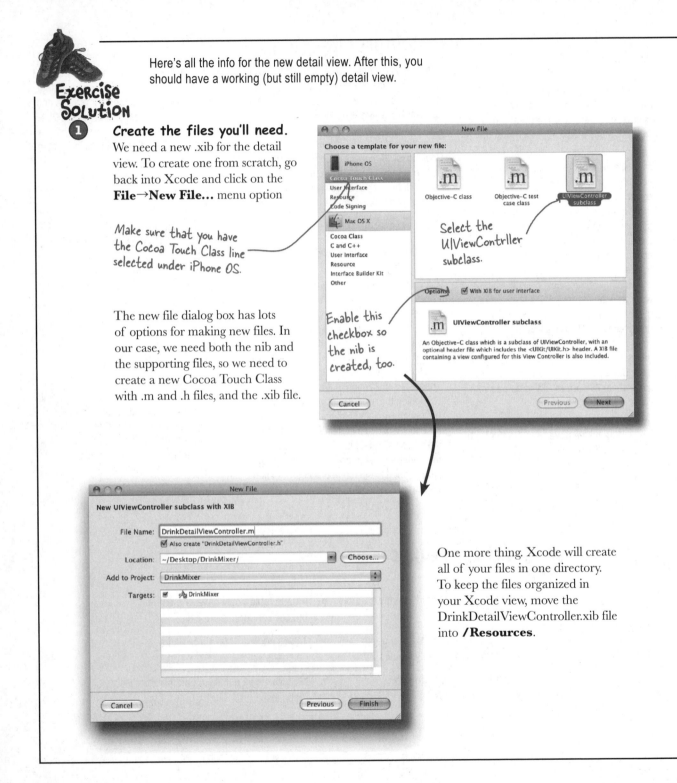

One more thing. Xcode will create all of your files in one directory. To keep the files organized in your Xcode view, move the DrinkDetailViewController.xib file into **/Resources**.

2 **Lay out the new view in Interface Builder.**

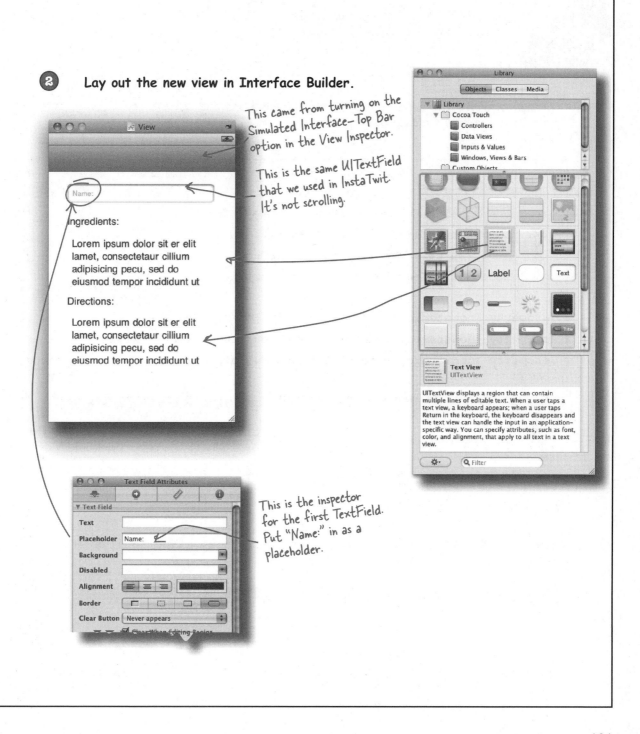

This came from turning on the Simulated Interface-Top Bar option in the View Inspector.

This is the same UITextField that we used in InstaTwit. It's not scrolling.

This is the inspector for the first TextField. Put "Name:" in as a placeholder.

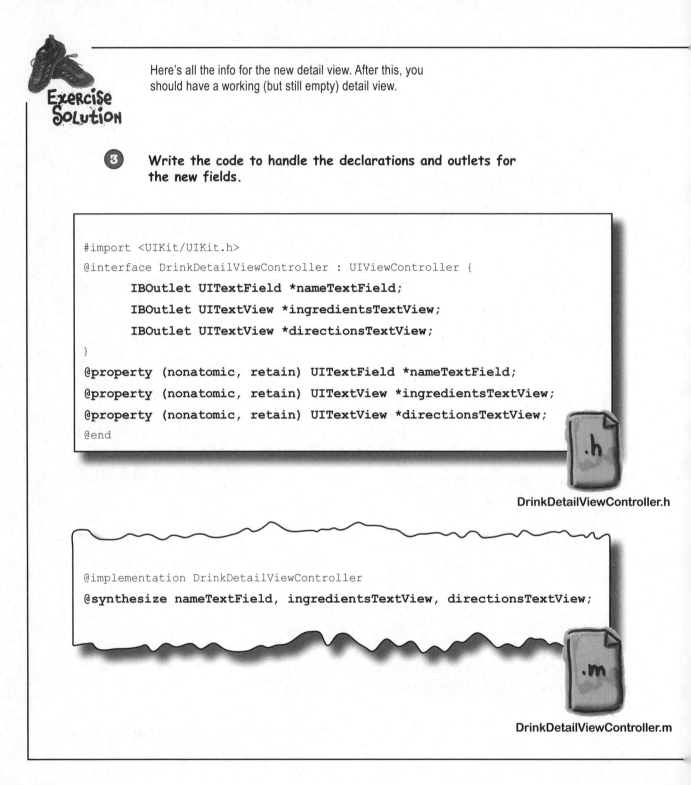

Here's all the info for the new detail view. After this, you should have a working (but still empty) detail view.

③ **Write the code to handle the declarations and outlets for the new fields.**

```objc
#import <UIKit/UIKit.h>
@interface DrinkDetailViewController : UIViewController {
    IBOutlet UITextField *nameTextField;
    IBOutlet UITextView *ingredientsTextView;
    IBOutlet UITextView *directionsTextView;
}
@property (nonatomic, retain) UITextField *nameTextField;
@property (nonatomic, retain) UITextView *ingredientsTextView;
@property (nonatomic, retain) UITextView *directionsTextView;
@end
```

DrinkDetailViewController.h

```objc
@implementation DrinkDetailViewController
@synthesize nameTextField, ingredientsTextView, directionsTextView;
```

DrinkDetailViewController.m

```
    -(void)
dealloc {

    [nameTextField release];

    [ingredientsTextView release];

    [directionsTextView release];

    [super dealloc];

}
@end
```

DrinkDetailViewController.m

4 **Connect the detail view to the new outlets.**
All three outlets, the directionsTextView, the
ingredientsTextView, and the nameTextField need to
be connected to their spot on the new view.

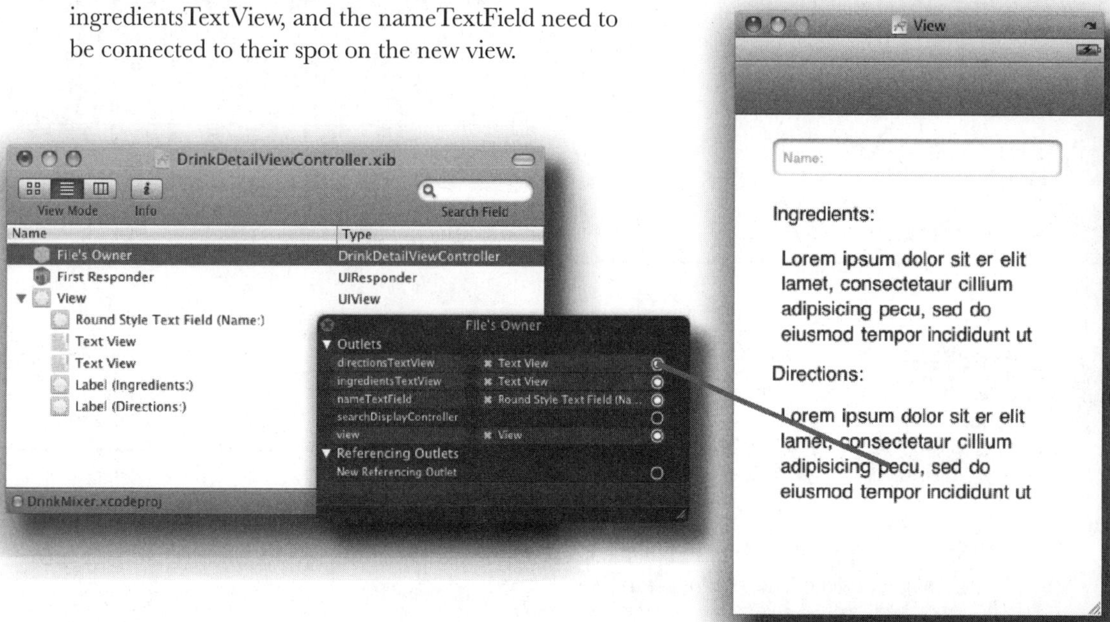

Exercise
Solution

Uncheck this
to freeze the
contents of the
UITextViews.

⑤ Make the text fields un-editable.
We need to disable both the UITextField and
the two UITextViews to prevent the user from
making changes. Simply click on each field and
toggle the **Enabled** checkbox to off.

Once those changes are made, the keyboard
issue goes away, because there won't be one!

Test Drive

Build and run your app. You just put in a lot of work,
and it's a good time to check for errors.

OK, so I have an order for a Melon Tree... but I still don't see the drink details.

Melon Tree ← Touch here

Rum Runner

We still need to get that detail view to load when Sam selects a drink.

Exercise

When your users browse through the drink information, they're going to need to switch between our list and detail views. Think about how we do that while keeping the user from getting lost.

1 How does the user navigate between views?

....

2 How can we keep track of what view to show?

....

3 How does the detail view know what drink to show?

....

4 How do you get the user back to the table view?

....

Exercise
Solution

When your users browse through the drink information, they're going to need to switch between our list and detail views. Think about how we do that and keep the user from getting lost.

In the simulator, Xcode will generate a back button with the text that says "DrinkMixer".

.ıll Carrier 🛜 2:21 PM 🔲
Drink Mixer
Lemon Drop
Letter Bomb
Long Island Ice Tea
Lost in Space
Manhattan
Melon Tree
Mexican Bomb
Miami Vice
Mojito
Music City Sunset

Name:

Ingredients:

Lorem ipsum dolor sit er elit lamet, consectetaur cillium adipisicing pecu, sed do eiusmod tempor incididunt ut

Directions:

Lorem ipsum dolor sit er elit lamet, consectetaur cillium adipisicing pecu, sed do eiusmod tempor incididunt ut

① How does the user navigate between views?   *The user is going to tap on the cell of the drink name that they want to see.*

② How can we keep track of what view to show?   *The navigation controller will keep track with back buttons and the title of the pane.*

③ How does the detail view know what drink to show?   *That's based on the table cell that the user selects.*

④ How do you get the user back to the table view?   *The navigation controller can supply a back button that can get us back to the main view.*

Use the navigation controller to switch between views

Now that we've got the table view populated and the detail view built, it's time to manage moving between the two views. The navigation-based template comes preloaded with the functionality we need:

 A view stack for moving between views
As users move back and forth, you can ask the navigation controller to display the appropriate view. The navigation controller keeps track of where the users are and gives them buttons to go back.

 A navigation bar for buttons and a title
The navigation controller interacts with the navigation bar to display buttons that interact with the view being shown, along with a title to help the users know where they are.

 A navigation toolbar for view-specific buttons
The navigation controller can display a toolbar at the bottom of the screen that shows custom buttons for its current view.

The UINavigationController supports a delegate, called the UINavigationControllerDelegate, that gets told when the controller is about to switch views, but for DrinkMixer we won't need this information. Since the views get told when they're shown and hidden, that's all we need for our app.

Now we need to get the table view and nav controller working together to display the detail view.

Navigation controllers maintain a stack of views

We've been dragging the navigation controller along since the beginning of this project, and now we finally get to put it to use. The navigation controller maintains a stack of views and displays the one on top. It will also automatically provide a back button, as well as the cool slide-in and out animations. We're going to talk more about the whole navigation controller stack in the next chapter, but for now, we're just going to push our new view onto the stack and let the controller take care of the rest. We just need to figure out how to get that new view.

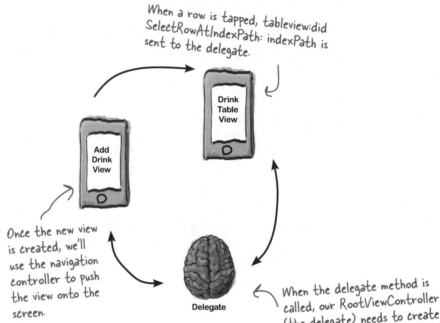

When a row is tapped, tableview:didSelectRowAtIndexPath: indexPath is sent to the delegate.

Once the new view is created, we'll use the navigation controller to push the view onto the screen.

When the delegate method is called, our RootViewController (the delegate) needs to create and push the detail view controller.

We'll use the tap notification in the table view delegate

When a table row is touched, the table view calls **tableview:didSelectRowA tIndexPath:** on its delegate. The table passes along an **NSIndexPath** (just like **cellForRowAtIndexPath**) that tells us which row was selected.

Here's where it gets interesting: **our RootViewController is our delegate**, so it needs to hand off control to the view controller for our detail view...

Instantiate a view controller like any other class

The only piece left to create is the view controller. Instantiating a view controller is no different than instantiating any other class, with the exception that you can pass in the nib file it should load its view from:

```
[[DrinkDetailViewController alloc] initWithNibName:@"DrinkDetailView
Controller" bundle:nil];
```

Once we've created the the detail view controller, we'll ask the NavigationController to push the new view controller onto the view stack. Let's put all of this together by creating the callback into the delegate and creating the new view controller to push onto the stack:

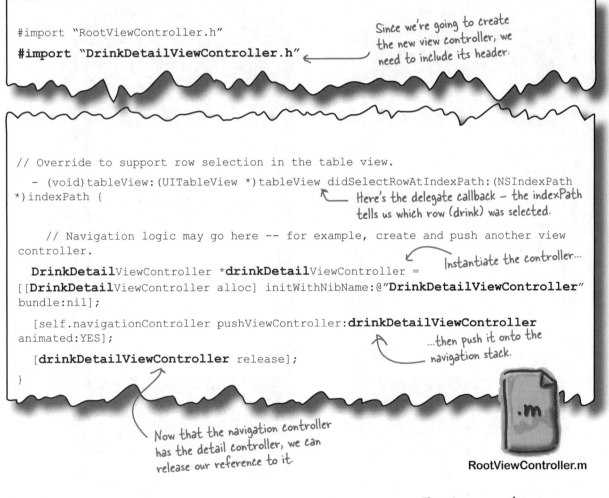

```
#import "RootViewController.h"
#import "DrinkDetailViewController.h"
```

Since we're going to create the new view controller, we need to include its header.

```
// Override to support row selection in the table view.
  - (void)tableView:(UITableView *)tableView didSelectRowAtIndexPath:(NSIndexPath
*)indexPath {
```

Here's the delegate callback — the indexPath tells us which row (drink) was selected.

```
    // Navigation logic may go here -- for example, create and push another view
controller.
    DrinkDetailViewController *drinkDetailViewController =
[[DrinkDetailViewController alloc] initWithNibName:@"DrinkDetailViewController"
bundle:nil];
```

Instantiate the controller...

```
    [self.navigationController pushViewController:drinkDetailViewController
animated:YES];
    [drinkDetailViewController release];
}
```

...then push it onto the navigation stack.

Now that the navigation controller has the detail controller, we can release our reference to it.

.m

RootViewController.m

Let's try this out...

TEST DRIVE

Now that both views can talk to each other, go ahead and build and run.

Tap here to make the detail view come up.

Try clicking in the text fields — no keyboard because they're not editable!

So, now we can get to the detail view from the drink list, but there aren't any details in there. We don't have that info in our plist, do we?

We've outgrown our array

All that's left is to get the ingredients and directions in the detail view, and we'll have a bartender's brain. To save you from having to type in the ingredients and directions, we put together a new file with all of the extra information. The problem is we can't just jam that information into an array. To add the drink details to this version, we need a different data model.

Exercise

Which options below are possible ways to load the drink data?

☐ Create a database with drink information

☐ Use dictionaries in our plist to hold the drink details

☐ Use an XML file to hold the drink details

☐ Create multiple arrays in our plist

Which of these options is the best for DrinkMixer? Why? ....

....

....

....

EXERCISE SOLUTION

Which options below are possible ways to load the drink data?

We could use a database to store drink information, but since nothing else in this app uses the database, we'd have to do some work to get DB support added... let's keep looking.

We already have a plist of strings—switching over to a plist of dictionaries won't be much work and gives us a data structure than can hold the drink info.

☐ Create a database with drink information

☑ Use dictionaries in our plist to hold the drink details

☐ Use an XML file to hold the drink details

☐ Create multiple arrays in our plist

This would work too, but has the same hurdle as using a DB. We're not parsing any XML right now, so we'd have to define the schema, then add parsing code.

This is basically the worst of all the options – we'd have to make sure multiple arrays line up to keep a single drink straight.

Which of these options is the best for DrinkMixer? Why? Since we already have code written that uses plists, we can change our plist to have an array of dictionaries instead of an array of strings without a lot of effort. This way we don't have to introduce SQL or XML into our project. However, we do lose out on the strong typing and data checking that both SQL and XML could give us. Since this is a smaller project, we're going to go with dictionaries.

Dictionaries store information as key-value pairs

Our current drink plist is just a single array of drink names. That worked great for populating the table view with just drink names, but doesn't help us at all with drink details. For this plist, instead of an array of strings, we created an array of dictionaries. Within each dictionary are three keys: **name**, **ingredients**, and **directions**. Each of these have string values with the corresponding information. Since NSDictionary adopts the NSCoding protocol, it can be saved and loaded in plists just like our basic array from before.

Key	Type	Value
▼ Root		
▼ Item 0	Array	(40 Items)
directions	Dictionary	(3 items)
ingredients	String	Shake vigorously and serve.
name	String	white creme de menthe, peach liqueur vodka, hot
▶ Item 1	String	After Dinner Mint
▶ Item 2	Dictionary	(3 items)
▶ Item 3	Dictionary	(3 items)
▶ Item 4	Dictionary	(3 items)
▶ Item 5	Dictionary	(3 items)
▶ Item 6	Dictionary	(3 items)
▶ Item 7	Dictionary	(3 items)
▶ Item 8	Dictionary	(3 items)
▶ Item 9	Dictionary	(3 items)
▶ Item 10	Dictionary	(3 items)
▶ Item 11	Dictionary	(3 items)
▶ Item 12	Dictionary	(3 items)
	Dictionary	(3 items)

there are no
Dumb Questions

Q: You keep talking about NSCoding. What is that?

A: NSCoding is a protocol that works with the encoding and decoding of objects. Working with this protocol means dealing with how an object can be stored on disk or distributed throughout the device. For more information about NSCoding, see the Apple documentation.

Q: Where did the back button in the detail view come from? We didn't do that...

A: It's automatic functionality that comes with the navigation controller. When you added a title for the main view, the navigation controller kept track of that name as part of the view stack for navigation, and added a back button with the title in it. So yeah, you did do that!

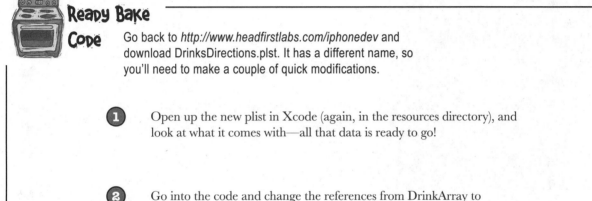

Ready Bake Code

Go back to *http://www.headfirstlabs.com/iphonedev* and download DrinksDirections.plst. It has a different name, so you'll need to make a couple of quick modifications.

1 Open up the new plist in Xcode (again, in the resources directory), and look at what it comes with—all that data is ready to go!

2 Go into the code and change the references from DrinkArray to DrinksDirections.

Test Drive

Build and run to see the new plist, and watch what happens...

TEST DRIVE

It crashed!

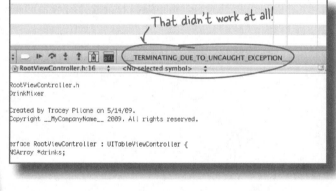

That didn't work at all!

TERMINATING_DUE_TO_UNCAUGHT_EXCEPTION

RootViewController.h:16   <No selected symbol>

RootViewController.h
DrinkMixer

Created by Tracey Pilone on 5/14/09.
Copyright __MyCompanyName__ 2009. All rights reserved.

erface RootViewController : UITableViewController {
NSArray *drinks;

Debugging—the dark side of iPhone development

Something has gone wrong, but honestly, this is a pretty normal part of the development process. There are lots of things that could cause our application to crash, so we need to figure out what the problem is.

Warnings can help find problems without debugging

In general, if your application doesn't build, Xcode won't launch it—but that's not true for warnings. Xcode will happily compile and run an application with warnings and your only indication will be a little yellow yield sign in the bottom right corner of Xcode. Two minutes spent investigating a warning can save hours of debugging time later.

3 errors and 3 warnings... the errors have to be fixed. The warnings should be investigated—and probably fixed, too.

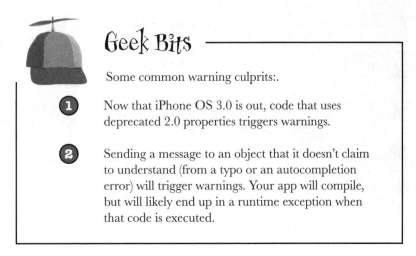

Geek Bits

Some common warning culprits:.

1 Now that iPhone OS 3.0 is out, code that uses deprecated 2.0 properties triggers warnings.

2 Sending a message to an object that it doesn't claim to understand (from a typo or an autocompletion error) will trigger warnings. Your app will compile, but will likely end up in a runtime exception when that code is executed.

That's not our problem, though: our code should be warning and compile-error-free. The good news is that when an app crashes in the Simulator, it doesn't go away completely (like it would on a real device). Xcode stops the app right before the OS would normally shut it down. Let's use that to see what's going on.

Time for some debugging...

First stop on your debugging adventure: the console

We need to figure out why our app crashed, and thankfully, Xcode has a lot of strong debugging capabilities. For now we're just going to look at the information it gave us about the crash, but later in the book we'll talk about some of the more advanced debugging features.

Since you ran the program in the simulator, the console should be up. Here's what ours looks like:

The toolbar contains typical debugging commands, like stopping your application, restarting it, and continuing after hitting a breakpoint.

The console has the information about what happened that caused our application to be shut down. It doesn't tell us why it happened, though...

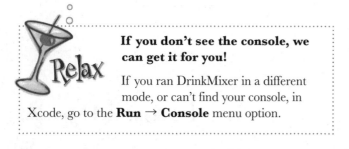

The console tells us that our app was shut down because of an uncaught exception, and what that exception was.

The console also gives us a stack trace of where our application was, but there's a much better view of that coming up in a second...

Interact with your application while it's running

The console is a very powerful debugging tool. Some of the best debugging techniques involve well-placed logging messages using NSLog(...). This information is printed into the console and can help you diagnose problems quickly. The console isn't just read-only, though; it is your window into your running application. We'll see log messages displayed in the console, and when your application hits a breakpoint, you'll be placed at the console prompt. From there you can use debugging commands like **print**, **continue**, **where**, **up**, and **down** to inspect the state of your application.

The console debugger is actually the open source gdb prompt, so nearly all gdb commands work here.

And when it's about to stop running

In this case, we're dealing with a nearly dead application, but the idea is the same. Since DrinkMixer has crashed, Xcode provides you with the basic information of what went wrong. In our case, an "unrecognized selector" was sent to an object. Remember that a selector is basically a method call—it means that some code is trying to invoke methods on an object and those methods don't exist.

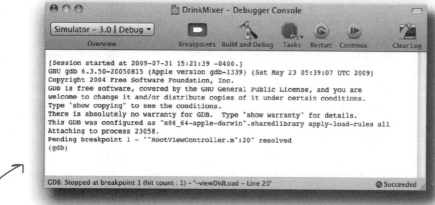

The console prompt lets you interact with your application at the command line.

But Xcode doesn't stop at the command line. It has a full GUI debugger built right in. Let's take a look...

Xcode supports you after your app breaks, too

So far we've used Xcode to write code and compile and launch our applications. Its usefulness doesn't stop once we hit the "Build and Debug" button. First, we can set breakpoints in our code to let us keep an eye on what's going on. Simply click in the gutter next to the line where you want to set a breakpoint. Xcode will put a small blue arrow next to the line and when your application gets to that line of code, it will stop and let you poke around using the console.

This switch indicates whether the breakpoints are on or not.

When the breakpoints are on, you'll get this cool can of bug spray icon...

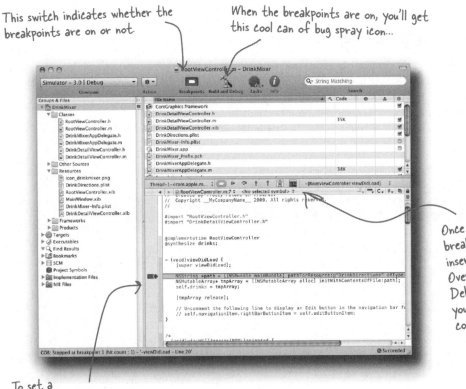

Once your app hits a breakpoint, Xcode will insert Step Into, Step Over, Continue, and Debugger buttons to let you walk through your code.

To set a breakpoint, just click here.

Click on the small bug spray icon or press Shift-⌘-Y to bring up the debugger...

The Xcode debugger shows you the state of your application

The debugger shows your code and also adds a stack view and a window to inspect variables and memory. When you click on a stack frame, Xcode will show you the line of code associated with that frame and set up the corresponding local variables. There isn't anything in the debugger window you couldn't do with the console, but this provides a nice GUI on top of it.

Here are the Step and Continue buttons to let you walk through your code.

Here's the stack from your app at the current breakpoint (or crash...). If you click on a frame, Xcode will show you the corresponding code.

Xcode shows you your app's variables (local, global, etc.) in this view.

TEST DRIVE

Since we know that we're having a problem near the array, try setting a breakpoint there. Then build and run and see what happens.

Test Drive

When you run it with the breakpoint at the point where you load the array, everything is OK:

To set a breakpoint, you'll need to click in the gutter, here.

But hit continue and...

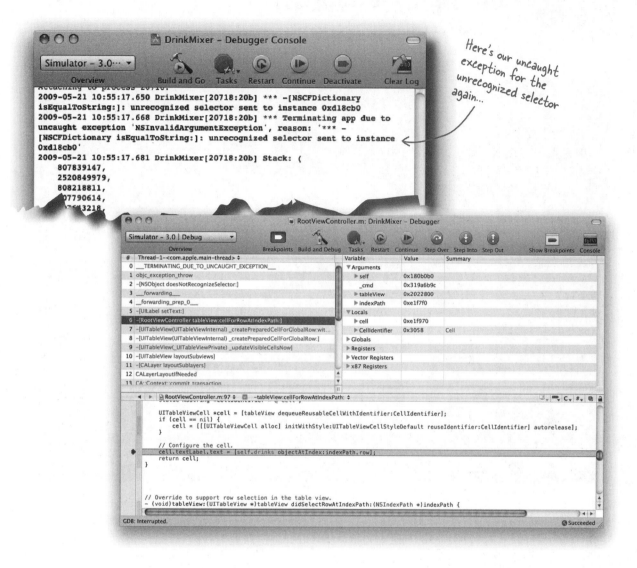

Here's our uncaught exception for the unrecognized selector again...

What the heck is going on?

Our application is crashing, and it's not at the array loading code. Open up the debugger and click on the topmost frame that contains our code. It will show you the line that's causing the problem... see what's wrong?

To be continued...

MultipleViewscross

Take what you've learned about the navigation controller and multiple views to fill in the blanks.

Across

3. The set of views that the nav controller deals with.
6. Dictionaries use _____ to organize data.
8. The screen that gives you output from the app.
9. A template that combines a table view and nav controls.
10. Has cells that need to be customized to work.

Down

1. A more versatile way to manage data beyond an array.
2. DrinkMixer is this type of app.
4. To use a new class you need to _____ it.
5. The @ symbol is shorthand for creating one of these.
7. A tool in Xcode to help fix broken code.

Your iPhone Toolbox

You've got Chapter 4 under your belt and now you've added multiple views and the navigation controller to your tool-box. For a complete list of tooltips in the book, go to http://www.headfirstlabs.com/iphonedev.

Navigation Template:

Comes with a table view and navigation control built in.

Is great for a productivity app.

Is designed to manage hierarchical data and multiple views.

Has cool animations built in to move between views.

Tables:

Are a collection of cells.

Come with support for editing contents, scrolling, and moving rows.

Can be customized so your cells look like more than one column.

UITableView:

Controls memory by only creating the cells requested in the view. Any other cells are destroyed if the iPhone needs the memory for something else.

Navigation Controller:

Maintains a view stack for moving between views.

Has a navigation bar for buttons and.a title.

Can support custom toolbars at the bottom of the view as needed.

Plists:

Supported by arrays and Xcode.

A great way to store information.

Are good for handling data, but have some limitations — we'll cover another option, core data, in a couple chapters coming up.

Debugging:

Has a built-in console with debugging and logging information.

Gives you errors and warnings as you compile to identify problems.

Has a built-in debugger that allows you to set breakpoints and step through the code to find the bug.

MultipleViewscross Solution

Take what you've learned about the navigation controller and multiple views to fill in the blanks.

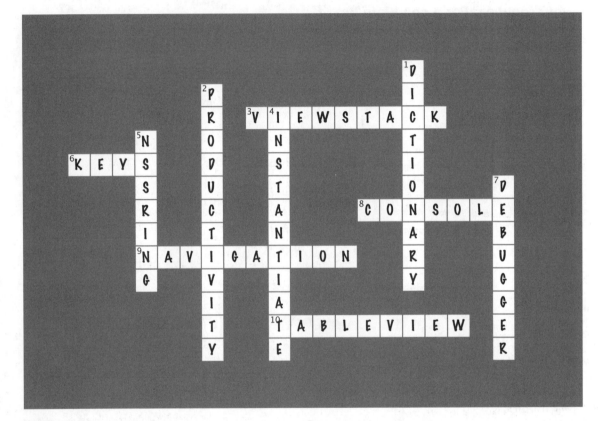

Across

3. The set of views that the nav controller deals with. [VIEWSTACK]
6. Dictionaries use _____ to organize data. [KEYS]
8. The screen that gives you output from the app. [CONSOLE]
9. A template that combines a table view and nav controls. [NAVIGATION]
10. Has cells that need to be customized to work. [TABLEVIEW]

Down

1. A more versatile way to manage data beyond an array. [DICTIONARY]
2. DrinkMixer is this type of app. [PRODUCTIVITY]
4. To use a new class you need to _____ it. [INSTANTIATE]
5. The @ symbol is shorthand for creating one of these. [NSSRING]
7. A tool in Xcode to help fix broken code. [DEBUGGER]

5 plists and modal views

Refining your app

This soup would be even better with the perfect cocktail, maybe a Neon Geek...

So you have this almost-working app...

That's the story of every app! You get some functionality working, decide to add something else, need to do some refactoring, and respond to some feedback from the App Store. Developing an app isn't ~~always~~ ever a linear process, but there's a lot to be learned in that process.

It all started with Sam...

Sam wanted an app to make his bartending work easier. You got one up and rolling pretty quick, but hit a snag filling in the details for each drink because of a plist of dictionaries.

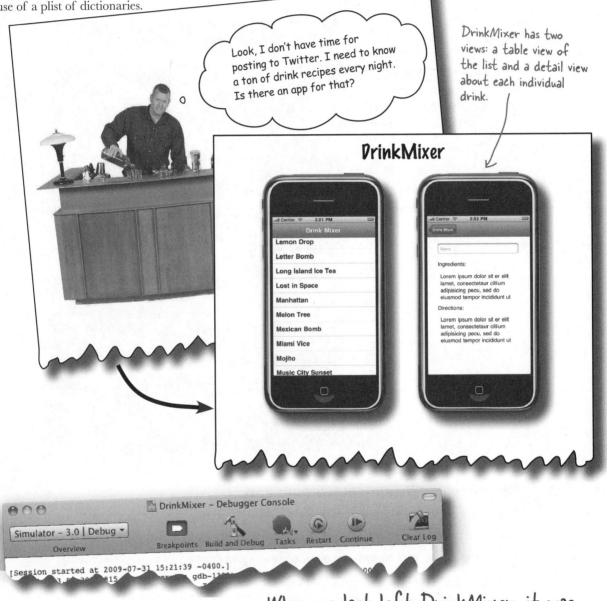

Look, I don't have time for posting to Twitter. I need to know a ton of drink recipes every night. Is there an app for that?

DrinkMixer has two views: a table view of the list and a detail view about each individual drink.

When we last left DrinkMixer, it was in the middle of being debugged...

Anatomy of a Crash

DrinkMixer started and ran happily until it hit our breakpoint at line 20. The debugger stopped our application and displayed the debugging console. By setting a breakpoint in our code, what we discovered at the end of Chapter 4 is that before your app got to the commands to import the file, there was no crash; so far so good.

Let's walk through loading our plist and make sure that works by typing **next** twice. The first "next" looks up the path to the plist, the second one actually loads the data.

Here's the Continue button.

You'll see buttons similar to these in Xcode, too.

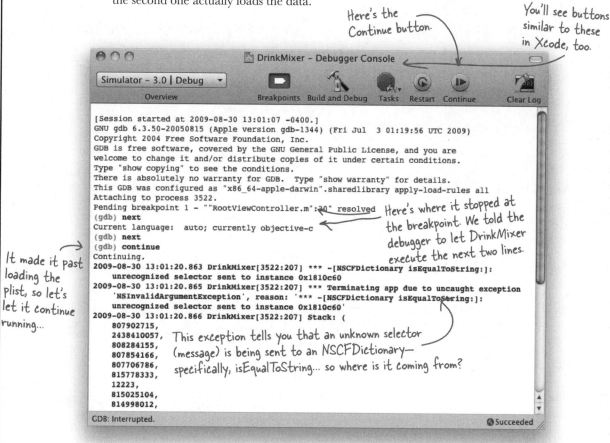

[Session started at 2009-08-30 13:01:07 -0400.]
GNU gdb 6.3.50-20050815 (Apple version gdb-1344) (Fri Jul 3 01:19:56 UTC 2009)
Copyright 2004 Free Software Foundation, Inc.
GDB is free software, covered by the GNU General Public License, and you are
welcome to change it and/or distribute copies of it under certain conditions.
Type "show copying" to see the conditions.
There is absolutely no warranty for GDB. Type "show warranty" for details.
This GDB was configured as "x86_64-apple-darwin".sharedlibrary apply-load-rules all
Attaching to process 3522.
Pending breakpoint 1 - ""RootViewController.m":20" resolved
(gdb) **next**
Current language: auto; currently objective-c
(gdb) **next**
(gdb) **continue**
Continuing.
2009-08-30 13:01:20.863 DrinkMixer[3522:207] *** -[NSCFDictionary isEqualToString:]:
  unrecognized selector sent to instance 0x1810c60
2009-08-30 13:01:20.865 DrinkMixer[3522:207] *** Terminating app due to uncaught exception
  'NSInvalidArgumentException', reason: '*** -[NSCFDictionary isEqualToString:]:
  unrecognized selector sent to instance 0x1810c60'
2009-08-30 13:01:20.866 DrinkMixer[3522:207] Stack: (
  807902715,
  2438410057,
  808284155,
  807854166,
  807706786,
  815778333,
  12223,
  815025104,
  814998012,

Here's where it stopped at the breakpoint. We told the debugger to let DrinkMixer execute the next two lines.

It made it past loading the plist, so let's let it continue running...

This exception tells you that an unknown selector (message) is being sent to an NSCFDictionary—specifically, isEqualToString... so where is it coming from?

Loading the plist worked fine; no problems there. The error must be coming after that. Let's have the application continue running and see where it fails. Hit the Continue button (or type **continue** in the console)... and there's our exception again. Where is this actually failing?

Use the debugger to investigate the crash

We can reliably get DrinkMixer to crash, and it doesn't seem to be our plist loading code. Xcode has suspended our application right before iPhoneOS shuts it down, so we can use the debugger to see exactly what it was trying to do before it crashed.

Switch back to the debugger and take a look at the stack in the upper left. This is the call stack that led to the crash.

The red stop sign icon will terminate your application.

Trying to continue now will just keep failing — DrinkMixer has been stopped by iPhoneOS.

The buttons along the top of the debugger function just like the buttons in the console.

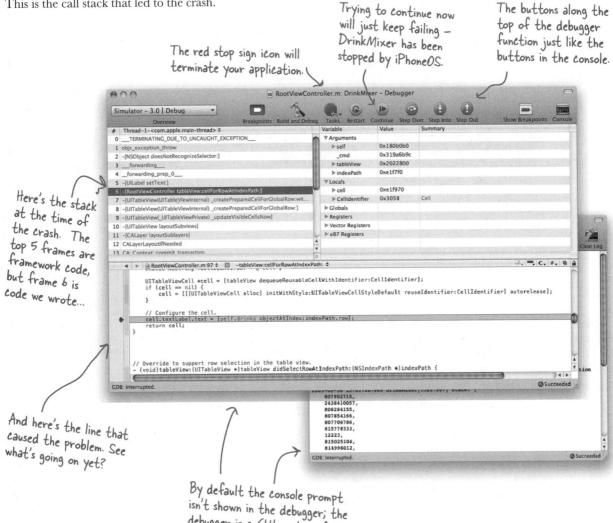

Here's the stack at the time of the crash. The top 5 frames are framework code, but frame 6 is code we wrote...

And here's the line that caused the problem. See what's going on yet?

By default the console prompt isn't shown in the debugger; the debugger is a GUI on top of it.

Sharpen your pencil

Using what you've learned so far, figure out what's going on!

The exception talked about NSCF Dictionary. What dictionary is it talking about? Where is it coming from?

....

....

Who's sending messages to the dictionary? Why did we get an unrecognized selector?

....

....

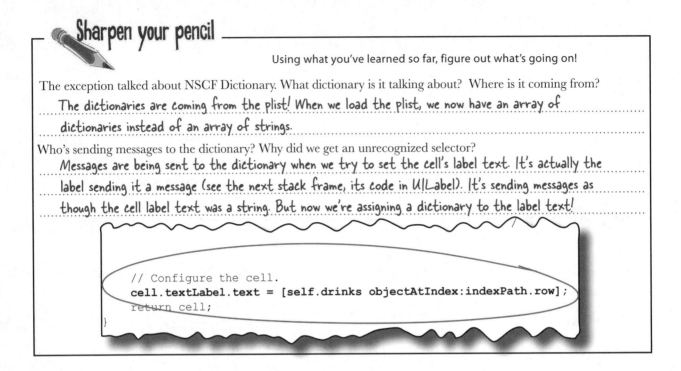

Sharpen your pencil

Using what you've learned so far, figure out what's going on!

The exception talked about NSCF Dictionary. What dictionary is it talking about? Where is it coming from?

The dictionaries are coming from the plist! When we load the plist, we now have an array of dictionaries instead of an array of strings.

Who's sending messages to the dictionary? Why did we get an unrecognized selector?

Messages are being sent to the dictionary when we try to set the cell's label text. It's actually the label sending it a message (see the next stack frame, its code in UILabel). It's sending messages as though the cell label text was a string. But now we're assigning a dictionary to the label text!

```
// Configure the cell.
cell.textLabel.text = [self.drinks objectAtIndex:indexPath.row];
return cell;
}
```

We're trying to stuff a dictionary into a string

Putting a dictionary into the text field of the label, which wants a string, isn't going to work. Our previous array was an array of strings, so that code worked fine. Now that we have an array of dictionaries, we need to figure out how to get the drink name value (a string) out of it, and then assign that to the text label. If you take another look at the DrinkDirections.plist, you'll see that we have an array of dictionaries — one for each drink. Dictionaries store their values using keys; they're just a collection of key-value pairs. To get a value out, you simply send the dictionary the `objectForKey:@"key"` message.

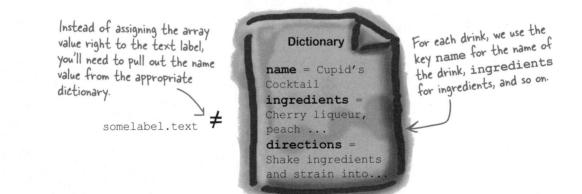

Instead of assigning the array value right to the text label, you'll need to pull out the name value from the appropriate dictionary.

`somelabel.text` ≠

Dictionary

name = Cupid's Cocktail
ingredients = Cherry liqueur, peach ...
directions = Shake ingredients and strain into...

For each drink, we use the key name for the name of the drink, ingredients for ingredients, and so on.

Update your code to handle a plist of dictionaries

Armed with the knowledge of how the dictionaries are put together, we can use this information to populate the detail view, too. If you give the detail view controller the dictionary of the selected drink, it can populate the view's fields before the view is shown to the user.

Each dictionary has everything we need for a drink. We need to get that dictionary to the datasource of the detail view.

Detail View

Datasource

View Controller

Sharpen your pencil

Go ahead and make the changes to your app. After this, it should know that you're using an array of dictionaries, not strings—and the detail view should have a reference to the drink it should display. Finally, the detail view should populate its fields before it appears on the screen.

1 **Change the way a table cell is configured.**
In RootViewController.m, fix the cell's textLabel.text property to use the name value from the appropriate dictionary.

Don't forget about the NSDictionary documentation if you want to know more about dictionaries.

2 **Add a reference to a drink dictionary in the detail view.**
In DrinkDetailViewController.h, add an NSDictionary* field named drink and the corresponding property declaration.

3 **Add drink to the DrinkDetailViewController.m file.**
Synthesize and dealloc the new dictionary reference.

We'll update the detail view controller to use the values in the new dictionary in a minute...

Sharpen your pencil
Solution

Go through the code and make sure that you've got everything right...

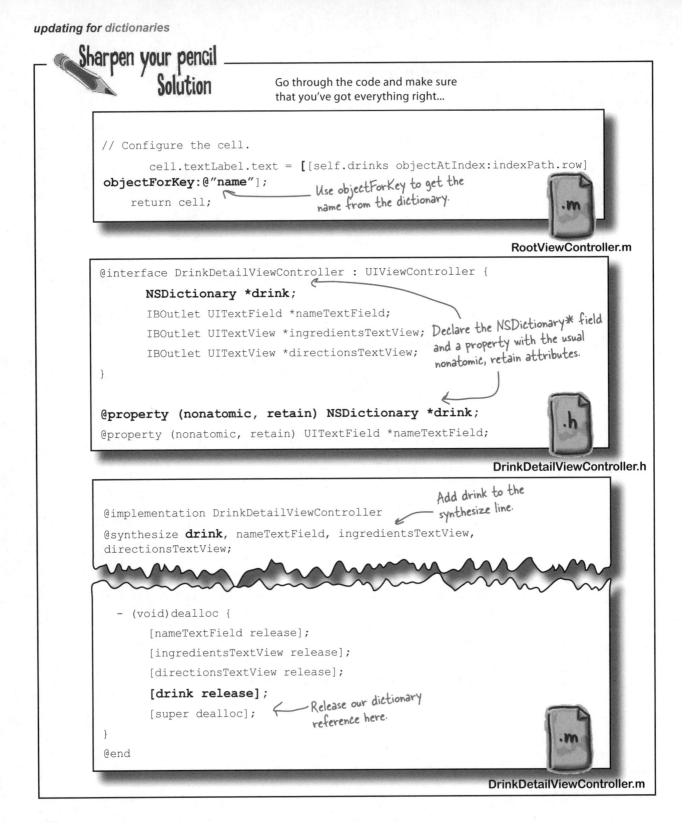

```
// Configure the cell.
        cell.textLabel.text = [[self.drinks objectAtIndex:indexPath.row]
objectForKey:@"name"];
    return cell;
```

Use objectForKey to get the name from the dictionary.

.m

RootViewController.m

```
@interface DrinkDetailViewController : UIViewController {
    NSDictionary *drink;
    IBOutlet UITextField *nameTextField;
    IBOutlet UITextView *ingredientsTextView;
    IBOutlet UITextView *directionsTextView;
}

@property (nonatomic, retain) NSDictionary *drink;
@property (nonatomic, retain) UITextField *nameTextField;
```

Declare the NSDictionary* field and a property with the usual nonatomic, retain attributes.

.h

DrinkDetailViewController.h

Add drink to the synthesize line.

```
@implementation DrinkDetailViewController
@synthesize drink, nameTextField, ingredientsTextView,
directionsTextView;
```

```
- (void)dealloc {
    [nameTextField release];
    [ingredientsTextView release];
    [directionsTextView release];
    [drink release];
    [super dealloc];
}
@end
```

Release our dictionary reference here.

.m

DrinkDetailViewController.m

Test Drive

Now that we've told DrinkMixer to deal with dictionaries, go ahead and build and run the app.

It's working again! Now that it's not crashing, it's time to fill in the details.

The detail view needs data

Now that you've figured out how to deal with dictionaries, it's time to fill in the drink details. But getting the details out of the array of dictionaries to give to the datasource requires another step.

This is the information in DrinkDirections.plist.

Key	Type	Value
▼ Root	Array	(40 items)
▼ Item 0	Dictionary	(3 items)
directions	String	Shake vigorously and serve.
ingredients	String	white creme de menthe, peach liqueur vodka, hot choc...
name	String	After Dinner Mint
▼ Item 1	Dictionary	(3 items)
directions	String	Pour the ingredients into a glass and stir.
ingredients	String	scotch whisky, coconut rum, cherry brand... lemonade
name	String	Aftershock
▼ Item 2	Dictionary	(3 items)
directions	String	Pour all ingredients into a shaker. Shake well and strain...
ingredients	String	Vodka, Sour Apple Schnapps, apple juice
name	String	Apple Martini
▼ Item 3	Dictionary	(3 items)
directions	String	Pour the liqueur into a glass, add the cider, and serve ...
ingredients	String	cinnamon schnapps, hard cider
name	String	Baked Apple
▶ Item 4	Dictionary	(3 items)
▶ Item 5	Dictionary	(3 items)
▶ Item 6	Dictionary	(3 items)
▶ Item 7	Dictionary	(3 items)
▶ Item 8	Dictionary	(3 items)
▶ Item 9	Dictionary	(3 items)
▶ Item 10	Dictionary	(3 items)
▶ Item 11	Dictionary	(3 items)
▶ Item 12	Dictionary	(3 items)
▶ Item 13	Dictionary	(3 items)
▶ Item 14	Dictionary	(3 items)

Melon Tree ◀— Touch here

View Controller

The datasource in this case is the plist.

Data-source

Detail View Controller

Remember this? We talked about this being the structure of the app.

Each dictionary has all the information we need

Right now we're just pulling the name of each drink into the app using the **name** key. In order to populate the ingredients and directions, we need to use the other keys. We could just type those right into our code, but we're better developers than that, so we'll pull them up into constants. The only thing left is getting the proper dictionary to the detail view controller so it can pull the information it needs. Go ahead and start setting everything up!

Exercise

The view controller needs direct access to the datasource, and the easiest way to get to that data is going to mean some quick code refactoring.

 Organize your dictionary constants to avoid bugs
Since we're going to need the **name**, **ingredients**, and **directions** keys in the view controller, we should clean up the code to start using real constants.

Create a new file called **DrinkConstants.h** (**File** → **New** then choose **Other** and a blank file). Add constants (#define's) for **name**, **ingredients**, and **directions**. Import DrinkConstants.h into DrinkDetailViewController.m and RootViewController.m. Finally, update the **@"name"** to the new constant, **NAME_KEY**.

 Set the detail view controller's drink property
After you instantiate the detail view controller when a cell is tapped, you need to set the drink property on the new controller to the selected drink.

3 **Add code to the detail view controller to populate the fields**
Before the detail view appears, the view controller should use the drink dictionary to set the contents of the name, ingredients, and directions components.

Exercise Solution

Here's all the added code to make the detail view work.

1. **DrinkConstants.h**

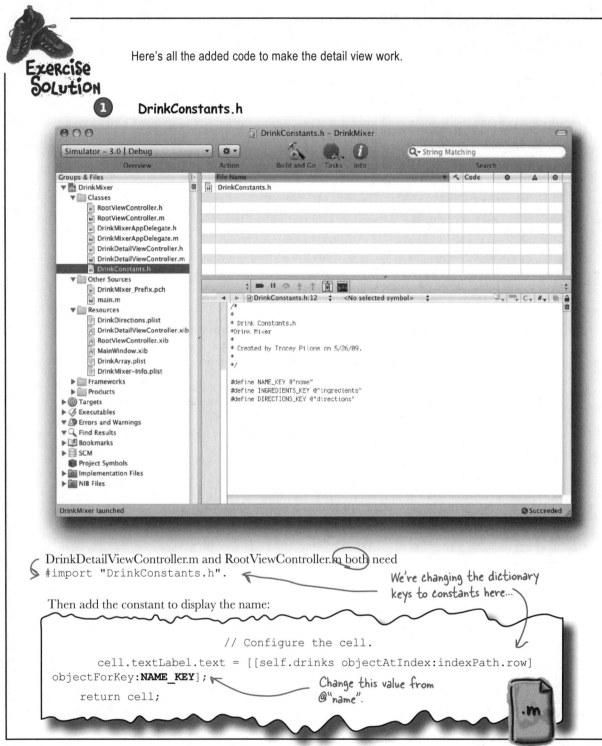

DrinkDetailViewController.m and RootViewController.m both need
`#import "DrinkConstants.h"`.

We're changing the dictionary keys to constants here...

Then add the constant to display the name:

```
                    // Configure the cell.

    cell.textLabel.text = [[self.drinks objectAtIndex:indexPath.row]
objectForKey:NAME_KEY];

    return cell;
```

Change this value from @"name".

RootViewController.m

② Set the detail view controller's drink property

```objectivec
// Override to support row selection in the table view.
 - (void)tableView:(UITableView *)tableView didSelectRowAtIndexPath:(NSIndexPath *)indexPath {


    // Navigation logic may go here -- for example, create and push
another view controller.
DrinkDetailViewController *drinkDetailViewController =
[[DrinkDetailViewController alloc] initWithNibName:@"DrinkDetailViewController" bundle:nil];
    drinkDetailViewController.drink = [self.drinks objectAtIndex:indexPath.row];
    [self.navigationController pushViewController:drinkDetailViewController animated:YES];
    [drinkDetailViewController release];
}
```

Add this whole line to grab a dictionary from the array.

RootViewController.m

③ Add a method to the detail view controller to populate the fields

```objectivec
- (void) viewWillAppear: (BOOL) animated {
    [super viewWillAppear:animated];
    nameTextField.text = [drink objectForKey:NAME_KEY];
    ingredientsTextView.text = [drink objectForKey:INGREDIENTS_KEY];
    directionsTextView.text = [drink objectForKey:DIRECTIONS_KEY];
}
```

This whole method is new.

DrinkDetailViewController.m

Test Drive

Compile and build and run again...

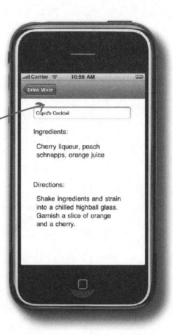

there are no Dumb Questions

Q: **We re-create the detail view every time someone taps on a drink. Couldn't I just reuse that view?**

A: For DrinkMixer it really won't matter too much; since the view is pretty lightweight, we won't suffer too much overhead re-creating it when a drink is tapped. However, for best performance you can refactor it to reuse the same detail view controller and just change the drink it should be showing when a row is tapped.

Q: **Why did we have to pull out the dictionary key names into a separate file?**

A: Having magic string values in your code is generally a bad idea—no matter what programming language or platform you're using. By pulling them up into constants using #define, they are checked by the compiler. So a typo like @"nme" instead of @"name" would end up as a bug at runtime, while mistyping NME_KEY instead of NAME_KEY would prevent things from even compiling.

Q: **I looked at the NSDictionary documentation and there's a valueForKey: and an objectForKey:. What's the difference?**

A: Great question. valueForKey: is used for what's called key value coding, which is a specific pattern typically used in Cocoa Binding. The subtle catch is that NSDictionary usually just turns a call to valueForKey: into a call to objectForKey, and it looks like either one will work. However, valueForKey actually checks the key you pass it and has different behavior depending on your key. That's almost never what you want (unless you're doing Cocoa binding stuff, of course). The correct method to use is objectForKey:.

Overheard at
Head First
Lounge

Is that app up on the App Store? Then I can just download it on my phone and start making even more tips!

Sam, ready for your app to make his (and your) wallet fatter...

Looks like there's a market there!
A quick submission to Apple and...

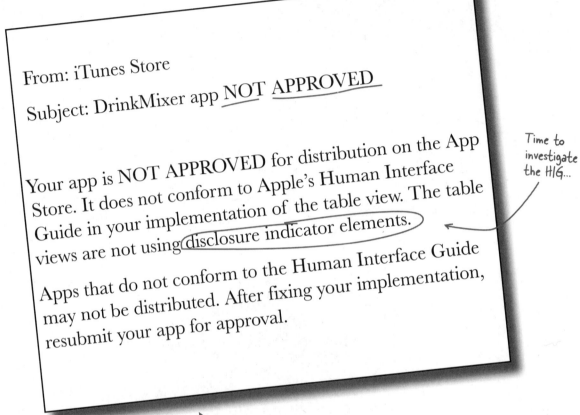

From: iTunes Store

Subject: DrinkMixer app NOT APPROVED

Your app is NOT APPROVED for distribution on the App Store. It does not conform to Apple's Human Interface Guide in your implementation of the table view. The table views are not using disclosure indicator elements.

Apps that do not conform to the Human Interface Guide may not be distributed. After fixing your implementation, resubmit your app for approval.

Time to investigate the HIG...

Seriously, this can and will happen if you don't follow the HIG. It happened to, um, a friend of the authors... twice.

Relax

We'll go through the approval process later.

Later in the book, we'll take you step by step through the process of preparing an app for approval. For now, just worry about how to fix DrinkMixer!

We have a usability problem

We know that the user needs to touch the name of the drink
to see the details about each individual drink, but how is
the user supposed to know that? The HIG has a number of
recommendations for how to deal with drill-down, hierarchical
data. We're already on the right track using table views but the
HIG has a number of additional recommendations for helping
the user understand how to navigate the app.

Table cells have a number of built-in usability
items that help users understand how to use
your app – even if it's the first time they've
run it.

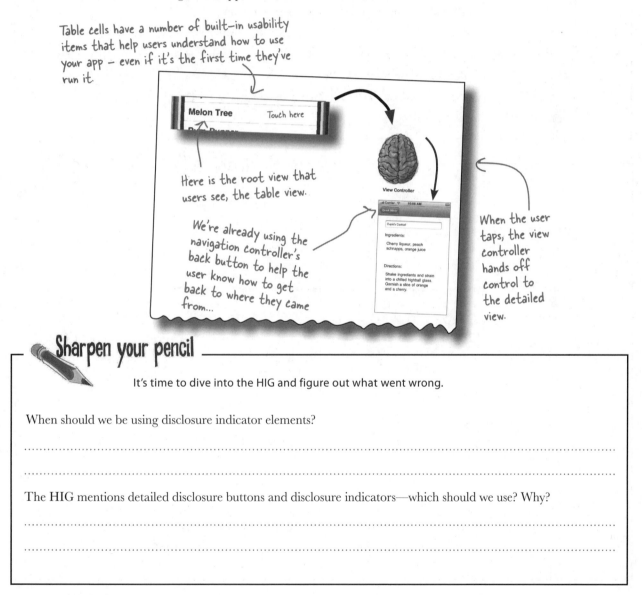

Here is the root view that
users see, the table view.

We're already using the
navigation controller's
back button to help the
user know how to get
back to where they came
from...

When the user
taps, the view
controller
hands off
control to
the detailed
view.

Sharpen your pencil

It's time to dive into the HIG and figure out what went wrong.

When should we be using disclosure indicator elements?

....

....

The HIG mentions detailed disclosure buttons and disclosure indicators—which should we use? Why?

....

....

Sharpen your pencil
Solution
It's time to dive into the HIG and figure out what went wrong.

When should we be using disclosure indicator elements?

In the HIG, Chapter 8, the "Configuring a Table View" section, you can pretty quickly find out why you're in violation over those disclosure indicators:

> **"The disclosure indicator element... is necessary if you're using the table to present hierarchical information."**

The HIG mentions detailed disclosure buttons and disclosure indicators—which should we use? Why?

The disclosure indicator denotes that there is an additional level of information available about an item when you click it (like drink details); it selects that row and shows the additional data. The button can do something besides select the row — it can kick off an action. That's more than we'll need here, so we'll just stick with the disclosure indicator.

Table Cells Up Close

So, what exactly is the disclosure indicator element, and where does it go? Let's look a little deeper in the HIG:

imageView — used to show images associated with a cell.

textLabel — the main text area in a cell.

Big Font Info
small detailed text

detailTextLabel — depending on what cell style you use, it can show up in different places, fonts, and colors.

accessoryType — common ones are disclosure indicator, detailed disclosure indicator, and checkmark.

DrinkMixer uses really basic cells, but you can easily customize your cells for a different app, besides just adding disclosure indicators. Even though the table only supports one column, you can make it look like more by adding a thumbnail, for example. You can also adjust the font sizes to open up some room for each table cell if you need to.

Most really polished apps use some kind of table cell customizing, so keep that in mind while you're looking through the API. For now, we just need to add the disclosure icon to our cells to indicate there's more information available if a user taps on them.

Use a disclosure indicator if your cell leads to more information

TableViewCells have a lot of built-in functionality—we're just scratching the surface. Adding a disclosure indicator is simply a matter of telling the cell what type of accessory icon it should use. Take a look at the UITableViewCell documentation for some of the other options.

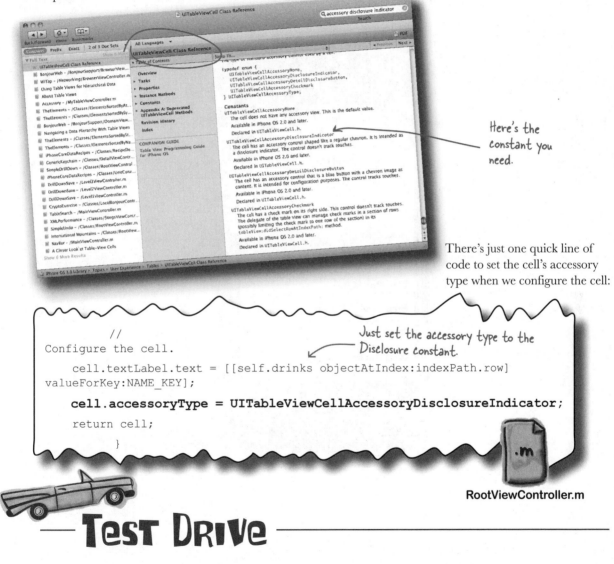

Here's the constant you need.

There's just one quick line of code to set the cell's accessory type when we configure the cell:

Just set the accessory type to the Disclosure constant.

```
        //
Configure the cell.

    cell.textLabel.text = [[self.drinks objectAtIndex:indexPath.row]
valueForKey:NAME_KEY];

    cell.accessoryType = UITableViewCellAccessoryDisclosureIndicator;

    return cell;
    }
```

RootViewController.m

TEST DRIVE

Go ahead and build and Run....make sure it's working!

TEST DRIVE

One little line of code fixed all of your App Store approval issues.

> There are those disclosure elements—now the user knows what to do!

After resubmitting to the App Store,
DrinkMixer is up on iTunes!

Sales report - DrinkMixer - Week 1

Overall sales - 400 downloads

Price - $1.99

Overall revenue - $796

Wow, just for one week!

Remember that Apple will take a percentage of this...

The reviews are coming in...

Sales were going strong...

But then bad reviews started coming in. What's going on?

The reviews are bad...

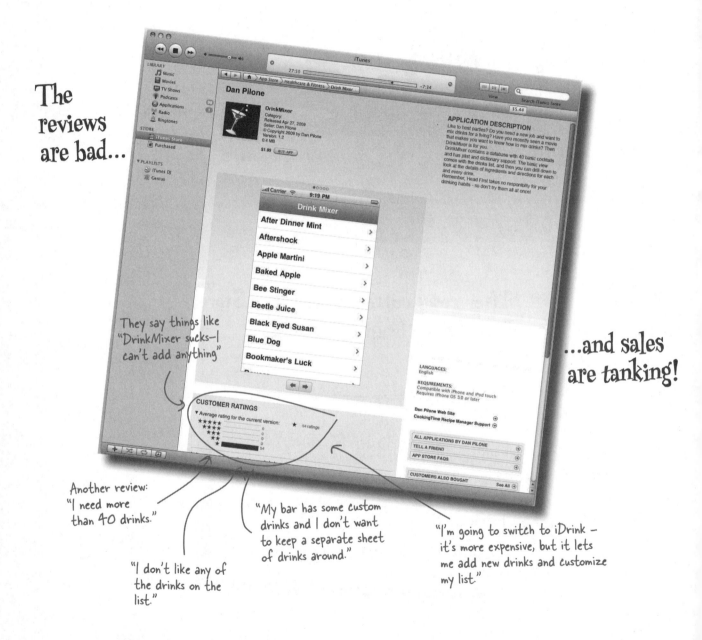

They say things like "DrinkMixer sucks—I can't add anything"

...and sales are tanking!

Another review: "I need more than 40 drinks."

"I don't like any of the drinks on the list."

"My bar has some custom drinks and I don't want to keep a separate sheet of drinks around."

"I'm going to switch to iDrink — it's more expensive, but it lets me add new drinks and customize my list."

Sharpen your pencil

Think about how you originally designed DrinkMixer and the feedback, and figure out what you'll do next.

1   What would address the users' concerns?

....

....

....

....

2   Given the structure of DrinkMixer, how would you refactor the code to fix the problem?

....

....

....

....

3   Is there an easy way to fix the code? A hard way?

....

....

....

....

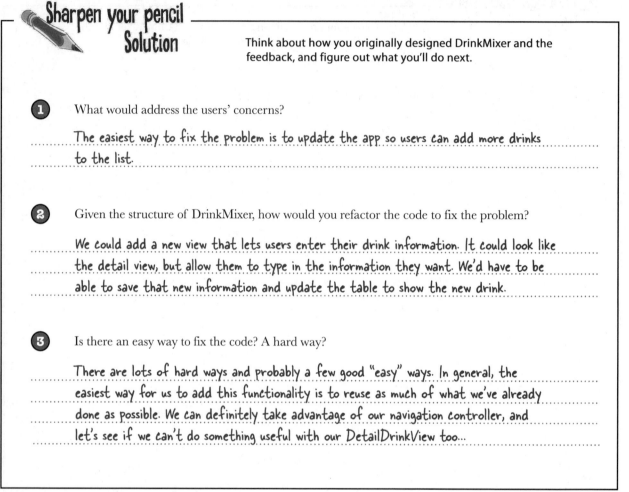

Sharpen your pencil Solution

Think about how you originally designed DrinkMixer and the feedback, and figure out what you'll do next.

1 What would address the users' concerns?

The easiest way to fix the problem is to update the app so users can add more drinks to the list.

2 Given the structure of DrinkMixer, how would you refactor the code to fix the problem?

We could add a new view that lets users enter their drink information. It could look like the detail view, but allow them to type in the information they want. We'd have to be able to save that new information and update the table to show the new drink.

3 Is there an easy way to fix the code? A hard way?

There are lots of hard ways and probably a few good "easy" ways. In general, the easiest way for us to add this functionality is to reuse as much of what we've already done as possible. We can definitely take advantage of our navigation controller, and let's see if we can't do something useful with our DetailDrinkView too...

BRAIN POWER

How would you go about implementing a view where users can add drinks to DrinkMixer?

APP LAYOUT CONSTRUCTION

Here is the table view for DrinkMixer with two possible designs. Based on aesthetics, usability, and standard iPhone App behavior, which one is better for showing the users where they should add a drink?

Some kind of button in the navigation controller to kick off a new view.

Add a new toolbar with some buttons below the nav controller.

You'd have room for an add button and others, when you need them.

Option #1

Option #2

Which interface is better? ....

Why? (Be specific.) ....

....

Why not the other? ....

APP LAYOUT CONSTRUCTION SOLUTION

Here are two designs. Based on aesthetics, usability, and standard iPhone App behavior, which one is better for showing the users where they should add a drink?

The navigation controller comes with built-in button support.

This type of interface is good when you have several new views to add, not just one.

The toolbar will cover up part of the table view, too.

Option #1   **Option #2**

Which interface is better? *Option #1.*

Why? (Be specific.) *Because by putting the icon in the nav controller, you don't take up more space away from the table view. There's also built-in support for that button in the nav controller already.*

Why not the other? *Option #2 makes the interface a bit more cluttered, and requires more code.*

Use navigation controller buttons for editing

So far we've used the navigation controller to move between views. But if you've spent much time with other iPhone apps, you know it's capable of much more. Since a UITableView is almost always embedded in a navigation controller, table editing is usually done through buttons on the controller itself. Let's start out by adding a + button to the navigation controller that will let the users add a drink when they tap it.

Users will be able to tap the + button to add a drink.

 Sharpen your pencil

Using Xcode, add the button to the Nav controller and the associated IBActions and IBOutlets.

1 **Open RootViewController.xib in Interface Builder.**
Scroll through the library and drag a Bar Button Item to the Main Window (this will add it to the list after the table view). It won't show up on the navigation controller in Interface Builder—we'll need to add code so it shows up at runtime.

It won't show up because the navigation controller in Interface Builder is SIMULATED, not real.

2 **Add the IBAction, IBOutlet, and property declaration for addButtonItem.**
Just like any other button, we'll have an IBAction for when it gets clicked and a reference to the button itself—all in RootViewController.h.

3 **Add the synthesize, dealloc, and addButtonPressed method for addButtonItem.**
Synthesize the property, release the reference, and implement the addButtonPressed to log a message when the button is clicked—all in RootViewController.m

4 **Finish up in Interface Builder.**
Open up RootViewController.xib again, and link the new Bar Button Item to the actions and outlets within the Main Window.

Finally, pull up the inspector for the Bar Button Item and change the **Identifier** to **Add**.

Sharpen your pencil
Solution

Using Xcode, add the button to the nav controller and the associated IBActions and IBOutlets.

1 **Open RootViewController.xib in Interface Builder.**
Scroll through the library and drag a Bar Button Item to the Main Window (it will get added to the list).

2 **Add the IBAction, IBOutlet, and property declaration for addButtonItem.**

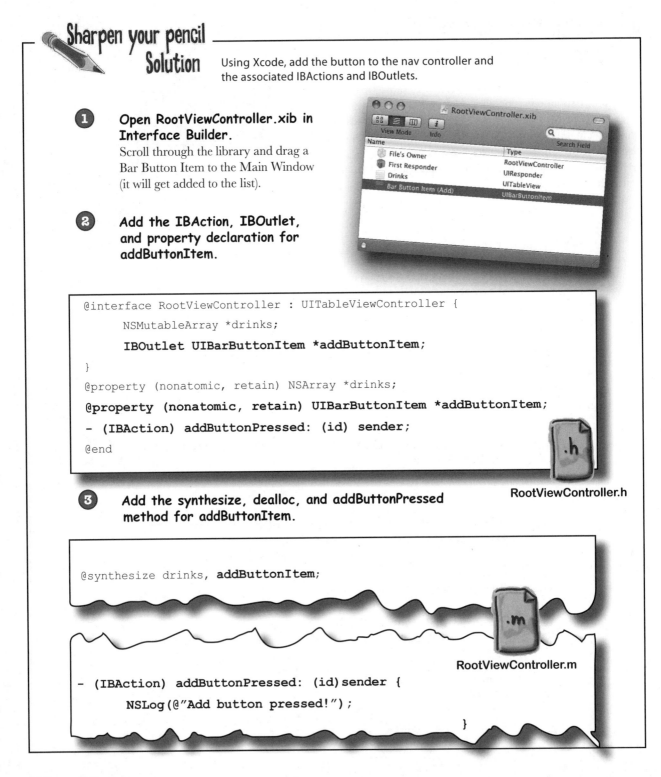

```
@interface RootViewController : UITableViewController {
    NSMutableArray *drinks;
    IBOutlet UIBarButtonItem *addButtonItem;
}
@property (nonatomic, retain) NSArray *drinks;
@property (nonatomic, retain) UIBarButtonItem *addButtonItem;
- (IBAction) addButtonPressed: (id) sender;
@end
```

RootViewController.h

3 **Add the synthesize, dealloc, and addButtonPressed method for addButtonItem.**

```
@synthesize drinks, addButtonItem;
```

RootViewController.m

```
- (IBAction) addButtonPressed: (id) sender {
    NSLog(@"Add button pressed!");
}
```

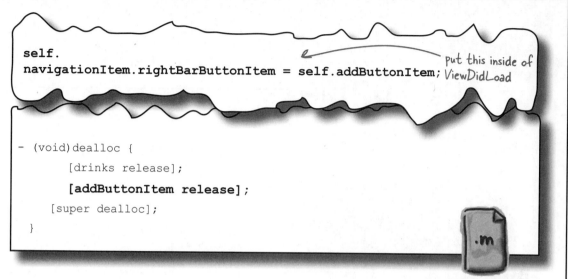

```
self.
navigationItem.rightBarButtonItem = self.addButtonItem;
```

put this inside of ViewDidLoad

```
- (void)dealloc {
    [drinks release];

    [addButtonItem release];

    [super dealloc];
}
```

RootViewController.m

4 **Finish up in Interface Builder.**

Open up RootViewController.xib again, and link the new Bar Button Item to the actions and outlets within the Main Window, right clicking and using the menus that pop up.

Finally, pull up the inspector for the Bar Button Item and change the **Identifier** to **Add**.

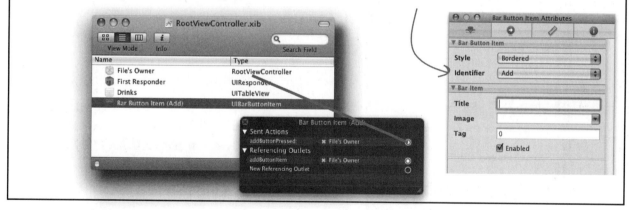

TEST DRIVE

Go ahead; build and run the app...

Test Drive

Go ahead; build and run the app...

The button works! Now you get an affirmative message in the console...

The button shows up in the view, but now what?

The button should create a new view

Our new button works: the action gets called, but really doesn't do anything useful yet. We need to give our user a place to enter the new drink information and we can do that with a new view. Just like with the detailed view, we can let the navigation controller handle the transition.

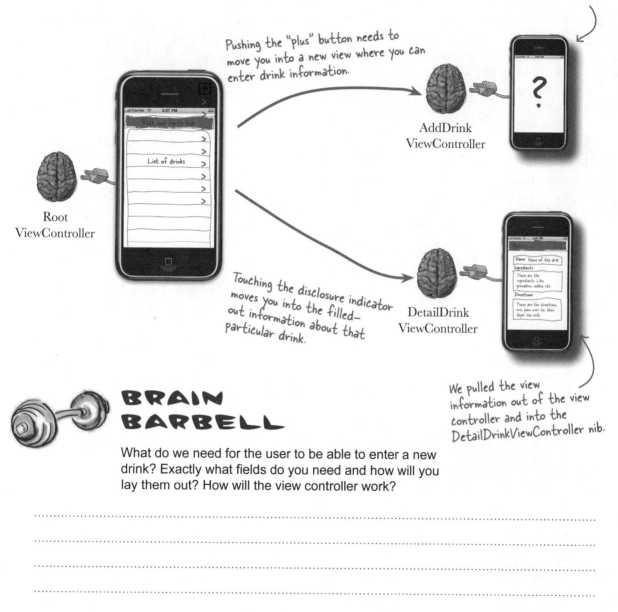

What do we need for the AddViewController's UI? Where does it go?

Pushing the "plus" button needs to move you into a new view where you can enter drink information.

AddDrink
ViewController

Root
ViewController

List of drinks

Touching the disclosure indicator moves you into the filled-out information about that particular drink.

DetailDrink
ViewController

We pulled the view information out of the view controller and into the DetailDrinkViewController nib.

BRAIN BARBELL

What do we need for the user to be able to enter a new drink? Exactly what fields do you need and how will you lay them out? How will the view controller work?

....

....

....

....

We need a view... but not necessarily a <u>new</u> view

Our "new drink" view is really just an editable version of our detailed view. So instead of creating a whole new nib, let's take advantage of the fact that the UI (the nib) is separate from our behavior (the UIView subclass in the .m file), and reuse the detail view.

Up until now we've had a one-to-one pairing between our nibs and our view controllers. That's definitely the norm, but our view controllers are really just normal Objective-C classes. We can use object-oriented extension mechanisms like inheritance to add the behavior we want.

We need to support different behavior than the detail view controller, though. We'll need a new view controller.

The add drink view needs to contain exactly the same fields as the detail view—it just needs to be editable.

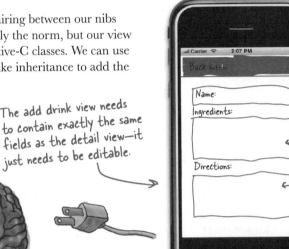

When you click on these text fields, the keyboard will pop up and let you enter new information.

AddDrink
ViewController

DrinkDetailViewController.xib

Really, a new view controller but not a new nib? I thought they always go together.

Not necessarily.

Remember that a nib is just the XML representation of a view. Using nibs is a lot easier than trying to lay out your view using code. And since the nib is just graphical information, you need to put the actual code somewhere. That's where the view controller comes in...

The view controller defines the behavior for the view

From the user's perspective we'll have three views: the table view, the detailed view, and the new drink view. But, since we're reusing the .xib to create the "new" view, all we need is a new view controller class that supports adding a drink. That means there isn't any Interface Builder work to do at all!

Here's the new view we need to create. It will look the same, so we can reuse the nib.

When we instantiate the DrinkDetailViewController, we tell it to initialize with a specific nib.

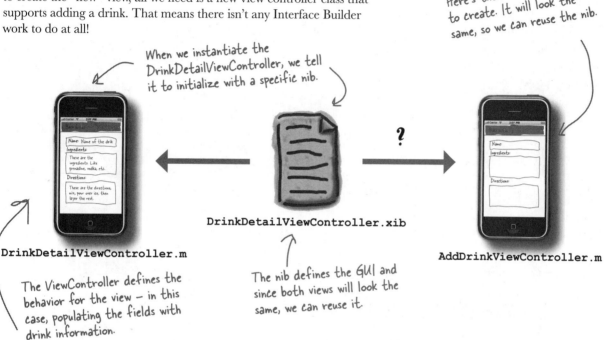

?

DrinkDetailViewController.xib

DrinkDetailViewController.m

AddDrinkViewController.m

The ViewController defines the behavior for the view — in this case, populating the fields with drink information.

The nib defines the GUI and since both views will look the same, we can reuse it.

Separating the UI from behavior helps you reuse your view.

BRAIN BARBELL

Reusing both the the nib file and the detail view controller is also an option... but where could we run into problems?

A nib file contains the UI components and connections...

One way we could reuse the nib is to create a new ViewController and pass it the DrinkDetailViewController.xib file when we initialize it. There are a few challenges with that, though. Remember, we don't just use Interface Builder to lay out the interface; we use it to wire up the components to the class that will load the nib.

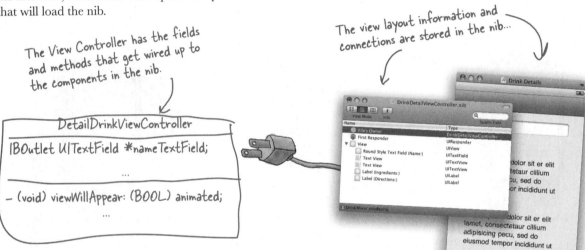

The View Controller has the fields and methods that get wired up to the components in the nib.

The view layout information and connections are stored in the nib...

DetailDrinkViewController

IBOutlet UITextField *nameTextField;

...

– (void) viewWillAppear: (BOOL) animated;

...

...and information about the nib's File's Owner

The nib doesn't actually contain the ViewController class it's setup up to be wired to. Instead, it does this through the nib's File's Owner. When you pass the nib to the view controller, it will deserialize the nib and begin making connections to the outlet names stored in the nib file. This means if we want to pass that nib into another, new view controller, we need to make sure we have the same outlets with the same names, the same actions, etc.

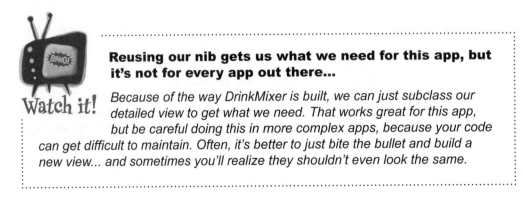

Watch it!

Reusing our nib gets us what we need for this app, but it's not for every app out there...

Because of the way DrinkMixer is built, we can just subclass our detailed view to get what we need. That works great for this app, but be careful doing this in more complex apps, because your code can get difficult to maintain. Often, it's better to just bite the bullet and build a new view... and sometimes you'll realize they shouldn't even look the same.

You can subclass and extend views like any other class

Instead of reusing just the nib and having to re-create all of the outlets and actions, we can just subclass the DetailedViewController and add the behavior we need. Our AddDrinkViewController is the same as a DetailedViewController; it just has the ability to create and save an entirely new drink. Everything else—showing the name, showing the description, etc.—are all exactly the same as the DetailedViewController.

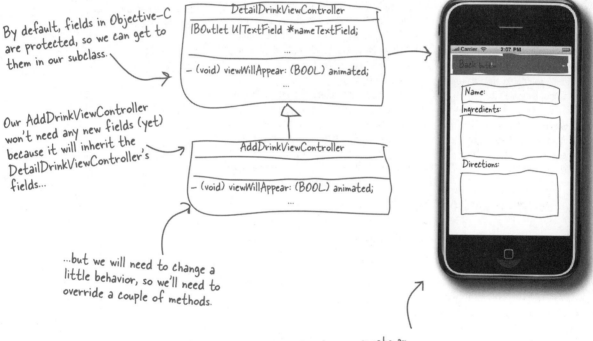

By default, fields in Objective-C are protected, so we can get to them in our subclass.

Our AddDrinkViewController won't need any new fields (yet) because it will inherit the DetailDrinkViewController's fields...

...but we will need to change a little behavior, so we'll need to override a couple of methods.

DetailDrinkViewController

IBOutlet UITextField *nameTextField;

...

– (void) viewWillAppear: (BOOL) animated;

...

AddDrinkViewController

– (void) viewWillAppear: (BOOL) animated;

...

So when we create an AddDrinkDetailViewController, it will ask its superclass, the DetailDrinkViewController, to load the DetailDrinkViewController.xib.

First, we need to create the new view controller.

there are no
Dumb Questions

Q: I still don't get it about the new view controller without a new nib.

A: There's nothing in that nib that you couldn't create in normal Objective-C by hand. As you've likely discovered with Interface Builder, nibs are generally a lot easier to work with than trying to lay out your view using code, so when you create a new view, you typically create a nib to go with it. But really, you could build an entire application without a single nib.

In our case, we're going to do something somewhere in the middle: we're going to create a new view but reuse the UI information from another view.

Q: So why the "Watch it" warning about reusing the nib? Is this a good idea or not?

A: Unfortunately, the answer is: it depends. For DrinkMixer, we can reuse our DetailDrinkView and its nib since we want the layouts to look the same and the DetailDrinkView doesn't really do anything specific. However, in a more complex application, you might run into problems where you're constantly fighting between the two view controllers or you have to expose so much information to the subclass that your code becomes unmaintainable. This isn't a problem unique to iPhone development; you always have to be careful when you start subclassing things.

For our app, subclassing works fine, and you'll see it in some of Apple's example applications, too (which is part of the reason we included it here). But it's equally likely that in some other application you'll want views to be similar, but not quite exactly the same. In those cases, create a new view controller and nib.

Use Xcode to create a view controller without a nib

What we'll do is create a new ViewController in Xcode that doesn't have its own nib, and then tweak it to inherit from the DetailDrinkViewController. This new view will get all of the fields, behavior (which we'll change), and the nib we need.

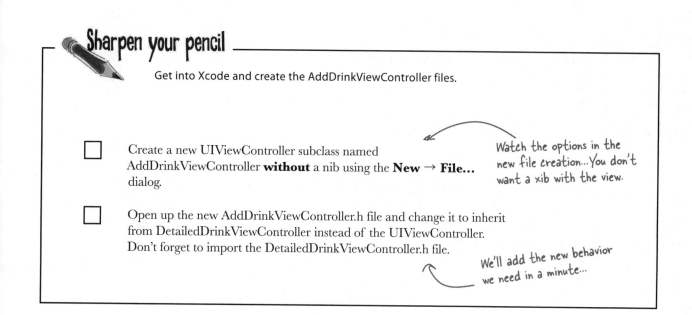

Sharpen your pencil

Get into Xcode and create the AddDrinkViewController files.

☐ Create a new UIViewController subclass named AddDrinkViewController **without** a nib using the **New → File...** dialog.

Watch the options in the new file creation... You don't want a xib with the view.

☐ Open up the new AddDrinkViewController.h file and change it to inherit from DetailedDrinkViewController instead of the UIViewController. Don't forget to import the DetailedDrinkViewController.h file.

We'll add the new behavior we need in a minute...

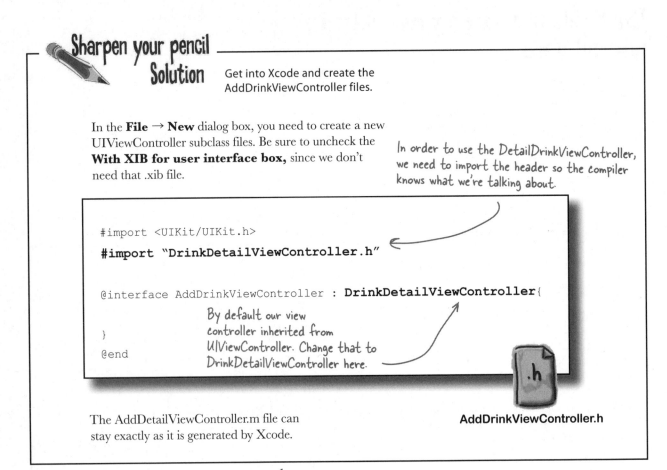

Sharpen your pencil Solution

Get into Xcode and create the AddDrinkViewController files.

In the **File → New** dialog box, you need to create a new UIViewController subclass files. Be sure to uncheck the **With XIB for user interface box,** since we don't need that .xib file.

In order to use the DetailDrinkViewController, we need to import the header so the compiler knows what we're talking about.

```
#import <UIKit/UIKit.h>
#import "DrinkDetailViewController.h"

@interface AddDrinkViewController : DrinkDetailViewController{

}
@end
```

By default our view controller inherited from UIViewController. Change that to DrinkDetailViewController here.

The AddDetailViewController.m file can stay exactly as it is generated by Xcode.

AddDrinkViewController.h

there are no Dumb Questions

Q: Wait, why aren't we just passing the nib into the AddDrinkViewController? Why all this subclassing stuff?

A: We could do that, but the problem is we're not just dealing with GUI layout. We have text fields and labels in there that need to get populated. Our DetailedDrinkViewController already has outlets for all of the fields we need, plus it has the functionality to populate them with a drink before it's shown. We'd have to reimplement that in our new view controller if we didn't subclass.

Q: Is this some kind of contrived Head First example or should I really be paying attention?

A: You should be paying attention. This pattern shows up pretty often and a lot of Apple's example applications use it. It's very common, particularly in table-driven applications, to have one view that just displays the data and another to edit it when the user puts the table in editing mode (we'll talk about that more later). Sometimes you should use totally different views; sometimes you can reuse one you have.

Q: You mentioned that fields are protected by default. What if I wanted private fields in my class?

A: It's easy—just put @private (or @public for public fields) in your interface definition before you declare the fields. If you don't put an access specifier there, Objective-C defaults to protected for fields.

Frank

Joe

Jim

Jim: Now we have an AddDrinkViewController class, so all we have to do is push it on the stack like we did with the detail view, right?

Joe: That makes sense—we used the navigation controller to drill down into the data just by pushing a detailed view on the stack...

Frank: Adding a new drink to our list is a little different, though.

Jim: Why?

Frank: Well, adding a new drink is really a sub-task.

Joe: Huh?

Frank: The users are stepping out of the usual browsing drinks workflow to create a new drink.

Joe: Oh, that's true. Now they're typing, not reading and mixing a drink.

Frank: Right, so for times like this, it's important to communicate to the users that they have to complete the task. Either by finishing the steps or—

Joe: —or by cancelling.

Frank: So, what kind of view is that?

BRAIN POWER

Which of these views better communicates what the user needs to do? Is one more ambiguous than the other?

Drink Mixer		Cancel	Done

After Dinner Mint

Ingredients:

white creme de menthe,
peach liqueur vodka, hot
chocolate

Directions:

Shake vigorously and serve.

After Dinner Mint

Ingredients:

white creme de menthe,
peach liqueur vodka, hot
chocolate

Directions:

Shake vigorously and serve.

Modal views focus the user on the task at hand...

When users navigate through your app, they are used to seeing views pushed and popped as they move through the data. However, some tasks are different than the normal drill-down navigation and we really need to call the users attention to what's going on. iPhone does this through modal views. These are normal views from the developer perspective, but feel different to the user in a few ways:

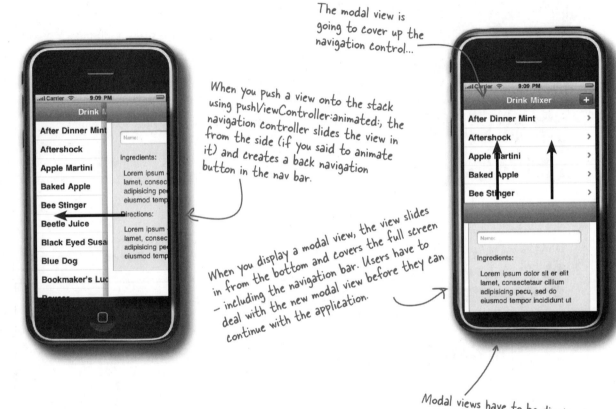

The modal view is going to cover up the navigation control...

When you push a view onto the stack using pushViewController:animated:, the navigation controller slides the view in from the side (if you said to animate it) and creates a back navigation button in the nav bar.

When you display a modal view, the view slides in from the bottom and covers the full screen – including the navigation bar. Users have to deal with the new modal view before they can continue with the application.

Modal views have to be dismissed – either by saving the changes or cancelling out of the view.

...like adding or editing items

We're going to use a modal view when users want to add a new drink to DrinkMixer. They have to either save the added drink, or discard (cancel) it, before they can return to the main DrinkMixer app.

Any view can present a modal view

Up until now we've presented new views using our navigation controller. Things are a little different for modal views: any UIViewController can show a modal view, then hide it when necessary. To display a modal view on top of the current view, simply send the current view the presentModal ViewController:animated: message. Since our RootViewController is the view controller that needs to show the modal view, we can just send this message to ourselves, using **self**, like this:

```
[self presentModalViewController:addViewController animated:YES];
```

self is the Objective-C keyword for the object that is currently executing the method. It's similar to this in Java or C++.

This is the view controller you want displayed as a modal view, in our case, the new AddDrinkViewController.

If you say NO to animated, then the view just appears. By saying YES, we get the smooth slide in from the bottom.

Sharpen your pencil

Update the RootViewController.m file to display our AddDrinkViewController in a UINavigationController when the + button is tapped.

☐ You'll need to import the AddDrinkViewController.h so the RootViewController knows what class you're talking about.

☐ Change the addButtonPressed:sender: method to create an AddDrinkViewController, and present it as a modal view. Be careful about your memory management—don't leak references to the controllers.

Sharpen your pencil
Solution

Update the RootViewController.m file to display our AddDrinkViewController in a UINavigationController when the + button is tapped.

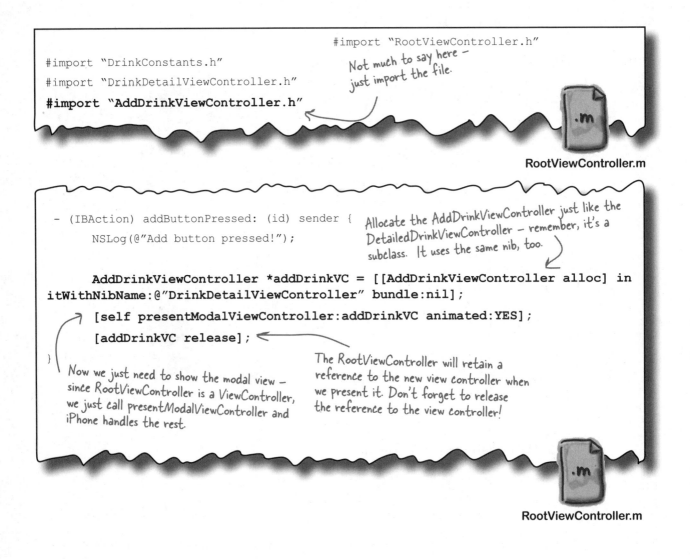

```
#import "RootViewController.h"
```
Not much to say here — just import the file.

```
#import "DrinkConstants.h"
#import "DrinkDetailViewController.h"
#import "AddDrinkViewController.h"
```

RootViewController.m

```
- (IBAction) addButtonPressed: (id) sender {
    NSLog(@"Add button pressed!");

    AddDrinkViewController *addDrinkVC = [[AddDrinkViewController alloc] initWithNibName:@"DrinkDetailViewController" bundle:nil];
    [self presentModalViewController:addDrinkVC animated:YES];
    [addDrinkVC release];
}
```

Allocate the AddDrinkViewController just like the DetailedDrinkViewController — remember, it's a subclass. It uses the same nib, too.

Now we just need to show the modal view — since RootViewController is a ViewController, we just call presentModalViewController and iPhone handles the rest.

The RootViewController will retain a reference to the new view controller when we present it. Don't forget to release the reference to the view controller!

RootViewController.m

Test Drive

Now that the add view is fully implemented, build and run the project. Make sure you try out all of the functionality: scrolling, drilling down to details, and finally adding a drink. Make sure you try adding a new drink name...

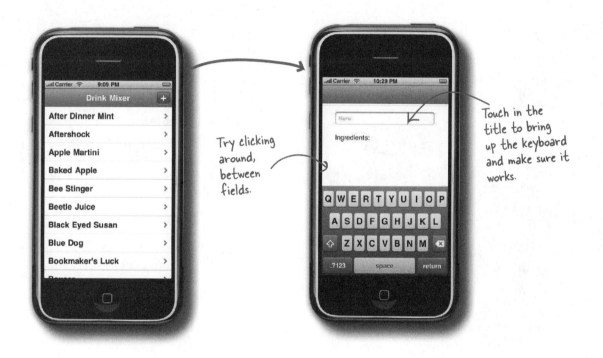

Try clicking around, between fields.

Touch in the title to bring up the keyboard and make sure it works.

Watch it!

If your keyboard isn't working, your fields might still not be editable.

Back in Chapter 4, we had you make the fields uneditable in Interface Builder. If your keyboard isn't appearing, try going back into Interface Builder and checking that the fields are now editable.

But what about after you finish typing?

That's great, but after I type in the drink, nothing happens! I can't get the view to go away, and I can't add the drink.

That's a problem.

Actually, it's two problems that are related. The add drink detail view needs to go away one of two ways: either the user cancels out or saves the drink. We need to handle both.

BRAIN BARBELL

How should we lay out the save and cancel buttons?

Save

Cancel

Our view doesn't have a navigation bar

To be consistent with the rest of DrinkMixer, we really should put the save and
cancel buttons at the top of the view in a navigation bar. The problem is, we
don't have one in our modal version of the detail view.

A modal view covers the navigation control.

Drink detail view

Add drink detail view
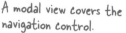

The detail view is pushed on top of the table view, preserving the nav controller.

We could add one by hand, but remember we're sharing the detail drink view
nib, which gets its navigation bar from the navigation controller. Since we're
showing the add drink view as a modal view, we cover up the navigation bar.

Instead of trying to solve this from within the detail drink view nib, we can
embed our add drink view in a navigation controller of its own, like this:

Instead of presenting our addDrinkVC, we present the addNavCon view controller.

This will add a nav controller to wrap the add drink detail view.

```
UINavigationController *addNavCon = [[UINavigationController alloc]
initWithRootViewController:addDrinkVC];
```

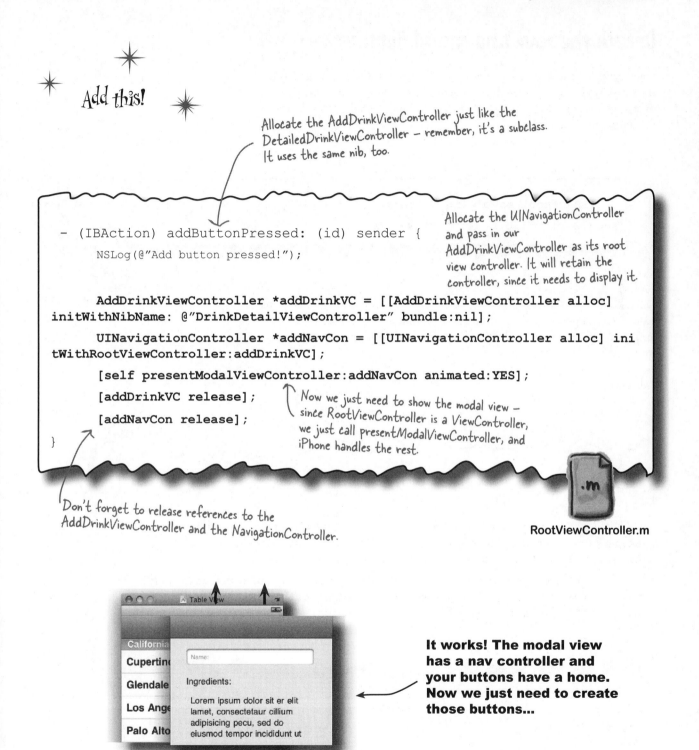

Add this!

Allocate the AddDrinkViewController just like the DetailedDrinkViewController – remember, it's a subclass. It uses the same nib, too.

Allocate the UINavigationController and pass in our AddDrinkViewController as its root view controller. It will retain the controller, since it needs to display it.

```
- (IBAction) addButtonPressed: (id) sender {
    NSLog(@"Add button pressed!");

    AddDrinkViewController *addDrinkVC = [[AddDrinkViewController alloc]
initWithNibName: @"DrinkDetailViewController" bundle:nil];

    UINavigationController *addNavCon = [[UINavigationController alloc] ini
tWithRootViewController:addDrinkVC];

    [self presentModalViewController:addNavCon animated:YES];

    [addDrinkVC release];

    [addNavCon release];

}
```

Now we just need to show the modal view – since RootViewController is a ViewController, we just call presentModalViewController, and iPhone handles the rest.

Don't forget to release references to the AddDrinkViewController and the NavigationController.

RootViewController.m

It works! The modal view has a nav controller and your buttons have a home. Now we just need to create those buttons...

Create the save and cancel buttons

Since both the save and cancel buttons need to dismiss the modal view, let's start by wiring them up to do that. We'll need some actions, and the buttons themselves. We've covered how to do that in Interface Builder, so we'll write them in code this time.

```
- (IBAction) save: (id) sender;

- (IBAction) cancel: (id) sender;
```

These go just before the @end.

AddDrinkViewController.h

Since we're using the navigation bar, we get built-in support for left and right-hand buttons. We just need to create those buttons and assign them to our leftBarButtonItem and rightBarButtonItem to have them placed where we want them.

Just like when we made an add button, we're going to use the navigation controller's left and right buttons for save and cancel.

This time we'll build the buttons in code.

```
- (void)viewDidLoad {
    [super viewDidLoad];

    self.navigationItem.leftBarButtonItem = [[[UIBarButtonItem
alloc] initWithBarButtonSystemItem:UIBarButtonSystemItemCancel
target:self action:@selector(cancel:)] autorelease];

    self.navigationItem.rightBarButtonItem = [[[UIBarButtonItem
alloc] initWithBarButtonSystemItem:UIBarButtonSystemItemSave
target:self action:@selector(save:)] autorelease];
```

AddDrinkViewController.m

Notice our "autorelease" here – normally we alloc a class, assign it to where it needs to go, then release our reference to it. By autoreleasing when we create it we ask Objective-C to handle releasing it for us later. Not quite as efficient as explicitly handling it ourselves, but a little cleaner-looking in the code.

Write the save and cancel actions

When the user clicks either Save or Cancel, we need to exit the modal view by asking the view controller that presented the view to dismiss it. However, to make things easier, we can send the modal view the dismiss message, and it will automatically forward the message to its parent view controller. Since the AddDrinkViewController is the modal view and gets the button call back, we can just send ourselves the dismiss message and the controller stack will handle it correctly. We need to send ourselves the `dismissModalViewControllerAnimated:` message, like this:

```
[self dismissModalViewControllerAnimated:YES];
```

Use this code to write out the save and cancel methods to log which one was called, then clear the modal view. We'll tackle actually saving a new drink once this works.

Start this at the bottom of the file, just before the dealloc.

```
#pragma mark -
#pragma mark Save and Cancel

- (IBAction) save: (id) sender {
    NSLog(@"Save pressed!");
    [self dismissModalViewControllerAnimated:YES];
}
- (IBAction) cancel: (id) sender {
    NSLog(@"Cancel pressed!");
    [self dismissModalViewControllerAnimated:YES];
}
```

Since we are in the modal view, this dismiss message will be delegated up to our parent view controller, which will actually make the view go away.

.m

AddDrinkViewController.m

Now, to see if those buttons work...

— Test Drive —

The modal view can be dismissed now, and the keyboard works too!

Just like that, the buttons are in the detail view.

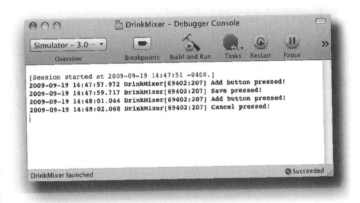

```
[Session started at 2009-09-19 14:47:51 -0400.]
2009-09-19 14:47:57.972 DrinkMixer[69402:207] Add button pressed!
2009-09-19 14:47:59.717 DrinkMixer[69402:207] Save pressed!
2009-09-19 14:48:01.044 DrinkMixer[69402:207] Add button pressed!
2009-09-19 14:48:02.068 DrinkMixer[69402:207] Cancel pressed!
```

Congratulations, the modal view is working!

This chapter, you've learned how to add a view and pass it through the navigation stack to pop the view, plus you reused the nib you already created and wired it up for a new use! Not only that, but your add view is modal, and you can dismiss it, too.

there are no
Dumb Questions

Q: **Why don't we need an outlet for the save/cancel button? And what about Interface Builder?**

A: The navigation controller API has support for both left and right buttons; you just need to initialize them with the buttons you want to use (save and cancel buttons, for instance). After that, all you need are the matching actions.

So can I add some new drinks yet? I just learned how to make this cool new one from another bartender and want to put it in my app.

To be continued...

iPhoneDevcross

Using all the stuff you've learned about how to work
with different plists and views, fill in the puzzle...

Across

1. The navigation controller has support for _____
   buttons to fix stuff.
5. Use these to organize names of things.
7. Views can be _____ and extended like any other
   class.
8. You can create _____ bars in the IB or in code.
9. _____ is easier when the UI is separated from
   the behavior.
10. User _____ on iTunes stick with the app even
    after a new version is released.

Down

2. The HIG requires some kind of _____ element in a
   cell if there is more information availible.
3. An _____ specifies what a button should look
   like.
4. A nib file has UI _____.
6. A _____ view has to be dealt with by the user before
   doing anything else.

Your iPhone Toolbox

You've got Chapter 5 under your belt and now you've added plists and modal views to your toolbox. For a complete list of tooltips in the book, go to http://www.headfirstlabs.com/iphonedev.

Debugging

If you know where your problem is likely to be, set the breakpoint there.

You can use the debugger to step through the problem area.

If you have no idea where to start, you can step through the entire app!

iTunes Basics

1. Submitting your app to the store means it HAS TO CONFORM TO THE HIG.

2. Approvals can take weeks, so try and get it right the first time.

3. Once your app is up for sale, the reviews stay with it, even with updates.

Dictionaries

Are useful ways to expand the contents of a plist.

Need to be properly handled inside the app.

Views

Are pushed onto the stack via the table view or buttons.

Can be subclassed and extended like any other class.

Modal views force the user to interact with them before they can be dismissed.

iPhoneDevcross Solution

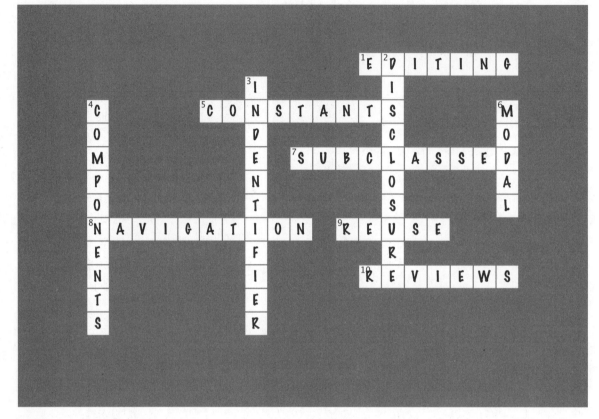

Across

1. The navigation controller has support for _____ buttons to fix stuff. [EDITING]
5. Use these to organize names of things. [CONSTANTS]
7. Views can be _____ and extended like any other class. [SUBCLASSED]
8. You can create _____ bars in IB or in the code. [NAVIGATION]
9. _____ is easier when the UI is separated from the behavior. [REUSE]
10. User _____ on iTunes stick with the app even after a new version is released. [REVIEWS]

Down

2. The HIG requires some kind of _____ element in a cell if there is more information availible. [DISCLOSURE]
3. An _____ specifies what a button should look like. [INDENTIFIER]
4. A nib file has UI _____. [COMPONENTS]
6. A _____ view has to be dealt with by the user before doing anything else. [MODAL]

6 saving, editing, and sorting data

*Everyone's an editor...

If these records were on an iPhone and I could edit them life would be grand!

Displaying data is nice, but adding and editing information is what makes an app really hum. DrinkMixer is great—it uses some cell customization, and works with plist dictionaries to display data. It's a handy reference application, and you've got a good start on adding new drinks. Now, it's time to give the user the ability to modify the data—saving, editing, and sorting—to make it more useful for everyone. In this chapter we'll take a look at editing patterns in iPhone apps and how to guide users with the nav controller.

Sam is ready to add a Red-Headed School Girl...

A new drink at the Lounge.

Sam went to try DrinkMixer with the new add view, and ran into problems right away.

Sam was clicking around, ready to add his new drink.

The directions field is hidden under the keyboard.

You can't see the directions at all, and part of the ingredients information is covered up.

Sam, the bartender

We have a problem with our view, since we can't get to some of the fields.

...but the keyboard is in the way

We're back to the keyboard problem we saw earlier with InstaTwit. When Sam taps on a control, it gets focus (becomes the first responder) and asks iPhoneOS to show the keyboard. Generally, that's a good thing. However...

We had a similar problem in InstTwit where the user couldn't get to the controls under the keyboard.

When Sam taps in the Drink name field, the keyboard appears like it's supposed to—that's good.

He can even try to tap into the Ingredients field and type in some of the ingredients... but he runs under the keyboard.

And the keyboard completely covers the Directions field!

BRAIN BARBELL

How did we deal with the keyboard last time? Will that work this time? What do you want the view to **do** when the keyboard appears?

....

....

....

....

BRAIN BARBELL

How did we deal with the keyboard last time? Will that work this time?
What do you want the view to *do* when the keyboard appears?

Resigning first responder worked last time. In DrinkMixer it would be fine for the name field, but
what about the directions and the ingredients fields? As soon as they keyboard comes up, they're
covered. The user has a smaller screen to work with once the keyboard shows up — we need to set up
the view to scroll things in when the user needs them. We can do this with a UIScrollView.

UIScrollView Up Close

UIScrollView is just like the basic UIView we've been using except that it can handle having items (like
buttons, text fields, etc.) that are off the screen and then scroll them into view. The scroll view draws
and manages a scroll bar, panning and zooming, and what part of the content view is displayed. It
does all of this by knowing how big the area it needs to show is (called the contentSize) and how
much space it has to show it in (the frame). UIScrollView can figure out everything else from there.

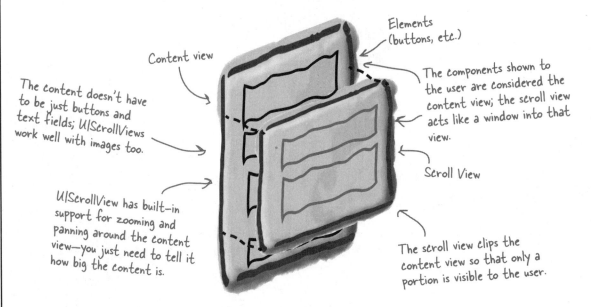

Content view

The content doesn't have
to be just buttons and
text fields; UIScrollViews
work well with images too.

UIScrollView has built-in
support for zooming and
panning around the content
view—you just need to tell it
how big the content is.

Elements
(buttons, etc.)

The components shown to
the user are considered the
content view; the scroll view
acts like a window into that
view.

Scroll View

The scroll view clips the
content view so that only a
portion is visible to the user.

Remember, in CocoaTouch, components are subclasses of UIView. All a scroll view needs to care
about are the subviews it has to manage. It doesn't matter if it's one huge UIImageView that shows a
big image you can pan around, or if it's lots of text fields, buttons, and labels.

To get a scrollable view, we need to move our components into a UIScrollView instead of a UIView.
Time to get back into Interface Builder...

We need to wrap our content in a scroll view

We want the user to be able to scroll through our controls when the keyboard covers some of them up. In order to do that, we need to add a UIScrollView to our view and then tell it about the controls (the content view) we want it to handle.

All of these components need to be children of the scroll view.

The scroll view will be the size of the entire view (minus the nav control)

The scroll view needs to hold these components now.

> This is really annoying. You mean we have to pull all those components off and then lay out the view again? Isn't there an easier way?

You've got a point.

Remember when we said sometimes Interface Builder makes things (a lot) easier? This is one of those times...

EASY GUI RECONSTRUCTION

Apparently we aren't the only people to realize after we've built a view that it needs to be scrollable. Interface Builder has built-in support for taking an existing view and wrapping it in a UIScrollView.

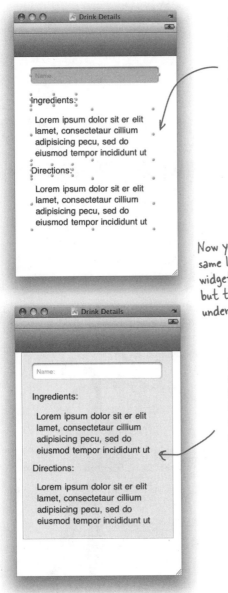

Highlight all of the widgets (as shown here) in the detail view, then go to the **Layout → Embed Objects In → Scroll View** menu option. Interface Builder will automatically create a new scrolled view and stick all the widgets in the same location on the scrolled view.

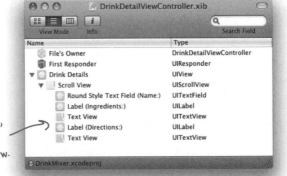

Now you have the same listing of widgets as before, but they are under a scroll view.

Interface Builder will create a UIScrollView just big enough to hold all of our components. Since we want the whole view to scroll, grab the corners of the new UIScrollView and drag them out to the corners of the screen, right up to the edge of the navigation bar (we don't want that to scroll).

How will this new scroll view know how much content needs to be scrolled?

The scroll view is the same size as the screen

Interface Builder created the UIScrollView, but there are a few finishing touches we must do manually to make this work the way we want. We need to tell the UIScrollView how big its content area is so it knows what it will need to scroll. We do that by setting its `contentSize` property. You'll need to add an outlet and property for the UIScrollView, then wire it up in Interface Builder so we can get to it.

So how do we figure out how big the `contentSize` should be? When the UIScrollView is the same size as our screen, we don't have anything outside of the visible area that it needs to worry about. Since the scroll view is the same size as our UIView that it's sitting in, we can grab the size from there, like this:

```
scrollView.contentSize = self.view.frame.size;
```

Once you've added that line, you'll have a scroll view that takes up all of the available space, and it thinks its content view is the same size.

Once you resize it, the UIScrollView and its contentSize are the same size. We just need to tell that to the scroll view.

Sharpen your pencil

Update DrinkDetailViewController.h and DrinkDetailViewController.m to handle our new UIScrollView.

1 Add an attribute named `scrollView` to DrinkDetailViewController to hold a reference to the UIScrollView. You'll need the field declaration and IBOutlet property, then you will synthesize it in the .m and release it in dealloc.

2 Wire up the new property to the UIScrollView in Interface Builder by adding a new Referencing Outlet to the UIScrollView connected to your scrollView property.

3 Set the initial `contentSize` for the `scrollView` in `viewDidLoad:`. Remember, we're telling the scrollView that its content is the same size as the view it's sitting in.

Sharpen your pencil
Solution

Update your DrinkDetailViewController.h and
DrinkDetailViewController.m to handle our new UIScrollView.

1 Add an attribute named `scrollView` to DrinkDetailViewController to hold a
reference to the UIScrollView. You'll need the field declaration, an IBOutlet property,
synthesize it in the .m and release it in dealloc.

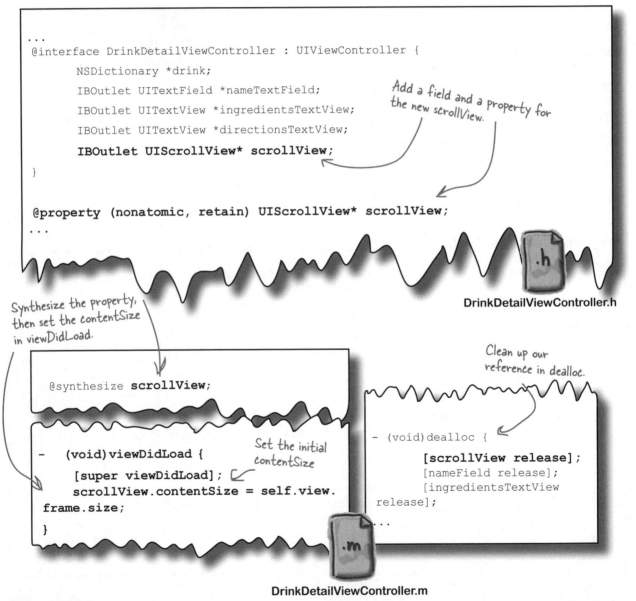

```
...
@interface DrinkDetailViewController : UIViewController {
    NSDictionary *drink;
    IBOutlet UITextField *nameTextField;
    IBOutlet UITextView *ingredientsTextView;
    IBOutlet UITextView *directionsTextView;
    IBOutlet UIScrollView* scrollView;
}

@property (nonatomic, retain) UIScrollView* scrollView;
...
```

Add a field and a property for the new scrollView.

DrinkDetailViewController.h

Synthesize the property, then set the contentSize in viewDidLoad.

```
@synthesize scrollView;
```

```
- (void)viewDidLoad {
    [super viewDidLoad];
    scrollView.contentSize = self.view.
frame.size;
}
```

Set the initial contentSize

Clean up our reference in dealloc.

```
- (void)dealloc {
    [scrollView release];
    [nameField release];
    [ingredientsTextView
release];
    ...
```

DrinkDetailViewController.m

2 Wire up the new property to the UIScrollView in Interface Builder.

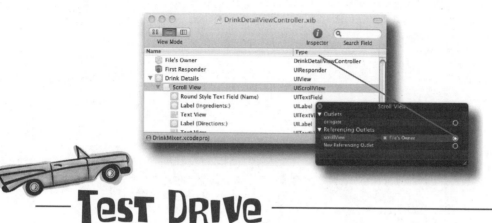

TesT DRive

Tap in the text field
and the keyboard
appears... but nothing's
scrolling!

⚛BRAIN POWER

Why isn't it working yet? Think about all the things
that you have going into this view—the scroll view,
the main view, and the keyboard...

The keyboard changes the visible area

The problem is the keyboard changes the visible area but the scroll
view has no idea that just happened. The scroll view still thinks it has
the whole screen to display its content, and from its perspective, that's
plenty of room. We need to tell the scroll view that the visible area is
smaller now that the keyboard is there.

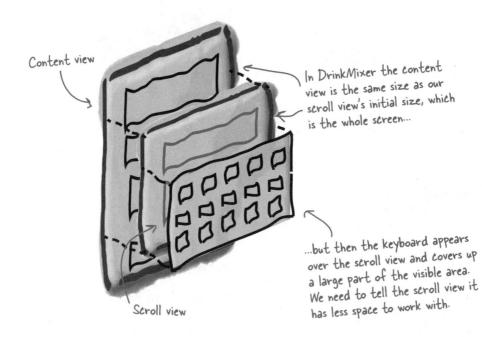

Content view

In DrinkMixer the content
view is the same size as our
scroll view's initial size, which
is the whole screen...

...but then the keyboard appears
over the scroll view and covers up
a large part of the visible area.
We need to tell the scroll view it
has less space to work with.

Scroll view

**iPhone tells you about the keyboard,
but doesn't tinker with your views.**

Just because iPhone knows that the keyboard
is there, it doesn't know how your app wants
to handle it. That's up to you!

Wouldn't it be dreamy if iPhone could just tell the app when the keyboard appears? But I know it's just a fantasy…

iPhone notifies you about the keyboard

Interacting with the keyboard and the scroll view brings us to a part of the iPhone OS we haven't talked about yet, called **Notifications**. Just like component events being passed around our application, there are system-level events, called Notifications, that are being passed by the iPhone OS. The secret to knowing what's going on with the keyboard is tapping into these events.

 Sam taps in the Drink name field and the field becomes the first responder. Now the iPhone OS needs to show the keyboard.

2 The iPhone OS posts a notification to the default NSNotificationCenter named UIKeyboardDidShowNotification.

Event	Object	Selector
UIKeyboardDidShowNotification	DetailDrinkViewController	keyboardDidShow

NSNotificationCenter

4 The NSNotificationCenter invokes the target selector and passes it information about the object that triggered the event, along with event specific details.

```
[registeredObject
keyboardDidShow:eventInfo];
```

3 NSNotificationCenter looks up the event to see if anyone is registered to be told when that event happens. Objects are registered by providing a selector (method) to call if the event is triggered.

Register with the default notification center for events

The iPhone OS supports more than one NSNotificationCenter, but unless you have specific needs for your own, you can just use the default system-level one. You can get a reference to the default one by calling:

```
[[NSNotificationCenter defaultCenter];
```

With the notification center, you can register for events by passing the object you want the notification center to call back to (usually yourself), the method to call, an event you are interested in (or nil for any event), and, optionally, the sender you want to listen to (or nil for all senders).

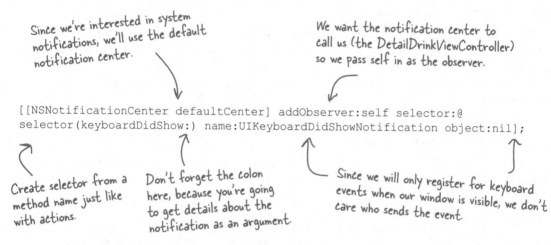

Since we're interested in system notifications, we'll use the default notification center.

We want the notification center to call us (the DetailDrinkViewController) so we pass self in as the observer.

```
[[NSNotificationCenter defaultCenter] addObserver:self selector:@
selector(keyboardDidShow:) name:UIKeyboardDidShowNotification object:nil];
```

Create selector from a method name just like with actions.

Don't forget the colon here, because you're going to get details about the notification as an argument.

Since we will only register for keyboard events when our window is visible, we don't care who sends the event.

Then unregister when you're done

Just like memory management, we need to clean up our registrations from the notification center when we don't need them any longer. We'll register for events in viewWillAppear: and unregister in viewWillDisappear:. Unregistering for an event is easy—just ask the notification center to removeObserver for the object you registered.

```
[[NSNotificationCenter defaultCenter] removeObserver:self];
```

Make sure you unregister from the same notification center you registered with.

We simply ask the notification center to remove us from everything we've registered for. If you only want to stop receiving certain notifications, you can specify the notification as well.

The notification center exposed

This week's interview:
Why do you talk so much?

Head First: Um, this is embarrassing but I'm not entirely sure I have the right Notification Center here...

Notification Center: Well, unless you need something weird, it's probably me. I'm the guy everybody goes to by default. Heads up! An app's shuttin' down. Be with you in a second.

Head First: Wow—so you know about every app that starts and stops?

Notification Center: Yup. I'm the default center; all the system events go through me. Now, not everybody is interested in what's going on, but if they want to know, I'm the guy to see.

Head First: So when someone wants to know what's going on, they tell you what they're interested in, right?

Notification Center: Exactly. If somebody wants to know about somethin' in the system, they register with me. They tell me the notification they want me to watch for, who I should tell when it happens, and, if they're really picky, who should have sent it.

Head First: So then you tell them when that notification happens?

Notification Center: Right—they tell me what message to send them when I see the notification they were interested in. I package up the notification information into a nice object for them and then call their method. Doesn't take me long at all; the sender almost always waits for me to finish telling everyone what happened before it does anything else.

Interviewer: Almost always?

Notification Center: Well, the sender could use a notification queue to have me send out the notifications later, when the sender isn't busy, but that's not typically how it's done.

Head First: Hmm, this sounds a lot like message passing. The sender wants to tell somebody that something happened, you call a method on that somebody... what's different?

Notification Center: It's similar to message passing, but there are some differences. First, the senders don't need to know who to tell. They just tell me that something happened and I'll figure out if anyone cares. Second, there might be lots of people interested in what's going on. In normal message passing the senders would have to tell each one individually. With notifications they just tell me once and I'll make sure everyone knows. Finally, the receiver of the notification doesn't need to care who's sending the message. If some object wants to know that the application is shutting down, it doesn't care who's responsible for saying the app's quitting, the object just trusts me to make sure they'll know when it happens.

Head First: So can anyone send notifications?

Notification Center: Sure. Anybody can ask me to post a notification and if anyone's registered to get it, I'll let them know.

Head First: How do they know which notifications to send?

Notification Center: Ah, well that's up to the sender. Different frameworks have their own messages they pass around, you'll have to check with the framework to see what they'll send out. If you're going to be posting your own notifications, you almost certainly don't want to go blasting out someone else's notifications; you should come up with your own. They're just strings—and a dictionary if you want to include some extra info—nothing fancy.

Head First: I see. Well, this has been great, Notification Center. Thanks for stopping by!

Sharpen your pencil

Fill in the blanks and get a plan for the next step!

We need to .... for the ....:

and .... events in ....

We'll add two........................... that will be called by the ....

when the notifications are posted.

We'll adjust the size of the .... when the keyboard appears and disappears.

We need to... for events in ....:

Sharpen your pencil Solution

Now you have a plan for what to do next.

We need to .... register .... for the UIKeyboardDidShowNotification

and ...UIKeyboardDidHideNotification... events in .....viewWillAppear....:

We'll add two ...methods... that will be called by the ....notification center....

when the notifications are posted.

We'll adjust the size of the .....scroll view..... when the keyboard appears and disappears.

We need to .... unregister .... for events in .....viewWillDisappear....:

---

there are no Dumb Questions

Q: I can't find the list of notifications that are sent by the iPhone OS. Where are they listed?

A: There isn't a central list of all the notifications that could be sent. Different classes and frameworks have different notifications they use. For example, the UIDevice class offers a set of notifications to tell you about when the battery is being charged or what's happening with the proximity sensor. Apple's documentation is usually pretty clear about what notifications are available and what they mean. The keyboard notifications are described in the UIWindow class documentation.

Q: Why would I want to create my own notifications?

A: It depends on your application. Remember, notifications let you decouple the sender from the receiver. You could use this in your application to let multiple distinct views know that something happened in your application.

For example, let's say you had a view that let you add or remove items from your application and your app has several different ways to view those things. Notifications could give you a nice way to announce to all of the other views that something has changed without your add/remove view needing to have a reference to each of them.

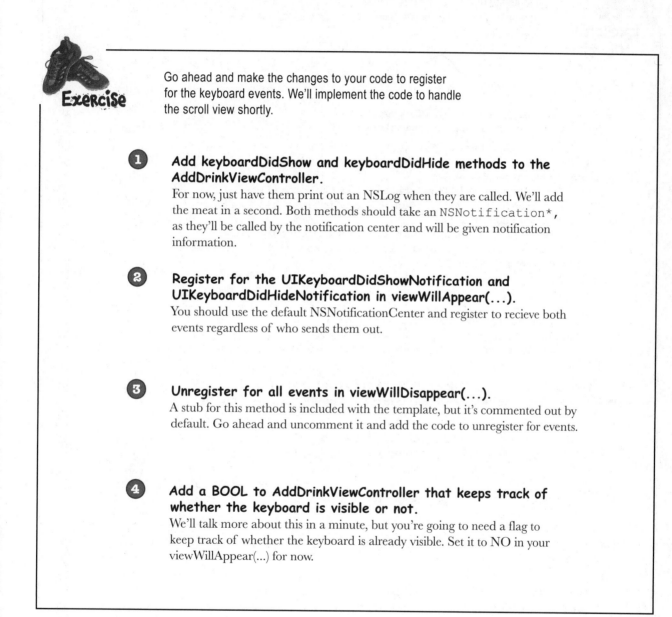

Go ahead and make the changes to your code to register
for the keyboard events. We'll implement the code to handle
the scroll view shortly.

① **Add keyboardDidShow and keyboardDidHide methods to the AddDrinkViewController.**

For now, just have them print out an NSLog when they are called. We'll add the meat in a second. Both methods should take an NSNotification*, as they'll be called by the notification center and will be given notification information.

② **Register for the UIKeyboardDidShowNotification and UIKeyboardDidHideNotification in viewWillAppear(...).**

You should use the default NSNotificationCenter and register to recieve both events regardless of who sends them out.

③ **Unregister for all events in viewWillDisappear(...).**

A stub for this method is included with the template, but it's commented out by default. Go ahead and uncomment it and add the code to unregister for events.

④ **Add a BOOL to AddDrinkViewController that keeps track of whether the keyboard is visible or not.**

We'll talk more about this in a minute, but you're going to need a flag to keep track of whether the keyboard is already visible. Set it to NO in your viewWillAppear(...) for now.

Exercise Solution

Go ahead and make the changes to your code to register
for the keyboard events. We'll implement the code to handle
the scroll view shortly.

These are both new methods for the keyboard notifications in the implementation file. We'll get to those in a minute.

```
- (void)viewWillAppear: (BOOL)animated {
    [super viewWillAppear:animated];

    NSLog(@"Registering for keyboard events");
    [[NSNotificationCenter defaultCenter] addObserver:self selector:@
selector(keyboardDidShow:)
    name:UIKeyboardDidShowNotification object:nil];
[[NSNotificationCenter defaultCenter] addObserver:self selector:@
selector(keyboardDidHide:)
    name:UIKeyboardDidHideNotification object:nil];
    // Initially the keyboard is hidden, so reset our variable
    keyboardVisible = NO;
}
```

We need to keep track of whether the keyboard is
showing or not. More on this in a minute.

If you don't give it a notification to unregister from, it will remove you from anything you've registered for.

```
- (void)viewWillDisappear: (BOOL)animated {
    NSLog(@"Unregistering for keyboard events");
    [[NSNotificationCenter defaultCenter] removeObserver:self];
}

- (void)keyboardDidShow: (NSNotification *)notif {
    NSLog(@"Received UIKeyboardDidShowNotification.");
}

- (void)keyboardDidHide: (NSNotification *)notif {
    NSLog(@"Received UIKeyboardDidHideNotification.");
}
```

.m

AddDrinkViewController.h

```
@interface AddDrinkViewController : DrinkDetailViewController {
    BOOL keyboardVisible;
}
- (void)keyboardDidShow: (NSNotification*) notif;
- (void)keyboardDidHide: (NSNotification*) notif;
}
```

.h

AddDrinkViewController.h

Keyboard events tell you the keyboard state and size

The whole point of knowing when the keyboard appears or disappears is to tell the scroll view that the visible area has changed size. But, how do we know the new size? The iPhone OS sends out the keyboard notification events (UIKeyboardDidShowNotification and UIKeyboardDidHideNotification) when the keyboard appears and disappears and includes with this event all of the information we need.

The notification object contains the name of the notification and the object it pertains to (or nil if there's no related object).

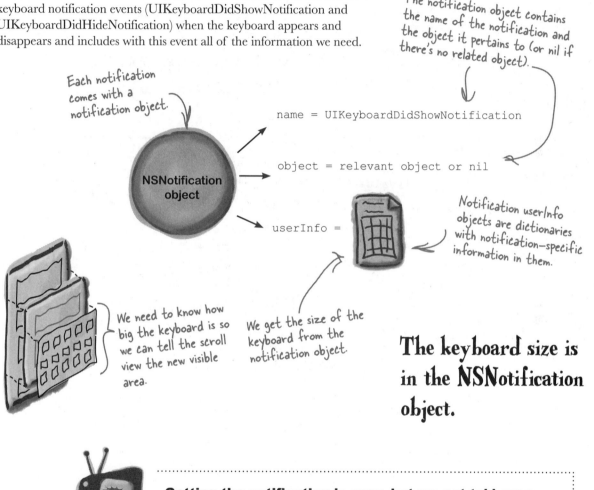

Each notification comes with a notification object.

NSNotification object

name = UIKeyboardDidShowNotification

object = relevant object or nil

userInfo =

Notification userInfo objects are dictionaries with notification-specific information in them.

We need to know how big the keyboard is so we can tell the scroll view the new visible area.

We get the size of the keyboard from the notification object.

The keyboard size is in the NSNotification object.

Getting the notification is easy, but we get told every time the keyboard is shown, even if it's already there.

That's why we need the BOOL to keep track of whether or not the keyboard is currently displayed. If the keyboard isn't visible when we get the notification, then we need to tell our scroll view its visible size is smaller. If the keyboard is hidden, we set the scroll view back to full size.

Watch it!

Keyboard Code Magnets Part I

Below are the code magnets you'll need to implement the keyboardDidShow method. Use the comments in the code on the right to help you figure out what goes where.

```objc
CGRect viewFrame = self.view.frame;
viewFrame.size.height -= keyboardSize.height;
```

```objc
NSValue* aValue = [info objectForKey:UIKeyboardBoundsUserInfoKey];
CGSize keyboardSize = [aValue CGRectValue].size;
```

```objc
scrollView.frame = viewFrame;
keyboardVisible = YES;
```

```objc
NSLog(@"Resizing smaller for keyboard");
```

```objc
if (keyboardVisible) {
    NSLog(@"Keyboard is already visible.  Ignoring notification.");
    return;
}
```

```objc
NSDictionary* info = [notif userInfo];
```

```
- (void)keyboardDidShow:(NSNotification *)notif {




        // The keyboard wasn't visible before



        // Get the size of the keyboard.






        // Resize the scroll view to make room for the keyboard




}
```

AddDrinkViewController.m

Keyboard Code Magnets Part II

Below are the code magnets you'll need to implement the keyboardDidHide method. Use the comments in the code on the right to help you figure out what goes where.

```
scrollView.frame = viewFrame;
keyboardVisible = NO;
```

```
NSLog(@"Resizing bigger with no keyboard");
```

```
if (!keyboardVisible) {
        NSLog(@"Keyboard already hidden.  Ignoring notification.");
        return;
}
```

```
NSDictionary* info = [notif userInfo];
```

```
NSValue* aValue = [info objectForKey:UIKeyboardBoundsUserInfoKey];
CGSize keyboardSize = [aValue CGRectValue].size;
```

```
CGRect viewFrame = self.view.frame;
viewFrame.size.height += keyboardSize.height;
```

```
- (void)keyboardDidHide:(NSNotification *)notif {




    // The keyboard was visible


    // Get the size of the keyboard.




    // Reset the height of the scroll view to its original value



}
```

AddDrinkViewController.m

Keyboard Code Magnets Solution

Below are the code magnets to work with the keyboard...

```objc
- (void)keyboardDidShow:(NSNotification *)notif {

    if (keyboardVisible) {
      NSLog(@"Keyboard is already visible.  Ignoring notification.");
      return;
    }
```

We will get this notification whenever the user switches text fields, even if the keyboard is already showing. So we keep track of it and bail if it's a repeat.

```objc
    // The keyboard wasn't visible before

    NSLog(@"Resizing smaller for keyboard");

    // Get the size of the keyboard.

    NSDictionary* info = [notif userInfo];
```

NSNotification contains a dictionary with the event details; we pull that out here.

```objc
    NSValue* aValue = [info objectForKey:UIKeyboardBoundsUserInfoKey];
    CGSize keyboardSize = [aValue CGRectValue].size;
```

We get the keyboard size from the dictionary...

```objc
    // Resize the scroll view to make room for the keyboard

    CGRect viewFrame = self.view.frame;
    viewFrame.size.height -= keyboardSize.height;
```

...then figure out how big the scroll view really is now (basically how big our view is, minus the size of the keyboard).

```objc
    scrollView.frame = viewFrame;
    keyboardVisible = YES;
}
```

Finally, update the scroll view with the new size and mark that the keyboard is visible.

AddDrinkViewController.m

Keyboard Code Magnets Part II Solution

Below are the code magnets to work with the keyboard...

Handling the UIKeyboardDidHideNotification works almost exactly the same way, except this time the scroll view needs to be expanded by the size of the (now missing) keyboard.

```objc
- (void)keyboardDidHide:(NSNotification *)notif {

    if (!keyboardVisible) {
        NSLog(@"Keyboard already hidden.  Ignoring notification.");
        return;
    }
```

Ignore this notification if we know the keyboard isn't visible.

```objc
    // The keyboard was visible
    NSLog(@"Resizing bigger with no keyboard");
```

Just like before, we pull the keyboard size from the event...

```objc
    // Get the size of the keyboard.

    NSDictionary* info = [notif userInfo];

    NSValue* aValue = [info objectForKey:UIKeyboardBoundsUserInfoKey];
    CGSize keyboardSize = [aValue CGRectValue].size;


    // Reset the height of the scroll view to its original value

    CGRect viewFrame = self.view.frame;
    viewFrame.size.height += keyboardSize.height;

    scrollView.frame = viewFrame;
    keyboardVisible = NO;
```

...and resize the scroll view to the new visible area.

```objc
}
```

AddDrinkViewController.m

Test Drive

Go ahead and build and run. Once you get into the detail view, you should be able to scroll the view to the right field, and the messages in the console help you keep track of what's going on.

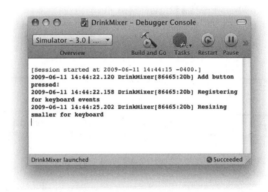

there are no Dumb Questions

Q: Manipulating that scroll view size is kind of tricky—how would I have figured that out without magnets?

A: A great reference for the code samples and information for programming apps in general is the *iPhone Application Programming Guide* that is available on the Apple developer website. That has sample code for common problems like handling the keyboard events, using the GPS, etc.

Q: Tell me again why we need to keep track of whether the keyboard is already visible? Isn't iPhone doing that?

A: The iPhone OS knows the state of the

keyboard, but it sends keyboard events out when different controls get focus. So, when the user taps in the first field, you'll get a UIKeyboardWillShowNotification followed by a UIKeyboardDidShowNotification. When the user taps into another field, you'll get another UIKeyboardDidShowNotification so you know they keyboard focus has changed, but you won't get the keyboard hide event, since it never actually went away. You need to keep track of whether you already knew it was visible so you don't resize the scroll view to the wrong size.

Q: The scroll view works, but depending on what the users pick, they still have to scroll to the widget?

A: Yes—and that's not ideal. You can

ask the scroll view to scroll to a particular spot on the content view if you keep track of which control has the focus. The *iPhone Application Programming Guide* has good sample code for that.

Q: Do we really need to use the keyboard size stuff in the notification? Isn't it always the same?

A: It's not always the same! If your application is landscape. your keyboard is wider than it is tall. If your app is portrait, then it's taller than it is wide. Apple also makes it clear that they may change the size of the keyboard if necessary and you should never assume you know how big it is. Always get size information directly from the keyboard notifications.

Everything scrolls OK, and I can put a drink in, but as soon as I get back to the list, it's gone!

Sam's drink is missing!

As soon as he leaves the drink detail view. the new drink no longer shows up in the main list. We need to figure out how to keep it around longer...

Sharpen your pencil

Answer the following and think about what it means for our app.

What happens to new drinks when the user hits save?

....

Where do we need to add code?

....

How are we going to save the new drink?

....

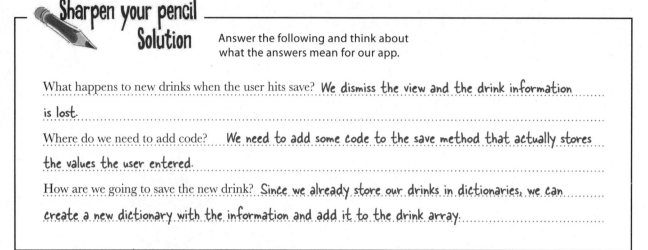

Sharpen your pencil
Solution

Answer the following and think about what the answers mean for our app.

What happens to new drinks when the user hits save? We dismiss the view and the drink information is lost.

Where do we need to add code? We need to add some code to the save method that actually stores the values the user entered.

How are we going to save the new drink? Since we already store our drinks in dictionaries, we can create a new dictionary with the information and add it to the drink array.

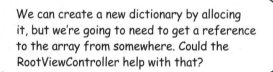

> We can create a new dictionary by allocing it, but we're going to need to get a reference to the array from somewhere. Could the RootViewController help with that?

We need to give the AddDrinkViewController a reference to the whole drink array.

Creating a new NSMutableDictionary is easy enough, we can do that by allocing and initializing it. We can set the drink on the dictionary using the setObjectForKey:. What's going to take a little more work is adding it to the drink array. We could have the RootViewController pass the new drink in after we've created it...

Exercise

Go back and update the RootViewController and AddDrinkViewController to support saving new drinks.

Give the AddDrinkController a reference to the master drink array.
You're going to need to add a field to the class, a property, and then synthesize it and release the reference in dealloc. Finally, you need to make sure that the RootViewController passes on a reference to the drink array when it's setting up the AddDrinkController.

Create and add a new dictionary to the array.
You need to update the save: method to get the drink details from the controls and store them in a new dictionary. After that, add the dictionary to the master drink array using `addObject:`.

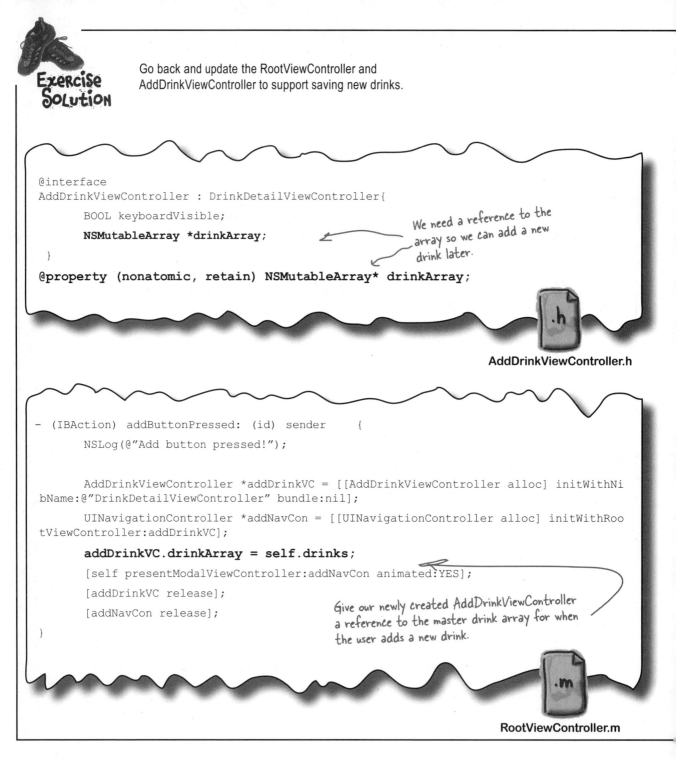

Exercise Solution

Go back and update the RootViewController and
AddDrinkViewController to support saving new drinks.

```objc
@interface
AddDrinkViewController : DrinkDetailViewController{
    BOOL keyboardVisible;
    NSMutableArray *drinkArray;
}
@property (nonatomic, retain) NSMutableArray* drinkArray;
```

We need a reference to the array so we can add a new drink later.

AddDrinkViewController.h

```objc
- (IBAction) addButtonPressed: (id) sender     {
    NSLog(@"Add button pressed!");

    AddDrinkViewController *addDrinkVC = [[AddDrinkViewController alloc] initWithNibName:@"DrinkDetailViewController" bundle:nil];
    UINavigationController *addNavCon = [[UINavigationController alloc] initWithRootViewController:addDrinkVC];
    addDrinkVC.drinkArray = self.drinks;
    [self presentModalViewController:addNavCon animated:YES];
    [addDrinkVC release];
    [addNavCon release];
}
```

Give our newly created AddDrinkViewController a reference to the master drink array for when the user adds a new drink.

RootViewController.m

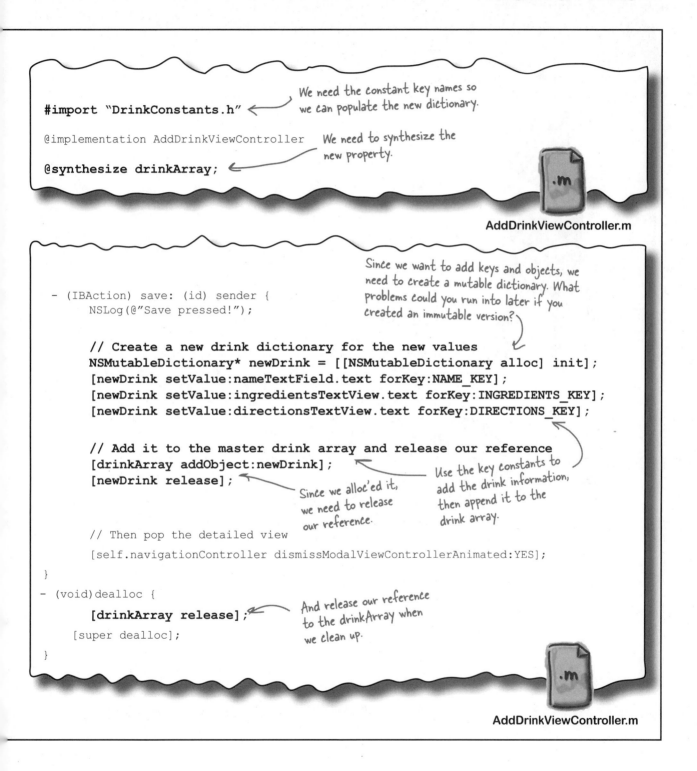

```
#import "DrinkConstants.h"
```
We need the constant key names so we can populate the new dictionary.

```
@implementation AddDrinkViewController
```
We need to synthesize the new property.

```
@synthesize drinkArray;
```

AddDrinkViewController.m

Since we want to add keys and objects, we need to create a mutable dictionary. What problems could you run into later if you created an immutable version?

```
- (IBAction) save: (id) sender {
    NSLog(@"Save pressed!");

    // Create a new drink dictionary for the new values
    NSMutableDictionary* newDrink = [[NSMutableDictionary alloc] init];
    [newDrink setValue:nameTextField.text forKey:NAME_KEY];
    [newDrink setValue:ingredientsTextView.text forKey:INGREDIENTS_KEY];
    [newDrink setValue:directionsTextView.text forKey:DIRECTIONS_KEY];

    // Add it to the master drink array and release our reference
    [drinkArray addObject:newDrink];
    [newDrink release];

    // Then pop the detailed view
    [self.navigationController dismissModalViewControllerAnimated:YES];
}
- (void)dealloc {
    [drinkArray release];
    [super dealloc];
}
```

Use the key constants to add the drink information, then append it to the drink array.

Since we alloc'ed it, we need to release our reference.

And release our reference to the drinkArray when we clean up.

AddDrinkViewController.m

Nicole, ready to pamper her VIP guests.

Five-Minute Mystery

The Case of the Missing Reservations

Nicole has been a Maitre d' at Chez Platypus since it opened nearly 10 years ago. This upscale restaurant has a number of distinguished customers who like their dining experience to be just perfect. The VIP guest list hasn't changed in years and Nicole knows everyone's face. She sends them right to their favorite table when they show up and makes sure everything is just right. She's extremely efficient and the restaurant couldn't do without her... that is, until her recent, tragic, mistake.

Earlier this month Chez Platypus got a new investor. A prominent if eccentric Nobel Prize-winning scientist who is known for his particular tastes. Restaurant management dug up the dusty VIP list and added the scientist's name at the bottom, along with all the detailed instructions for making sure everything was "just so" when he arrived. They trusted that Nicole would would take good care of him and didn't give it another thought.

Last night, their new investor arrived a few minutes before some of the other VIP guests. Nicole didn't even notice him. She continued to move the regular VIPs to their seats and, for all she knew, their new investor did not even exist.

Why would Nicole ignore such an important new guest?

TEST DRIVE

That was a lot of code! Run the app and make sure everything is working. Here's a drink to add to the list (it's the new house drink in the Head First Lounge).

Add this to your app.

Red-Headed School Girl

Canadian whiskey

Cream soda

Add the whiskey, then the cream soda to a

shot glass and drink.

Test Drive

To properly test the app now, click the add button and enter the data for the new drink in the detail view. When you're finished, click save.

Now, what happens back in the list view?

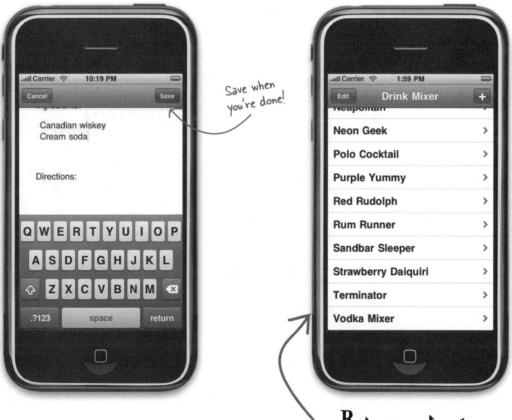

Save when you're done!

But your drink still isnt' there!

Exercise
Debugging

Something's wrong. We implemented the save method, created a new drink, added it to the array... and we're pretty sure all that code works. Before we move on, let's use the debugger and do a quick sanity check. Uncomment the `viewWillAppear` in RootViewController.m and set a breakpoint. Click "Build and Run" to start the application...

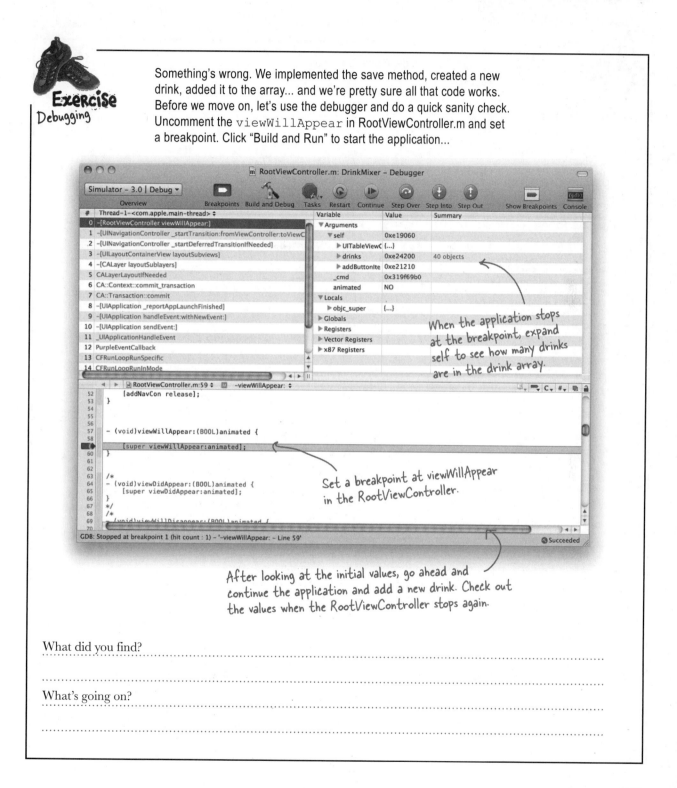

When the application stops at the breakpoint, expand self to see how many drinks are in the drink array.

Set a breakpoint at viewWillAppear in the RootViewController.

After looking at the initial values, go ahead and continue the application and add a new drink. Check out the values when the RootViewController stops again.

What did you find?
....
....

What's going on?
....
....

Exercise
Solution

Debugging

Now we're going to use the debugger to help us
figure out what's going on.

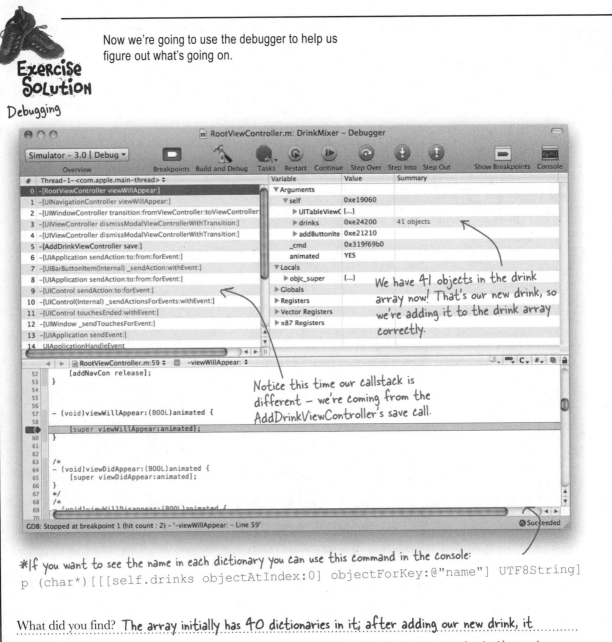

We have 41 objects in the drink
array now! That's our new drink, so
we're adding it to the drink array
correctly.

Notice this time our callstack is
different — we're coming from the
AddDrinkViewController's save call.

*If you want to see the name in each dictionary you can use this command in the console:
`p (char*)[[[self.drinks objectAtIndex:0] objectForKey:@"name"] UTF8String]`

What did you find? The array initially has 40 dictionaries in it; after adding our new drink, it
has one more. If we use that console command we can step through them and see that it's right.

What's going on? The tableview isn't picking up the new drink. We've added it to the drink array,
but it's not getting added to the actual view. It's like the table view doesn't know it's there...

The Case of the Missing Reservations Solved

Why would Nicole ignore such an important new guest?

Nicole hasn't needed to look at the VIP list in years. She was so concerned that their important customers feel welcome that she didn't want to have to do something as crass as go back and read a list every time someone arrived. She made a point of memorizing that list so when they came to the restaurant she could recognize and seat them immediately. As far as Nicole knew, there were 10 VIPs on that list and she knew them all.

The problem was that the list was changed and no one told her. All it would have taken was a simple "heads up" to Nicole that there was a change to the list and the restaurant's newest investor wouldn't have disappeared... along with his money.

Five-Minute Mystery Solved

The table view doesn't know its data has changed

The table view does a number of things to improve performance as much as possible. As a result, if you just change values in the datasource without telling it, it won't know that something has changed. In our case, we added a new value to the array used by our datasource but didn't let the table view know about it.

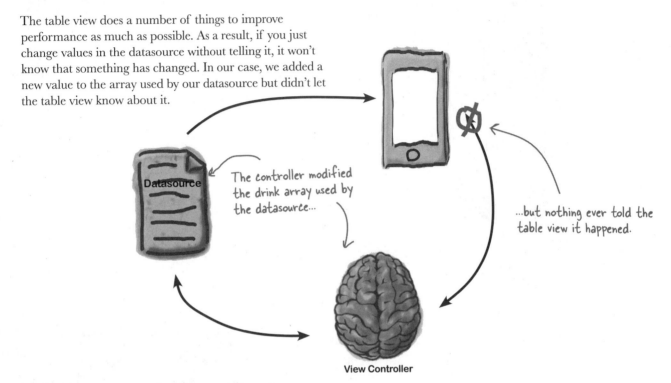

The controller modified the drink array used by the datasource...

...but nothing ever told the table view it happened.

View Controller

You need to ask the table view to reload its data

Since we're modifying the underlying data used by the datasource, the easiest way to refresh the table is to ask it to reload its data. You do this by sending it the `reloadData` message. This tells the tableview to reconstruct everything—how many sections it thinks it has, the headers and footers of those sections, its data rows, etc.

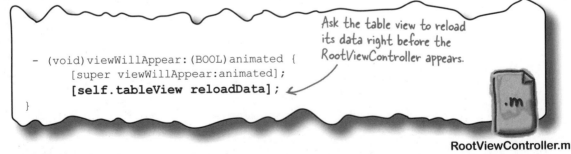

Ask the table view to reload its data right before the RootViewController appears.

```
- (void)viewWillAppear:(BOOL)animated {
    [super viewWillAppear:animated];
    [self.tableView reloadData];
}
```

RootViewController.m

Test Drive

Update your RootViewController.m to tell the table view to
refresh its data before the tableview is shown, and let's try
adding a new drink again.

Add this to
your app.

Red-Headed School Girl

Canadian whiskey

Cream soda

Add the whiskey, then the cream soda to a
shot glass and drink.

TEST DRIVE

To properly test the app now, click the add button and enter the data for the new drink in the detail view. When you're finished, click save.

Now, what happens back in the list view?

Save when you're done!

Canadian wiskey
Cream soda

Directions:

Drink Mixer

Polo Cocktail
Purple Yummy
Red Rudolph
Rum Runner
Sandbar Sleeper
Strawberry Daiquiri
Terminator
Vodka Mixer
Red-Headed School Girl

There it is...

there are no
Dumb Questions

Q: Telling the table to reload all its data seems pretty drastic. Is that really how I should do it?

A: It's the simplest way to refresh the table data, but not necessarily the most efficient. It depends on what you're doing to the table. If you're modifying the table while it's visible, you can call `beginUpdates` and `endUpdates` to tell it you're about to make a number of changes and it will animate those changes for you and let you avoid a `reloadData` call. There are also versions that only reload the specified rows or for a given section. Which you use depends on your application, how much you know about what changed in your data, and how big your dataset is.

Q: We didn't add any code to the cancel button. Don't we have to do something there?

A: Nope—the cancel button is coded to just dismiss the AddDrinkViewController. This will clean up any memory associated with the controller and throw away any data the user entered in the fields. As long as we don't manipulate the drink array, we've properly canceled any action the user started.

Q: Why can't I see the drink information in the debugger when I expand the drinks array and dictionaries?

A: This is one of the disadvantages of using a generic class like `NSMutableDictionary` for storing our drinks. The debugger knows the class is a dictionary, but that's about all it can tell us, since all of the keys and values are dynamic. You can get to them through the debugging console, but that's not as convenient as seeing real attributes on classes when you debug something.

Q: Did we really need to use the debugger back there? Couldn't I have just printed out how many items were in the array using NSLog?

A: Sure, but then you wouldn't have been able to practice debugging again... :-)

Uhh—that drink is at the end of the list, not in with the Rs.

⚛BRAIN POWER

Look back at our debugging work. Why is the drink showing up at the bottom of the table? What do we need to do?

The array is out of order, too

Our table view gets its information directly from our drink array. In fact, we just map the row number into an index in our array in `cellForRowAtIndexPath:`.

RootViewController.m

```
    // Configure the cell.
    cell.textLabel.text = [[self.drinks objectAtIndex:indexPath.row]
valueForKey:NAME_KEY];
```

We map the row number right into an index value for the array. So, row 41 is going to be whatever we have in the 41st spot in the array — namely, our new drink.

We can sort our array using NSSortDescriptor

In order to get the table view properly sorted, we need to sort our data array. NSSortDescriptors can do exactly that. You tell descriptors what to compare by specifying a property, how to compare them with an optional selector, and then which order to display the information in. In our case, we're looking for alphabetical sorting by the name of the drink.

We want the NSSortDescriptor to sort based on drink names.

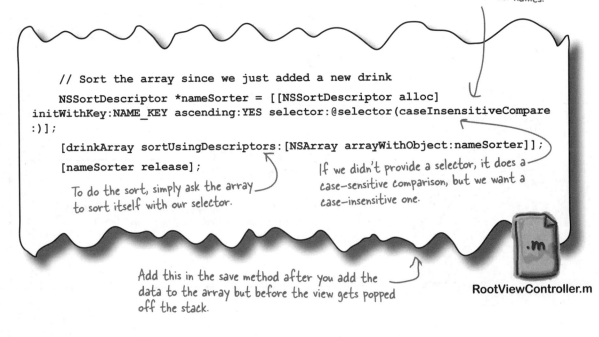

```
    // Sort the array since we just added a new drink

    NSSortDescriptor *nameSorter = [[NSSortDescriptor alloc]
initWithKey:NAME_KEY ascending:YES selector:@selector(caseInsensitiveCompare
:)];

    [drinkArray sortUsingDescriptors:[NSArray arrayWithObject:nameSorter]];

    [nameSorter release];
```

To do the sort, simply ask the array to sort itself with our selector.

If we didn't provide a selector, it does a case-sensitive comparison, but we want a case-insensitive one.

Add this in the save method after you add the data to the array but before the view gets popped off the stack.

.m

RootViewController.m

Test Drive

Add the sorting code to AddDrinkViewController, then run the app. Let's add another drink; this one should end up in the right place.

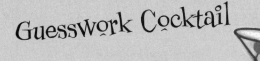

Guesswork Cocktail

Peach schnapps, gin, dry sherry, passion fruit juice, pineapple juice and lime juice

Shake together, strain into a cocktail glass and serve.

Great, that new drink is there, but what about the Red-Headed Schoolgirl from before? Don't we need to deal with saving more permanently?

All our data is lost when we quit...

We're positive we're updating the array with our new drink, but obviously that new array doesn't survive quitting and restarting our app.

What do we need to do? When should it happen?

Frank

Joe

Jim

Jim: OK, so we should save the array after each new drink is added, right? That will make sure we always have the right data.

Frank: Not so fast. Keep in mind the whole speed/memory management thing.

Joe: What's the problem? It's just a little array.

Frank: But that means you could be saving out every time you add a drink.

Jim: Oh, I see, that means we'll have to go through reading in the array and saving it back out multiple times. That does seem like a waste.

Joe: Well then, when are we supposed to do it?

Frank: When we exit! The app will keep the data present until it closes, then it's lost without some kind of save.

Jim: How do we do that? How can we tell when the user exits?

Frank: Hmm... what about that applicationWillTerminate method on our app delegate?

Joe: But the app delegate doesn't know anything about our drink list or where to save it...

Frank: Good point. The UIApplicationDelegate says there's a notification that goes out too. I bet we could use that...

there are no
Dumb Questions

Q: What notification tells us the application is quitting?

A: The iPhone OS will send out an UIApplicationWillTerminateNotification before your app exits.

Q: Do I need to register to receive it?

A: Yup—just like any other notification.

Q: What if the user hits the home button or the phone rings or...?

A: Anytime your application exits normally, either through your code or the user hitting a button or something else triggers the iPhone to switch applications (like a phone call the user decides to answer), you'll get the applicationWillTerminate. There's really only one case where you won't...

Q: What happens if my app crashes?

A: Then you're not going to get the notification. The data would be lost in this case. You need to balance how critical it is to make sure no data is lost with the performance impact of saving more frequently. In our case, we're just going to save on exit.

Sharpen your pencil

Use your skills at working with the API and what Jim, Frank, and Joe were discussing to figure out what to implement to save the array. Update your RootViewController.m and RootViewController.h to handle saving.

1 **Add the code to save out the new plist of dictionaries.**
Implement the method that will be called when the UIApplicationWillTerminateNotification is sent to save the plist. We're going to give you a little code snippet to use. This code will only work on the simulator, but we'll revisit this issue in Chapter 7.

```
NSString *path = [[NSBundle mainBundle]
    pathForResource:@"DrinkDirections" ofType:@"plist"];

[self.drinks writeToFile:path atomically:YES];
```

2 **Register for the UIApplicationWillTerminateNotification.**
We know that the applicationWillTerminate: method will be called on the AppDelegate when the application shuts down, but our RootViewController really owns all of the data. Have the RootViewController register for the UIApplicationWillTerminateNotification just like the AddDrinkViewController did, except add the registration and unregistration code to viewDidLoad and viewDidUnload, respectively.

 **Watch it!**

This code will only work in the simulator!

The code used to save the plist will work fine on the simulator, but fail miserably on a real device. The problem is with file permissions and where apps are allowed to store data. We'll talk a lot more about this in Chapter 7, but for now, go ahead with this version. This is a perfect example of things working on the simulator but behaving differently on a real device.

Sharpen your pencil
Solution

Use your skills at working with the API and what Jim, Frank, and Joe were discussing to figure out what to implement to save the array. Update your RootViewController.m and RootViewController.h to handle saving.

RootViewController.m

Add this to viewDidLoad.

```
// Register for application exiting information so we can save data
[[NSNotificationCenter defaultCenter] addObserver:self
     selector:@selector(applicationWillTerminate:)
     name:UIApplicationWillTerminateNotification object:nil];
```

Don't forget to declare this in RootViewController.h, too.

```
- (void)applicationWillTerminate:(NSNotification *)notification {
    NSString *path = [[NSBundle mainBundle]
         pathForResource:@"DrinkDirections" ofType:@"plist"];
    [self.drinks writeToFile:path atomically:YES];
}
```

This is the code that's going to give us problems on a real device. We'll run into this again (and fix it) in the next chapter—bear with us for now....

Add this to viewDidUnload.

```
// Unregister for notifications
[[NSNotificationCenter defaultCenter] removeObserver:self];
```

TEST DRIVE

Here it is!

Purple Crayon

Raspberry liqueur, vodka, and pineapple juice

Pour the liqueur and vodka over ice and then fill with pineapple juice and garnish with a grape.

Make sure when you run DrinkMixer the second time you tap on the icon in the simulator; don't hit Build and Debug again!

Author's note: we thought about showing the same screenshot twice, but figured that still wouldn't prove that it saves after hitting the home key and coming back in.

Watch it!

The stop and "Build and Run" in Xcode are NOT the same as the home key and relaunching the app in the simulator!

When you stop the app using Xcode's stop button, you are killing the app right then and there. No termination notifications are sent, no saving is done—it's just stopped. Likewise, when you click Build and Debug, Xcode will reinstall the application on your device before launching it. To test our load and save code, make sure you restart the app by tapping the icon in the simulator.

there are no
Dumb Questions

Q: So arrays know how to save themselves... Can I just put any object in there and have it save to a plist?

A: No —not just any old object. Arrays load and save using a Cocoa technique called NSCoding. Any objects you want to load an save must conform to the NSCoding protocol, which includes `initWithCoder` and `encodeWithCoder` method— basically, load and save. You'd need to conform to the NSCoding protocol and provide those methods to be serializable in and out of an array. However, NSDictionaries do conform to NSCoding (as do the strings inside of them), and that's why we can load and save so easily.

Q: What is the deal with giving us code that won't work on the device? What happens?

A: Well, to find out what happens, we encourage you to run it on a real device. Then think about why it isn't working the way you'd expect. We'll talk a lot more about this in the next chapter. To give you a hint, it has to with where we're trying to save the data. This is also a real world example of something working just fine in the simulator only to behave differently on a real device. You always need to test on both.

Q: Instead of registering for that quit notification, couldn't we have just updated the AppDelegate to get the drink array from the RootViewController and save it in the delegate?

A: Yes, you could. It's more of a style and design question than anything else. Right now the AppDelegate doesn't know anything about our plist, our drink array, or even the RootViewController, for that matter (other than making it visible). You could argue we'd be breaking encapsulation if we exposed what needs to be loaded and saved for each view up to the AppDelegate. Since we only need to save a single array, it's not a big deal either way, but if you have a number of views that need to save information or complex persistence code, it can often be cleaner to leave it with the class that needs to know about it rather than lumping it all into the AppDelegate. Technically speaking, though, either one would work.

Q: Why did we register and unregister in the viewDidLoad and viewDidUnload methods instead of the *Appear methods?

A: The problem is when and how often those methods are called. `viewWillAppear` is called whenever the view is about to be shown. That starts out OK—we'll get that call before the table view shows up and we can register. However,

the `viewWillDisappear` will be called right before we show the detail or add drink view controllers (since our RootViewController is about to be hidden).

If we unregister there we won't get the termination notification if the user decides to quit while looking at the details for a drink.

For example, say the user adds a new drink, goes back to the RootViewController then taps on his drink to make sure he entered it correctly. We show the detailed view, he's happy, then he quits the app. Our RootViewController has unregistered for the termination notification and the drink is lost. Instead, we use the load and unload methods, which are called when the view is loaded from the nib or unloaded. Since that view is in use throughout the application, those won't be called except at startup and shutdown.

Q: What's the deal with hitting "Build and Run" versus tapping on the icon to start DrinkMixer the second time?

A: It's because of how we're saving the data. We'll talk more about it in the next chapter, but the problem is when you hit "Build and Debug," Xcode compiles and installs the application onto the simulator. This means it's replacing the modified drink plist with the one that we ship with the application and you lose your drink. Which, everyone can agree, is very, very sad.

That's great! Now I can add the extra drinks I need. But there are a couple of other things that I need to really make this app work for me.

1 Delete drinks that aren't used to keep the list small and easy to use.

2 Edit the ingredients for drinks that were already in the list.

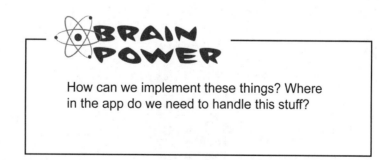

BRAIN POWER

How can we implement these things? Where in the app do we need to handle this stuff?

Table views have built-in support for editing and deleting

Good news! The table view comes complete with almost everything we need for deleting data. This is behavior that acts a bit like implementing a save or cancel button, and a lot of it comes preloaded.

Editing mode adds an edit button to the navigation control in the main view, and when it's pressed, indicators appear to the left of the table cell that can be selected and deleted like this:

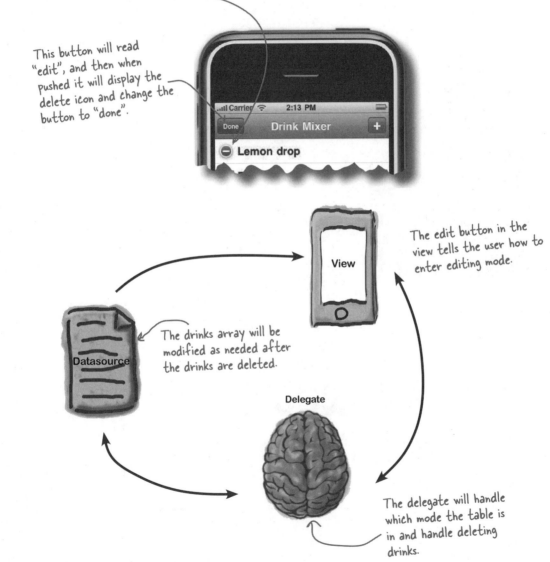

This button will read "edit", and then when pushed it will display the delete icon and change the button to "done".

The edit button in the view tells the user how to enter editing mode.

The drinks array will be modified as needed after the drinks are deleted.

The delegate will handle which mode the table is in and handle deleting drinks.

EDITING VIEW CONSTRUCTION

Using the view below, write what each part of the editing view does.

EDITING VIEW CONSTRUCTION SOLUTION

Using the view below, write what each part of the editing view does.

The Done button turns off editing mode and puts the table back to normal.

The + button is unchanged: it lets us add a new drink.

The delete icons let the user delete a row from the table.

When tapping on a row in edit mode, we should be able to edit a drink instead of just displaying it.

Exercise

The Xcode template comes with a good bit of the code we'll need, and at this point you're pretty familiar with the RootViewController and the table view. We'll give you some hints on what to implement next, but let you take it from here.

Add the edit button to the root view.

We need an edit button in the upper left of the navigation bar. The templated code for the UITableViewController comes with everything we need built-in; it's just a matter of uncommenting the line in viewDidLoad.

Implement the tableView:commitEditingStyle:forRowAtIndexPath.

Once the table view is in editing mode, we'll get a call when the user tries to delete a row either by swiping across the row or tapping the delete indicator. Most of this method is stubbed out for us too, but you'll need to add code to update the datasource with the change. Remember, we've been mapping rows to indexes in our array. Lastly, you don't need to call reloadData after this change because we ask the tableView to explicitly remove the row.

Update the didSelectRowAtIndexPath to add a drink.

Our AddDrinkViewController has nearly everything we need to be able to edit an existing drink. Update didSelectRowAtIndexPath to invoke the AddDrinkViewController instead of the DrinkDetailViewController if we're in editing mode.

4 Make sure Interface Builder knows it's editable.

Check that "Allow Selection While Editing" is checked for the Drinks table view.

5 Add the ability to edit a drink in our AddDrinkViewController.

You'll need to tell the app that it must edit a drink instead of creating a new one, then have it populate the controls with the existing information, and finally update the drink on save.

Exercise Solution

The Xcode template comes with a good bit of the code we'll need, and at this point you're pretty familiar with the RootViewController and the table view. We'll give you some hints on what to implement next, but let you take it from here.

1 **Add the edit button to the root view.**
We need an edit button in the upper left of the navigation bar. The templated code for the UITableViewController comes with everything we need built-in; it's just a matter of uncommenting the line in viewDidLoad.

In viewDidLoad

```
// Uncomment the following line to display an Edit button in the navigation bar
for this view controller.
self.navigationItem.leftBarButtonItem = self.editButtonItem;
```

The UITableViewController comes with built-in support for an edit button. All we need to do is add it to the nav bar.

RootViewController.m

2 **Implement the tableView:commitEditingStyle:forRowAtIndexPath.**
Once the table view is in editing mode, we'll get a call when the user tries to delete a row either by swiping across the row or tapping the delete indicator. Most of this method is stubbed out for us too, but you'll need to add code to update the datasource with the change. Remember, we've been mapping rows to indexes in our array. Lastly, you don't need to call reloadData after this change because we ask the tableView to explicitly remove the row.

```
// Override to support editing the table view.
- (void)tableView:(UITableView *)tableView commitEditingStyle:(UITableViewCellEdit
ingStyle)editingStyle forRowAtIndexPath:(NSIndexPath *)indexPath {
    if (editingStyle == UITableViewCellEditingStyleDelete) {
        // Delete the row from the data source.
        [self.drinks removeObjectAtIndex:indexPath.row];
        [tableView deleteRowsAtIndexPaths:[NSArray arrayWithObject:indexPath]
            withRowAnimation:UITableViewRowAnimationFade];
    }
    else if (editingStyle == UITableViewCellEditingStyleInsert) {
    }
}
```

Use removeObjectAtIndex to clean up our datasource.

RootViewController.m

Update the didSelectRowAtIndexPath to add a drink.
Our AddDrinkViewController has nearly everything we need to be able
to edit an existing drink. Update didSelectRowAtIndexPath to invoke the
AddDrinkViewController instead of the DrinkDetailViewController if we're in
editing mode.

```
// Override to support row selection in the table view.
- (void)tableView:(UITableView *)tableView didSelectRowAtIndexPath:(NSIndexPath *)
indexPath {
  if (!self.editing) {
    DrinkDetailViewController *drinkDetailViewController =
[[DrinkDetailViewController alloc] initWithNibName:@"DrinkDetailViewController"
bundle:nil];
    drinkDetailViewController.drink = [self.drinks objectAtIndex:indexPath.row];
    [self.navigationController pushViewController:drinkDetailViewController
animated:YES];
    [drinkDetailViewController release];
  }
  else {
    AddDrinkViewController *editingDrinkVC = [[AddDrinkViewController
alloc] initWithNibName:@"DrinkDetailViewController" bundle:nil];
    UINavigationController *editingNavCon = [[UINavigationController alloc]
initWithRootViewController:editingDrinkVC];
    editingDrinkVC.drink = [self.drinks objectAtIndex:indexPath.row];
    editingDrinkVC.drinkArray = self.drinks;
    [self.navigationController presentModalViewController:editingNavCon
animated:YES];
    [editingDrinkVC release];
    [editingNavCon release];
  }
}
```

First we need to check to see if we're
in editing mode. If not, just display
the normal detail view.

If we are in editing mode, create an
AddDrinkViewController and set the drink to
edit in addition to our drink array. We'll fix
up the AddDrinkViewController in a minute...

.m

RootViewController.m

④ **Make sure Interface
Builder knows it's
editable.**
Check that "Allow Selection
While Editing" is checked
for the Drinks table view.

Table View

Style	Plain
Separator	Single Line
Section Index Row Count	0

☑ Allow Selection While Editing
☑ Show Selection On Touch

Scroll View

**Just the
AddDrink
ViewController
left...**

Exercise Solution

The Xcode template comes with a good bit of the code we'll need, and at this point you're pretty familiar with the RootViewController and the table view. We'll give you some hints on what to implement next, but let you take it from here.

⑤ Add the ability to edit a drink in our AddDrinkViewController.
You'll need to tell it that it must edit a drink instead of creating a new one, then have it populate the controls with the existing information, and finally update the drink on save.

```objc
- (void)viewWillAppear: (BOOL)animated {
    [super viewWillAppear:animated];

    NSLog(@"Registering for keyboard events");
    [[NSNotificationCenter defaultCenter] addObserver:self
            selector:@selector(keyboardWillShow:)
            name:UIKeyboardWillShowNotification object:self.view.window];

    [[NSNotificationCenter defaultCenter] addObserver:self
            selector:@selector(keyboardWillHide:)
            name:UIKeyboardDidHideNotification object:nil];

    // Initially the keyboard is hidden, so reset our variable
    keyboardVisible = NO;

    if (self.drink != nil) {
        nameTextField.text = [self.drink objectForKey:NAME_KEY];
        ingredientsTextView.text = [self.drink objectForKey:INGREDIENTS_
KEY];

        directionsTextView.text = [self.drink objectForKey:DIRECTIONS_
KEY];
    }
}
```

If we have a drink set, that means we're supposed to edit that drink rather than create a new one. We'll need to populate our fields with the current drink information.

AddDrinkViewController.m

```
- (IBAction) save: (id) sender {
        NSLog(@"Save pressed!");

        if (drink != nil) {
            // We're working with an existing drink, so let's remove
            // it from the array to get ready for a new one
            [drinkArray removeObject:drink];
            self.drink = nil; // This will release our reference too
        }


        // Now create a new drink dictionary for the new values
        NSMutableDictionary* newDrink = [[NSMutableDictionary alloc] init];
        [newDrink setValue:nameTextField.text forKey:NAME_KEY];
        [newDrink setValue:ingredientsTextView.text forKey:INGREDIENTS_KEY];
        [newDrink setValue:directionsTextView.text forKey:DIRECTIONS_KEY];


        // Add it to the master drink array and release our reference
        [drinkArray addObject:newDrink];
        [newDrink release];


        // Then sort it since the name might have changed with an existing
        // drink or it's a completely new one.
    NSSortDescriptor *nameSorter = [[NSSortDescriptor alloc] initWithKey:NAME_KEY
ascending:YES selector:@selector(caseInsensitiveCompare:)];
        [drinkArray sortUsingDescriptors:[NSArray arrayWithObject:nameSorter]];
    [nameSorter release];


        // Then pop the detailed view
        [self.navigationController dismissModalViewControllerAnimated:YES];
}
```

If there's a drink set, then we need to update it. We can either update the existing object or replace it. Since we need to resort the whole array anyway (in case the drink name changed), we just remove the old one and re-add it.

AddDrinkViewController.m

TEST DRIVE

Make the editing changes to your app and give it a shot. You should be able to remove drinks and fine-tune them all you want. Remember to restart your app by tapping on the icon, though; otherwise, you'll lose your changes.

Resubmit your app to the store and...

Here's DrinkMixer at #1!
Congratulations!

NavigationControllercross

Let's check your scroll view, nav control, and table view buzz words!

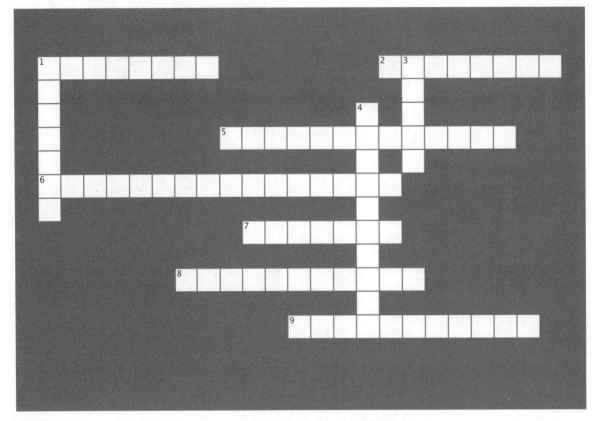

Across

1. A field that the user can change is _____.
2. Arrays load and save using _____.
5. System-level events that can be passed are called _____.
6. Sort data using the _____.
7. All the sytem events go through the _____ center.
8. The scroll view won't work without setting the _____.
9. viewWillAppear and _____ are called at different times.

Down

1. Table views have built-in support for _____.
3. Keyboard events tell you about the _____ and size of the keyboard.
4. The _____ handles the scroll bar, panning, zooming, and what content is displayed in the view.

Q: I like the automatic editing support in the table view, but how do I do those cool "Add New Address" rows that the iPhone has when you edit a contact?

A: It's a lot easier than you think. Basically, when you're in editing mode you tell the table view you have one more row than you actually have in your data. Then, in cellForRowAtIndexPath, check to see if the row the table view is asking for is one past the end. If it is, return a cell that says "Add New Address" or whatever. Finally, in your didSelectRowAtIndexPath, check to see if the selected row is one past your data, and if so, you know it was the selected row.

Q: We haven't talked about moving rows around, but I've seen tables do that. Is it hard?

A: No, the table view part is really easy; it's the datasource part that can be tricky. If you support moving rows around, simply implement the method tableview:move RowAtIndexPath:toIndexPath (the tableview checks to see if you provide this method before allowing the user to rearrange cells). The users will see a row handle on the side of the cells when they're in editing mode. When they move a row, you'll get a call to your new method that provides the IndexPath the row started at and the IndexPath for the new position. It's your job to update your datasource to make sure they stay that way. You can also implement

tableview:canMoveRowAtIndexPath to only allow the users to move certain rows. There are even finer-grained controls in the delegate if you're interested, such as preventing the users from moving a cell to a certain section.

Q: What if I don't want the users to be able to delete a row? Can I still support editing for some of the rows?

A: Absolutely. Just implement tableview: canEditRowAtIndexPath: and return NO for the rows you don't want to be editable.

Q: When we edit a drink, we replace the object in the array. What if we had some other view that had a reference to the original?

A: Great question. The short answer is you're going to have a problem, no matter how you handle it. If some other view has a reference to the object we removed, that's not tragic since the retain count should still be at least 1; the object won't get dealloced when we remove it. However, the other views obviously won't see any of the changes the user made since we're putting them in a new dictionary. Even if they had the old dictionary, they wouldn't have any way of knowing the values changed. There are a few ways you could handle this. One option is you could change our code to leave the original object in the array and modify it in place, then make sure that any other view you have refreshes itself on viewWillAppear

or something along those lines. Another option is you could send out a custom notification that the drink array changed or that a particular drink was modified. Interested views can register to receive that notification.

Q: Aren't we supposed to be concerned about efficiency? Isn't removing the drink and reading it inefficient?

A: It's not the most efficient way since it requires finding the object in the array and removing it before reinserting it, but for the sake of code clarity we decided it was simpler to show. We'd have to re-sort the array regardless of which approach we took, however, since the name of the drink (and its place alphabetically) could change with the edit.

Q: We added the edit button on the left-hand side of the detail view, but what about a back button? Isn't that where they usually go?

A: That's true. When you get into having an add button, an edit button, and a back button, you run into a real estate problem. The way we solved it was fine, but you'll need to make sure that your app flows the way you need it to when your navigation controller starts to get crowded.

NavigationControllercross Solution

Let's check your scroll view, nav control, and table view buzz words!

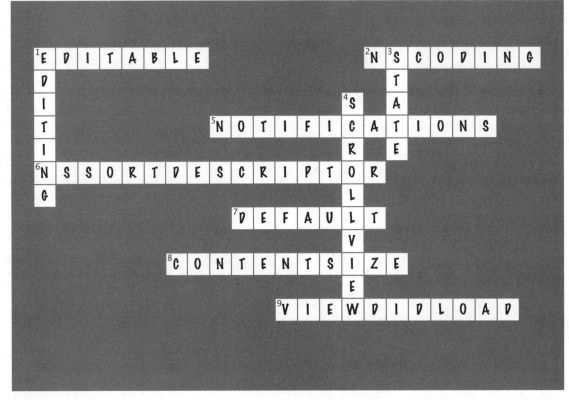

Across

1. A field that the user can change is _____.
   [EDITABLE]
2. Arrays load and save using _____. [NSCODING]
5. System-level events that can be passed are called
   _____. [NOTIFICATIONS]
6. Sort data using the _____.
   [NSSORTDESCRIPTOR]
7. All the sytem events go through the _____
   center. [DEFAULT]
8. The scroll view won't work without setting the
   _____. [CONTENTSIZE]
9. viewWillAppear and _____ are called at different
   times. [VIEWDIDLOAD]

Down

1. Table views have built-in support for _____.
   [EDITING]
3. Keyboard events tell you about the _____ and size of
   the keyboard. [STATE]
4. The _____ handles the scroll bar, panning,
   zooming, and what content is displayed in the view.
   [SCROLLVIEW]

300   Chapter 6

Your iPhone Development Toolbox

**You've got Chapter 6 under your belt
and now you've added saving, editing,
and sorting data to your toolbox. For a
complete list of tooltips in the book, go to
http://www.headfirstlabs.com/iphonedev.**

Scroll View

Acts like a lens to show only the
part of the view you need and
scrolls the rest off the screen.

Needs to be given a contentSize
to work properly.

Can be easily constructed in
Interface Builder

Sorting

Arrays can be sorted using
NSSortDescriptors.

Table View Editing

There's built-in support for
editing a table view.

The edit button comes with lots
of functionality, including methods
to delete rows from the table
view.

Notifications

Are system-level events that you
can monitor and use in your app.

The default notification center
handles most notifications.

Different frameworks use
different notifications, or you can
create your own.

7 tab bars and core data

~~Bounty hunter apps~~ Enterprise apps

Here's what I 've found: we just can't be competitive anymore without an iPhone app!

Enterprise apps mean managing more data in different ways.

Companies large and small are a significant market for iPhone apps. A small handheld device with a custom app can be huge for companies that have staff on the go. Most of these apps are going to manage lots of data, and iPhone 3.x has built in Core Data support. Working with that and another new controller, the tab bar controller, we're going to build an app for justice!

HF bounty hunting

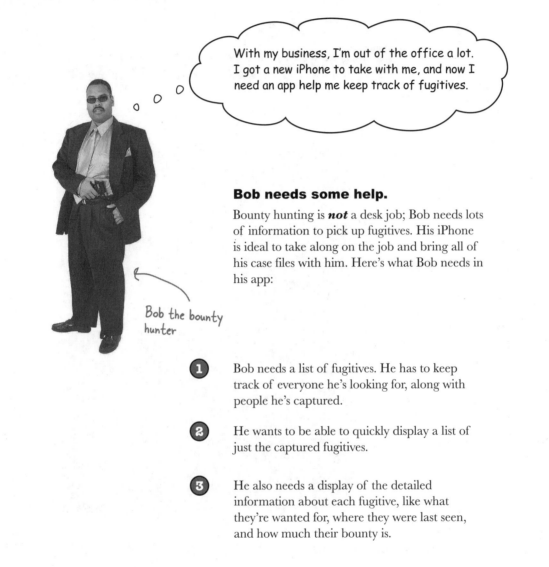

With my business, I'm out of the office a lot. I got a new iPhone to take with me, and now I need an app help me keep track of fugitives.

Bob the bounty hunter

Bob needs some help.

Bounty hunting is *not* a desk job; Bob needs lots of information to pick up fugitives. His iPhone is ideal to take along on the job and bring all of his case files with him. Here's what Bob needs in his app:

1. Bob needs a list of fugitives. He has to keep track of everyone he's looking for, along with people he's captured.

2. He wants to be able to quickly display a list of just the captured fugitives.

3. He also needs a display of the detailed information about each fugitive, like what they're wanted for, where they were last seen, and how much their bounty is.

Sharpen your pencil

Time for some design work. You have Bob's requirements—take them and sketch up what you think we'll need for this app.

Sharpen your pencil
Solution

We're going to need three views. Using Bob's
parameters, here's what we came up with.

1 Bob needs a list of fugitives. He keeps
track of everyone he's looking for or
has captured.

2 Joe wants to be able to quickly display a
list of just the captured fugitives.

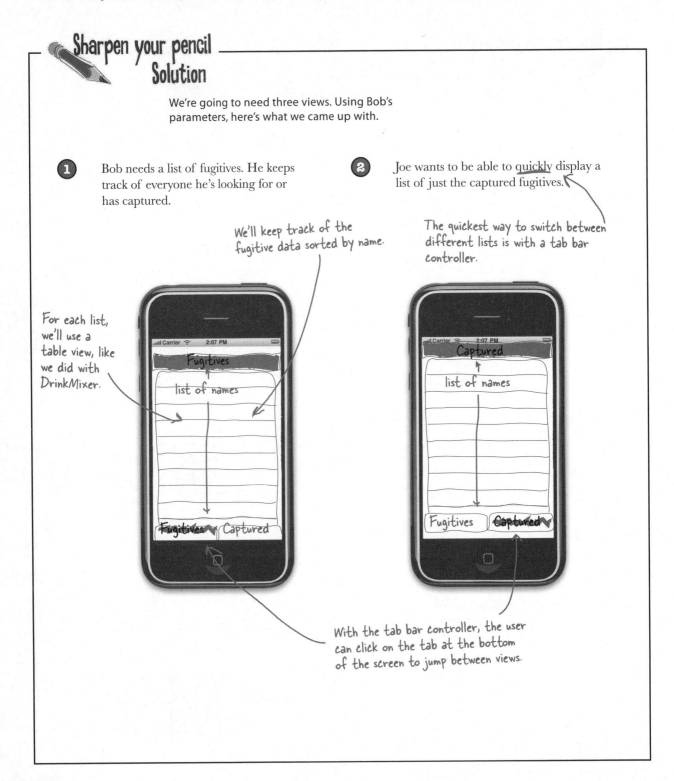

We'll keep track of the
fugitive data sorted by name.

The quickest way to switch between
different lists is with a tab bar
controller.

For each list,
we'll use a
table view, like
we did with
DrinkMixer.

With the tab bar controller, the user
can click on the tab at the bottom
of the screen to jump between views.

Sharpen your pencil
Solution

3 Bob wants a display of the detailed information about each fugitive.

For managing the data we're going to use new iPhone 3.x technology, Core Data. It can manage a lot of different data types for your app.

The detail view for each fugitive will be available by clicking on any name.

This area is for notes and details about the fugitive

The tab bar controller will still be visible.

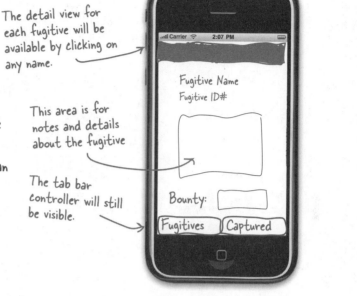

Fugitive Name
Fugitive ID#

Bounty:

| Fugitives | Captured |

Tab Bar Up Close

The tab bar controller is another common iPhone interface. Unlike the navigation controller, there isn't really a stack. All of the views are created up front and easily accessed by clicking the tab, with each tab being tied to a specific view.

Tab bars are better suited to tasks or data that are related, but not necessarily hierarchical. The UITabBarController keeps track of all of the views and swaps between them based on user input.

Standard iPhone apps that have tab bar controllers include the phone app, and the iPod.

The tab bar can contain any view you need.

The tabs themselves can contain text and/or an image.

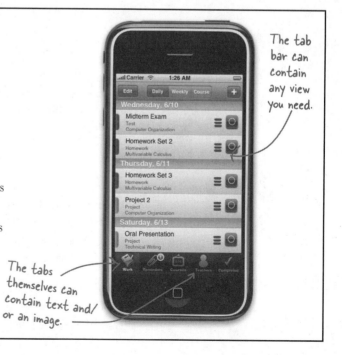

Choose a template to start iBountyHunter

This time around, we have a lot going on in our app. A navigation controller, a tab bar, and Core Data, too. Core Data is an optional add-on to many of the templates, including the basic window-based app. We're going to start with the window-based app and add the tab bar and the navigation controller with interface builder and a little bit of code.

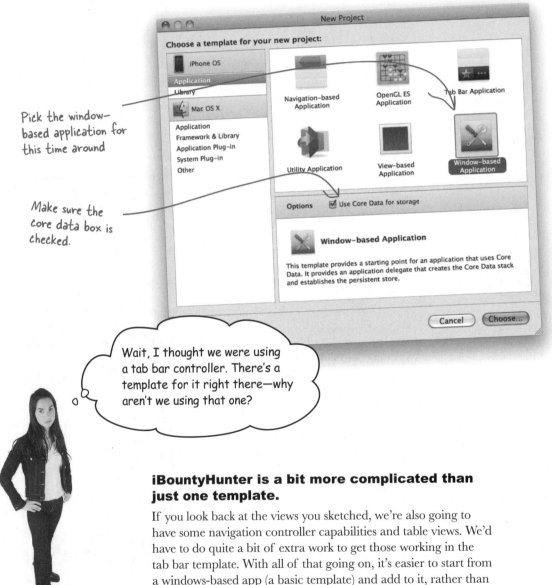

Pick the window-based application for this time around

Make sure the core data box is checked.

Wait, I thought we were using a tab bar controller. There's a template for it right there—why aren't we using that one?

iBountyHunter is a bit more complicated than just one template.

If you look back at the views you sketched, we're also going to have some navigation controller capabilities and table views. We'd have to do quite a bit of extra work to get those working in the tab bar template. With all of that going on, it's easier to start from a windows-based app (a basic template) and add to it, rather than working with a template that doesn't quite fit our needs.

Jim

Joe

Frank

Jim: OK, what do we do now? All we have is an empty view.

Joe: Well, we need to add two table views, the tab bar navigation controller to switch between those views, and the detail view.

Frank: So do we need a bunch of new nib files to handle all these views and controls?

Jim: Ugh. This basic template gave us nothing!

Joe: It's not so bad. I like to think of it as a blank slate. Let's see, we can start with the tab bar and tab bar controller...

Frank: Right, that will switch between the two table views for Fugitive and Captured. Those views will each need nav controllers as well, to get in and out of the detailed view.

Joe: So do we need separate nibs for the tab bar and those two views? It seems like maybe we could have all those controls in just one nib, for the tab bar and the two views, since they're basically the same.

Jim: Yeah, but we'd still need view controllers, headers, and .m files for each of those views.

Joe: Yup, they're the views that need the tables in them. We'd also need a detail view with it's own nib and view controller, with the .h and .m files, right?

Frank: That sounds about right. We can use Interface Builder to create the tab bar and navigation controllers.

Joe: What do we do about the rest of the stuff? Add new files in Xcode?

Frank: That'll work—like before, we just need to specify that the nib files are created at the same time, and we should be good to go.

Jim: I think that all makes sense—it's a lot to keep track of.

Joe: Well, we're combining like three different things now, so it's definitely going to get more complicated! Maybe it would help to diagram how this will all fit together?

Drawing how iBountyHunter works...

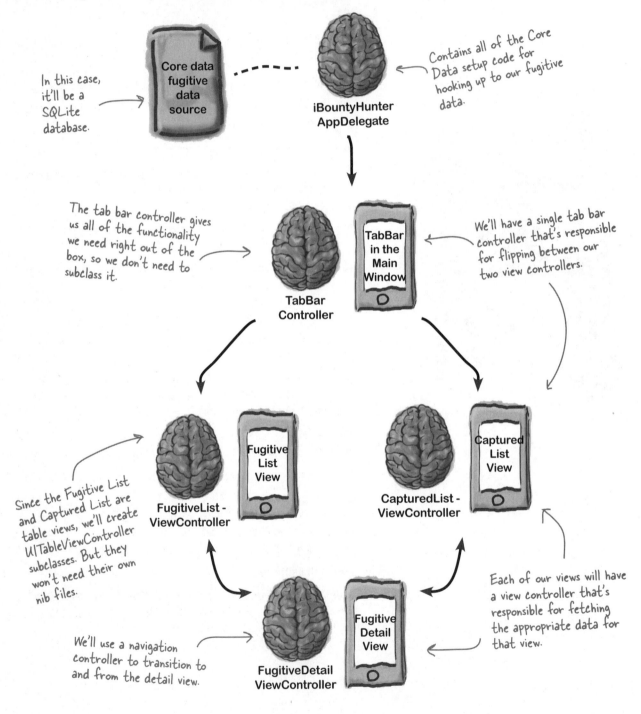

In this case, it'll be a SQLite database.

Core data fugitive data source

iBountyHunter AppDelegate

Contains all of the Core Data setup code for hooking up to our fugitive data.

The tab bar controller gives us all of the functionality we need right out of the box, so we don't need to subclass it.

TabBar Controller

TabBar in the Main Window

We'll have a single tab bar controller that's responsible for flipping between our two view controllers.

Since the Fugitive List and Captured List are table views, we'll create UITableViewController subclasses. But they won't need their own nib files.

FugitiveList - ViewController

Fugitive List View

CapturedList - ViewController

Captured List View

We'll use a navigation controller to transition to and from the detail view.

FugitiveDetail ViewController

Fugitive Detail View

Each of our views will have a view controller that's responsible for fetching the appropriate data for that view.

Joe: That helps a lot. So we only need two nibs, one to handle the controls for the tab bar switching between Fugitive and Captured views, and another to handle the detail view.

Frank: I get it. We need to put the table view components somewhere, and we can either create new nibs for each view and have the tab controller load them...

Jim: ...or we can just include it all in one nib. Easy!

Frank: Exactly. Since we don't plan to reuse those table views anywhere else and they're not too complicated, we can keep everything a bit simpler with just one nib.

Jim: And we need view controllers for the two table views, along with the detail view. They'll handle gettting the right data, depending on which view the user is in.

Frank: Plus a navigation controller for the table views to transition to and from the detail view.

Joe: I think we're ready to start building!

iBountyHunter To Do List

1. Create view controllers (both .h and .m files) for the Fugitive and Captured views
2. Create the tab bar view, and add the tab bar controller to it along with a reference from the app delegate.
3. Add the nav controllers for the Fugitive and Captured views.
4. Build the table views for the Fugitive and Captured views.
5. Create a detail view with a nib, and a view controller with .h and .m files.

there are no
Dumb Questions

Q: Why are we using a tab bar controller *and* a table view?

A: Our Fugitive data is hierarchical and lends itself well to a table view. The problem is, we have two table views: the fugitive list and the captured list. To support two top-level lists, we chose a tab bar.

Q: Couldn't you have done something similar with a toggle switch, like a UISegmentControl?

A: Yes, we could have. It's really a UI design choice. The two lists are really different lists, not just different ways of sorting or organizing the same data. It's subjective, though.

Q: OK, I'm still a bit confused about the business with using just one nib for the tab controller and the two table views.

A: Well, there is a lot going on in this app, and we could have done this a different way. We could create two more nibs, each with a nav controller and a table view in it. Then we'd tell the tab bar controller to load the first one as the Fugitive List and the second one as the Captured List. Rather than do that, we just put all those controls for the list in the same nib as the tab bar. Remember, the nib is just the UI controls, not the behavior.

Q: Seriously, though—this is a better approach than just using the Tab Bar template and adjusting it based on what we need?

A: That is definitely an option. However, if we look at using the TabBar template, it comes with two branches, with one broken out into a nib to show that you can do it and the other right in the same nib (to show you could do that too). So we'd have to change one, or continue splitting the approach, which can get ugly pretty quick. We'd also have to change a ton of the default configurations, half of which are in another nib, and half of which are embedded. In the end, this approach was less complicated and built on the methods you've already learned thus far.

Do this!

Add an icon for your app.
You're about to whip up a lot of code. Before you dive in, go to http://www.headfirstlabs.com/iphonedev and download the iBountyHunter icon (ibountyicon.png) and drop it in your new project in the **/Resources** folder. Then open up iBountyHunter-info.plist in Xcode and type the name of the file in the icon entry.

Icon files need to be 57 x 57 pixels.

Key	Value
▼ Information Property List	(12 items)
Localization native development re	English
Bundle display name	${PRODUCT_NAME}
Executable file	${EXECUTABLE_NAME}
Icon file	ibountyicon.png
Bundle identifier	com.yourcompany.${PRODUCT_NAME:rfc1034identifier}
InfoDictionary version	6.0
Bundle name	${PRODUCT_NAME}
Bundle OS Type code	APPL
Bundle creator OS Type code	????
Bundle version	1.0
LSRequiresIPhoneOS	☑
Main nib file base name	MainWindow

Create your two new classes for the Fugitive and Captured
views in Xcode, and then add your tab bar controller in
Interface Builder.

①   **Create two new classes with .m, and .h. files.**
These will be the view controllers for the Fugitive List
and the Captured List. FugitiveListViewController.h
and .m and CapturedListViewController.h and .m both
need to be subclasses of UITableViewController, so select
"UIViewController subclass" and check UITableViewController
subclass.

②   **Add the tab bar controller.**
In Interface Builder, open the MainWindow.xib to get started,
and drop the tab bar controller in the view.

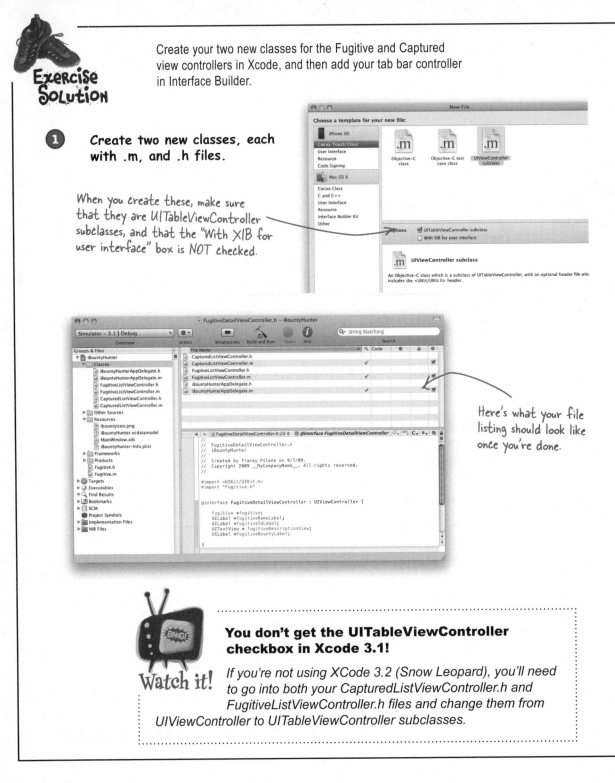

Create your two new classes for the Fugitive and Captured
view controllers in Xcode, and then add your tab bar controller
in Interface Builder.

Exercise Solution

① **Create two new classes, each with .m, and .h files.**

When you create these, make sure that they are UITableViewController subclasses, and that the "With XIB for user interface" box is NOT checked.

Here's what your file listing should look like once you're done.

You don't get the UITableViewController checkbox in Xcode 3.1!

If you're not using XCode 3.2 (Snow Leopard), you'll need to go into both your CapturedListViewController.h and FugitiveListViewController.h files and change them from UIViewController to UITableViewController subclasses.

Watch it!

② **Add the tab bar controller.**

The window template doesn't give us a whole
lot out of the box. We're going to use Interface
Builder to assemble our views and view
controllers the way we want them.

*The template comes with an empty
UIWindow. It's the window that our app
delegate will display when it starts.*

Drag the tab bar controller from the Library into your
main window listing. This will create your TabController
view:

*The tab bar
controller comes
with a tab bar and
two built-in view
controllers, but we're
going to change those
shortly...*

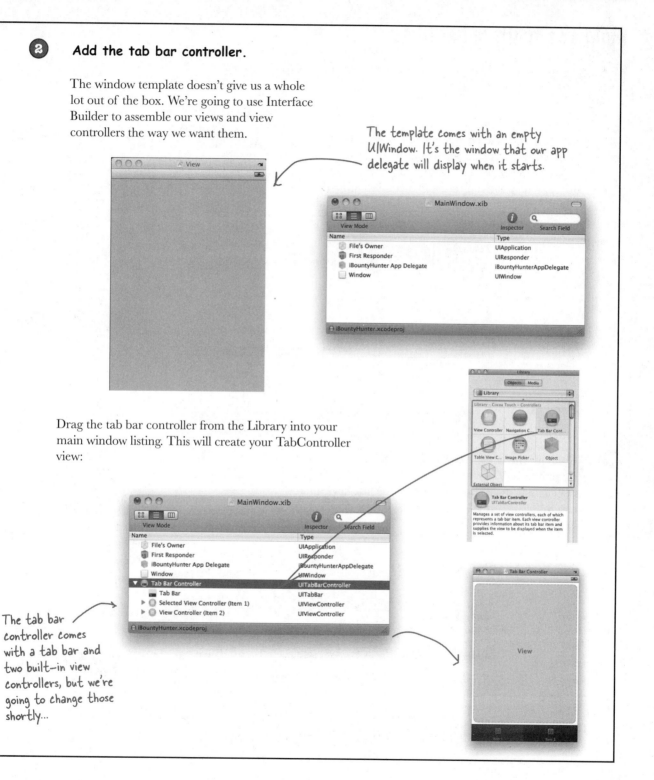

Build the fugitive list view

We're going to focus on the Fugitive List first, but the same steps will apply to the Captured List when we get to it.

 Delete those two view controllers and replace them with navigation controllers.
Since we want all of the functionality that comes with a nav controller, delete those the view controllers and drag two new nav controllers in their place from the Library. Make sure they're listed underneath the tab bar controller.

Nothing's changed in the view—the main window listing just reflects what you've updated

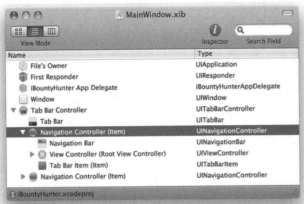

② Change the view controller to the FugitiveListView controller.
Highlight the view controller under the first navigation controller and use ⌘4 to change the **Class** to FugitiveListViewController.

The navigation controller comes with a default UIViewController. We don't want the default; we want it to use our Fugitive List view controller.

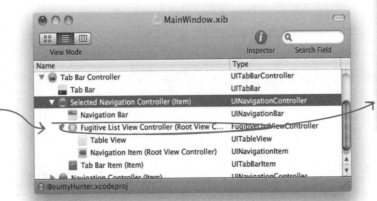

3 **Add the table view.**

Now that you've changed your first navigation controller to use the FugitiveListViewController, it needs a view. Drag a table view from the Library over as a child for that view controller.

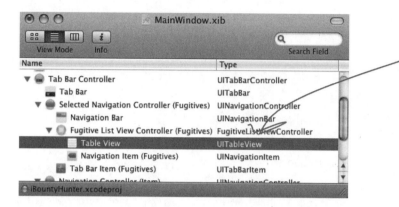

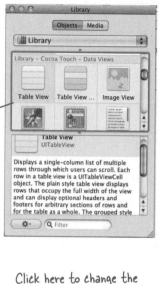

4 **Set the names in the tabbar and navbar.**

To change the title for the Fugitive List view controller, double-click on the title in the nav bar and type "Fugitives". For the tab, click on the first item, ⌘1, change the **Bar Item Title** to "Fugitives".

Click here to change the view controller title.

Updated nav controller title is changed with the badge item.

Updated bar item title

What's next?

Next up: the captured view

You've just gone through and created the classes for your two table views, and
dropped in a tab controller to switch between the two.

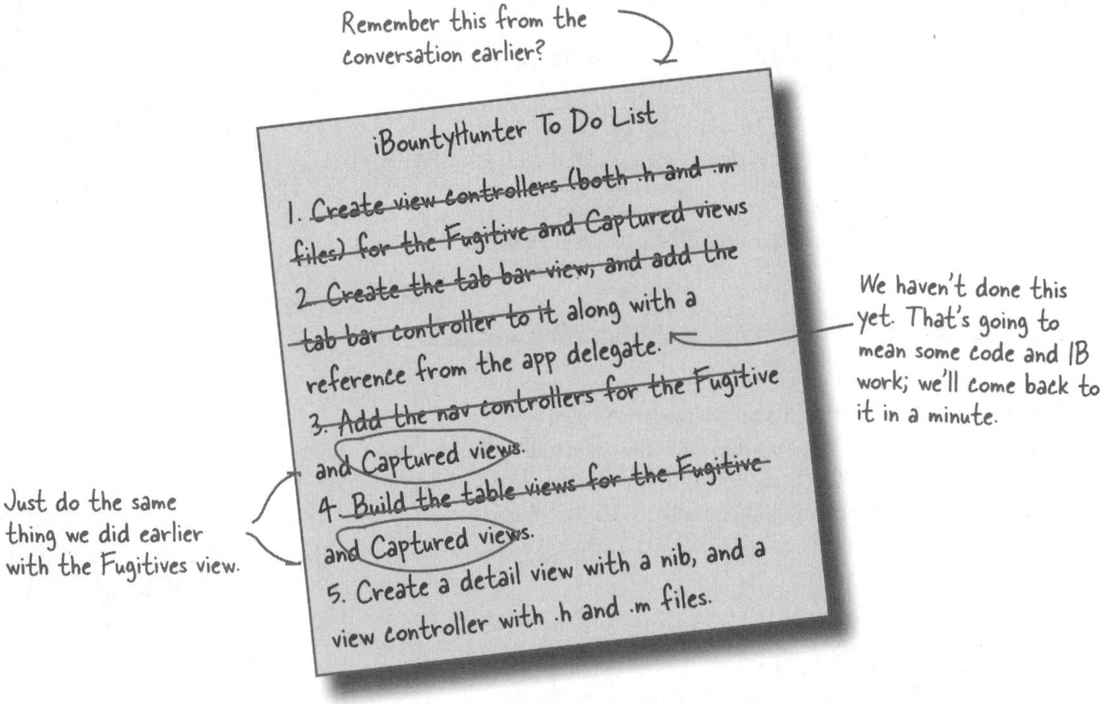

Remember this from the
conversation earlier?

iBountyHunter To Do List

1. ~~Create view controllers (both .h and .m~~
~~files) for the Fugitive and Captured views~~
2. ~~Create the tab bar view, and add the~~
~~tab bar controller to it~~ along with a
reference from the app delegate.
3. ~~Add the nav controllers for the Fugitive~~
and Captured views.
4. ~~Build the table views for the Fugitive~~
and Captured views.
5. Create a detail view with a nib, and a
view controller with .h and .m files.

We haven't done this
yet. That's going to
mean some code and IB
work; we'll come back to
it in a minute.

Just do the same
thing we did earlier
with the Fugitives view.

BE the Developer
Your job is to be developer and finish up the work in Xcode and Interface Builder to get the Fugitive and Captured views working with the tab bar controller. Use the to-do list from Jim, Frank, and Joe to figure out what's left.

It's up to you to create the captured view, and then connect the views up with the tab bar controller...

BE the Developer Solution

Your job is to be the developer and finish up the work in Xcode and Interface Builder to get the Fugitive and Captured views working.

Create your captured view.

Follow the same steps from earlier for creating the Fugitive view.

You should end up with a list that looks like this.

Then wire up the tab bar controller.

To do this, we need to go back to the AppDelegate. Right now, there isn't an outlet to connect the tab bar controller to anything, so it won't work. You should be pretty familiar with how to do this by now. Here's the outlet you need for a tab controller:

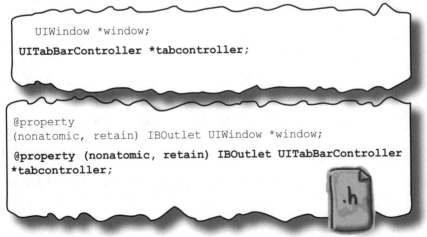

```
    UIWindow *window;

UITabBarController *tabcontroller;
```

```
@property
(nonatomic, retain) IBOutlet UIWindow *window;

@property (nonatomic, retain) IBOutlet UITabBarController
*tabcontroller;
```

iBountyHunterAppDelegate.h

Almost there...

Here we'll need to wire up the App Delegate to the Tab Bar Controller.

```
@synthesize window;
@synthesize tabcontroller;
```

iBountyHunterAppDelegate.m

```
[persistentStoreCoordinator release];

[tabcontroller release];
```

there are no Dumb Questions

Q: We have a lot jammed in our main window nib. It still seems kinda strange to me.

A: The nib for iBountyHunter contains five controllers (the tab bar, two nav controllers, and our FugitiveListViewController and CapturedListViewController) and their associated components. If you're still having trouble with the idea, it might help to open the MainWindow.xib file in Interface Builder and view it in tree mode. Expanding the hierarchy shows the structure of our app. We have a single nib with a tab bar controller, which internally has two nav controllers nested underneath it that are instances of FugitiveListViewController and CapturedListViewController, respectively.

Q: Can I add icons to the tab bar tabs?

A: Absolutely. The easiest way is to pick a standard icon using Interface Builder. To do that, click on the question mark icon on the tab you want to change, then change the Identifier in the Inspector. If you want to use a custom image, set the Identifier to custom, then select your image in the Image field (you'll need to add it to your project, just like we did with the application icon earlier). There are a couple of peculiarities with Tab Bar icons, though: they should be 30x30 and the alpha values in the icon are used to actually create the image. You can't specify colors or anything like that.

Q: How many views can I have in a tabbar?

A: As many as you want. If you add more views than can fit across the tab bar at the bottom, the UITabBarController will automatically add a "More" item and show the rest in a table view. By default, the UITabBarController also includes an Edit button that lets the user edit which tabs are on the bottom bar.

Q: Is there anyway of knowing when a user switches tabs?

A: Yes, there's a UITabBarDelegate protocol you can conform to and set as the tab bar delegate. You'll be notified when the users are customizing the bottom bar and when they change tabs.

Q: Why did we add a reference to the tab bar controller in the App Delegate?

A: We've added the tab bar controller to the nib, but there's a little more tweaking we're going to have to do to get everything displaying properly. Go ahead and give it a Test Drive to see what's going on...

Test Drive

You've just done a lot of work on your app—new view controllers, new nav controllers, table views—all from scratch. Build and run to make sure that everything's working.

Ugh! Nothing! Why isn't the tab bar controller (or anything else) being displayed?

Sharpen your pencil

Figure out what's going on. Look at what we did earlier in Interface Builder and see if you can figure out where we went wrong...

....

....

....

....

....

....

....

....

....

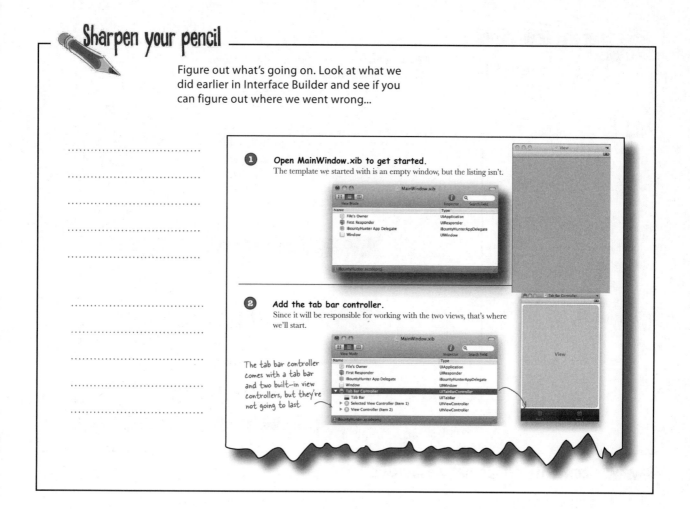

1 **Open MainWindow.xib to get started.**
The template we started with is an empty window, but the listing isn't.

2 **Add the tab bar controller.**
Since it will be responsible for working with the two views, that's where we'll start.

The tab bar controller comes with a tab bar and two built-in view controllers, but they're not going to last.

Sharpen your pencil
Solution

Figure out what's going on. Look at what we did earlier in Interface Builder and see if you can figure out where we went wrong...

The problem is that the tab bar is a top-level element in the nib. The AppDelegate has the UIWindow as its window, so the delegate will display that window. But the UIWindow doesn't contain anything—it has no subviews.

We need to embed the tab bar controller into the UIWindow.

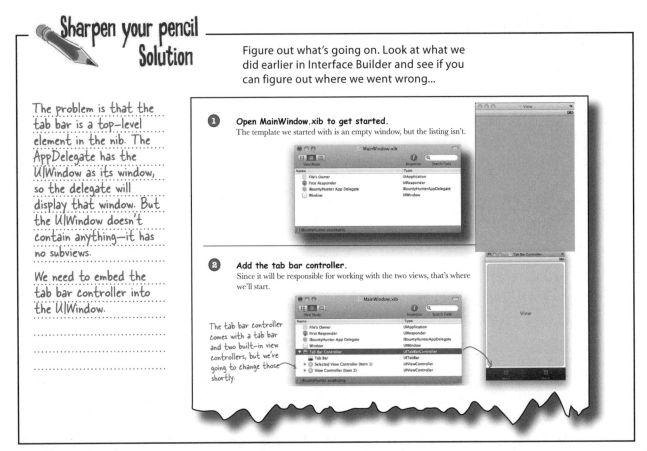

1 **Open MainWindow.xib to get started.**
The template we started with is an empty window, but the listing isn't.

2 **Add the tab bar controller.**
Since it will be responsible for working with the two views, that's where we'll start.

The tab bar controller comes with a tab bar and two built-in view controllers, but we're going to change those shortly.

A view's contents are actually subviews

All of the UI components we've used are subclasses of UIView. By dropping them into a view we've made them subviews of some bigger, container view. We need to do the same thing with our tab bar; however, the problem is that we can't get to the UIWindow's view in Interface Builder. We'll need to do this in code.

Anything you do in Interface Builder can also be done in code.

```
- (void)applicationDidFinishLaunching:(UIApplication *)application {
    // Override point for customization after app launch
    [window addSubview:tabcontroller.view];
    [window makeKeyAndVisible];
}
```

We need to make the tab bar a subview of the UIWindow. You can do this in the ApplicationDidFinishLaunching method.

iBountyHunterAppDelegate.m

Test Drive

We're close. There are a few more connections we need to put together in Interface Builder to wrap it up.

The table views also need to be connected to both view controllers, as well as outlets from the App Delegate to both the fugitive controller and the captured controller.

Name	Type
File's Owner	UIApplication
First Responder	UIResponder
I Bounty Hunter App Delegate	iBountyHunterAppDelegate
Window	UIWindow
▼ Tab Bar Controller	UITabBarController
Tab Bar	UITabBar
▼ Navigation Controller (Fugitives)	UINavigationController
Navigation Bar	UINavigationBar
▼ Fugitive List View Controller (Fugitives)	FugitiveListViewController
Table View	UITableView
Navigation Item (Fugitives)	UINavigationItem
Tab Bar Item (Fugitives)	UITabBarItem
▼ Selected Navigation Controller (Captured)	UINavigationController
Navigation Bar	UINavigationBar
▼ Captured List View Controller (Capt...	CapturedListViewController
Table View	UITableView
Navigation Item (Captured)	UINavigationItem
Tab Bar Item (Captured)	UITabBarItem

MainWindow.xib

View Mode   Inspector   Search Field

iBountyHunter.xcodeproj

Tab View

▼ Outlets
  dataSource   ✖ Captured List View Contro...
  delegate   ✖ Captured List View Contro...
▼ Referencing Outlets
  New Referencing Outlet

For both table views, the delegates and datasources need to be connected to their parent view controller.

Test Drive

It's time to see everything working. Build and run and you can see both tab views working with tables.

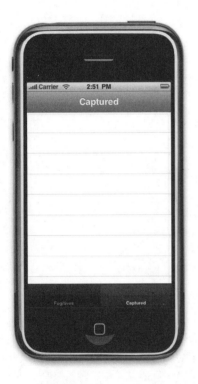

Remember that icon we installed earlier? Go ahead and hit the home key to check it out.

After a quick meeting with Bob...

Looks great so far. Here's my list of fugitives. Right now it's pretty old school—just a typed list from the court.

Managing Bob's data is the next step.

Now that the app is up and running, you need to fill in the blanks. The list is pretty simple right now, so we can make the data into any form we want and then import it.

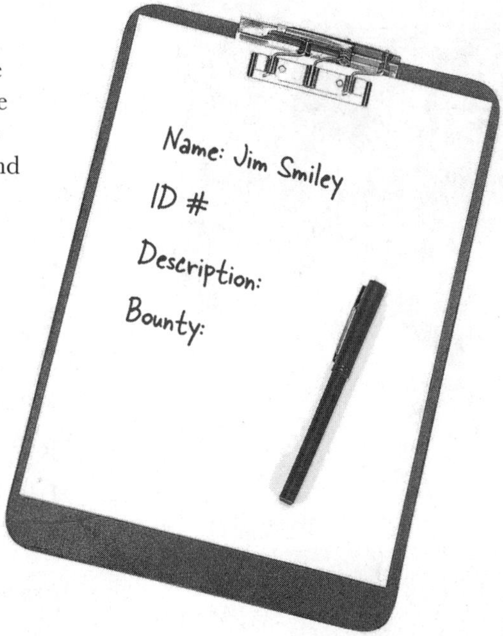

Name: Jim Smiley

ID #

Description:

Bounty:

✹ BRAIN POWER

How should we represent the data?

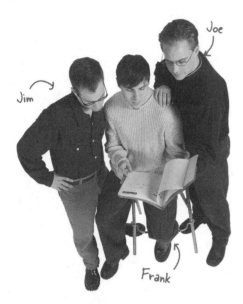

Jim

Joe

Frank

Frank: I was thinking—I'm not sure a plist is such a good idea this time.

Jim: Why not? We used it for DrinkMixer, and it worked fine.

Frank: Well, this list could get pretty big—remember, the list of fugitives is going to be ongoing: the ones that Bob is trying to catch and those that he already has.

Joe: So?

Frank: So... a big list means lots of memory.

Joe: Oh, that's right—and the plist loaded the entire thing every time.

Frank: Exactly.

Jim: What about that Core Data thing, that's supposed to handle large amounts of data, right?

Frank: That's the new 3.x data framework. That would probably work.

Jim: Why use that and not just a database? Doesn't iPhone have SQLite support?

Frank: It does, but I'm not a SQL expert, and Core Data can support all kinds of data, including SQL, but you don't have to talk to it directly.

Joe: I thought you said we weren't using SQLite?

Frank: We are, but we'll use Core Data to access it.

Joe: How does that work?

Frank: Core Data handles all of the dirty work for us, we just need to tell it what data we want to load and save...

BRAIN POWER

What are some other limitations with how we stored data in plists and dictionaries with DrinkMixer?

Core Data lets you focus on your app

Loading and saving data, particularly lots of data, is a major part of most applications. We've already spent a lot of time working with plists and moving objects in and out of arrays. But what if you wanted to sort that data in a bunch of different ways, or only see fugitives worth more than $1,000,000, or handle 100,000 fugitives? Writing code to handle that kind of persistence gets really old, really quickly. Enter Core Data...

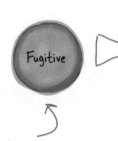  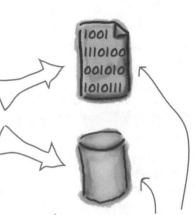

Core Data works with objects. You define what your classes (called Entities) look like.

Core Data handles the loading and saving code necessary...

...and can store them in a number of different formats, like in a database or simple binary file.

But wait, there's more!

Core Data makes loading and saving your data a snap, but it doesn't stop there. It's a mature framework that Apple brought over from Mac OS X to the iPhone in version 3.0 and gives you:

- **The ability to load and save your objects**
  Core Data automatically loads and saves your objects based on Entity descriptions. It can even handle relationships between objects, migrating between versions of your data, required and optional fields, and field validation.

- **Different ways to store your data**
  Core Data hides how your data is actually stored from your application. You could read and write to a SQLite database or a custom binary file by simply telling Core Data how you want it to save your stuff.

- **Memory management with undo and redo**
  Core Data can be extremely efficient about managing objects in memory and tracking changes to objects. You can use it for undo and redo, paging through huge databases of information, and more.

But before we do any of that, we need to tell Core Data about our objects...

Core Data needs to know what to load

We need Core Data to load and save the fugitive information and we need to populate our detailed view. If you think back to DrinkMixer, we used dictionaries to hold our drink information and accessed them with keys, like this:

```
nameTextField.text = [drink objectForKey:NAME_KEY];
ingredientsTextView.text = [drink objectForKey:INGREDIENTS_KEY];
directionsTextView.text = [drink objectForKey:DIRECTIONS_KEY];
```

The problem with dictionaries and plists was that we had to store all of our data using basic types and get to this data with dictionary keys. We could have easily had a bug if we put the wrong type in the Dictionary or used the wrong key and caused lots of problems later. What we really want is to use normal Objective-C classes and objects where we can declare properties for the fields, use real data types, etc. That's exactly what Core Data lets us do.

DrinkMixer used dictionaries to store drink information. It worked, but was pretty primitive.

Use Core Data to populate this.

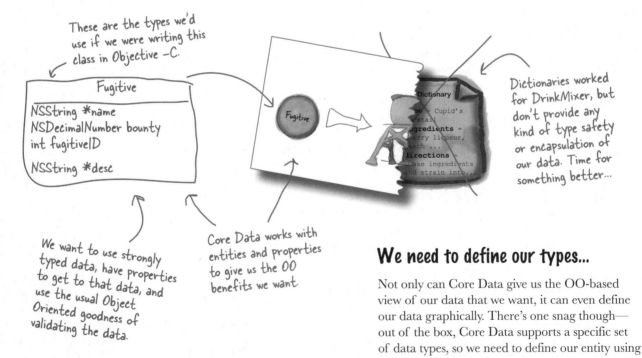

These are the types we'd use if we were writing this class in Objective -C.

Fugitive

NSString *name
NSDecimalNumber bounty
int fugitiveID

NSString *desc

Dictionaries worked for DrinkMixer, but don't provide any kind of type safety or encapsulation of our data. Time for something better...

We want to use strongly typed data, have properties to get to that data, and use the usual Object Oriented goodness of validating the data.

Core Data works with entities and properties to give us the OO benefits we want.

We need to define our types...

Not only can Core Data give us the OO-based view of our data that we want, it can even define our data graphically. There's one snag though—out of the box, Core Data supports a specific set of data types, so we need to define our entity using the types it offers...

WHO DOES WHAT?

Match each field we need to implement for the data view to it's Core Data type.

Field for the Detail View

Name

Bounty

Fugitive ID#

Description

Core Data Type

Int32   A 32 bit integer

String

Equivalent to an NSString attribute

Boolean

A BOOL value (YES or NO)

Decimal

A fixed-point decimal number

Date

Date and Time information

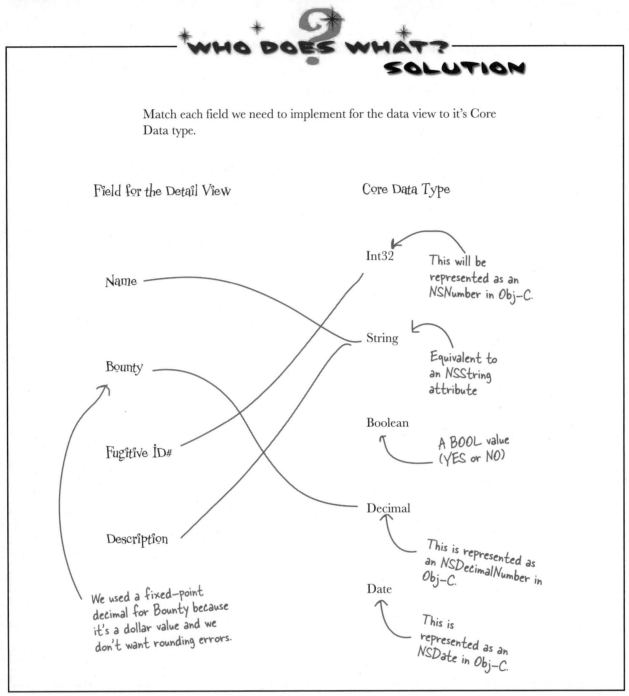

WHO DOES WHAT?
SOLUTION

Match each field we need to implement for the data view to it's Core Data type.

Field for the Detail View   Core Data Type

Name

Bounty

Fugitive ID#

Description

Int32

> This will be represented as an NSNumber in Obj-C.

String

> Equivalent to an NSString attribute

Boolean

> A BOOL value (YES or NO)

Decimal

> This is represented as an NSDecimalNumber in Obj-C.

Date

> This is represented as an NSDate in Obj-C.

> We used a fixed-point decimal for Bounty because it's a dollar value and we don't want rounding errors.

Core Data describes entities with a Managed Object Model

Entities controlled by Core Data are called Managed Objects. The way you capture your entity descriptions (properties, relationships, type information, etc.) for Core Data is through a Managed Object Model. Core Data looks at that Managed Object Model at runtime to figure out how to load and save data from its persistence store (e.g., a database). The Xcode template we used comes with an empty Managed Object Model to get us started.

Our template comes with an empty Managed Object Model in the Resources group called iBountyHunter.xcdatamodel. Click on that to get this view.

The Managed Object Model describes the objects we're going to ask for or try to save.

It also contains all of the information Core Data needs to read and write this data from storage.

The template is set up so that Core Data will try to load all of the Managed Object Models defined in your application at startup. We'll only need this one.

By default, our object model is empty; we'll need to define the Fugitive entity.

Technically you can create a Managed Object Model in code or by hand, but the Xcode tools make it much, much easier.

Let's go ahead and create our Fugitive entity...

Build your Fugitive entity

We need to create a Fugitive entity in our Managed Object Model. Since our Fugitive doesn't have any relationships to other classes, we just need to add properties. Open up `iBountyHunter.xcdatamodel` in the Resources group to create the Fugitive data type.

1 To add the Fugitive entity, click the "plus" button here, and change the **name** to "Fugitive".

The property editor lets you enter constraints for your properties too, min, max, whether it's required, etc. We're not going to use these just yet...

A data model is called an "Entity"

Each data field is an "attribute."

2 Once the entity exists, you can add attributes to the data model, using a plus button again.

3 Use these fields to edit the name and type of the property. You should use your normal property naming convention when naming these.

This diagram is automatically generated to give you a visual representation of the data being managed.

If we had multiple entities you'd see the others here too, along with their relationships.

MANAGED OBJECT MODEL CONSTRUCTION

Finish building the Fugitive entity in the Managed Object Model based on the Fugitive information we want to store. Remember, Core Data Types won't match our Objective-C types exactly. Make sure you name your properties the same as we have in the Fugitive diagram shown below.

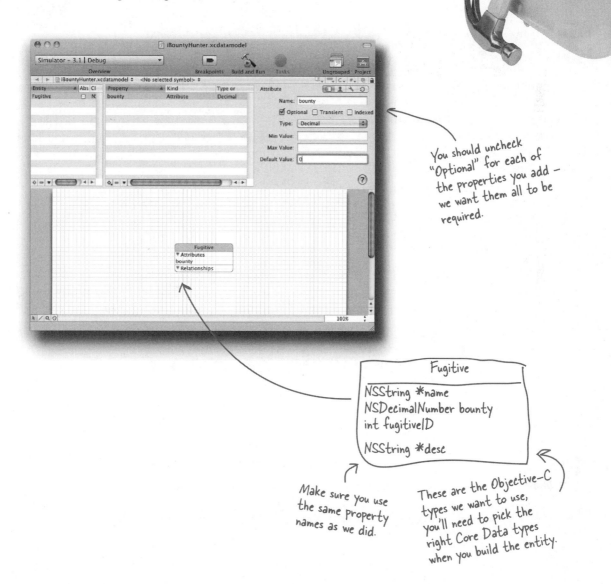

You should uncheck "Optional" for each of the properties you add — we want them all to be required.

Fugitive

NSString *name
NSDecimalNumber bounty
int fugitiveID

NSString *desc

Make sure you use the same property names as we did.

These are the Objective-C types we want to use, you'll need to pick the right Core Data types when you build the entity.

MANAGED OBJECT MODEL CONSTRUCTION SOLUTION

Finish building the Fugitive entity in the Managed Object Model based on the Fugitive information we want to store. Remember, Core Data Types won't match our Objective-C types exactly. Make sure you name your properties the same as we used in the Fugitive diagram.

Check that you used the same types for your properties as we did.

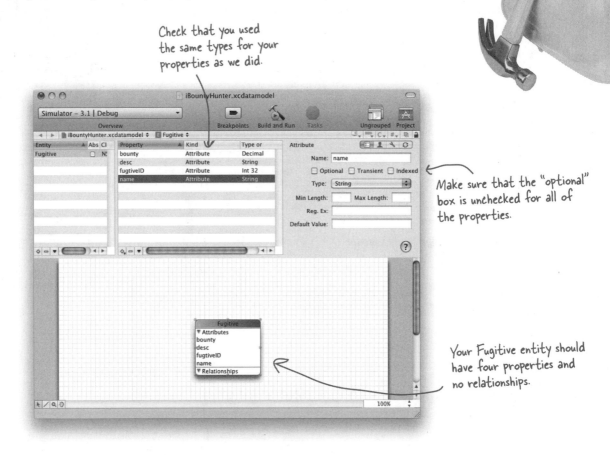

Make sure that the "optional" box is unchecked for all of the properties.

Your Fugitive entity should have four properties and no relationships.

Make sure your object model matches ours exactly!

When you're writing your own apps, there are lots of ways to set up your data model, but since we're going to give you a database for iBountyHunter, your model must match ours exactly!

Q: Why did you use an NSDecimalNumber for the bounty? Why not a float or a double?

A: We're going to store a currency value in the bounty field, so we want precision with the decimal part of the figure. Floats and Doubles are approximations, so you tend to get things like $9.999999998 instead of $10.00 when using them for currency calculations. Our choice of NSDecimalNumber for the bounty has nothing to do with Core Data and everything to do with what we're trying to store.

Q: What are the transient and indexed checkboxes for in Xcode when you create properties?

A: The transient checkbox indicates that Core Data doesn't need to load or save that property. Transient properties are typically used to hold values that you only want to calculate once for performance or convenience reasons, but can be calculated based on the other data you save in the Entity. If you use transient properties, you typically implement a method named awakeFromFetch: that is called right after Core Data loads your Entity. In that method you can calculate the values of your transient properties and set them.

The indexed checkbox tells Core Data it should try and create an index on that property. Core Data can use indexes to speed up searching for items, so if you have a property that you use to look up your entities (customer IDs, account numbers, etc.), you can ask Core Data to index them for faster searching. Indexes take up space and can slow down inserting new data into the store, so only use them when they can actually improve search performance.

Q: I've seen constants declared with k's in front of them. Are they different somehow?

A: Nope. It's just a naming convention. C and C++ programmers tend to use all caps, while Apple tends to use the lowercase "k" instead.

Q: What if I need to use a type that Core Data doesn't support?

A: The easiest way is obviously to try and make your data work with one of the built-in types. If that doesn't work, you create custom types and implement methods to help Core Data load and save those values. Finally, you could stick your data into a binary type (binary data or BLOB) and write some code to encode and decode it at runtime.

Q: What other types of persistance does Core Data support?

A: Core Data supports three types of persistence stores on the iPhone: Binary files, SQLite DBs, and in-memory. The SQLite store is the most useful and what we're using for iBountyHunter. It's also the default. Binary files are nice because they're atomic, meaning either everything is successfully stored at once or nothing is. The problem with them is that in order to be atomic, the iPhone has to read and write the whole file whenever something changes. They're not used too often on the iPhone. The in-memory persistence store is a type of store that isn't actually ever saved on disk, but lets you use all of the searching, sorting, and undo-redo capabilities that Core Data offers with data you keep in-memory.

Q: What SQL datatypes/table structures does Core Data use when it writes to a SQLite database?

A: The short answer is you don't need to know. Even though it's writing to a SQLite database the format, types, and structures are not part of the public API and could potentially be changed by Apple. You're supposed to treat the SQLite database as a blackbox and only access it through Core Data.

Q: So this is a nice GUI and all, but I don't see what this gets us over dictionaries yet. It seems like a lot of work.

A: We had to tell Core Data what kind of information we're working with. Now that we've done that, we can start putting it to work.

Core Data Up Close

Core Data is about managing objects

So far we've talked about how to describe our objects to Core Data, but not how we're actually going to do anything with them. In order to do that, we need to a take a quick look inside Core Data.

Inside of Core Data is a stack of three critical pieces: the Managed Object Context, the Persistent Store Coordinator, and the Persistent Object Store.

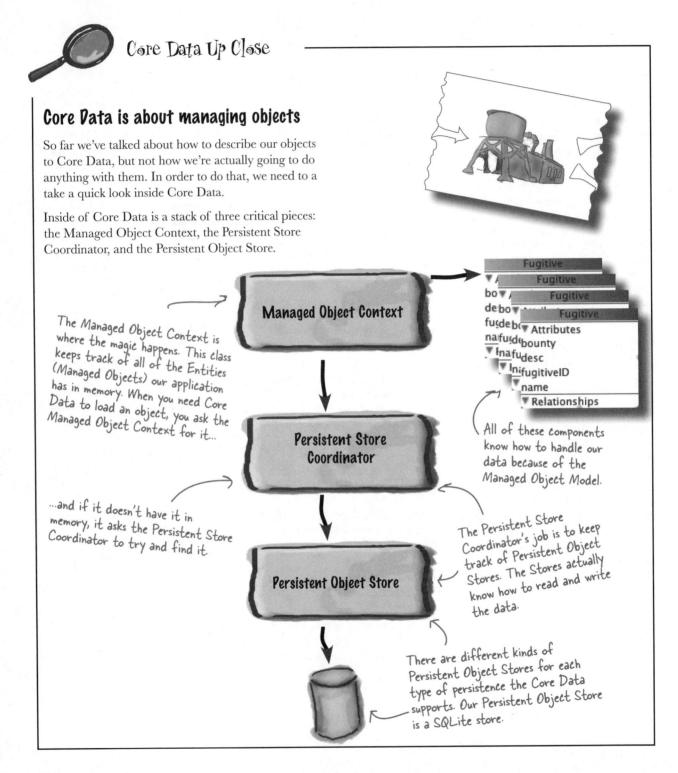

Managed Object Context

The Managed Object Context is where the magic happens. This class keeps track of all of the Entities (Managed Objects) our application has in memory. When you need Core Data to load an object, you ask the Managed Object Context for it...

Fugitive
Fugitive
Fugitive
Fugitive
▼ Attributes
bounty
desc
fugitiveID
name
▼ Relationships

All of these components know how to handle our data because of the Managed Object Model.

Persistent Store Coordinator

...and if it doesn't have it in memory, it asks the Persistent Store Coordinator to try and find it.

The Persistent Store Coordinator's job is to keep track of Persistent Object Stores. The Stores actually know how to read and write the data.

Persistent Object Store

There are different kinds of Persistent Object Stores for each type of persistence the Core Data supports. Our Persistent Object Store is a SQLite store.

So, if we want to load or save anything using Core Data, we need to talk to the Managed Object Context...

Exactly!

The question is how do we get data in and out of it...?

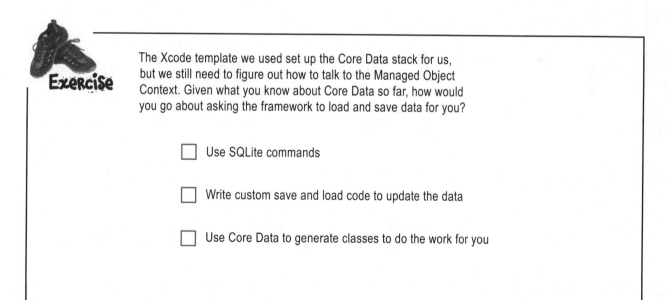

Exercise

The Xcode template we used set up the Core Data stack for us, but we still need to figure out how to talk to the Managed Object Context. Given what you know about Core Data so far, how would you go about asking the framework to load and save data for you?

☐ Use SQLite commands

☐ Write custom save and load code to update the data

☐ Use Core Data to generate classes to do the work for you

Exercise Solution

The Xcode template we used set up the Core Data stack for us, but we still need to figure out how to talk to the Managed Object Context. Given what you know about Core Data so far, how would you go about asking the framework to load and save data for you?

☐ Use SQLite commands ←

We're using a SQLite store, but Core Data supports other kinds of stores. Everything about how it uses SQLite is hidden from you. Trying to access it with straight SQL would be dangerous.

☐ Write custom save and load code to update the data ←

This has two problems: first, you still don't know how the data is actually stored (or even the type of store being used), and second, one of the big reasons we're using Core Data is to avoid writing this kind of code.

☑ Use Core Data to generate classes to do the work for you ←

This is what we're after! Because of our Managed Object Model Core Data knows everything it needs to know to create classes for us and do all of the loading and saving, we just need to ask it.

BULLET POINTS

- Core Data is a **persistence framework** that offers loading, saving, versioning and undo-redo.

- **Core Data** can be built on top of SQLite databases, binary files, or temporary memory.

- The **Managed Object Model** defines the **Entities** we're going to ask Core Data to work with.

- The **Managed Object Context** is our entry point to our data. It keeps track of active **Managed Objects**.

- The Persistent Object Store is part of the Core Data stack that handles reading and writing our data.

Whip up a Fugitive class without writing a line

Xcode can create a Fugitive class from our Managed Object Model that we can use like any other class.

 Select the iBountyHunter.xcdatamodel and click on the Fugitive Entity

You need to have a Core Data entity selected before you ask Xcode to generate a class for you.

 Create a new Managed Object Class...

Select **File→New File...** There will be a new type of file that you can add, the **Managed Object Class.** Select this file and click **Next.**

Make sure you select "Cocoa Touch Class" under iPhone OS.

Now when you create a Cocoa Touch Class you should have an option to create a Managed Object Class.

 ...based on the Fugitive Entity

You will be asked which entity you want to create and you should select Fugitive. Click **Finish.**

This window will show you the Entities available.. We only have one, so pick the Fugitive.

 And generate the .h and .m

Click Finish and you should have a Fugitive.h and a Fugitive.m added to your project. Go ahead and drag these up to the **Classes** group.

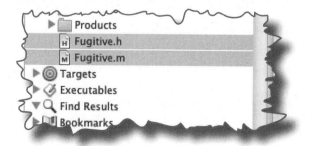

Our generated Fugitive class matches our Managed Object Model

Xcode created two new files from our Fugitive entity: a Fugitive.h header file and a Fugitive.m implementation file. Open up both files and let's take a look at what was created.

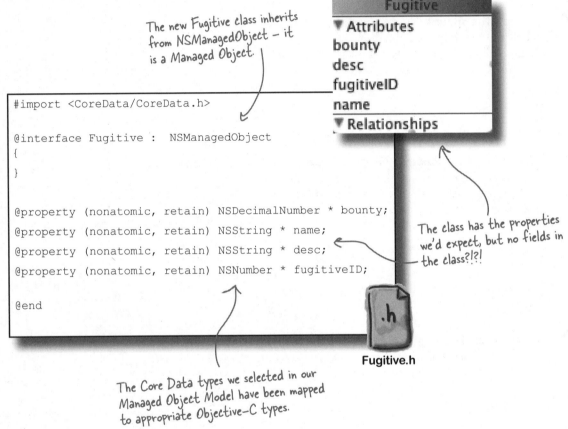

The new Fugitive class inherits from NSManagedObject — it is a Managed Object.

```
#import <CoreData/CoreData.h>

@interface Fugitive :  NSManagedObject
{

}

@property (nonatomic, retain) NSDecimalNumber * bounty;
@property (nonatomic, retain) NSString * name;
@property (nonatomic, retain) NSString * desc;
@property (nonatomic, retain) NSNumber * fugitiveID;

@end
```

Fugitive

▼ **Attributes**
bounty
desc
fugitiveID
name
▼ **Relationships**

The class has the properties we'd expect, but no fields in the class?!?!

Fugitive.h

The Core Data types we selected in our Managed Object Model have been mapped to appropriate Objective-C types.

NSManagedObject handles storage and memory for generated properties

The generated Fugitive class has properties for name, description, etc., but no fields in the class. The Core Data framework (and NSManagedObject in particular) are responsible for handling the memory associated with those properties. You can override this if you want, but in most cases this does exactly what you need.

Things get even more interesting in Fugitive.m...

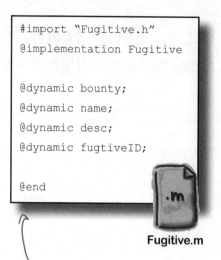

```
#import "Fugitive.h"
@implementation Fugitive

@dynamic bounty;
@dynamic name;
@dynamic desc;
@dynamic fugtiveID;

@end
```

Fugitive.m

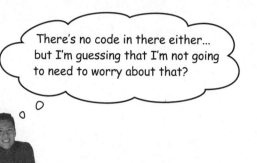

There's no code in there either... but I'm guessing that I'm not going to need to worry about that?

Right! The Core Data framework takes care of it.

The Fugitive.m class is nearly empty, and instead of synthesizing the properties, they're declared with a new directive, @dynamic.

The implementation of the Fugitive class is almost completely empty!

NSManagedObject also implements the properties

The new @dynamic directive tells the compiler not to worry about the getter and setter methods necessary for the properties. They need to come from somewhere, though, or else code is going to crash at runtime when someone tries to access those properties. This is where NSManagedObject steps in again. Because NSManagedObject handles the memory for the fields backing the properties, it also provides runtime implementations for the getter and setter methods. By having NSManagedObject implement those methods, you get a number of other neat benefits:

 The NSManagedObject knows when properties are changed, can validate new data, and can notify other classes when changes happen.

NSManagedObject can be lazy about fetching property information until someone asks for it. For example, it does this with relationships to other objects.

 NSManagedObject can keep track of changes to properties and provide undo-redo support.

You get all of this without writing a line of code!

Now it's just a matter of asking Core Data to load a Fugitive...

Use an NSFetchRequest to describe your search

In order to tell the Managed Object Context what we're looking for, we need to create an NSFetchRequest. The NSFetchRequest describes what kind of objects we want to fetch, any conditions we want when it fetches them (like bounty > 1,000), and how Core Data should sort the results when it gives them back.

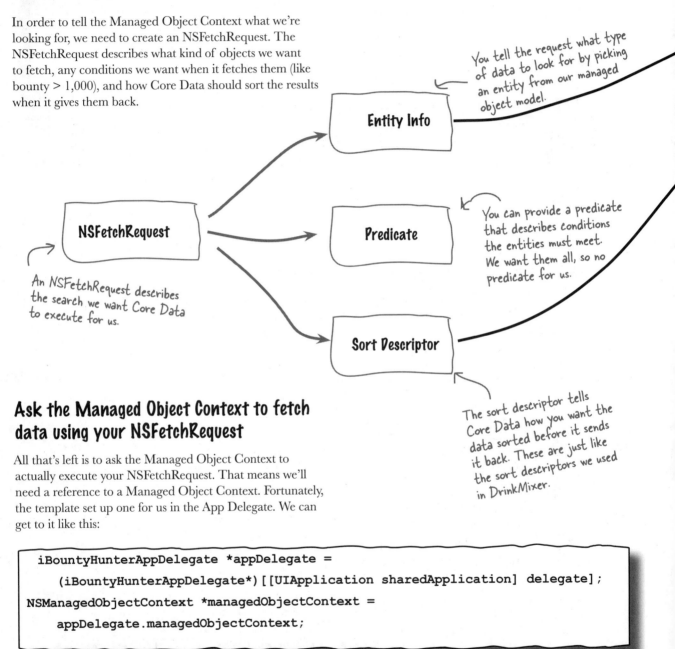

You tell the request what type of data to look for by picking an entity from our managed object model.

Entity Info

NSFetchRequest

An NSFetchRequest describes the search we want Core Data to execute for us.

Predicate

You can provide a predicate that describes conditions the entities must meet. We want them all, so no predicate for us.

Sort Descriptor

The sort descriptor tells Core Data how you want the data sorted before it sends it back. These are just like the sort descriptors we used in DrinkMixer.

Ask the Managed Object Context to fetch data using your NSFetchRequest

All that's left is to ask the Managed Object Context to actually execute your NSFetchRequest. That means we'll need a reference to a Managed Object Context. Fortunately, the template set up one for us in the App Delegate. We can get to it like this:

```
iBountyHunterAppDelegate *appDelegate =
    (iBountyHunterAppDelegate*)[[UIApplication sharedApplication] delegate];
NSManagedObjectContext *managedObjectContext =
    appDelegate.managedObjectContext;
```

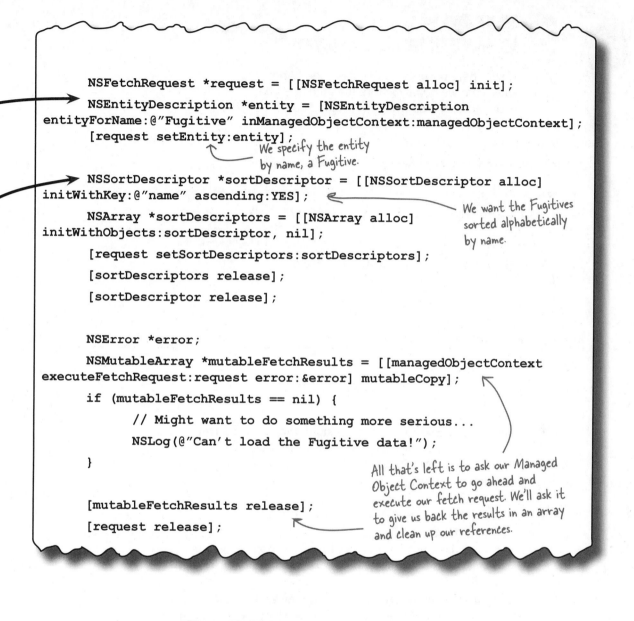

```
    NSFetchRequest *request = [[NSFetchRequest alloc] init];
    NSEntityDescription *entity = [NSEntityDescription
entityForName:@"Fugitive" inManagedObjectContext:managedObjectContext];
    [request setEntity:entity];
```
We specify the entity
by name, a Fugitive.

```
    NSSortDescriptor *sortDescriptor = [[NSSortDescriptor alloc]
initWithKey:@"name" ascending:YES];
```
We want the Fugitives
sorted alphabetically
by name.

```
    NSArray *sortDescriptors = [[NSArray alloc]
initWithObjects:sortDescriptor, nil];

    [request setSortDescriptors:sortDescriptors];

    [sortDescriptors release];

    [sortDescriptor release];


    NSError *error;

    NSMutableArray *mutableFetchResults = [[managedObjectContext
executeFetchRequest:request error:&error] mutableCopy];

    if (mutableFetchResults == nil) {
        // Might want to do something more serious...
        NSLog(@"Can't load the Fugitive data!");
    }


    [mutableFetchResults release];

    [request release];
```

All that's left is to ask our Managed
Object Context to go ahead and
execute our fetch request. We'll ask it
to give us back the results in an array
and clean up our references.

BRAIN BARBELL

Now, where do we put all of this code? And
where are we going to store the results? What
about actually displaying the fetched data?

BRAIN BARBELL SOLUTION

Now, where do we put all of this code? And where are we going to store the results? What about actually displaying the fetched data?

Since Bob is going to want to see his list as soon as his view shows up, the fetching code needs to go into viewWillAppear in FugitiveViewController.m.

As for storing the results, we'll get back an array, but we release it right away. We need to keep a reference to that array in our view controller.

In order to actually show this data, we're going to need to implement the cellForRowAtIndexPath to pull the data from the array.

Sharpen your pencil

Let's get all of these pieces into the app.

1 **Create the mutable array to hold the fetched items.**
Create an array in the FugitiveViewController called `items` to hold the results of the fetch. Don't forget to synthesize the property and clean up memory.

2 **Import the appropriate headers into FugitiveViewController.m.**
Make sure that you `#import` headers for the App Delegate and the Fugitive classes into FugitiveListViewController.m.

3 **Implement the fetch code inside viewWillAppear.**
Take what we learned on the previous couple of pages and get the fetch working. You'll need to get the Managed Object Context from the delegate, create the fetch, then execute it. Remember to update the code to actually hang onto the results by assigning them to the array we just created.

Table Cell Magnets

Use the code snippets below to customize the table cells for the fugitive list.

```objc
_____

_____ (UITableView *)tableView {
        return 1;
}


// Customize the number of rows in the table view.
 - (NSInteger)tableView:(UITableView *)tableView numberOfRowsInSection:
(NSInteger)section {

        _____

}


// Customize the appearance of table view cells.
 - (UITableViewCell *)tableView:(UITableView *)tableView cellForRowAtIndexPath:
(NSIndexPath *)indexPath {

        _____


        UITableViewCell *cell = _____
CellIdentifier];
        if (cell == nil) {
                cell = [[[UITableViewCell alloc] initWithStyle:
                                                    autorelease];
        }
        // Set up the cell...

_____

_____

_____

}
```

```
return [items count];
```

```
return cell;
```

```
= fugitive.name;
```

```
Fugitive *fugitive
```

```
UITableViewCellStyleDefault reuseIdentifier:CellIdentifier]
```

```
tableView dequeueReusableCellWithIdentifier:
```

```
cell.textLabel.text
```

```
#pragma mark table view methods
```

```
- (NSInteger) numberOfSectionsInTableView:
```

```
static NSString *CellIdentifier = @"Cell";
```

```
= [items objectAtIndex:indexPath.row];
```

Sharpen your pencil
Solution

It's a lot of code to implement, but when you're done, Core Data
will be fetching the data you need for the fugitive list.

1 **Create the mutable array to hold the fetched items.**

```
#import <UIKit/UIKit.h>
@interface FugitiveListViewController : UITableViewController {
      NSMutableArray *items;
}
@property(nonatomic, retain) NSMutableArray *items;
@end
```

FugitiveListViewController.h

2 **Import the appropriate headers into
FugitiveViewController.m.**

```
#import "FugitiveListViewController.h"
#import "iBountyHunterAppDelegate.h"
#import "Fugitive.h"
@implementation FugitiveListViewController
@synthesize items;
```

FugitiveListViewController.m

```
- (void)dealloc {
    [items release];
    [super dealloc];
}
```

3 Implement the fetch code inside viewWillAppear.

```objc
- (void) viewWillAppear:(BOOL)animated {
    [super viewWillAppear:animated];
    iBountyHunterAppDelegate *appDelegate =
(iBountyHunterAppDelegate*)[[UIApplication sharedApplication] delegate];
    NSManagedObjectContext *managedObjectContext = appDelegate.
managedObjectContext;
    NSFetchRequest *request = [[NSFetchRequest alloc] init];
    NSEntityDescription *entity = [NSEntityDescription
entityForName:@"Fugitive" inManagedObjectContext:managedObjectContext];
    [request setEntity:entity];

    NSSortDescriptor *sortDescriptor = [[NSSortDescriptor alloc]
initWithKey:@"name" ascending:YES];
    NSArray *sortDescriptors = [[NSArray alloc]
initWithObjects:sortDescriptor, nil];
    [request setSortDescriptors:sortDescriptors];
    [sortDescriptors release];
    [sortDescriptor release];

    NSError *error;
    NSMutableArray *mutableFetchResults = [[managedObjectContext
executeFetchRequest:request error:&error] mutableCopy];
    if (mutableFetchResults == nil) {
        // Handle the error.
    }

    self.items = mutableFetchResults;
    [mutableFetchResults release];
    [request release];
}
```

FugitiveListViewController.m

Table Cell Magnets Solution

Use the code snippets below to customize the table cells for the fugitive list.

```objc
#pragma mark table view methods

- (NSInteger) numberOfSectionsInTableView:    (UITableView *)tableView {
    return 1;
}


// Customize the number of rows in the table view.
 - (NSInteger)tableView:(UITableView *)tableView numberOfRowsInSection:
(NSInteger)section {
    return [items count];
}


// Customize the appearance of table view cells.
 - (UITableViewCell *)tableView:(UITableView *)tableView cellForRowAtIndexPath:
(NSIndexPath *)indexPath {
    static NSString *CellIdentifier = @"Cell";

    UITableViewCell *cell = tableView dequeueReusableCellWithIdentifier:
CellIdentifier];
    if (cell == nil) {
        cell = [[[UITableViewCell alloc] initWithStyle:
UITableViewCellStyleDefault reuseIdentifier:CellIdentifier]    autorelease];
    }

    // Set up the cell...
    Fugitive *fugitive = [items objectAtIndex:indexPath.row];
    cell.textLabel.text = fugitive.name;
    return cell;
}
```

Here's Core Data at work. The data is stored in normal Objective-C Fugitive objects. No more magic dictionary keys here...

Do this! ➡ To completely wire up your table view, in Interface Builder make sure that the table view in the Fugitive List has its datasource as the FugtiveListViewController.

WHO DOES WHAT?

Match each Core Data concept to what it does.

Managed Object Model

Describes the search you want to execute on your data. Includes type of information you want back, any conditions the data must meet, and how the results should be sorted.

NSManagedObject

Responsible for keeping track of managed objects active in the application. All your fetch and save requests go through this.

Managed Object Context

Captures how data should be sorted in a generic way. You specify the field the data should be sorted by and how it should be sorted.

Describes entities in your application, including type information, data constraints, and relationships between the entities.

NSFetchRequest

A Objective-C version of a Core Data entity. Subclasses of this represent data you want to load and save through Core Data. Provides the support for monitoring changes, lazy loading, and data validation.

NSSortDescriptor

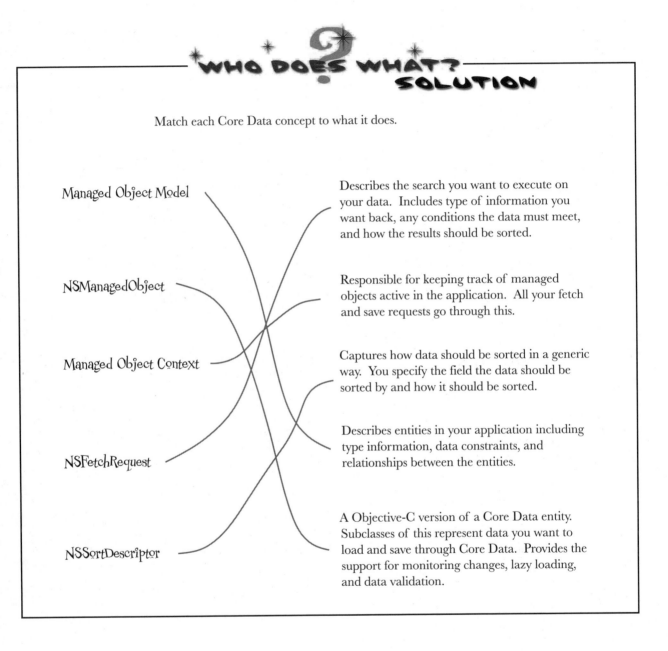

WHO DOES WHAT?
SOLUTION

Match each Core Data concept to what it does.

Managed Object Model

NSManagedObject

Managed Object Context

NSFetchRequest

NSSortDescriptor

Describes the search you want to execute on your data. Includes type of information you want back, any conditions the data must meet, and how the results should be sorted.

Responsible for keeping track of managed objects active in the application. All your fetch and save requests go through this.

Captures how data should be sorted in a generic way. You specify the field the data should be sorted by and how it should be sorted.

Describes entities in your application including type information, data constraints, and relationships between the entities.

A Objective-C version of a Core Data entity. Subclasses of this represent data you want to load and save through Core Data. Provides the support for monitoring changes, lazy loading, and data validation.

Here's a URL for the data I'm getting. Turns out I can do that instead of getting that paper list from the court...

You'll need to download your copy of the fugitive list.

Browse over to *http://www.headfirstlabs.com/iphonedev* and download iBountyHunter.sqlite. Right-click on the iBountyHunter project and select **Add→Existing Files...,** and make sure it is copied into the project.

How do we tell Core Data to load from this file?

Add the database as a resource

We have all of this code already in place to load data—it came with the Core Data template. But how do we get from there to actually loading the database?

We've handled the object model, the Managed Object Context, and the Fugitive Class.

Now we need to look at the other end. We need to connect Core Data to our Fugitive Database.

Back to the Core Data stack

Remember the Core Data stack we talked about earlier? We've gotten everything in place with the Managed Object Context, and now we're interested in where the data is actually coming from. Just like with the Managed Object Context, the template set up the rest of the stack for us.

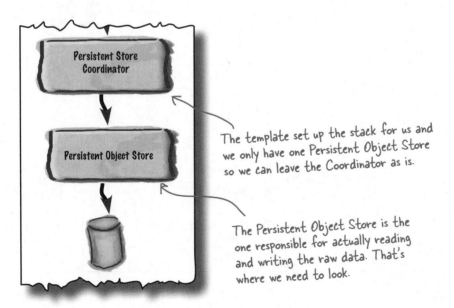

The template set up the stack for us and we only have one Persistent Object Store so we can leave the Coordinator as is.

The Persistent Object Store is the one responsible for actually reading and writing the raw data. That's where we need to look.

Let's take a look at the template code in the App Delegate...

The template sets things up for a SQLite DB

The Core Data template set up the Persistent Store Coordinator to use a SQLite database named after our project. As long as the database is named iBountyHunter.sqlite, then Core Data should be ready to go.

```
- (NSPersistentStoreCoordinator *)persistentStoreCoordinator {
    if (persistentStoreCoordinator != nil) {
      return persistentStoreCoordinator;
    }

    NSURL *storeUrl = [NSURL fileURLWithPath: [[self
applicationDocumentsDirectory] stringByAppendingPathComponent:
@"iBountyHunter.sqlite"]];
      NSError *error = nil;
    persistentStoreCoordinator = [[NSPersistentStoreCoordinator alloc] i
nitWithManagedObjectModel:[self managedObjectModel]];

    if (![persistentStoreCoordinator addPersistentStoreWithType:NSSQLite
StoreType configuration:nil URL:storeUrl options:nil error:&error]) {

  NSLog(@"Unresolved error %@, %@", error, [error userInfo]);

  abort();

    }

  return persistentStoreCoordinator;

}
```

The template sets things up to use a DB named the same as your project.

The template code adds a Persistent Object Store to the coordinator configured with the NSSQLiteStoreType.

.m

iBountyHunterAppDelegate.m

Test Drive

Now that the database is in place, and the Persistent Object Store can be used as-is, go ahead and run the app.

Test Drive

Where is the data?

> We added the database to the project. The code looks right. This all worked with DrinkMixer. What's the deal??

Core Data is looking somewhere else.

Our problem is with how Core Data looks for the database. Well, it's actually a little more complicated than that.

iPhone Apps are read-only

Back in DrinkMixer, we loaded our application data from a plist using the application bundle. This worked great and our data loaded without a problem. But remember how we talked about how this would only work in the simulator? It's time to sort that out. As part of iPhone security, applications are installed on the device read-only. You can get to any resources bundled with your application, but you can't modify them. The Core Data template assumes you're going to want to read and write to your database, so it doesn't even bother checking the application bundle.

Watch it!

This code will only work in the simulator!!

The code used to save the plist will work fine on the miserably on a real device. The problem is with file apps are allowed to store data. We'll talk a lot more

The Core Data template looks in the application documents directory for the database, not the application bundle.

```objc
NSURL *storeUrl = [NSURL fileURLWithPath: [[self
applicationDocumentsDirectory] stringByAppendingPathComponent:
@"iBountyHunter.sqlite"]];
```

iBountyHunterAppDelegate.m

We need to take a closer look at how those directories are set up...

The iPhone's application structure defines where you can read and write

For security and stability reasons, the iPhone OS locks down the filesystem pretty tight. When an application is installed, the iPhone OS creates a directory under /User/Applications on the device using a unique identifier. The application is installed into that directory, and a standard directory structure is created for the app.

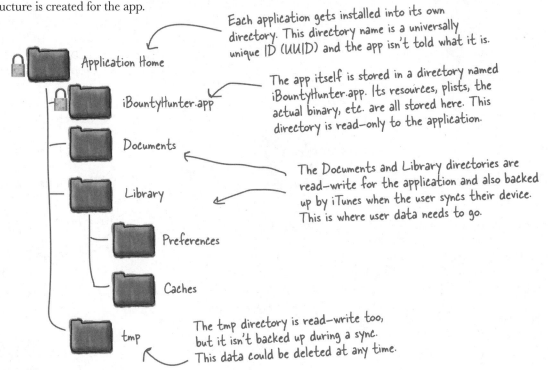

Each application gets installed into its own directory. This directory name is a universally unique ID (UUID) and the app isn't told what it is.

The app itself is stored in a directory named iBountyHunter.app. Its resources, plists, the actual binary, etc. are all stored here. This directory is read-only to the application.

The Documents and Library directories are read-write for the application and also backed up by iTunes when the user syncs their device. This is where user data needs to go.

The tmp directory is read-write too, but it isn't backed up during a sync. This data could be deleted at any time.

Use the Documents directory to store user data

Since most Core Data applications want to read and write data, the template sets up our Core Data stack to read and write from the Documents directory. An application can figure out where its local directories are by using the NSSearchPathForDirectoriesInDomains, just like the template does in the App Delegate:

```
- (NSString *)applicationDocumentsDirectory {

  return [NSSearchPathForDirectoriesInDomains(NSDocumentDirectory,
      NSUserDomainMask, YES) lastObject];

}
```

Copy the database to the correct place

When the application first starts, we need to check to see if there's a copy of the database in our Documents directory. If there is, we don't want to mess with it. If not, we need to copy one there.

You'll need to delcare this method in iBountyHunterAppDelegate.h.

```objc
- (void) createEditableCopyOfDatabaseIfNeeded {

    // First, test for existence - we don't want to wipe out a user's DB
    NSFileManager *fileManager = [NSFileManager defaultManager];
    NSString *documentsDirectory = [self applicationDocumentsDirectory];
    NSString *writableDBPath = [documentsDirectory stringByAppendingPathCompo
nent:@"iBountyHunter.sqlite"];

    BOOL dbexists = [fileManager fileExistsAtPath:writableDBPath];
    if (!dbexists) {
    // The writable database does not exist, so copy the default to the
    appropriate location.
    NSString *defaultDBPath = [[[NSBundle mainBundle] resourcePath] stringByA
ppendingPathComponent:@"iBountyHunter.sqlite"];

    NSError *error;
    BOOL success = [fileManager copyItemAtPath:defaultDBPath
toPath:writableDBPath error:&error];
    if (!success) {
    NSAssert1(0, @"Failed to create writable database file with message
'%@'.", [error localizedDescription]);
        }
    }
}
```

Here we grab the master DB from our application bundle; this is the read-only copy.

Copy it from the read-only to the writable directory.

```objc
- (void) applicationDidFinishLaunching:
(UIApplication *) application {
        [self createEditableCopyOfDatabaseIfNeeded];
}
```

iBountyHunterAppDelegate.m

Do this!

Now that the app knows how to copy the database, you need to uninstall the old version of your app to delete the empty database that Core Data created earlier. When you build and run again, our new code will copy the correct DB into place.

TEST DRIVE

Now that the app knows where to find the database, it should load.

All the data
is in there!

Q: Why didn't we have to do all of this directory stuff with the plist in DrinkMixer?

A: We only ran DrinkMixer in the simulator, and the simulator doesn't enforce the directory permissions like the real device does. We'd basically have the same problem with DrinkMixer on a device. The reason this was so obvious with iBountyHunter is that Core Data is configured to look in the correct place for a writeable database, namely the application's Documents directory.

Q: How do I get paths to the other application directories?

A: Just use NSSearchPathForDirectoriesInDomains but with different NSSearchPathDirectory constants. Most of them you won't ever need; NSDocumentsDirectory is the most common. You should never assume you know what the directory structure is or how to navigate it; always look up the specific directory you want.

Q: So what happens to the data when someone uninstalls my application?

A: When an application is removed from a device, the entire application directory is removed, so data, caches, preferences, etc., are all deleted.

Q: The whole Predicate thing with NSFetchRequest seems pretty important. Are we going to talk about that any more?

A: Yes! We'll come back to that in Chapter 8.

Q: So is there always just one Managed Object Context in an application?

A: No, there can be multiple if you want them. For most apps, one is sufficient, but if you want to separate a set of edits or migrate data from one data source to another you can create and configure as many Managed Object Contexts as you need.

Q: I don't really see the benefit of the Persistent Store Coordinator. What does it do?

A: Our application only uses one Persistent Object Store, but Core Data supports multiple stores. For example, you could have a customer information coming from one database but product information coming from another. You can configure two separate persistent object stores and let the persistent store coordinator sort out which one is used based on the database attached.

Q: How about object models? Can we have more than one of those?

A: Yup—in fact we're going to take a look at that in Chapter 8.

Q: Do I always have to get my NSManagedObjects from the Managed Object Context? What if I want to create a new one?

A: No, new ones have to be added to the context—however, you can't just alloc and init them. You need to create them from their entity description, like this: [NSEntityDescription insertNewObjectForEntityForName:@"Fugitive" inManagedObjectContext:managedObjectContext];

That will return a new Fugitive instance and after that you can use it like normal.

Now we need to build the
detail view, right?

Exactly.

We have the database loading with
detailed information, but the user can't
see it yet. Now, we just need to build out
the detail view to display that information
as well.

You're almost done
with your list!

iBountyHunter To Do List

1. ~~Create view controllers (both .h and .m~~
~~files) for the Fugitive and Captured views.~~
2. ~~Create the tab bar view, and add the~~
~~tab bar controller to it along with a~~
~~reference from the app delegate.~~
3. ~~Add the nav controllers for the Fugitive~~
~~and Captured views.~~
4. ~~Build the table views for the Fugitive~~
~~and Captured views.~~
5. Create a detail view with a nib, and a
view controller with .h and .m files.

And you definitely
know how to do this...

Long Exercise

Building the detail view isn't anything new for you—so get to it! Here is what you're working with from our earlier sketch for the detail view.

☐ Create a new view controller and nib called the FugitiveDetailViewController.

☐ Lay out the nib using Interface Builder to have the fields we need.

☐ Then update the new view controller to have outlets for the fields we'll need to set and a reference to the Fugitive it's displaying.

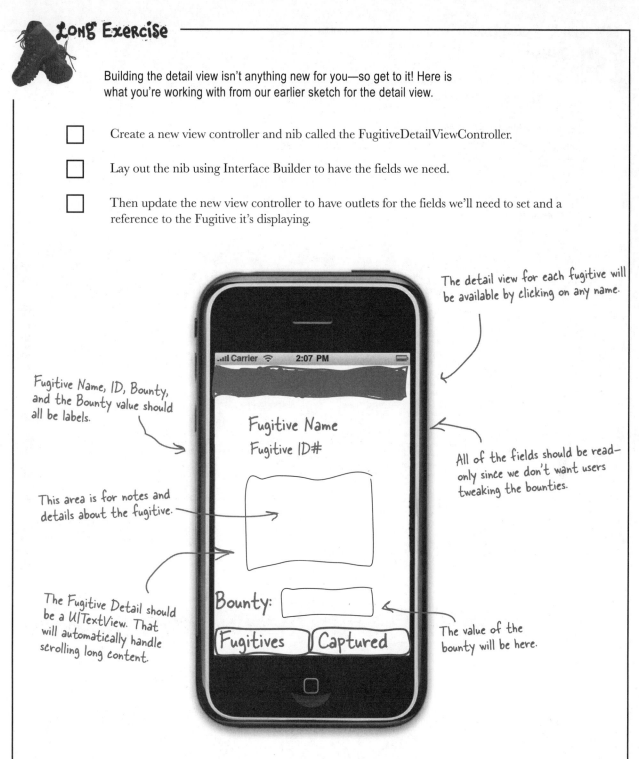

The detail view for each fugitive will be available by clicking on any name.

Fugitive Name, ID, Bounty, and the Bounty value should all be labels.

All of the fields should be read-only since we don't want users tweaking the bounties.

This area is for notes and details about the fugitive.

The Fugitive Detail should be a UITextView. That will automatically handle scrolling long content.

The value of the bounty will be here.

Long Exercise Solution

Go through and check the code, outlets, declarations, and dealloc.

The files that you need for the new view are: FugitiveDetailViewController.h, FugitiveDetailViewController.m, and FugitiveDetailViewController.xib.

To create them, just select **File → New** and check the box that says "With XIB for User Interface". After that, you'll need to move the .xib file into **/Resources** within Xcode.

When you create the new class files, you'll have the .m, .h, and .xib files.

Make sure you move the DetailController.xib file into the /Resources folder.

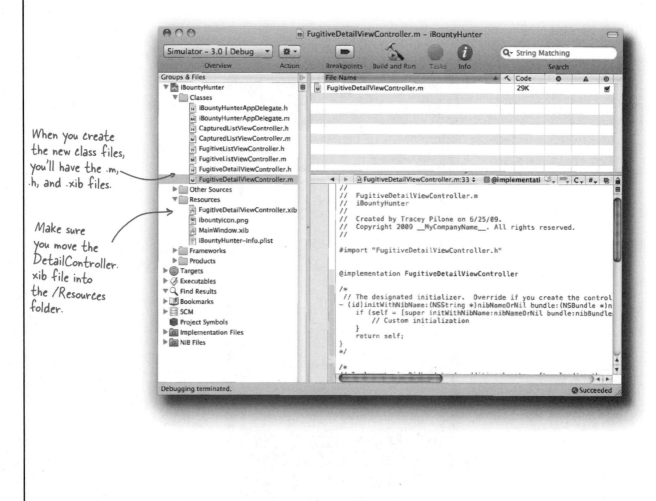

```objective-c
@class Fugitive;
@interface FugitiveDetailViewController : UIViewController {
    Fugitive *fugitive;
    UILabel *fugitiveNameLabel;
    UILabel *fugitiveIdLabel;
    UITextView *fugitiveDescriptionView;
    UILabel *fugitiveBountyLabel;
}
@property (nonatomic, retain) Fugitive *fugitive;
@property (nonatomic, retain) IBOutlet UILabel *fugitiveNameLabel;
@property (nonatomic, retain) IBOutlet UILabel *fugitiveIdLabel;
@property (nonatomic, retain) IBOutlet UITextView *fugitiveDescriptionView;
@property (nonatomic, retain) IBOutlet UILabel *fugitiveBountyLabel;
@end
```

FugitiveDetailViewController.h

```objective-c
#import "FugitiveDetailViewController.h"
#import "Fugitive.h"

@implementation FugitiveDetailViewController

@synthesize fugitive, fugitiveNameLabel, fugitiveIdLabel,
fugitiveDescriptionView, fugitiveBountyLabel;
```

FugitiveDetailViewController.m

```objective-c
- (void)dealloc {
    [fugitive release];
    [fugitiveNameLabel release];
    [fugitiveIdLabel release];
    [fugitiveDescriptionView release];
    [fugitiveBountyLabel release];
    [super dealloc];
}
@end
```

LONG EXERCISE SOLUTION

Now build the view in Interface Builder.

Here's the final listing of the components of the detail view.

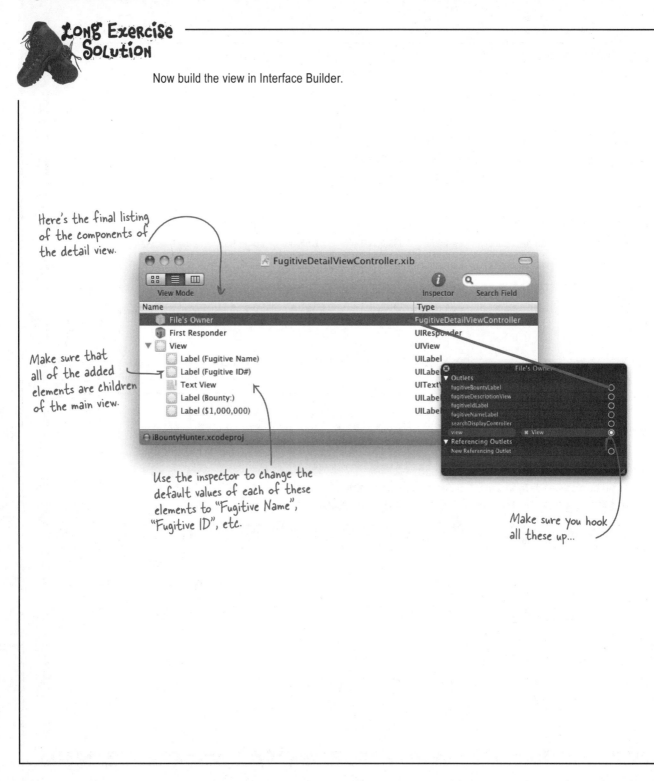

Make sure that all of the added elements are children of the main view.

Use the inspector to change the default values of each of these elements to "Fugitive Name", "Fugitive ID", etc.

Make sure you hook all these up...

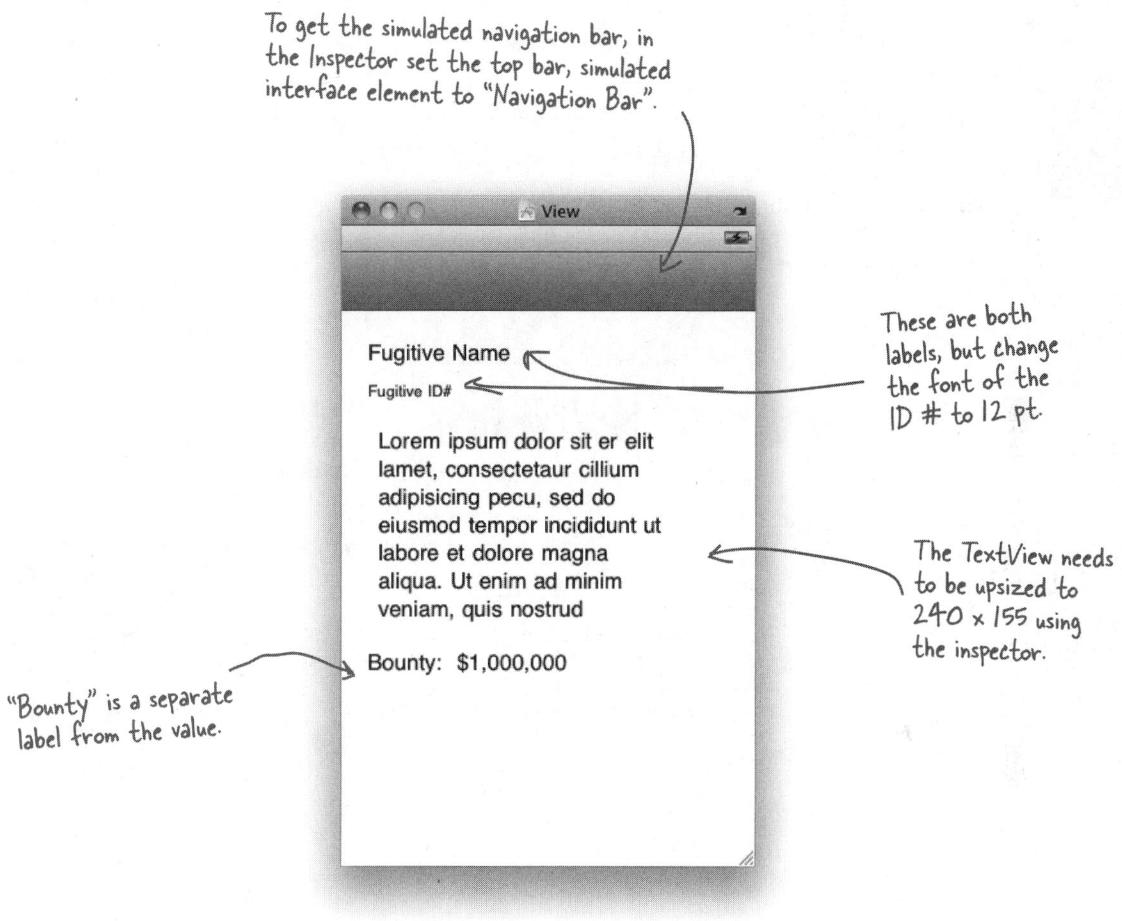

To get the simulated navigation bar, in the Inspector set the top bar, simulated interface element to "Navigation Bar".

View

Fugitive Name

Fugitive ID#

Lorem ipsum dolor sit er elit lamet, consectetaur cillium adipisicing pecu, sed do eiusmod tempor incididunt ut labore et dolore magna aliqua. Ut enim ad minim veniam, quis nostrud

Bounty: $1,000,000

These are both labels, but change the font of the ID # to 12 pt.

The TextView needs to be upsized to 240 x 155 using the inspector.

"Bounty" is a separate label from the value.

Geek Bits

We're going to add some spit and polish to this view. It's fine the way it is, but here's some iPhone coolness to add.

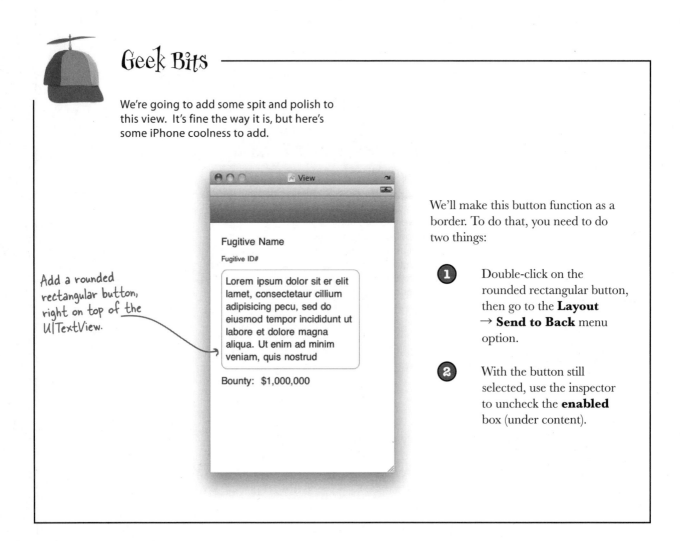

Add a rounded rectangular button, right on top of the UITextView.

We'll make this button function as a border. To do that, you need to do two things:

1 Double-click on the rounded rectangular button, then go to the **Layout → Send to Back** menu option.

2 With the button still selected, use the inspector to uncheck the **enabled** box (under content).

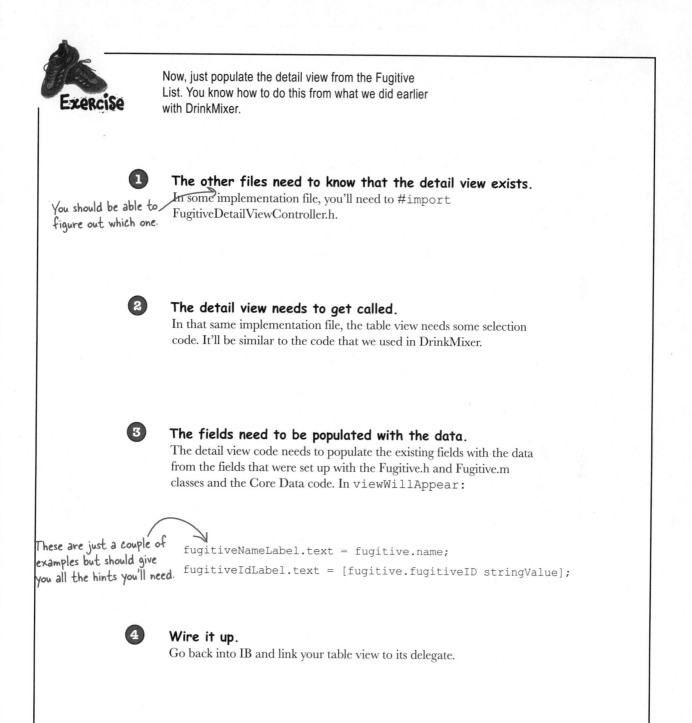

Exercise

Now, just populate the detail view from the Fugitive List. You know how to do this from what we did earlier with DrinkMixer.

1 **The other files need to know that the detail view exists.**
In some implementation file, you'll need to #import FugitiveDetailViewController.h.

You should be able to figure out which one.

2 **The detail view needs to get called.**
In that same implementation file, the table view needs some selection code. It'll be similar to the code that we used in DrinkMixer.

3 **The fields need to be populated with the data.**
The detail view code needs to populate the existing fields with the data from the fields that were set up with the Fugitive.h and Fugitive.m classes and the Core Data code. In `viewWillAppear:`

These are just a couple of examples but should give you all the hints you'll need.

```
fugitiveNameLabel.text = fugitive.name;
fugitiveIdLabel.text = [fugitive.fugitiveID stringValue];
```

4 **Wire it up.**
Go back into IB and link your table view to its delegate.

Exercise Solution

Now, just populate the detail view. You know enough from before to do this.

1 **The other files need to know that the detail view exists.**

In some implementation file, you'll need to #import FugitiveDetailViewController.h

Just add this to the top of the FugitiveListViewController.m file.

2 **The detail view needs to get called.**

In that same implementation file, the table view needs some selection code. It'll be similar to the code that we used in DrinkMixer.

```
-   (void)
tableView:(UITableView*)tableView didSelectRowAtIndexPath: (NSIndexPath
*)indexPath {

    FugitiveDetailViewController *fugitiveDetailViewController
= [[FugitiveDetailViewController alloc] initWithNibName:
@"FugitiveDetailViewController" bundle:nil];
    fugitiveDetailViewController.fugitive = [self.items
objectAtIndex:indexPath.row];
    [self.navigationController pushViewController:
fugitiveDetailViewController animated:YES];
    [fugitiveDetailViewController release];

}
```

Here we tell the detail view controller which fugitive it should display.

FugitiveListViewController.m

③ **The fields need to be populated with the data.**

```
#import "FugitiveDetailViewController.h"
#import "Fugitive.h"
@implementation FugitiveDetailViewController
@synthesize fugitive, fugitiveNameLabel, fugitiveIdLabel,
fugitiveDescriptionView, fugitiveBountyLabel;

-(void) viewWillAppear:(BOOL)animated {
    [super viewWillAppear:animated];

    fugitiveNameLabel.text = fugitive.name;
    fugitiveIdLabel.text = [fugitive.fugitiveID stringValue];
    fugitiveDescriptionView.text = fugitive.desc;
    fugitiveBountyLabel.text = [fugitive.bounty stringValue];
}
```

We're going to be accessing fields in the Fugitive class. We need to tell the compiler about it.

Adding the stringValue on the end of these two declarations handles the fact that they were not strings, but NSNumber and NSDecimalNumbers.

FugitiveDetailViewController.m

④ **Wire it up.**
In IB, the table view under the Fugitive List View Controller needs to have its delegate linked to that View Controller.

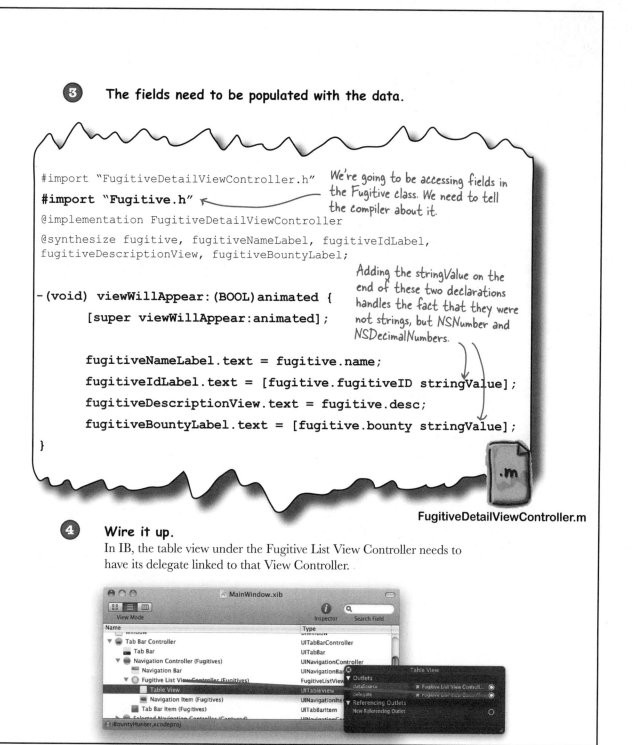

Test Drive

After populating the detail view, you can see
the information about each fugitive.

The back button is working thanks to
the nav control.

The labels
have been
replaced
with values
from the
database.

Now an
entry can be
selected in the
view.

The detail view
is fully populated.

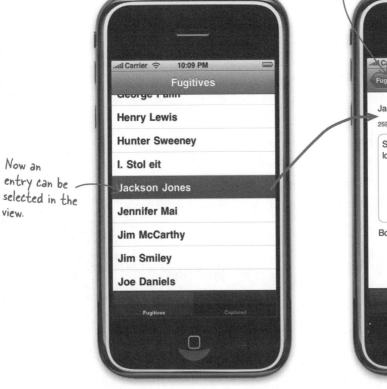

It all works!

It works great! Having all that information with me makes it much easier to catch outlaws. I should be able to almost double my business with this app!

Great!

After a couple of weeks, Bob is back with a new request...

That really worked! I've caught a ton of people already! How can I keep track of who I've caught?

To be continued...

CoreDatacross

There's a lot of terminology with Core Data; let's make sure you remember it!

Across

2. Each app has a _____ directory.
5. NS_____Descriptor captures how data should be sorted.
6. In the middle of the Core Data stack is the Persistent Store _____.
7. The _____ template is pretty basic.
8. _____ can manage different types of data.
10. The managed object _____ is the top of the Core Data stack.
11. NSFetch_____ describes a search.

Down

1. The Persistent Object Store is at the _____ of the Core Data stack.
3. Core Data has _____ and redo.
4. The _____ controller is good for switching views.
9. The managed _____ model describes entities.

Your Core Data Toolbox

You've got Chapter 7 under your belt and now you've added Core Data to your toolbox. For a complete list of tooltips in the book, go to http://www.headfirstlabs.com/iphonedev.

The Data Model

Works with entities that have properties called attributes.

Can be edited directly in Xcode.

Has several different data types.

Tab Bars

Each tab means a separate view.

Tabs work well with tasks that are not hierarchical.

Core Data

Provides a stack that manages the data so you don't have to.

Can manage different types of data.

Great for memory management and tracking changes.

BULLET POINTS

- Core Data is a **persistence framework** that offers loading, saving, versioning and undo-redo.

- **Core Data** can be built on top of SQLite databases, binary files, or temporary memory.

- The **Managed Object Model** defines the **Entities** we're going to ask Core Data to work with.

- The **Managed Object Context** is our entry point to our data. It keeps track of active **Managed Objects**.

- The Managed Object Context is part of the Core Data stack that handles reading and writing our data.

CoreDatacross Solution

So, did you remember all those words?

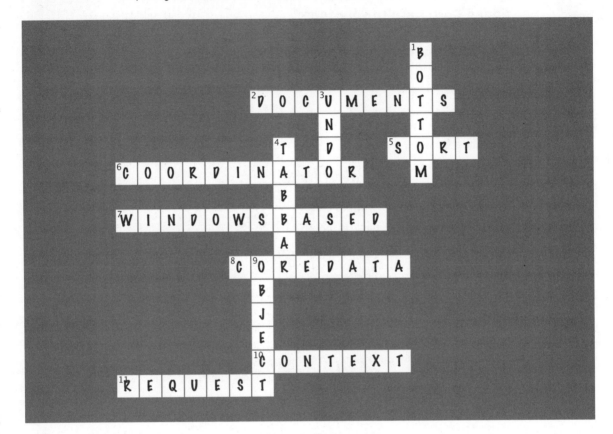

Across

2. Each app has a _____ directory. [DOCUMENTS]
5. NS_____Descriptor captures how data should be sorted. [SORT]
6. In the middle of the Core Data stack is the Persistent Store _____. [COORDINATOR]
7. The _____ template is pretty basic. [WINDOWSBASED]
8. _____ can manage different types of data. [COREDATA]
10. The managed object _____ is the top of the Core Data stack. [CONTEXT]
11. NSFetch_____ describes a search. [REQUEST]

Down

1. The Persistent Object Store is at the _____ of the Core Data stack. [BOTTOM]
3. Core Data has _____ and redo. [UNDO]
4. The _____ controller is good for switching views. [TABBAR]
9. The managed _____ model describes entities. [OBJECT]

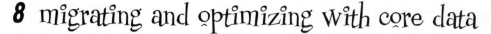

8 migrating and optimizing with core data

Things are changing

How about this one? I just can't seem to decide which outfit to wear...

We have a great app in the works.

iBountyHunter successfully loads the data that Bob needs and lets him view the fugitives in an easy way. But what about when the data has to change? Bob wants some new functionality, and what does that do to the data model? In this chapter you'll learn how to handle changes to your data model and how to take advantage of more Core Data features.

Bob needs documentation

To get paid, I need to be able to show who was captured when...

Bob needs to record more information.

Bob has to keep track of his work so he can be paid. That means that we need somewhere to store the day and time of a capture and then use that to build the captured view...

Remember that captured view we built in the last chapter?

How are we going to update iBountyHunter to handle the new information?

Sharpen your pencil

We need to figure out how to update iBountyHunter to handle this new data. Look at each piece of our application and write what, if anything, needs to change.

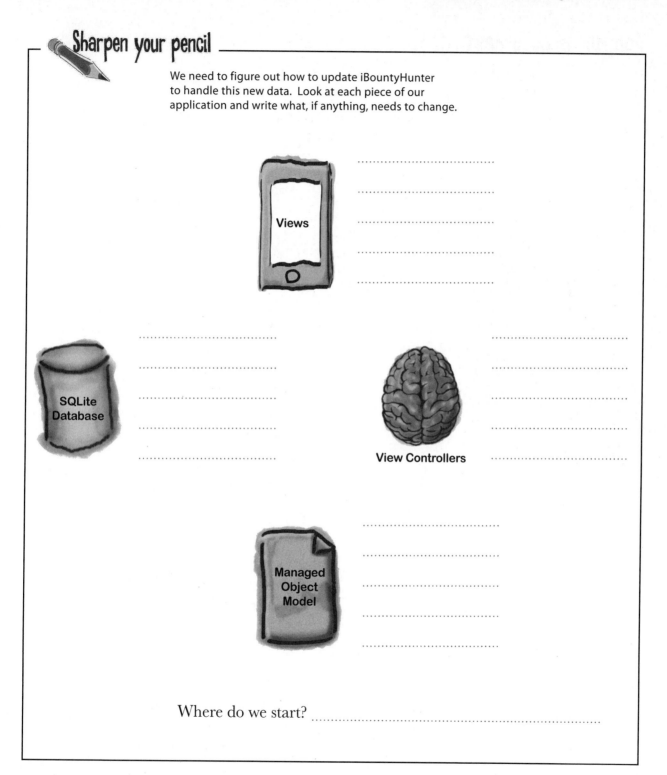

Views

....
....
....
....
....

SQLite Database

....
....
....
....
....

View Controllers

....
....
....
....

Managed Object Model

....
....
....
....
....

Where do we start? ....

Sharpen your pencil
Solution

We need to figure out how to update iBountyHunter to handle this new data. Look at each piece of our application and write what, if anything, needs to change.

Views

— A spot to mark fugitives as caught.

— Show the date and time of capture.

— Populate the captured list.

SQLite Database

— Add a captured flag to fugitives.

— Add the captured time for the fugitive.

— Add the captured date for the fugitive.

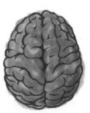

View Controllers

— Fill in the date and time of capture data.

— Display only the captured fugitives in the captured view.

Managed Object Model

— Add information about the changes to the data for display in the app.

Where do we start?   Since nearly everything depends on the new data we need to add, let's get that in our object model first; then we can update the rest.

Everything stems from our object model

From what we figured out in the exercise, the Fugitive entity needs a few more fields: the date and time, and something to indicate whether or not the fugitive has been captured. The database is built from the data model, so we can just update the data model to add the information we need. The Core Data date type includes both a date and time, so we only need two more properties on our Fugitive entity:

Since all fugitives will be either captured or not, it needs to exist for all of them.

captured
- Boolean
- NOT Optional
- NO by default

This provides both the date and the time.

captdate
- Date
- Optional

Since this field will only exist for the captured fugitives, it's optional.

Sharpen your pencil

Update the data model with the new captured fields.

☐ Use the data model editor to update the model with the two new fields.

☐ After you update the model, you'll need to delete the two old fugitive class files and generate new ones with the new fields included.

Sharpen your pencil
Solution

Use the tools that Xcode comes with to
quickly make those changes.

☑ Use the data model editor to update the model with the two new fields.

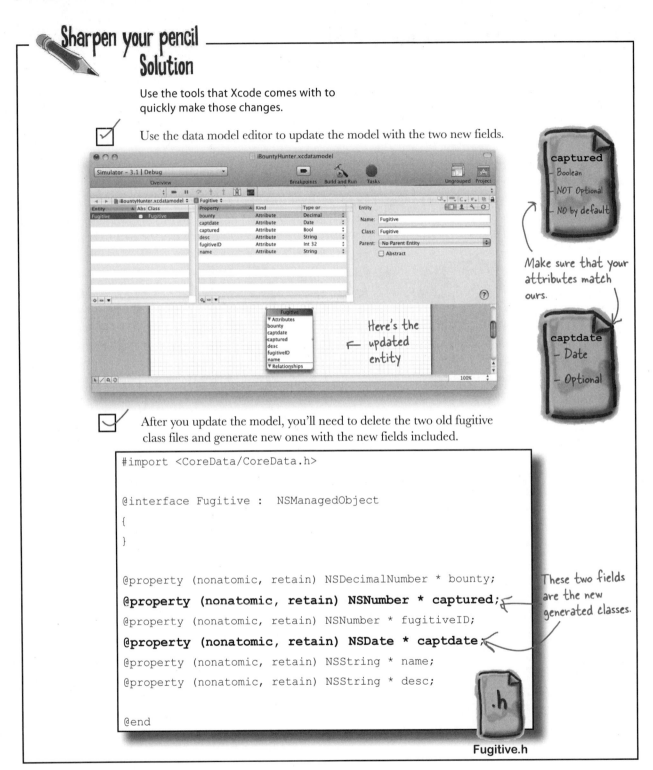

Make sure that your
attributes match
ours.

captured
- Boolean
- NOT Optional
- NO by default

captdate
- Date
- Optional

Here's the
updated
entity

☑ After you update the model, you'll need to delete the two old fugitive
class files and generate new ones with the new fields included.

```objc
#import <CoreData/CoreData.h>


@interface Fugitive :  NSManagedObject
{
}


@property (nonatomic, retain) NSDecimalNumber * bounty;
@property (nonatomic, retain) NSNumber * captured;
@property (nonatomic, retain) NSNumber * fugitiveID;
@property (nonatomic, retain) NSDate * captdate;
@property (nonatomic, retain) NSString * name;
@property (nonatomic, retain) NSString * desc;


@end
```

These two fields
are the new
generated classes.

Fugitive.h

```
#import "Fugitive.h"


@implementation Fugitive


@dynamic bounty;
@dynamic captured;
@dynamic fugitiveID;
@dynamic captdate;
@dynamic name;
@dynamic desc;


@end
```

The new fields have been added as dynamic properties, just like the earlier ones.

Fugitive.m

TEST DRIVE

Once you've made the changes, go ahead and run iBountyHunter.

```
● ● ●                    iBountyHunter – Debugger Console
Simulator - 3.1 | Debug ▾    ▶           ⚒          ●        ●       ❚❚          ▦
   Overview              Breakpoints  Build and Run  Tasks   Restart  Pause    Clear Log

[Session started at 2009-09-09 21:43:29 -0400.]
2009-09-09 21:43:32.890 iBountyHunter[10952:207] Unresolved error Error
   Domain=NSCocoaErrorDomain Code=134100 UserInfo=0x3c23c80 "Operation could not be
   completed. (Cocoa error 134100.)", {
   metadata =         {
       NSPersistenceFrameworkVersion = 248;
       NSStoreModelVersionHashes =         {
           Fugitive = <e33370b6 e7ca3101 f91d2595 1e8bfe01 3e7fb4de 6ef2a31d 9e50237b
               b313d390>;
       };
       NSStoreModelVersionHashesVersion = 3;
       NSStoreModelVersionIdentifiers =         (
       );
       NSStoreType = SQLite;
       NSStoreUUID = "E711F65F-3C5A-4889-872B-6541E4B2863A";
       "_NSAutoVacuumLevel" = 2;
   };
   reason = "The model used to open the store is incompatible with the one used to
   create the store";
}
}
Debugging terminated.
```

It crashed!

BRAIN POWER

Why did the app crash?

The data hasn't been updated

If you take a close look at the console report of the crash, you can figure out what's wrong...

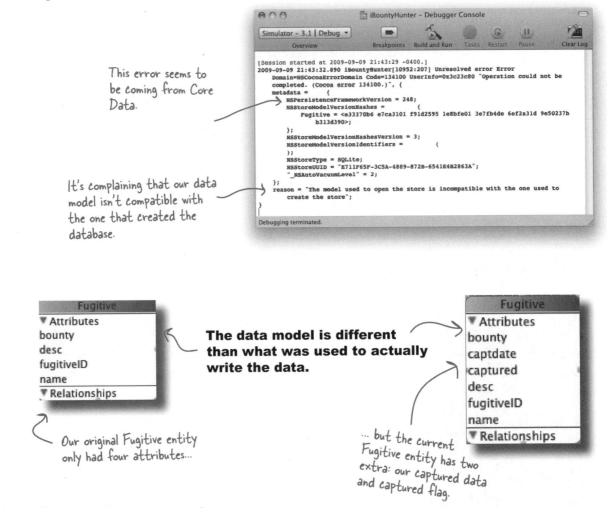

This error seems to be coming from Core Data.

It's complaining that our data model isn't compatible with the one that created the database.

The data model is different than what was used to actually write the data.

Our original Fugitive entity only had four attributes...

... but the current Fugitive entity has two extra: our captured data and captured flag.

Core Data caught a mismatch between our DB and our model

We created this problem when we added new fields to the Fugitive entity. Our initial fugitive database was created with the old model, and Core Data has no idea where to get those new fields from. Rather than risk data corruption, it aborted our application with an error. That's good, but we still need to figure out how to fix it.

Data migration is a common problem

Realizing you need to add new data or changing the way you store old data is a pretty common problem in application development. But just because it's common doesn't mean it's easy. Core Data works hard to make sure it doesn't corrupt or lose any data, so we're going to have to tell it what to do with our new Fugitive entity.

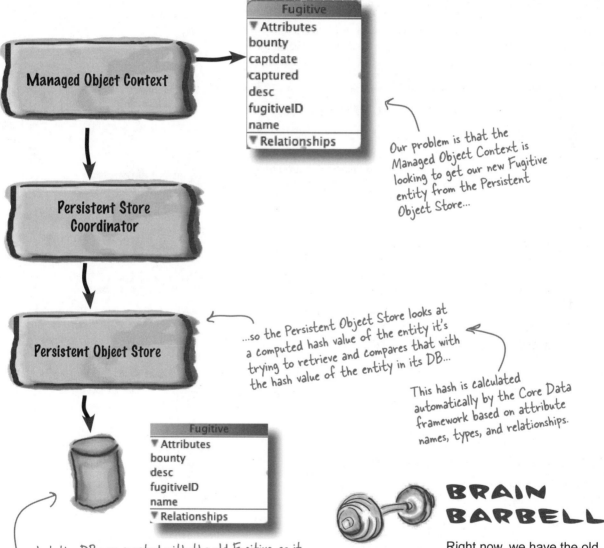

Managed Object Context

Persistent Store Coordinator

Persistent Object Store

Fugitive
▼ Attributes
bounty
captdate
captured
desc
fugitiveID
name
▼ Relationships

Fugitive
▼ Attributes
bounty
desc
fugitiveID
name
▼ Relationships

Our problem is that the Managed Object Context is looking to get our new Fugitive entity from the Persistent Object Store...

...so the Persistent Object Store looks at a computed hash value of the entity it's trying to retrieve and compares that with the hash value of the entity in its DB...

This hash is calculated automatically by the Core Data framework based on attribute names, types, and relationships.

...but the DB was created with the old Fugitive, so it has the old hash value. The Persistent Object Store fails to load the data, saying it can't load what's in that database into the new entity.

BRAIN BARBELL

Right now, we have the old data and the new data **model**. How can we get the new data?

We need to migrate the old data into the new model

We made the changes to the data model, but we need everything up and down the Core Data stack to be able to deal with those changes. In order to do that, we need to **migrate the data**.

To migrate anything, you need to go *from* somewhere *to* somewhere. Core Data needs to have both of these data models to make data migration work for the entire stack. We need a new approach to changing the data model, besides just changing the old one. Let's undo what we did earlier so we can load the data from the database again.

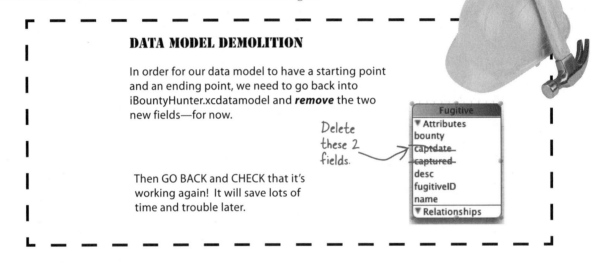

DATA MODEL DEMOLITION

In order for our data model to have a starting point and an ending point, we need to go back into iBountyHunter.xcdatamodel and *remove* the two new fields—for now.

Delete these 2 fields.

Then GO BACK and CHECK that it's working again! It will save lots of time and trouble later.

Our two models need different versions

It's easy enough to change the data model by hand, but Core Data needs to be able to work with both the old and new data. We need to give Core Data access to both, but tell them they're different versions of the same model. Even more importantly, we need to tell Core Data which one we consider our current version.

The Persistent Object Store needs to know that this is what we consider our current version.

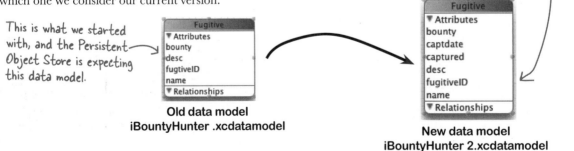

This is what we started with, and the Persistent Object Store is expecting this data model.

Old data model
iBountyHunter .xcdatamodel

New data model
iBountyHunter 2.xcdatamodel

Xcode makes it easy to version the data model

Fortunately, it's pretty easy to create a new version of your data model using Xcode:

 Highlight iBountyHunter.xcdatamodel.
Then go to the **Design → Data Model → Add Model Version** menu option.
That will generate a new directory called iBountyHunter.xcdatamodeld. Under that
directory, there will be two copies of the data model.

 Set the current version.
Inside the iBountyHunter.xcmodeld directory, select iBountyHunter 2.xcdatamodel,
which will be our new version. Go to the **Design → Data Model → Set Current
Version** menu option.

Here's what the final file listing will look like.

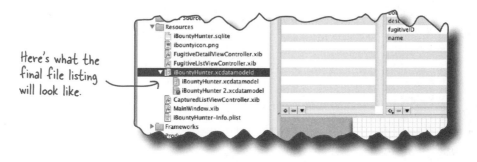

 Update the new data model.
Select iBountyHunter 2.xcdatamodel and re-edit the data model to add back in the
captdate and captured fields as we did before. Now the old version is preserved and
the changes are where they belong.

Geek Bits

Normally, you'd also need to delete and regenerate the
Fugitive class, but since we made the same changes to
the new file, the generated class would be the same.

**How does the app
map between the
two versions?**

Frank

Jim

Joe

Jim: Ugh. I guess we need to write a bunch of migration code or something.

Joe: Why?

Jim: I assume we're going to have to tell Core Data how to get from the old version of the data to the new one, right?

Frank: Well, actually, I think we can do it automatically.

Jim: What?

Frank: Core Data has a feature that allows you to tell the app about both models and it can migrate the data for you.

Jim: Nice! When does the data actually get migrated?

Frank: Runtime, when the Persistent Object Store sees that the data is in the old format. That means that we'll just need some code to tell iBountyHunter to actually do the migration.

Joe: OK, so it looks like some of that code is auto-generated, and some of it needs to be added.

Jim: This is great; so we can just change whatever we want?

Frank: There are certain data changes that Core Data can handle automatically, like adding new attributes. More complex changes to the data need to be handled manually.

Joe: Yeah, it says here that we can do automatic migration if we're adding attributes, or changing the optional status of an attribute.

Jim: What about renaming?

Frank: Renaming gets tricky—sometimes you can and sometimes you can't.

Joe: So, how can we migrate the data we have?

Core Data can "lightly" migrate data

Lightweight data migration is a powerful Core Data tool that allows you to cleanly update your underlying data to match a new data model without needing a mapping model. It only works with basic data changes: adding new attributes, changing a required attribute to an optional one, or making an optional attribute required with a default value. It can also handle limited renaming of attributes, but that gets trickier.

Automatic data migration happens at runtime, which means that your app needs to know that it's going to happen so that the data can be migrated. You'll do that in the AppDelegate:

```
- (NSPersistentStoreCoordinator *)persistentStoreCoordinator {

    if (persistentStoreCoordinator != nil) {
      return persistentStoreCoordinator;
    }

    NSURL *storeUrl = [NSURL fileURLWithPath: [[self applicationDocumentsDirectory]
stringByAppendingPathComponent: @"iBountyHunter.sqlite"]];

      NSError *error = nil;

    persistentStoreCoordinator = [[NSPersistentStoreCoordinator alloc] initWithManagedOb
jectModel:[self managedObjectModel]];

    NSDictionary *options = [NSDictionary dictionaryWithObjectsAndKeys:

    [NSNumber numberWithBool:YES], NSMigratePersistentStoresAutomaticallyOption,

    [NSNumber numberWithBool:YES], NSInferMappingModelAutomaticallyOption, nil];

      if (![persistentStoreCoordinator addPersistentStoreWithType:NSSQLiteStoreType
configuration:nil URL:storeUrl options:options error:&error])
```

Remember, by default Core Data will load all of the object models in your app bundle. That means it will see both the old version and the current version of our model.

iBountyHunterAppDelegate.m

We changed this from nil: options to pass the options to the persistentStoreCoordiator.

All we need to do to enable lightweight migration is turn it on.

TEST DRIVE

After adding the code to the app delegate, Build and Debug...

If you run into issues here, try Build->Clean first, then Build and Debug. Strangely, Xcode doesn't always properly recompile the first time you version your model, but cleaning should fix it.

TEST DRIVE

Fugitives

Kate Raines

Linda Lewis

Michael Merkins

Mike Smithson

Mike Thayer

N. Winner

Nick Forsee

Nicky Wolf

Fugitives — Captured

Awesome! It's working with a whole new data model.

The Persistent Object Store Exposed

**This week's interview:
Do you really have any
staying power?**

Head First: Hi Persistent Object Store, mind if I call you POS for short?

Persistent Object Store: I'd rather you didn't. Just "Store" is fine.

Head First: OK, Store, so I understand you're part of the Core Data stack?

Store: Yep—one of the most important parts, actually. It's my job to read and write your actual data.

Head First: Right, you're the guy who translates into a bunch of different formats.

Store: Exactly. When you use Core Data, you don't really need to know if your data is going into a simple file or a sophisticated database. You just ask me to read and write a bunch of data and I handle it.

Head First: That's convenient. I understand you can be pretty particular, though. I hear you don't take well to change.

Store: I don't think you're getting the whole picture. See, it's my job to make sure your data is loaded and saved exactly right.

Head First: I get that, but still, small changes are OK, right?

Store: Sure—I just need to make sure you really want me to do them. You need to tell me what data I'm looking at and then tell me how you want me to return it to you. Tell me it's OK to infer the differences and do the mapping and I'll take care of the rest.

Head First: So do you actually migrate the data or just translate it when you load it?

Store: Oh, I actually migrate the data. Now, here's where things get cool. Simple stores like the binary file ones just create a new file with the migrated data. But if I'm using a SQLite DB, I can usually do the migration right in place. Don't need to load the data and the whole migration is nearly instant.

Head First: Nice! I thought lightweight migration was kind of a noob's migration.

Store: Oh no, if you can let me do the migration through lightweight migration, that's definitely the way to go. Now if you need to do something more complicated, like splitting an old attribute into two new ones or change the type of something, you'll need to help me out.

Head First: And people do that through code?

Store: Sort of. Basically, you need to give me one more model, a mapping model. That tells me how to move your data from the old format to the new format.

Head First: Hmm, OK, makes sense. I guess this applies to renaming variables too?

Store: Actually, most of the time I can handle that too, as long as you tell me what the old name was. If you look at the details of an attribute in your object model, you can give me the old name of an attribute. If it's there, and I have to do a migration, I can handle renaming too.

Head First: Wow, you're not nearly as boring as I thought...

Store: Thanks, I guess.

there are no
Dumb Questions

Q: How may versions of a data model can I have?

A: As many as you need. Once you start adding versions, you'll need to keep track of your current version so that Managed Object Model knows what you want when you ask for an entity. By keeping all of the old versions around, Core Data can migrate from any prior version to the current one.

Q: When is renaming something OK for a lightweight migration? When isn't it?

A: You can rename variables as long as you don't change the type. If you rename them, click on the little wrench on the attribute properties in Xcode and specify the renaming identifier to be the old attribute. Core Data will handle the migration automatically from there.

Q: Can I use migration to get data I have in some other format into Core Data?

A: No. Migration (lightweight or otherwise) only works with existing Core Data. If you have legacy data you want moved into Core Data, you'll need to do that yourself. Typically, you just read the legacy data with your own code, create a new NSManagedObject to hold it, populate the new object, and save it using Core Data. It's not pretty, but it works. There are a couple other approaches you can look at if you have large amounts of data to migrate or streaming data (for example, from a network feed). Take a look at the Apple Documentation on Efficiently Importing Data with Core Data for more details.

Q: Does it make a difference if I use lightweight migration or migrate data myself?

A: Use lightweight migration if you can. It won't work for all cases, but, if it can be done, Core Data can optimize the migration if you're using a SQLite store. Migration time can be really, really small when done through lightweight migration.

Q: What do I do if I can't use lightweight migration?

A: You'll need to create a mapping model. You can do that in Xcode by selecting Design→Mapping Model, then picking the two models you want to map between. You'll need to select your source entities and attributes, then select the destination entities and attributes. You can enter custom expressions to do data conversions if you need to. To find out more information on mapping models, check out the Apple Documentation on Core Data Migration.

Q: Xcode lets me enter a hash modifier in the Versioning Settings for an attribute. What are those for?

A: Core Data computes a hash for entities using attribute information so it can determine if the model has changed since the data store was created. However, it's possible that you need to change the way your data is stored without actually changing the data model. For example, let's say you always stored your time values in seconds, but then decided you needed to store milliseconds instead. You can continue to store the value as an integer but use the version hash modifier to let Core Data know that you want two models to be considered different versions and apply your migration code at runtime.

BULLET POINTS

- Lightweight automatic migration needs **both versions** of the data model before it will work.

- Automatic migration can change a SQLite database **without** loading the data.

- Migration of data happens **at runtime**.

- You can use lightweight migration to **add variables**, make a required variable **optional**, make an optional one **required** with default, and to do some **renaming**.

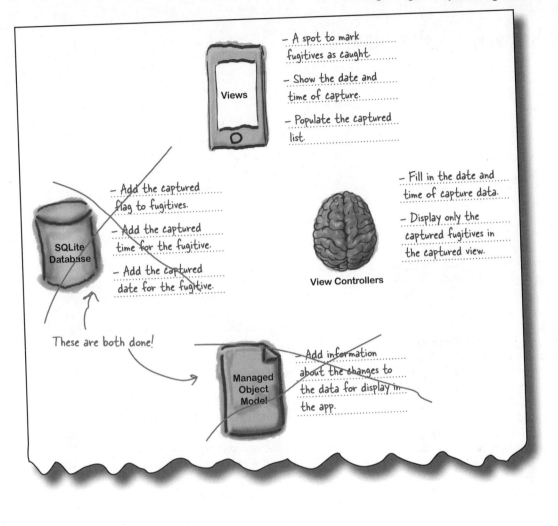

Views
- A spot to mark fugitives as caught.
- Show the date and time of capture.
- Populate the captured list.

- Add the captured flag to fugitives.
- Add the captured time for the fugitive.
- Add the captured date for the fugitive.

SQLite Database

These are both done!

View Controllers
- Fill in the date and time of capture data.
- Display only the captured fugitives in the captured view.

Managed Object Model
- Add information about the changes to the data for display in the app.

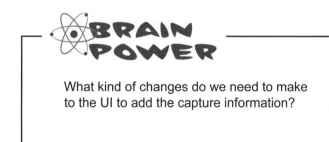

What kind of changes do we need to make to the UI to add the capture information?

Bob has some design input

I want all of this captured info on the detail view. Here, I sketched up some ideas.

View

Cancel   Save

Fugitive Name

Fugitive ID#

Lorem ipsum dolor sit er elit lamet, consectetaur cillium adipisicing pecu, sed do eiusmod tempor incididunt ut labore et dolore magna aliqua. Ut enim ad minim veniam, quis nostrud

Bounty: $1,000,000

Captured? Y/N

Capture Date & Time:

I was thinking I could just type in Y or N when I capture a guy? Then fill in the date and time below.

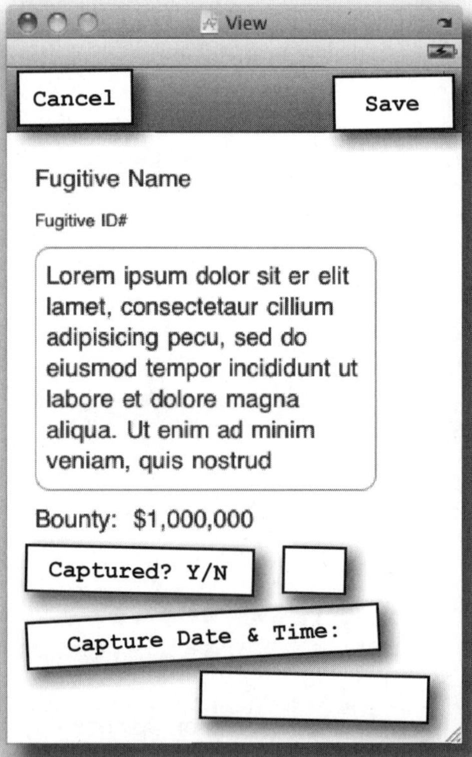

But Bob's sketch has some problems...

Sharpen your pencil

Bob's view needs some improving. As an experienced iPhone developer, you can probably come up with some better UI designs. Time for you to help him out.

1 Can Bob's view actually work with the app as it's currently written? (Circle one)   **Yes**   **No**

2 If not, why not? ....

....

....

3 To properly implement this view, you need to know what data is editable. What data can the user edit and what is the best way to handle that input? ....

....

....

3 Sketch up *your* plan for the final detail view:

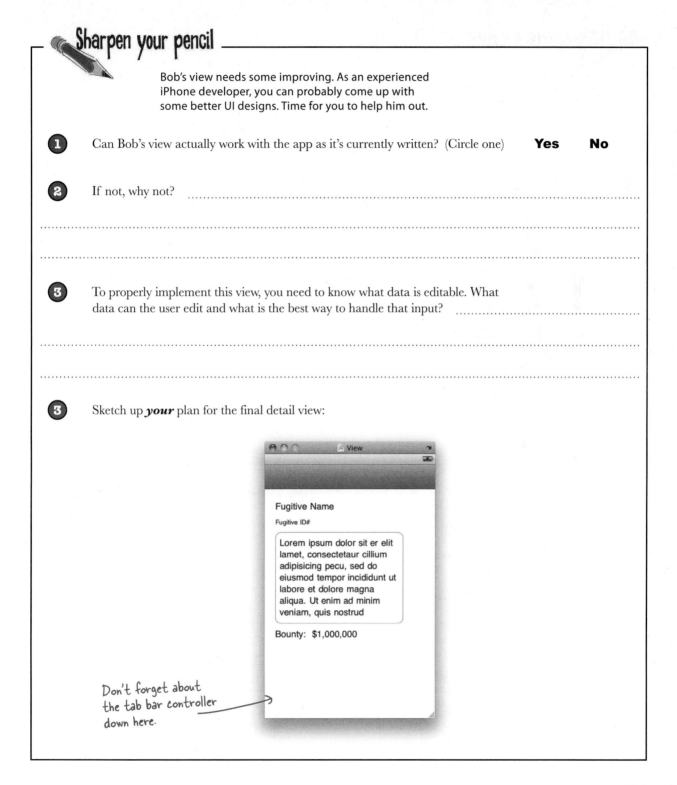

Fugitive Name

Fugitive ID#

Lorem ipsum dolor sit er elit lamet, consectetaur cillium adipisicing pecu, sed do eiusmod tempor incididunt ut labore et dolore magna aliqua. Ut enim ad minim veniam, quis nostrud

Bounty: $1,000,000

Don't forget about the tab bar controller down here.

Sharpen your pencil
Solution

Now that you've thought through the design implications,
what should the detail view look like?

1 Can Bob's view actually work as is with the app as written? (Circle one) **Yes** **No**

2 If not, why not?   We already have a "back" button where Bob wants to put a cancel button.
Asking the user to input the "Y" or "N" and type the date and time is not a great UI.

3 To properly implement this view, you need to know what data is editable.
What data can the user edit and what is the best way to handle input?   The only data that will need to
change is the captured field and the captured date and time. Since captured is a boolean,
a switch or some kind of control will work better than typing. Since Bob will hit the control when he
captures the bad guy, we can just get the current date and time from iPhone and save even more typing.

3 Sketch up *your* plan for the final detail view:

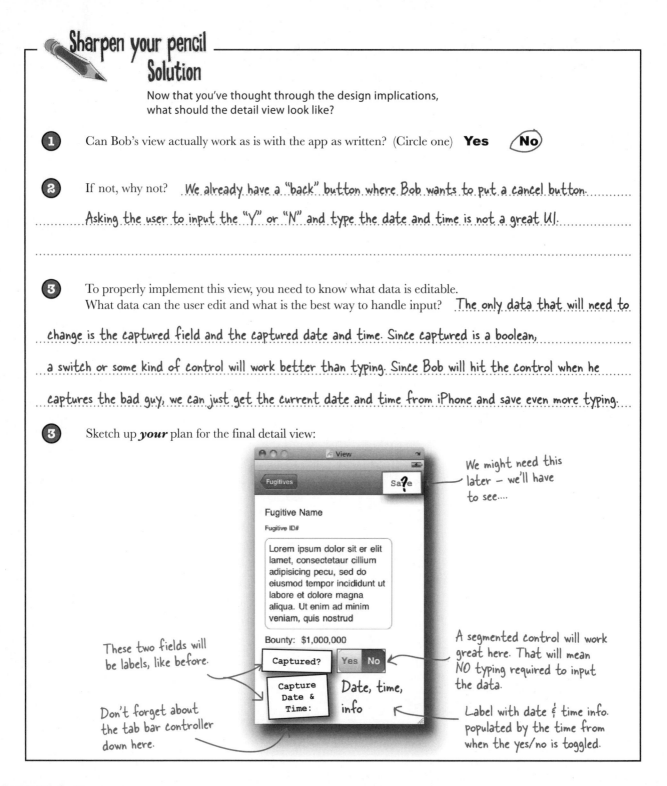

We might need this later – we'll have to see....

These two fields will be labels, like before.

Don't forget about the tab bar controller down here.

A segmented control will work great here. That will mean NO typing required to input the data.

Label with date & time info. populated by the time from when the yes/no is toggled.

Window contents:
View

Fugitives   Sa?e

Fugitive Name
Fugitive ID#

Lorem ipsum dolor sit er elit lamet, consectetaur cillium adipisicing pecu, sed do eiusmod tempor incididunt ut labore et dolore magna aliqua. Ut enim ad minim veniam, quis nostrud

Bounty: $1,000,000

Captured?   Yes No

Capture Date & Time: Date, time, info

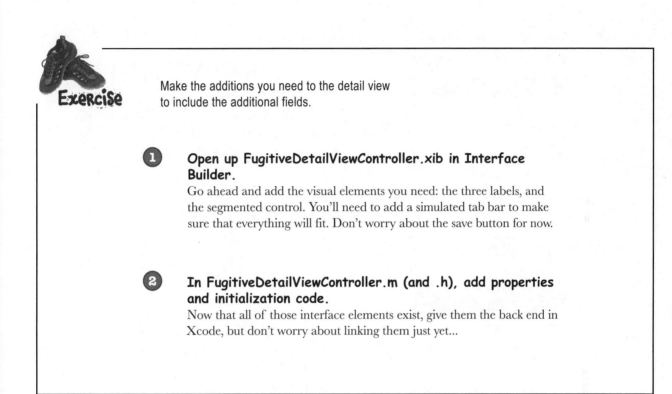

Make the additions you need to the detail view
to include the additional fields.

1 **Open up FugitiveDetailViewController.xib in Interface Builder.**

Go ahead and add the visual elements you need: the three labels, and the segmented control. You'll need to add a simulated tab bar to make sure that everything will fit. Don't worry about the save button for now.

2 **In FugitiveDetailViewController.m (and .h), add properties and initialization code.**

Now that all of those interface elements exist, give them the back end in Xcode, but don't worry about linking them just yet...

Exercise Solution

Here are the additions to the view,
and the code to support them.

① **Open up FugitiveDetailViewController.xib in Interface Builder.**

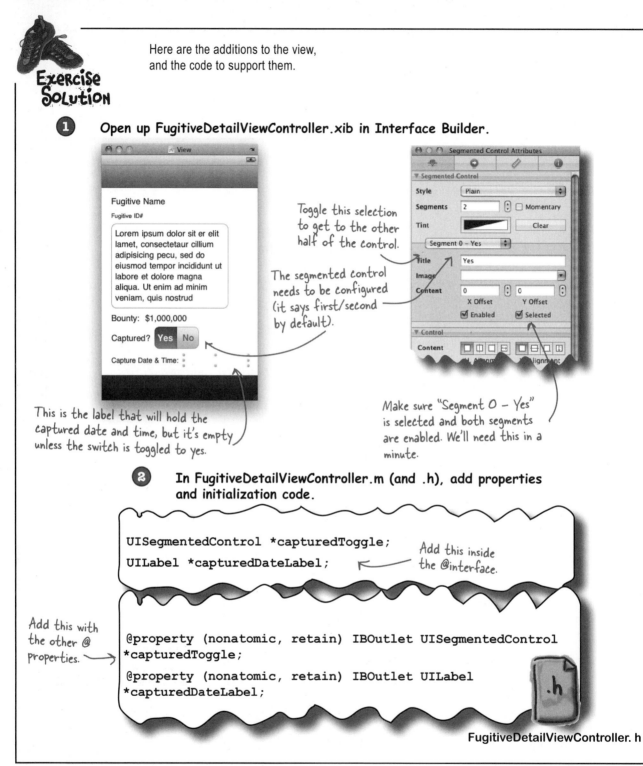

Toggle this selection to get to the other half of the control.

The segmented control needs to be configured (it says first/second by default).

This is the label that will hold the captured date and time, but it's empty unless the switch is toggled to yes.

Make sure "Segment 0 – Yes" is selected and both segments are enabled. We'll need this in a minute.

② **In FugitiveDetailViewController.m (and .h), add properties and initialization code.**

```
UISegmentedControl *capturedToggle;
UILabel *capturedDateLabel;
```

Add this inside the @interface.

Add this with the other @properties.

```
@property (nonatomic, retain) IBOutlet UISegmentedControl
*capturedToggle;
@property (nonatomic, retain) IBOutlet UILabel
*capturedDateLabel;
```

FugitiveDetailViewController. h

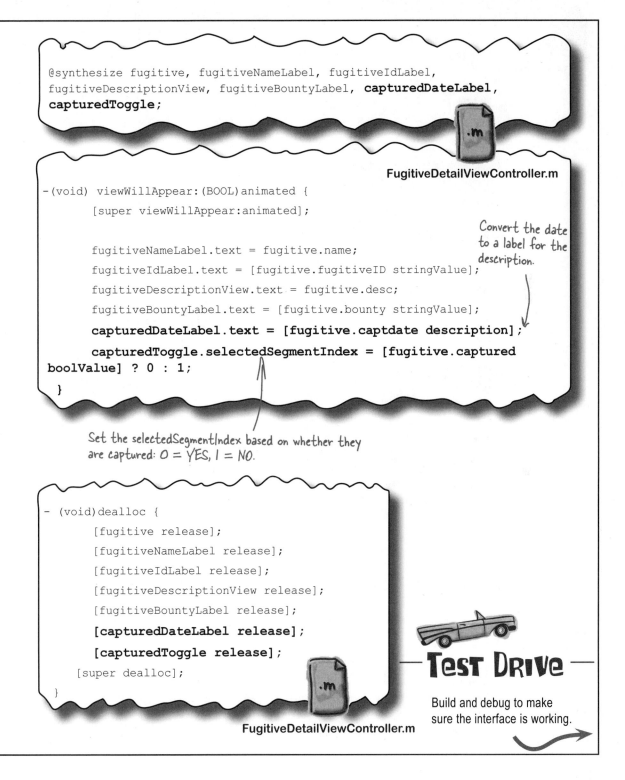

```
@synthesize fugitive, fugitiveNameLabel, fugitiveIdLabel,
fugitiveDescriptionView, fugitiveBountyLabel, capturedDateLabel,
capturedToggle;
```

FugitiveDetailViewController.m

```
-(void) viewWillAppear:(BOOL)animated {
    [super viewWillAppear:animated];

    fugitiveNameLabel.text = fugitive.name;
    fugitiveIdLabel.text = [fugitive.fugitiveID stringValue];
    fugitiveDescriptionView.text = fugitive.desc;
    fugitiveBountyLabel.text = [fugitive.bounty stringValue];
    capturedDateLabel.text = [fugitive.captdate description];
    capturedToggle.selectedSegmentIndex = [fugitive.captured
boolValue] ? 0 : 1;
}
```

Convert the date to a label for the description.

Set the selectedSegmentIndex based on whether they are captured: 0 = YES, 1 = NO.

```
- (void)dealloc {
    [fugitive release];
    [fugitiveNameLabel release];
    [fugitiveIdLabel release];
    [fugitiveDescriptionView release];
    [fugitiveBountyLabel release];
    [capturedDateLabel release];
    [capturedToggle release];
    [super dealloc];
}
```

FugitiveDetailViewController.m

— TEST DRIVE —

Build and debug to make sure the interface is working.

Test Drive

All the view elements look good! Now we just need to implement their behaviors...

there are no
Dumb Questions

Q: Why didn't we use the switch instead of the segmented control?

A: Because there's no Apple-sanctioned way to change the text of the switch. By default, the options are On and Off, which won't work for us.

Q: Why didn't we use a check box for the captured field?

A: It turns out that the check box isn't a standard control. It's certainly surprising, since you see them so often in iPhone apps.

They can be done, however, by creating a custom button with three images (an empty box, a selected box, and a checked box), and switching between them.

Toggle Code Magnets

Now that we have the controls laid out the way we want them, we need to actually give them some behavior. Use the magnets below to implement the method that will handle the segmented control switching. Then everything will be ready for linking to the segmented control in Interface Builder.

```objc
- (IBAction) capturedToggleChanged: (id) sender

        if (_____    _____) {

                _____ *now = [NSDate _____

                            _____ = now;

                    fugitive.captured = [NSNumber numberWithBool:YES];
                }
                else {

                            _____ = nil;

                    fugitive.captured = [NSNumber numberWithBool:NO];
                }


                capturedDateLabel.text = [_____];
        }
```

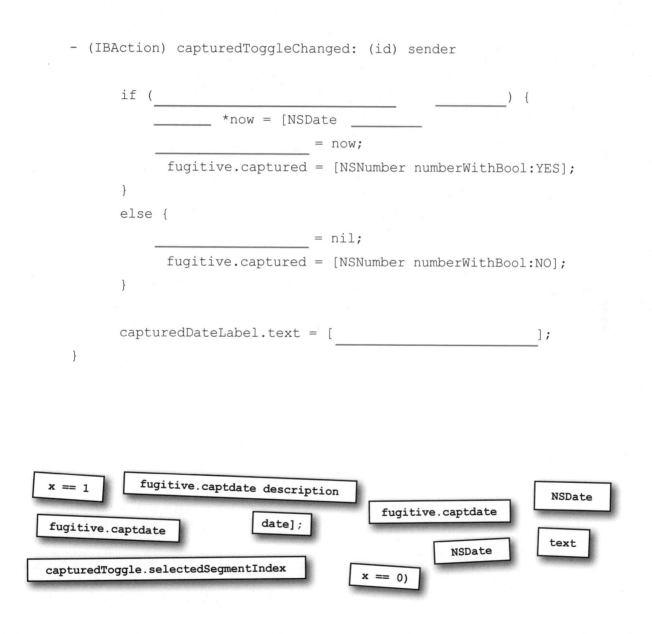

x == 1	
fugitive.captdate description	NSDate
fugitive.captdate	date]; fugitive.captdate
capturedToggle.selectedSegmentIndex	NSDate text
	x == 0)

Toggle Code Magnets Solution

Now that we have the controls laid out the way we want them, we need to actually give them some behavior. Use the magnets below to implement the method that will handle the segmented control switching. Then everything will be ready for linking to the segmented control in Interface Builder.

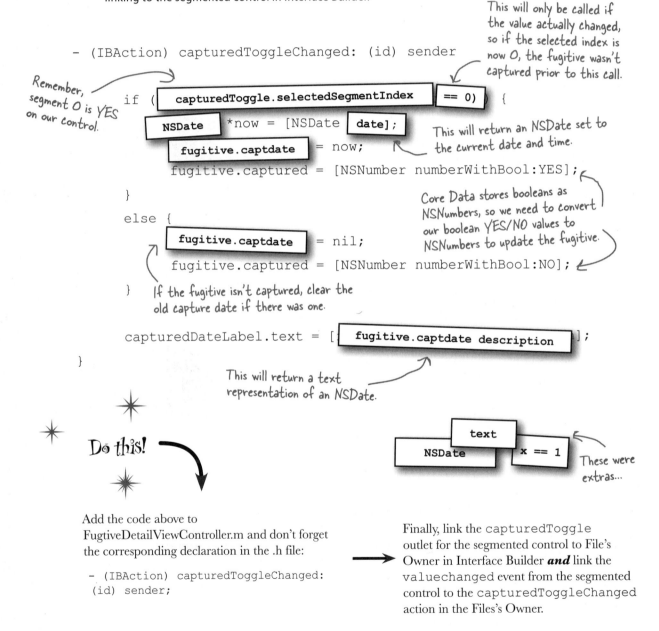

This will only be called if the value actually changed, so if the selected index is now 0, the fugitive wasn't captured prior to this call.

```
- (IBAction) capturedToggleChanged: (id) sender
```

Remember, segment 0 is YES on our control.

```
    if ( capturedToggle.selectedSegmentIndex == 0) {
        NSDate *now = [NSDate date];
        fugitive.captdate = now;
        fugitive.captured = [NSNumber numberWithBool:YES];
    }
    else {
        fugitive.captdate = nil;
        fugitive.captured = [NSNumber numberWithBool:NO];
    }
    capturedDateLabel.text = [ fugitive.captdate description ];
}
```

This will return an NSDate set to the current date and time.

Core Data stores booleans as NSNumbers, so we need to convert our boolean YES/NO values to NSNumbers to update the fugitive.

If the fugitive isn't captured, clear the old capture date if there was one.

This will return a text representation of an NSDate.

Do this!

NSDate   text   x == 1

These were extras...

Add the code above to FugtiveDetailViewController.m and don't forget the corresponding declaration in the .h file:

```
- (IBAction) capturedToggleChanged:
(id) sender;
```

Finally, link the capturedToggle outlet for the segmented control to File's Owner in Interface Builder **and** link the valuechanged event from the segmented control to the capturedToggleChanged action in the Files's Owner.

Test Drive

Now that all of that work is done, you should have a functioning detail view. Give it a try...

The view looks great and the segmented control is set to No, just like it should be.

If you toggle the segmented control, the date and time are filled in.

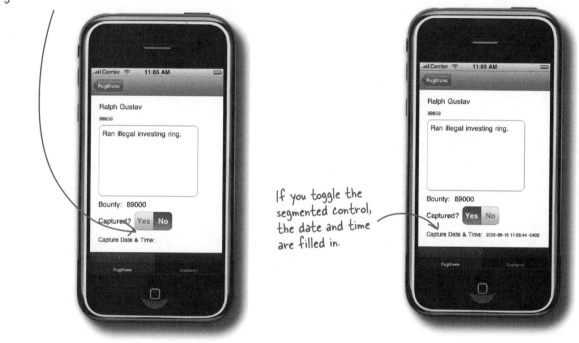

It's working! Spend some time moving around in and out of the table view, mark a fugitive as captured, and then come back into that same fugitive. Go ahead, quit the app and check again, we dare you. What's going on?

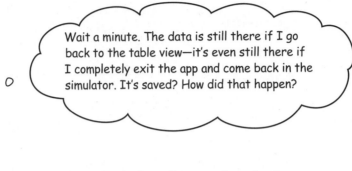

Wait a minute. The data is still there if I go back to the table view—it's even still there if I completely exit the app and come back in the simulator. It's saved? How did that happen?

Core Data handles saving, too!

Checking that Core Data box when you created the app did more for you than you realized—it enabled saving as well.

The Managed Object Context saves new or changed items

We've used the managed object context to load our Fugitives, but it is also responsible for coordinating saving your data, too. Remember how NSManagedObject can keep track of changes to entities? The Managed Object Context can take advantage of this information to tell if you if there are any changes in the objects it's managing. Similarly, if you create a new instance of an NSManagedObject, you need to tell it which Managed Object Context it belongs to and that Managed Object Context knows it has new entities to keep track of. The Core Data template takes advantage of this during application exit to see if the Managed Object Context has any new or changed data. If it does, the application simply asks the context to save them.

This code from iBountyHunterAppDelegate.m is checking for changes as you exit the app.

```
- (void)applicationWillTerminate:(UIApplication *)
application {


    NSError *error = nil;
    if (managedObjectContext != nil) {
        if ([managedObjectContext hasChanges] &&
![managedObjectContext save:&error])

    ...
```

there are no
Dumb Questions

Q: You said if I create new instances of NSManagedObjects I need to tell them which Managed Object Context they belong to. How do I do that?

A: It's part of the EntityDescription we mentioned in Chapter 7. If you want to create a new instance of an NSManagedObject, you just do this: [NSEntityDescription insertNewObjectForEntityForName:@"Fugitive" inManagedObjectContext:managedObject Context];. The Managed Object Context is provided right from the start.

Q: What's the "&error" that's being passed to the save call?

A: Most Core Data load/save operations point to an NSError in case something goes wrong. The "&" in Objective-C behaves just like it does in C or C++ and returns the "address of" the item. We declare a pointer to an NSError then pass the address of that pointer into the save method in case something happens. If the save call fails, Core Data will populate that error argument with more detailed information.

Q: Speaking of errors, what should I do if this comes back with an error?

A: That's really application-specific. Depending on when you detect the problem, you can warn the user and try to recover; other times there's not too much you can do. For example, if the error happens during the applicationWillTerminate method, there's not much you can do other than tell the user the save failed and possibly stash the data somewhere else.

Q: Should I only ever call save in applicationWillTerminate?

A: No, not at all. The Core Data template set it up this way for convenience, but you should save whenever it's appropriate in your application. In fact, if you're using a SQLite database backend for your data, saves are significantly faster than when we were working with plists in DrinkMixer. You should consider saving additions or changes to the data as soon as possible after they are made to try and avoid any kind of data loss.

Q: You said Core Data could do data validation; where does that fit into all of this?

A: At a minimum, Core Data will validate objects before they're stored in the Persistent Store. So, it's possible that you could get a validation error when you try to save your changes if you have invalid data in one of your managed objects. To avoid such late notice, you should validate your NSManagedObjects as close to the time of change as possible. You can explicitly validate a new NSManagedObject like this: [fugitive validateForInsert:&error]. Similarly, there are methods for validating updates and deletes. You can call these methods at any time to verify that the NSManagedObject is valid against constraints you put in the data model. If it's not, you can notify the user and ask them to correct the problem.

Q: What if I don't want to save the changes in the Managed Object Context? Can I reset it?

A: It's easier than that—just send it the `rollback:` message. When a Managed Object Context is told to rollback it will discard any newly inserted objects, any deletions, and any unsaved changes to existing objects. You can think of the Managed Object Context as managing transactions—changes to entities, including insertion and deletions, are either committed with a `save:` message or abandoned with a `rollback:` message.

A quick demo with Bob

After seeing the detailed view and all the captured stuff,
Bob's thrilled, but has one quick comment:

This is definitely way easier than what I came up with. But, um, where is that list of captured people?

After all that, we forgot to populate the captured list!

OK, I know how to populate the table cells and stuff—but how can I only pick captured guys?

We can use Core Data to filter our results.

We already have capture information in our Fugitive data; we just need to use it to get the captured list. We need a way to tell Core Data we only want Fugitives where the captured flag is true.

Where is a natural place to put this kind of filtering?

Use predicates for filtering data

In database languages all over the world, predicates are used to scope a search to only find data that matches certain criteria. Remember the NSFetchRequest we talked about in Chapter 7? We've used the Entity Information and Sort Descriptor but haven't needed the predicate support... until now.

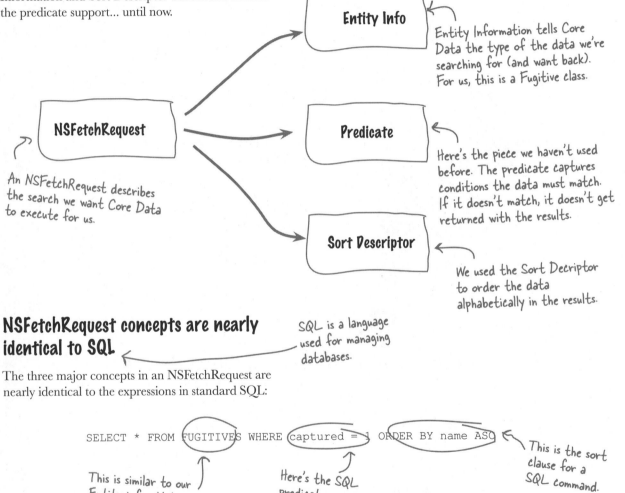

Entity Info

Entity Information tells Core Data the type of the data we're searching for (and want back). For us, this is a Fugitive class.

NSFetchRequest

An NSFetchRequest describes the search we want Core Data to execute for us.

Predicate

Here's the piece we haven't used before. The predicate captures conditions the data must match. If it doesn't match, it doesn't get returned with the results.

Sort Descriptor

We used the Sort Decriptor to order the data alphabetically in the results.

NSFetchRequest concepts are nearly identical to SQL

SQL is a language used for managing databases.

The three major concepts in an NSFetchRequest are nearly identical to the expressions in standard SQL:

```
SELECT * FROM FUGITIVES WHERE captured = 1 ORDER BY name ASC
```

This is similar to our Entity info.. Not exactly the same, but close.

Here's the SQL predicate...

This is the sort clause for a SQL command.

All we need to do is provide the predicate information to our NSFetchRequest and Core Data handles the rest. We can use an NSPredicate for that...

We need to set a predicate on our NSFetchRequest

NSPredicate is a deceptively simple class that lets us express logical constraints on our NSFetchRequest. You use entity and attribute names along with comparison operators to express your constraint information. You can create a basic NSPredicate with a string format syntax similar to NSString, like this:

```
NSPredicate *predicate = [NSPredicate predicateWithFormat:@"captured == YES"];
[request setPredicate:predicate];
```

But NSPredicates don't stop with simple attribute comparisons. Apple provides several subclasses like NSComparisonPredicate, NSCompoundPredicate, and NSExpression as well as a complex grammar for wildcard matching, object graph traversal, and more. For iBountyHunter, a simple attribute condition is all we need to get Bob's view working.

Exercise

Time to populate the captured view! There's some work to get the captured view updated to where the fugitive view is, and then a tweak to display what we need.

1 **Set some captured fugitives.**
Build and run the old version of the app and toggle a handful of the fugitives to captured before making any changes. You'll need that for testing.

2 **Get the captured view to match the fugitive view.**
Where we left off in Chapter 7, we hadn't yet done the work to populate the captured list. Since we're just going to be filtering the data that's in the fugitive list, the easiest way is to start with the entire list and then add the filtering code. Don't forget the tableview datasource and delegate methods.

3 **Add the predicate code.**
Update your NSFetchRequest to use an NSPredicate so it only finds captured fugitives. This needs to go into the viewWillAppear method in the CapturedViewController.m.

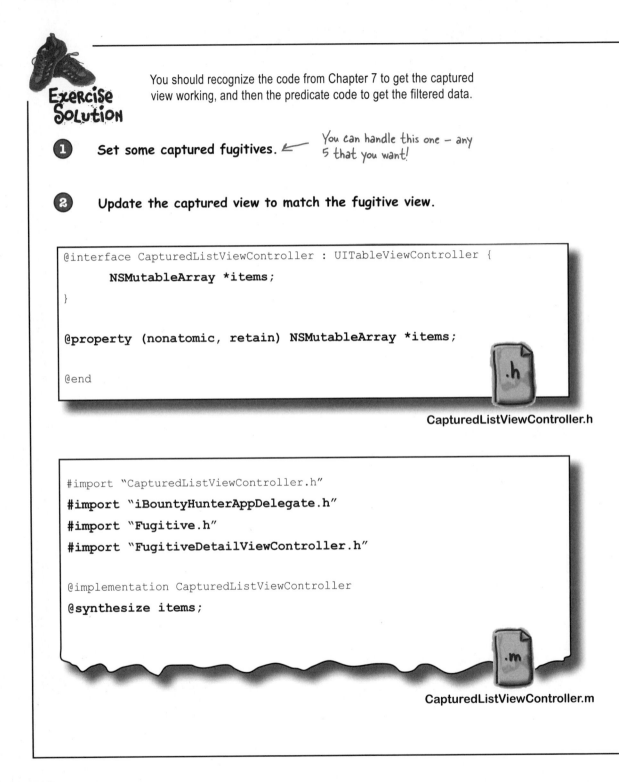

You should recognize the code from Chapter 7 to get the captured view working, and then the predicate code to get the filtered data.

① Set some captured fugitives. ← *You can handle this one – any 5 that you want!*

② Update the captured view to match the fugitive view.

```
@interface CapturedListViewController : UITableViewController {

    NSMutableArray *items;

}

@property (nonatomic, retain) NSMutableArray *items;

@end
```

CapturedListViewController.h

```
#import "CapturedListViewController.h"
#import "iBountyHunterAppDelegate.h"
#import "Fugitive.h"
#import "FugitiveDetailViewController.h"


@implementation CapturedListViewController
@synthesize items;
```

CapturedListViewController.m

```objc
- (void)viewWillAppear: (BOOL) animated {
    [super viewWillAppear:animated];

    iBountyHunterAppDelegate *appDelegate = (iBountyHunterAppDelegate*)
[[UIApplication sharedApplication] delegate];

    NSManagedObjectContext *managedObjectContext = appDelegate.
managedObjectContext;

    NSFetchRequest *request = [[NSFetchRequest alloc] init];

    NSEntityDescription *entity = [NSEntityDescription
entityForName:@"Fugitive" inManagedObjectContext:managedObjectContext];

    [request setEntity:entity];

    NSSortDescriptor *sortDescriptor = [[NSSortDescriptor alloc]
initWithKey:@"name" ascending:YES];

    NSArray *sortDescriptors = [[NSArray alloc]
initWithObjects:sortDescriptor, nil];

    [request setSortDescriptors:sortDescriptors];

    [sortDescriptors release];

    [sortDescriptor release];


    NSError *error;

    NSMutableArray *mutableFetchResults = [[managedObjectContext
executeFetchRequest:request error:&error] mutableCopy];

    if (mutableFetchResults == nil) {
        // Handle the error.
    }


    self.items = mutableFetchResults;

    [mutableFetchResults release];

    [request release];

    }
```

This code is exactly the same code that we used for the FugitiveListViewController.

CapturedListViewController.m

Exercise Solution

You should recognize the code from Chapter 7 to get the captured view working, and then the predicate code to get the filtered data.

2 **Get the captured view to match the fugitive view (continued).**

```objc
#pragma mark Table view methods


- (NSInteger)numberOfSectionsInTableView:(UITableView *)tableView {
    return 1;
}
// Customize the number of rows in the table view.
- (NSInteger)tableView:(UITableView *)tableView numberOfRowsInSection:(NSInteger)section {
    return [items count];
}
// Customize the appearance of table view cells.
- (UITableViewCell *)tableView:(UITableView *)tableView cellForRowAtIndexPath:(NSIndexPath *)indexPath {
    static NSString *CellIdentifier = @"Cell";
    UITableViewCell *cell = [tableView dequeueReusableCellWithIdentifier:CellIdentifier];
    if (cell == nil) {
    cell = [[[UITableViewCell alloc] initWithStyle:UITableViewCellStyleDefault reuseIdentifier:CellIdentifier] autorelease];
    }
    // Set up the cell...
    Fugitive *fugitive = [items objectAtIndex:indexPath.row];
    cell.textLabel.text = fugitive.name;
    return cell;
}
```

CapturedListViewController.m

```
- (void)tableView:(UITableView*)tableView didSelectRowAtIndexPath:(NSI
ndexPath *)indexPath {

        FugitiveDetailViewController *fugitiveDetailViewController =
[[FugitiveDetailViewController alloc] initWithNibName:@"FugitiveDetail
ViewController" bundle:nil];

        fugitiveDetailViewController.fugitive = [self.items
objectAtIndex:indexPath.row];

        [self.navigationController pushViewController:fugitiveDetailVie
wController animated:YES];

        [fugitiveDetailViewController release];

}


- (void)dealloc {

        [items release];

        [super dealloc];

@end
```

CapturedListViewController.m

3 Add the predicate code.

```
NSPredicate *predicate = [NSPredicate predicateWithFormat:@"captured ==
YES"];

[request setPredicate:predicate];
```

Put this in viewWillAppear just after
[request setEntity:entity];.

CapturedListViewController.m

Test Drive

Go ahead and fire it up—the captured
view should be ready to go!

Test Drive

It works! These are the four
fugitives we marked as captured.

Hang on—you said we should be careful with memory and performance and blah blah... Now we have two arrays of fugitives and we reload them every time the view appears. It seems pretty dumb. What if we moved this code to viewDidLoad so it's only done once per view?

True, we can make this a lot more efficient.

But not by moving it to `viewDidLoad`. If we move the code there, we're going to end up with two new problems. We need another solution...

BRAIN BARBELL

What problems would we introduce if we moved the fetching code to `viewDidLoad`? What else could we do to improve performance?

Core Data controller classes provide efficient results handling

The code for both the `FugitiveListViewController` and the `CapturedListViewController` is in `viewWillAppear`. The problem is that `viewWillAppear` gets called every time the view is shown, which means we're reloading all of the fugitives and all of the captured fugitives every time, regardless of whether anything's changed.

We could move the code to `viewDidLoad`, but that only gets called when the views are loaded from their nibs. That causes two problems. First, if we mark a fugitive as captured, the Captured List won't reflect that since it only loads its data once. The second problem is that `viewDidLoad` gets called *before* our `applicationDidFinishLaunching,` which means the views will try to get their data before the app delegate gets a chance to copy the master database in place. What we need is a better way to manage our fetched data.

Table views and NSFetchedResultsControllers are made for each other

Since UITableViews are such a common component and frequently deal with large amounts of data, there's a special Core Data class designed to support them. The NSFetchedResultsController works together with the Managed Object Context and your NSFetchRequest to give you some pretty impressive abilities:

Very efficient memory usage

The NSFetchedResultsController works with the NSFetchRequest and the ManagedObjectModel to minimize how much data is actually in memory. For example, even if we have 10,000 fugitives to deal with, the NSFetchedResultsController will try to keep only the ones the UITableView needs to display in memory, probably closer to 10 or 15.

High performance UITableView support

UITableView needs to know how many sections there are, how many rows there are in each section, etc. NSFetchedResultsController has built-in support for figuring that information out quickly, without needing to load all of the data.

Built-in monitoring for data changes

We've already talked about how the Managed Object Context knows when data is modified. NSFetchedResultsController can take advantage of that to let you (well, its delegate) know when data that matches your fetch results is modified.

Time for some high-efficiency streamlining

We need to do a little refactoring to get NSFetchedResultsController in there, but when it's done, Bob could give us a database of 100,000 fugitives and iBountyHunter wouldn't blink. We're going to do this for the CapturedListViewController, but the same refactoring will apply to the FugitiveListViewController too.

First, we need to replace our items array with an instance of an NSFetchedResultsController, like this:

We want the controller to tell us when data changes — we need to conform to its delegate protocol.

```objc
@interface CapturedListViewController : UITableViewController
<NSFetchedResultsControllerDelegate> {

        NSFetchedResultsController *resultsController;
}

@property (nonatomic, retain) NSFetchedResultsController
*resultsController;

@end
```

.h

CapturedListViewController.h

Remove the items array and its property.
We won't need those any longer.

```objc
@implementation CapturedListViewController
@synthesize resultsController;
```

Delete the reference to the items array here and release the new view controller.

```objc
- (void)dealloc {
    [resultsController release];
    [super dealloc];
}
@end
```

.m

CapturedListViewController.m

Next we need to change the search to use the controller...

Refactor viewWillAppear to use the controller

```
- (void) viewWillAppear:(BOOL)animated {
      [super viewWillAppear:animated];

      if (self.resultsController != nil) {
            return;
      }
      iBountyHunterAppDelegate *appDelegate = (iBountyHunterAppDelegate*)
[[UIApplication sharedApplication] delegate];
      NSManagedObjectContext *managedObjectContext = appDelegate.
managedObjectContext;
      NSFetchRequest *request = [[NSFetchRequest alloc] init];
      NSEntityDescription *entity = [NSEntityDescription entityForName:@"Fugitive"
inManagedObjectContext:managedObjectContext];
      [request setEntity:entity];

      NSPredicate *predicate = [NSPredicate predicateWithFormat:@"captured ==
YES"];
      [request setPredicate:predicate];

      NSSortDescriptor *sortDescriptor = [[NSSortDescriptor alloc]
initWithKey:@"name" ascending:YES];
      NSArray *sortDescriptors = [[NSArray alloc] initWithObjects:sortDescriptor,
nil];
      [request setSortDescriptors:sortDescriptors];
      [sortDescriptors release];
      [sortDescriptor release];

      NSFetchedResultsController *fetchedResultsController =
[[NSFetchedResultsController alloc] initWithFetchRequest:request
   managedObjectContext:managedObjectContext  sectionNameKeyPath:nil
   cacheName:@"captured_list.cache"];
      fetchedResultsController.delegate = self;
      NSError *error;
      BOOL success = [fetchedResultsController performFetch:&error];
      if (!success) {
            // Handle the error.
      }

      self.resultsController = fetchedResultsController;
      [request release];

      [self.tableView reloadData];
```

Since the NSFetchedResultsController can tell us when data changes, we only need to actually fetch once. If we've already done this (the view is being shown again), we can just bail.

Create and initialize the NSFetchedResultsController with our fetch request and the Managed Object Controller.

We're going to be the delegate so we're told when data changes.

Now instead of asking the Managed Object Model to perform the fetch, we ask the controller.

Tuck the controller away so we can get the data out.

Tell the table view our data has changed.

CapturedListViewController.m

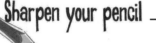

Hmm, so if we get rid of the array
of Fugitives, then we're going to have to
reimplement the datasource and delegate
methods too, right? My guess is we're going
to use the NSFetchedResultsController
there as well?

Yes.

The NSFetchedResultsController gives us everything we
need to access the fetched data. In fact, it can do it a lot
more efficiently.

Sharpen your pencil

We've given you the code to set up the
NSFetchedResultsController. Now you need to
update the tableview delegate and datasource
methods to use the controller instead of the view.

 **Refactor numberOfSectionsInTableView and
numberOfRowsInSection to use the controller.**
NSFetchedResultsController has a sections property
that is an array of NSFetchedResultsSectionInfo
objects. Use those to figure out how many sections there are and
how many rows in each section.

 **Refactor cellForRowAtIndexPath and
didSelectRowAtIndexPath to use the controller.**
NSFetchedResultsController makes it easy to
implement these methods using its objectAtIndexPath method.

Sharpen your pencil
Solution

Here is the final code for CapturedListViewController.m
table methods.

```objc
#pragma mark Table view methods
- (NSInteger)numberOfSectionsInTableView:(UITableView *)tableView {

    return [[self.resultsController sections] count];

}
```

For the number of sections we can just return
the count of the sections in the controller.

```objc
// Customize the number of rows in the table view.
- (NSInteger)tableView:(UITableView *)tableView numberOfRowsInSection:(NSInteger)
section {

    return [[[self.resultsController sections] objectAtIndex:section]
numberOfObjects];

}
```

You could have also done this using an id that conforms
to the NSFetchedResultsSectionInfo protocol.

```objc
// Customize the appearance of table view cells.
- (UITableViewCell *)tableView:(UITableView *)tableView cellForRowAtIndexPath:(NS
IndexPath *)indexPath {
    static NSString *CellIdentifier = @"Cell";

    UITableViewCell *cell = [tableView dequeueReusableCellWithIdentifier:CellIden
tifier];

    if (cell == nil) {
        cell = [[[UITableViewCell alloc] initWithStyle:UITableViewCellStyleDefault
reuseIdentifier:CellIdentifier] autorelease];

    }
// Set up the cell...
    Fugitive *fugitive = [self.resultsController
objectAtIndexPath:indexPath];

    cell.textLabel.text = fugitive.name;

    return cell;

}
```

Nothing fancy here – just get the
Fugitive at the given indexPath.

.m

CapturedListViewController.m

```
- (void)tableView:(UITableView*)tableView didSelectRowAtIndexPath:(NSIndexPath *)
indexPath {


        FugitiveDetailViewController *fugitiveDetailViewController =
[[FugitiveDetailViewController alloc] initWithNibName:@"FugitiveDetailViewControl
ler" bundle:nil];
```

One more lookup for the indexPath to get the Fugitive, and we're all set.

```
fugitiveDetailViewController.fugitive = [self.resultsController
objectAtIndexPath:indexPath];

[self.navigationController pushViewController:fugitiveDetailViewControlle
r animated:YES];

[fugitiveDetailViewController release];
```

CapturedListViewController.m

Test Drive

Go ahead and run iBountyHunter to make sure the changes didn't break anything. The views should be loading just like they were... sort of. Do some quick testing—if you mark a fugitive as captured, does he switch lists? What if you exit and come back into the app using the home key?

Test Drive

Now that you're using the controller instead of just a predicate, the behavior of the app should be the same. But people are showing up in the captured list even when they're not marked as captured!

BRAIN POWER

Why aren't fugitives properly changing lists when you change their captured status?

We need to refresh the data

The fugitives aren't properly changing lists when you change their status because we're not refreshing the data every time the captured list view is displayed. We need to set up the NSFetchedResultsController to let us know when things have changed so we can update the table.

```
- (void)controllerDidChangeContent:(NSFetchedResultsController *)controller
{
        [self.tableView reloadData];
}
```

You can add this anywhere in the CapturedListViewController.m file.

The table view will completely reload the data when it detects a change.

NSFetchedResultsController can check for changes

Now that we've set up the app to work with the NSFetchedResultsController instead of just an array, we can leverage the methods embedded with the controller to help us. The view controller has built-in support for monitoring the data for changes through a delegate. We had set ourselves up as that delegate but never implemented the code to handle data changing.

Having the view completely reload when it detects a change can become cumbersome if you are dealing with a large amount of data; however, the FetchedResultsController delegate also has support built-in for notifying you of the specific cell that is changed, and you can modify just that. Check Apple's documentation for more details.

TEST DRIVE

Implement the controllerDidChangeContent method that we listed above, and make sure everything's working.

Test Drive

Do the same thing you did last time, build and run, and
then change the status of one of the fugitives to pull
him dynamically out of the captured list.

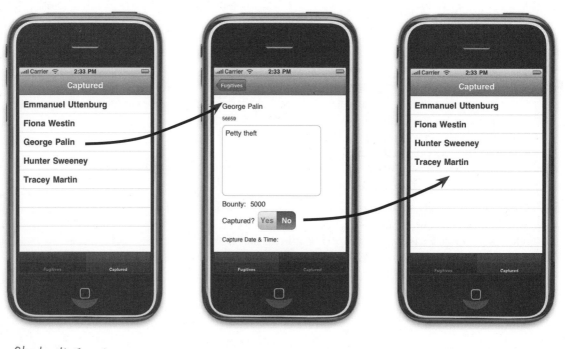

Start with 5 captured
fugitives...

...remove one from the list...

...and he's immediately gone!

It works!

This is awesome! The advantage I'm going to have over the competition is great, and having all that information with me means that I'll be making way fewer trips back to the police station. Thanks!

There's nothing like a satisfied customer!

there are no
Dumb Questions

Q: Where can I find the full syntax for NSPredicate?

A: NSPredicate has a pretty complex syntax available for expressing constraints on your data. There's a simple summary available in the NSPredicate class documentation but Apple has an entire document available to help you write advanced predicates.

Q: It seems like it would be pretty easy to make a mistake typing predicate syntax into code like that. Isn't that sort of like embedding SQL?

A: Yes, and Xcode can offer a lot of help here. Instead of embedding your predicates in code, you can build them graphically using Xcode's data modeller, just like we did with the Managed Object Model. To build a predicate graphically, select an entity in Xcode, then click on the plus as though you were adding an attribute. Select "Add Fetch Request" to create a new fetch request and click Edit Predicate to bring up the graphical editor. You can name your fetch requests whatever you like. You'll need to retrieve them in code like this:

```
NSFetchRequest *fetchRequest
= [managedObjectModel
fetchRequestFromTemplateWithName:
@"capturedFugitives" substitutionVariables:[
NSDictionary dictionaryWithObject:capturedF
lag forKey:@"captured"]];
```

Then just use that fetch request instead of one created in code. You can also use Xcode's builder to assemble a predicate, then just cut and paste that into your code if you'd prefer to keep them there.

Q: Reloading the whole table when data changes seem pretty inefficient. Aren't we trying to optimize things?

A: Yes it is, and yes, we are. There are a number of delegate methods you can implement to get finer-grained information about what's happening with the Managed Object Context. With that information, you can find out if you just need to update a specific table view cell, insert a cell, or remove a cell. We took the easier route and just asked the table view to reload completely.

Q: What's with that cache value we gave to the results controller?

A: The results controller will use that file name to cache information like the number of items, number of sections, etc. It will keep an eye on the data store and regenerate the cache if something changes. You can also forcibly ask it to remove a cache, but in general you shouldn't need to.

Q: Our results controller only has one section. How do I get it to split things into multiple sections?

A: Just provide an attribute name for the sectionNameKeyPath. The NSFetchedResultsController will group your results using that attribute and return each grouping as a section. You can get really sophisticated and create a transient property if you want to group them by something you're not actually storing in the database and calculate the value using a custom getter added to your object model.

BULLET POINTS

- NSFetchRequest can take an NSPredicate to **filter data** based on logical conditions.

- You can express NSPredicate **conditions** in code or using Xcode's predicate builder.

- NSFetchedResultsController provides highly efficient memory management and **change monitoring** for UITableViews

- Be careful about what you put in viewWillAppear, as it will be called **every time** your view is shown.

DataMigrationcross

We have some new data lingo to try out, so flex those verbal skills...

Across

2. viewDidLoad and view_____ both load views, but with different frequency.
5. The _____ is responsible for reading and writing data.
7. Automatic migration is called _____ data migration.
8. To update the data, we need to _____ it.
9. The FetchedResultsController is good at _____ management.
10. NSFetchResultsController can _____ for changes.

Down

1. _____ concepts are similar to NSFetchResults concepts.
3. _____ are used for filtering data.
4. The new model is the current _____.
6. The Managed Object Context saves new or _____ items.

DataMigrationcross

We have some new data lingo to try out, so flex those verbal skills...

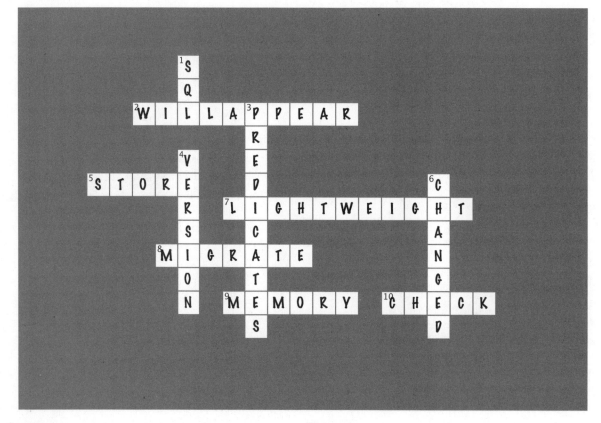

Across

2. viewDidLoad and view_____ both load views, but with different frequency. [WILLAPPEAR]
5. The _____ is responsible for reading and writing data. [STORE]
7. Automatic migration is called _____ data migration. [LIGHTWEIGHT]
8. To update the data, we need to _____ it. [MIGRATE]
9. The FetchedResultsController is good at _____ management. [MEMORY]
10. NSFetchResultsController can _____ for changes. [CHECK]

Down

1. _____ concepts are similar to NSFetchResults concepts. [SQL]
3. _____ are used for filtering data. [PREDICATES]
4. The new model is the current _____. [VERSION]
6. The Managed Object Context saves new or _____ items. [CHANGED]

Your Data Toolbox

You've got Chapter 8 under your belt and now you've added migrating and optimizing data to your toolbox. For a complete list of tooltips in the book, go to http://www.headfirstlabs.com/iphonedev.

Data Migration

Core data can use lightweight migration to automatically make database changes.

Versioning is used to keep track of the data migrations.

Lightweight migration can be used to add attributes or changing optional status.

Persistent Obj Store

Actually reads and writes the data.

Does data migration, sometimes without actually needing to load the data.

Uses mapping models if the changes are too much for lightweight migration.

Saving

The Managed Object Context handles saving new or changed items.

NSFetch-ResultsControllers

Maximizes memory efficiency.

Has high-performance UITableView support.

Built-in support for monitoring data changes.

Filtering Data

Predicates are used for filtering results data.

The predicate needs to be set on the NSFetchRequest.

It's a good thing
iPhone comes with
a camera...

9 camera, map kit, and core location

Proof in the real world

I can take a perfectly fine picture with this. I don't need a fancy iPhone...

The iPhone knows where it is and what it sees.

As any iPhone user knows, the iPhone goes way beyond just managing data: it can also take pictures, figure out your location, and put that information together for use in your app. The beauty about incorporating these features is that just by tapping into the tools that the iPhone gives you, suddenly you can import pictures, locations, and maps without much coding at all.

For Bob, payment requires proof!

Bob is working hard on getting as many fugitives off the street as he can, but to get paid he has to document his captures.

> I need a picture of the arrest when it happens, and since my phone has a camera, I was thinking you might be able to help out...

That should be easy enough.

Bob wants a picture of his catch and he's going to need it to be pretty big—so let's go ahead and put it on its own view.

Those pictures will be great for advertising, not to mention that it will speed up payment!

Sharpen your pencil

Here's what the app looks like so far. Where
and how should we add photo support?

Your ideas go here.

Sharpen your pencil
Solution

Here's what we came up with for the photo view.
It's similar to the way most utility apps work.

Space is getting a bit tight down here. If we shrink up the space for the description, we can move the capture info up and leave room for the new button.

You'll need to shrink this up a bit.

Caught photo.

This is the bottom of the image.

Flip over.

Done button to flip the picture back over.

Captured

Emmanuel Uttenburg

23454

Stealing cool names from other industries.

Bounty: 23000

Captured? Yes No

Capture Date & Time: 2009-09-16 10:23:23 -0400

Done

Flip over for the detail view!

It's about time we used some real animation in our app. Since we'll only want the photo after drilling down through to the detail view (what Bob will use to find his fugitive), it makes sense to stick it on the back of the detail view.

This is a really common interface for the utility apps on the iPhone. Typically, there will be two views, one with an info button on it, and another that is revealed by flipping over when the info button is clicked. Our app isn't a utility app, but we can steal the idea to give a nice baseball-card look to our fugitive detail view.

The flipping is just another transition that comes with UIKit. We're going to want a modal view for that last view.

Author's note: These are hints for the next exercise, so pay attention!

Long Exercise

Enough planning and hints. Build the view
and get it implemented!

1 Start with the FugitiveDetailViewControler updates.
The detail view needs a new info button, and an action to trigger the
new flip view. The info button is just a regular button with the Info Dark
type.

*Don't forget to connect the button
and the IBAction in Interface Builder!*

**2 Use a custom animation to show the new view when the
info button is pressed.**
You already know how to present a modal view, but this time we want
to do it with a custom animation. The animation you want to use is the
UIModalTransitionStyleFlipHorizontal. Take a look at the
UIViewController documentation if you're stuck on how to use it.

3 Build the new CapturedPhotoViewController.
That's going to mean a view with a UIImageView and a Done button.
Don't forget the action to tie in with the button and dismiss the view.

*Don't worry about an IBOutlet for the
UIImageView yet,; we'll get to that in a second.*

Long Exercise Solution

This one is a whole bunch of functionality that you added without much help! Here's what we came up with:

1 **Start with the FugitiveDetailViewController updates.**

Add the action to respond to the button press.

```
- (IBAction) showInfoButtonPressed: (id) sender;
@end
```

FugitiveDetailViewController.h

```
#import "CapturedPhotoViewController.h"
```

FugitiveDetailViewController.m

2 **Use a custom animation to show the new view when the info button is pressed.**

```
- (IBAction)showInfoButtonPressed: (id) sender {

    CapturedPhotoViewController *controller =
        [[CapturedPhotoViewController alloc] initWithNibName:
         @"CapturedPhotoViewController" bundle:nil];

    controller.modalTransitionStyle =
        UIModalTransitionStyleFlipHorizontal;
    [self presentModalViewController:controller animated:YES];
    [controller release];

}
```

Instantiate the view controller and open up the flip view nib.

FugitiveDetailViewController.m

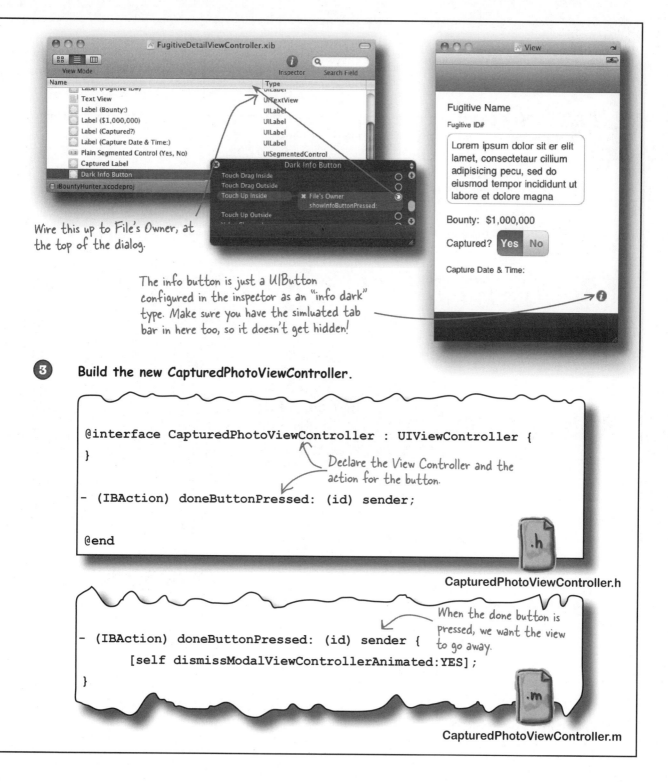

Wire this up to File's Owner, at the top of the dialog.

The info button is just a UIButton configured in the inspector as an "info dark" type. Make sure you have the simluated tab bar in here too, so it doesn't get hidden!

3 **Build the new CapturedPhotoViewController.**

```
@interface CapturedPhotoViewController : UIViewController {
}
```

Declare the View Controller and the action for the button.

```
- (IBAction) doneButtonPressed: (id) sender;


@end
```

CapturedPhotoViewController.h

When the done button is pressed, we want the view to go away.

```
- (IBAction) doneButtonPressed: (id) sender {
    [self dismissModalViewControllerAnimated:YES];
}
```

CapturedPhotoViewController.m

Long Exercise Solution

This one is a whole bunch of functionality that you added without much help! Here's what we came up with:

3 Build the new CapturedPhotoViewController (continued).

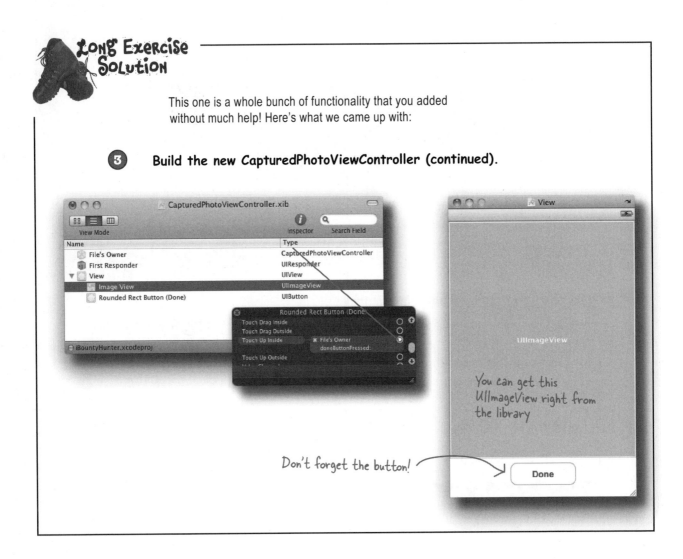

You can get this UIImageView right from the library

Don't forget the button!

Test Drive

Run the app and see the cool animation working!

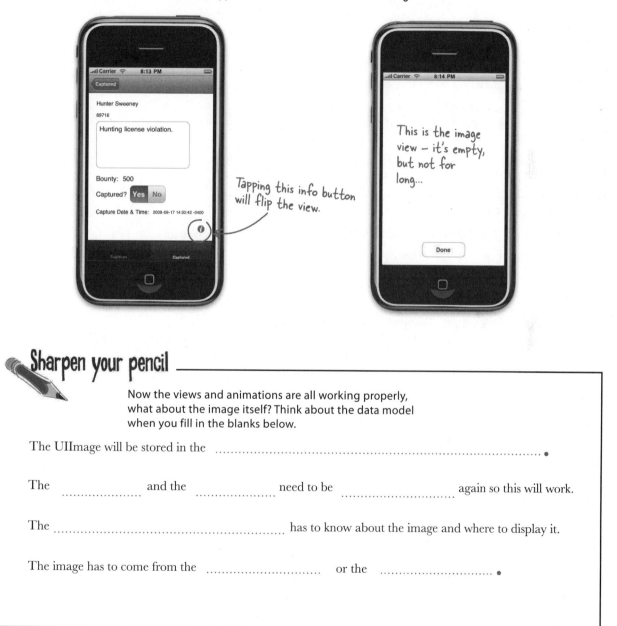

Tapping this info button will flip the view.

This is the image view – it's empty, but not for long...

Sharpen your pencil

Now the views and animations are all working properly, what about the image itself? Think about the data model when you fill in the blanks below.

The UIImage will be stored in the ....

The .... and the .... need to be .... again so this will work.

The .... has to know about the image and where to display it.

The image has to come from the .... or the ....

Sharpen your pencil Solution

Now the views and animations are all working properly, what about the image itself? Think about the data model when you fill in the blanks below.

The UIImage will be stored in the .... *database* .... •

The ...*database*... and the ...*data model*... need to be ......*migrated*...... again so this will work.

The ....*CapturedPhotoViewController*.... has to know about the image and where to display it.

The image has to come from the .....*camera*.......... or the ...*photo library*... •

Do this! You've migrated the database before, and you're going to need to do it again. Just so it's handled and out of the way, get into Xcode and do another database migration.

1 **Highlight iBountyHunter 2.xcdatamodel.**
Then go to the **Design → Data Model → Add Model Version** menu option. You will have iBountyHunter 3.xcdatamodel in the iBountyHunter.xcdatamodel directory.

2 **Set the current version.**
Inside the iBountyHunter.xcdatamodeld directory, select iBountyHunter 3.xcdatamodel, which will be our new version. Go to the **Design → Data Model → Set Current Version** menu option.

3 **Add the new field to the new data model and generate the new Fugitive class.**
For the image, we'll need a new attribute called "image" that is a binary data type. Then delete the old Fugitive.h and Fugitive.m files and generate new ones via the **New** menu option.

Check out Chapter 7 if you're still fuzzy on how to do this.

The way to the camera...

...is through the UIImagePickerController. Why? Because our real mission here is to pick an image. The iPhone implements image selection through a picker that allows you to get your image from different places, like the camera or the photo library.

The UIImagePickerController class has a lot of built-in functionality, plus it's modal, so once you implement it, a lot of things start happening without any additional code in your app:

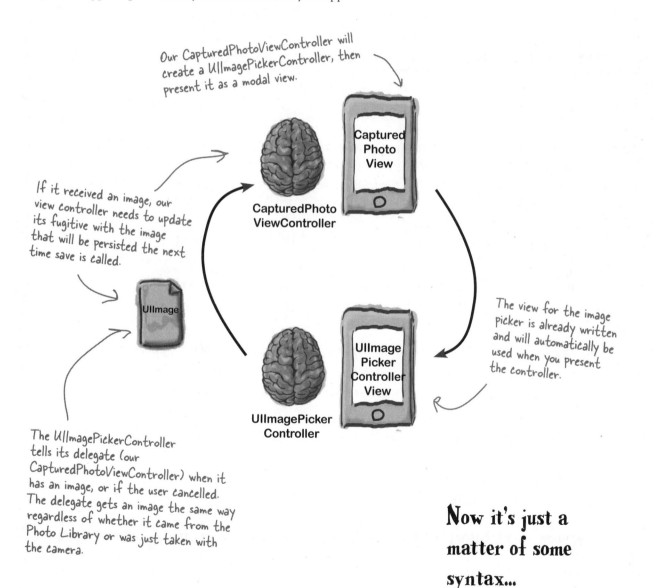

Our CapturedPhotoViewController will create a UIImagePickerController, then present it as a modal view.

If it received an image, our view controller needs to update its fugitive with the image that will be persisted the next time save is called.

The view for the image picker is already written and will automatically be used when you present the controller.

The UIImagePickerController tells its delegate (our CapturedPhotoViewController) when it has an image, or if the user cancelled. The delegate gets an image the same way regardless of whether it came from the Photo Library or was just taken with the camera.

Now it's just a matter of some syntax...

Ready Bake Code

Here is some code you'll need to tie the image picker together. This code goes in our CapturedPhotoViewController as part of the next exercise.

CapturedPhotoViewController
hints

```
- (void) viewWillAppear:(BOOL)animated {
    [super viewWillAppear:animated];
    self.fugitiveImage.image = [[[UIImage alloc]
      initWithData:fugitive.image] autorelease];
}
```

When the view appears, we're going to allocate the image in the database to the view if there is one.

```
- (IBAction) takePictureButton: (id) sender {
    NSLog(@"Taking a picture.");


    UIImagePickerController* picker =
      [[UIImagePickerController alloc] init];
    picker.sourceType = UIImagePickerControllerSourceTypePhotoLibrary |
                        UIImagePickerControllerSourceTypeCamera;
    picker.delegate = self;
    picker.allowsEditing = YES;


    [self presentModalViewController:picker animated:YES];

}


- (void)imagePickerController:(UIImagePickerController *)picker
            didFinishPickingImage:(UIImage *)image
            editingInfo:(NSDictionary *)editingInfo
{

    self.fugitive.image = UIImagePNGRepresentation(image);


    [self dismissModalViewControllerAnimated:YES];
    [picker release];
}
```

This allows the users to edit the photo they are choosing.

The picker is displayed asynchronously.

Once the image is chosen, this gets called.

Remove the picker interface and release the picker object.

Exercise

Time to get some images! Using the code for the image picker that we gave you, as well as some of your Objective-C skills, and let's get the images going.

1 **Import the Fugitive header file and declare a property for the fugitive.**
The CapturedPhotoViewController needs to know what fugitive it's working with. Add a Fugitive field and property named "fugitive" to the CapturedPhotoViewController.

2 **Store the image when it's selected and update the UIImageView.**
You need to set the image information on the fugitive when the picker gives us an image, then make sure the UIImageView is updated when the view is shown. You'll need an outlet for the UIImageView; then link it in Interface Builder.

3 **Add the code for the UIImagePickerController in the takePictureButton action.**
Use the code that we gave you to finish up the UIImagePickerController. You'll need to say our CapturedPhotoViewController conforms to the UIImagePickerControllerDelegate and UINavigationControllerDelegate protocols in order to make it the delegate.

4 **Add the "Take picture button".**
Using Interface Builder, you'll need to create a button that covers the entire UIImageView and is then set behind it. Don't forget to connect it to your takePictureButton action.

After you create the button, just select it and use the Layout → Send to Back menu option.

5 **Change the FugitiveDetailViewController's showInfoButtonPressed method to set the fugitive.**
You'll need to pass the fugitive information along to the CapturedPhotoViewController when it's created and before it's pushed.

Exercise

Here's all of the pieces put together to implement the button...

```
#import "Fugitive.h"        1      Import the Fugitive header file and
                                   declare a property for the fugitive.

@interface CapturedPhotoViewController : UIViewController
<UINavigationControllerDelegate, UIImagePickerControllerDelegate> {
        UIImageView *fugitiveImage;
        Fugitive* fugitive;              We'll need an outlet so we can update the UIImageView
}                                        with the selected image.


@property (nonatomic, retain) IBOutlet UIImageView *fugitiveImage;
@property (nonatomic, retain) Fugitive *fugitive;


- (IBAction) doneButtonPressed: (id) sender;
- (IBAction) takePictureButton: (id) sender;


@end
```

.h

CapturedPhotoViewController.h

```
#import "Fugitive.h"
                                    2    Store the image when it's
                                         selected and update the
@implementation CapturedPhotoViewController   UIImageView.
@synthesize fugitiveImage, fugitive;


- (void) viewWillAppear: (BOOL) animated {
      [super viewWillAppear:animated];
      self.fugitiveImage.image = [[[UIImage alloc]
                   initWithData:fugitive.image] autorelease];
}
```

.m

CapturedPhotoViewController.m

3 Add the code for the UIImagePickerController in the takePictureButton action.

```objc
- (IBAction) takePictureButton: (id) sender {
    NSLog(@"Taking a picture.");
    UIImagePickerController* picker =
        [[UIImagePickerController alloc] init];

    picker.sourceType = UIImagePickerControllerSourceTypePhotoLibrary |
                        UIImagePickerControllerSourceTypeCamera;

    picker.delegate = self;
    picker.allowsEditing = YES;

    [self presentModalViewController:picker animated:YES];
}

- (void)imagePickerController:(UIImagePickerController *)picker
            didFinishPickingImage:(UIImage *)image
            editingInfo:(NSDictionary *)editingInfo
{

    self.fugitive.image = UIImagePNGRepresentation(image);


    [self dismissModalViewControllerAnimated:YES];
    [picker release];
}

- (void)imagePickerControllerDidCancel:(UIImagePickerController *)picker
{

    [self dismissModalViewControllerAnimated:YES];

    [picker release];
}

- (void)dealloc {
    [fugitive release];
    [fugitiveImage release];
    [super dealloc];
}
@end
```

Logging the method here will let us see that it gets called in the debugger.

We set the delegate to be us so that we're notified when an image is selected (or the user hits cancel).

Then we present the picker and wait to see what happens...

...and we don't release the picker controller until we get the image callbacks.

Since Core Data wants to store binary data, we need to get the raw image information out of the UIImage. We convert it to a PNG representation for that.

You need to remember to release the picker controller once you've gotten the image.

CapturedPhotoViewController.m

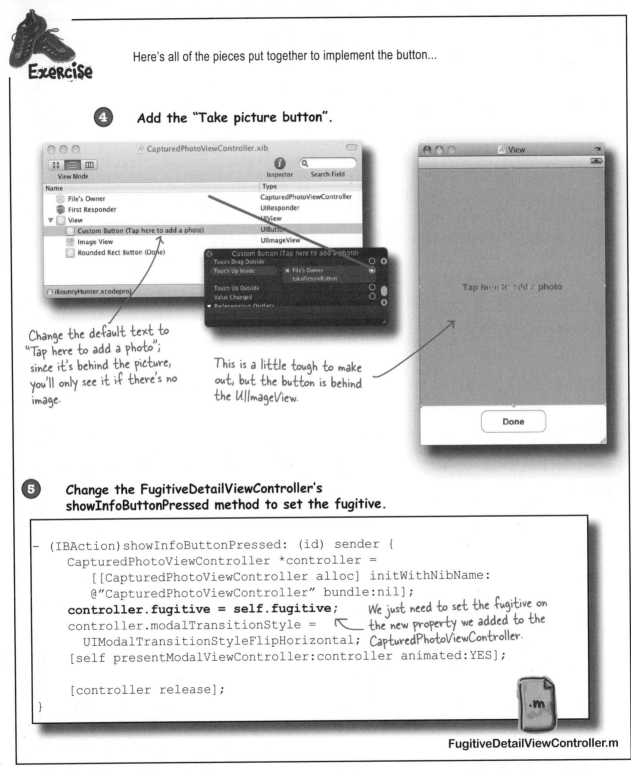

Exercise

Here's all of the pieces put together to implement the button...

④ **Add the "Take picture button".**

Change the default text to "Tap here to add a photo"; since it's behind the picture, you'll only see it if there's no image.

This is a little tough to make out, but the button is behind the UIImageView.

Tap here to add a photo

⑤ **Change the FugitiveDetailViewController's showInfoButtonPressed method to set the fugitive.**

```
- (IBAction)showInfoButtonPressed: (id) sender {
    CapturedPhotoViewController *controller =
        [[CapturedPhotoViewController alloc] initWithNibName:
        @"CapturedPhotoViewController" bundle:nil];
    controller.fugitive = self.fugitive;          We just need to set the fugitive on
    controller.modalTransitionStyle =             the new property we added to the
        UIModalTransitionStyleFlipHorizontal;     CapturedPhotoViewController.
    [self presentModalViewController:controller animated:YES];

    [controller release];
}
```

FugitiveDetailViewController.m

Test Drive

Build and run to see your new picture view in action.

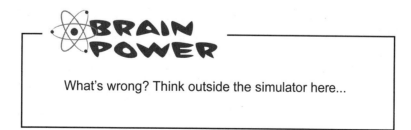

```
000                    iBountyHunter – Debugger Console
Simulator – 3.1 | Debug ▼      ▶         ⚒         ●        ⓖ        ⏸        📋
       Overview             Breakpoints  Build and Run  Tasks  Restart   Pause      Clear Log

[Session started at 2009-09-21 21:17:01 -0400.]
2009-09-21 21:17:05.446 iBountyHunter[84808:207] View did load....
2009-09-21 21:17:05.542 iBountyHunter[84808:207] Captured View did load....
2009-09-21 21:17:06.415 iBountyHunter[84808:207] Toggling the captured toggle.
2009-09-21 21:17:09.135 iBountyHunter[84808:207] Taking a picture.
2009-09-21 21:17:09.213 iBountyHunter[84808:207] *** Terminating app due to uncaught
    exception 'NSInvalidArgumentException', reason: 'Source type 1 not available'
2009-09-21 21:17:09.214 iBountyHunter[84808:207] Stack:
    30901419,
    2444488521,
    4463855,
    18020,
    2746211,
    3153546,
    3162283,
    3157495,
    2851099,
    2759444,
    2786203,
    38998841,
    30686160,

Debugging terminated.                                         ❌ Succeeded ⚠ 1
```

What does this mean?

Agh! It crashed!

⚛ BRAIN POWER

What's wrong? Think outside the simulator here...

Right! And neither does an iPod Touch.

The simulator is reacting to the fact that you are asking for the camera and it doesn't have one. But more than the simulator not having the camera, the iPod touch doesn't either.

Who cares? Apple.

The iPhone isn't the only device using apps

One of the things that Apple requires when you release an app is that it can work on all devices that can run apps, which for now includes the iPod Touch and the iPhone. Part of the approval process for apps is that they are checked for compatibility with the iPod Touch.

All this means that you need to be aware of when your app may be straying into areas where an iPhone behaves differently than the iPod Touch.

Author's note:

We don't have insider information or anything; we're just assuming that as time goes on this list will grow.

How many differences are there, really?

Pool Puzzle

Your **job** is to take items from the pool and place them into the list for the iPhone or iPod Touch. You may **not** use the same item more than once, and you won't need to use all the items listed. Your **goal** is to make a complete list of the functionality for the iPhone and iPod Touch.

<u>iPod Touch</u>   <u>iPhone</u>

Note: each thing from the pool can only be used once!

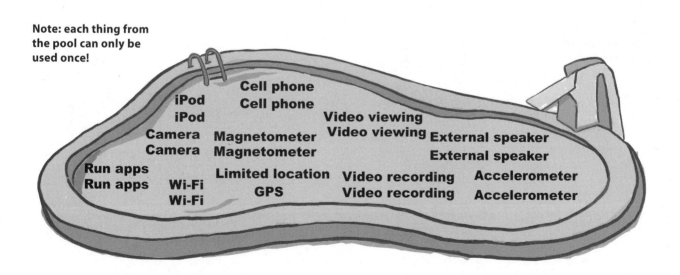

iPod
iPod
Camera
Camera
Run apps
Run apps

Cell phone
Cell phone

Wi-Fi
Wi-Fi

Magnetometer
Magnetometer

Limited location
GPS

Video viewing
Video viewing

Video recording
Video recording

External speaker
External speaker

Accelerometer
Accelerometer

Pool Puzzle Solution

Your **job** is to take functionality from the pool and place them into the list for the iPhone or iPod Touch. You may **not** use the same item more than once, and you won't need to use all the items listed. Your **goal** is to make a complete list of the functionality for iPhone and iPod Touch.

Watch it!

This list will change.

Apple is always coming out with new devices and updating capabilities. You need to check!

iPod Touch

iPod

Run apps

Video viewing

→ **Limited location**

Accelerometer

Wi-Fi

You can get some info about location from Wi-Fi.

This one can be an issue.

iPhone

iPod

Run apps

Video viewing

→ **GPS**

Accelerometer

Wi-Fi

Cell phone

Camera

External speaker

Video recording

Magnetometer

You may have noticed some random stuff on this list— who would've thought about the speaker?

Only on the 3GS

Note: each thing from the pool can only be used once!

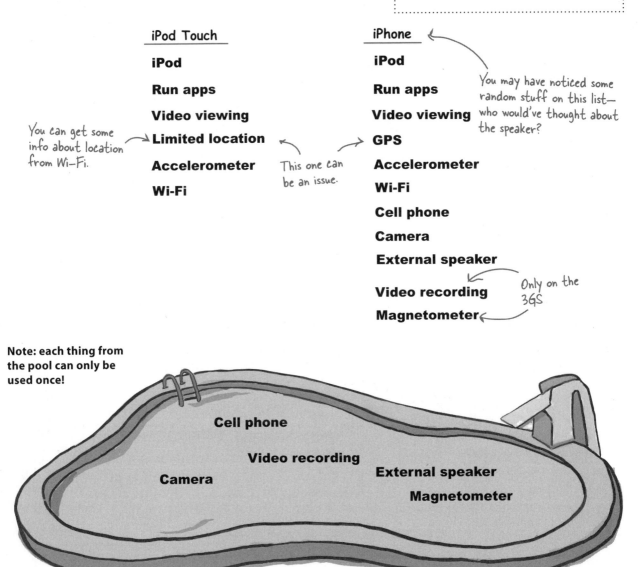

Cell phone

Video recording

Camera

External speaker

Magnetometer

There's a method for checking

With all of these little things that can be different between
devices, pretty much every time you go to use something from the
device, you need to check and see if it's there. For the camera, the
`UIImagePickerController` has a method to check.

```
[UIImagePickerController
    isSourceTypeAvailable:UIImagePickerControllerSourceTypeCamera]
```

*Since we're getting the info from
a source, we need to check and see
if the source you want is there.*

In our case, we have another option: the photo library. If there's no
camera, we can get an image from there instead.

BRAIN POWER

So what happens when the user taps the "Take
a photo" button? You check for the camera, then
what? What's the user flow?

Prompt the user with action sheets

Action sheets slide up from the bottom of the page and give the user options to proceed. It's similar to a modal view because the user has to address the action sheet before they can move on to anything else. Action sheets are really straightforward to use: they take strings for their buttons and have built-in animations for appearing and disappearing. Our code for the action sheet has some standard stuff included:

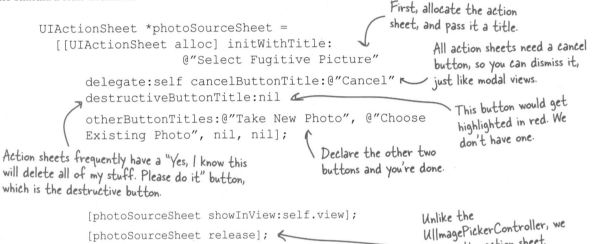

```
UIActionSheet *photoSourceSheet =
    [[UIActionSheet alloc] initWithTitle:
                @"Select Fugitive Picture"
        delegate:self cancelButtonTitle:@"Cancel"
        destructiveButtonTitle:nil
        otherButtonTitles:@"Take New Photo", @"Choose
        Existing Photo", nil, nil];
```

First, allocate the action sheet, and pass it a title.

All action sheets need a cancel button, so you can dismiss it, just like modal views.

This button would get highlighted in red. We don't have one.

Declare the other two buttons and you're done.

Action sheets frequently have a "Yes, I know this will delete all of my stuff. Please do it" button, which is the destructive button.

```
[photoSourceSheet showInView:self.view];

[photoSourceSheet release];
```

Unlike the UIImagePickerController, we release the action sheet immediately.

We'll use action sheets to let the user pick the image source

We know that our options are to use the camera, use the photo library, or cancel, so we'll need to implement the behavior for each option.

What happens with each of these buttons?

Go to the camera, take a picture, and then come back and put your new image into the Fugitive. Once you hand off to `UIImagePickerControllerSourceTypeCamera`, *it'll handle the rest.*

Go to the photo library, pick an image, and then come back and stuff that image into the Fugitive. Here, the `UIImagePickerControllerSourceTypePhotoLibrary` *handles the rest.*

Go back to the image view.

Sharpen your pencil

Implement the action sheet! There's a lot here to think about since we're changing the flow of the app a bit.

1 **Modify the takePictureButton action to include the action sheet.**

iBountyHunter needs to check for the camera, and if there is one, the user gets to pick whether to use the camera or an existing picture. If not, the app should just go straight into the photo library.

> This is where the action sheet comes in.

2 **Implement the delegate methods for the action sheet.**

Here's enough to get you started. Think about the options for case 1 and the default, and make sure you release the picker and present the view. Also don't forget to declare the UIActionSheetDelegate in the header file.

```objc
- (void)actionSheet:(UIActionSheet *)actionSheet
      didDismissWithButtonIndex:(NSInteger)buttonIndex {

    UIImagePickerController* picker =
        [[UIImagePickerController alloc] init];

    picker.delegate = self;

    picker.allowsEditing = YES;


    switch (buttonIndex) {
        case 0:

            NSLog(@"User wants to take a new picture.");
            picker.sourceType =
                UIImagePickerControllerSourceTypeCamera;
            break;
```

3 **Make your code readable!**

We divvied up the implementation code into three #pragmas: the takePictureButton code, the UIImagePickerController code, and the action sheet delegate methods.

Sharpen your pencil

The action sheet should be ready to go and
your app has a good user flow now...

1 Modify the **takePictureButton** action to include the action
sheet.

```
- (IBAction) takePictureButton: (id) sender {
      NSLog(@"Taking a picture.");
      if ([UIImagePickerController
      isSourceTypeAvailable:UIImagePickerControllerSourceTypeCamera]) {
         NSLog(
           @"This device has a camera, ask the user what they want to
  do.");

         UIActionSheet *photoSourceSheet =
           [[UIActionSheet alloc] initWithTitle:@"Select Fugitive Picture"
                                 delegate:self cancelButtonTitle:@"Cancel"
                                 destructiveButtonTitle:nil
         otherButtonTitles:@"Take New Photo", @"Choose Existing Photo",
                           nil, nil];
         [photoSourceSheet showInView:self.view];
         [photoSourceSheet release];
      }
      else { // No camera, probably a touch
         NSLog(@"No camera available on the device.  Defaulting to library.");
         UIImagePickerController* picker = [[UIImagePickerController alloc] init];
         picker.sourceType = UIImagePickerControllerSourceTypePhotoLibrary;
         picker.delegate = self;
         picker.allowsEditing = YES;
         [self presentModalViewController:picker animated:YES];
      }
}
```

Change this to `SourceTypePhotoLibary` *if
you want to see the action sheet working on the
simulator.*

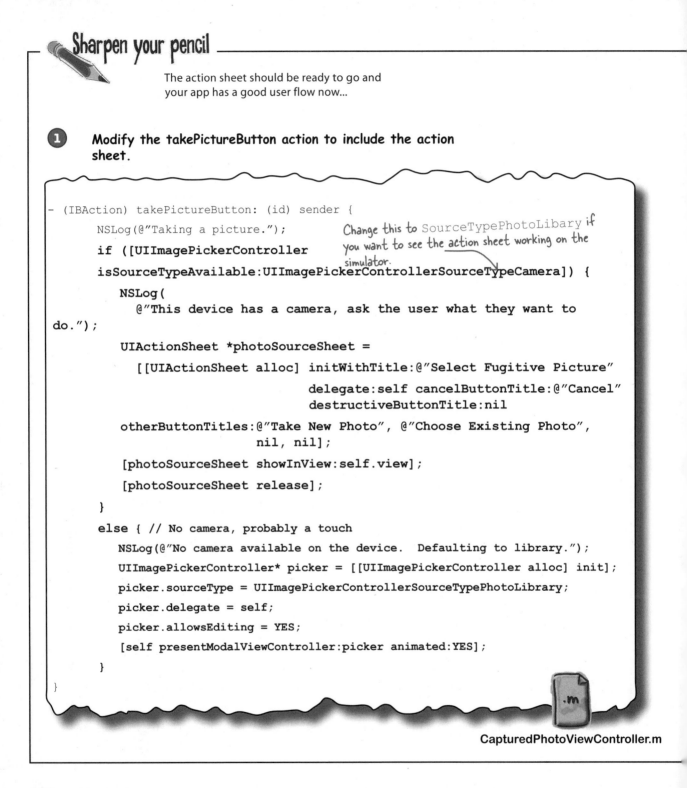

CapturedPhotoViewController.m

② **Implement the delegate methods for the action sheet.**

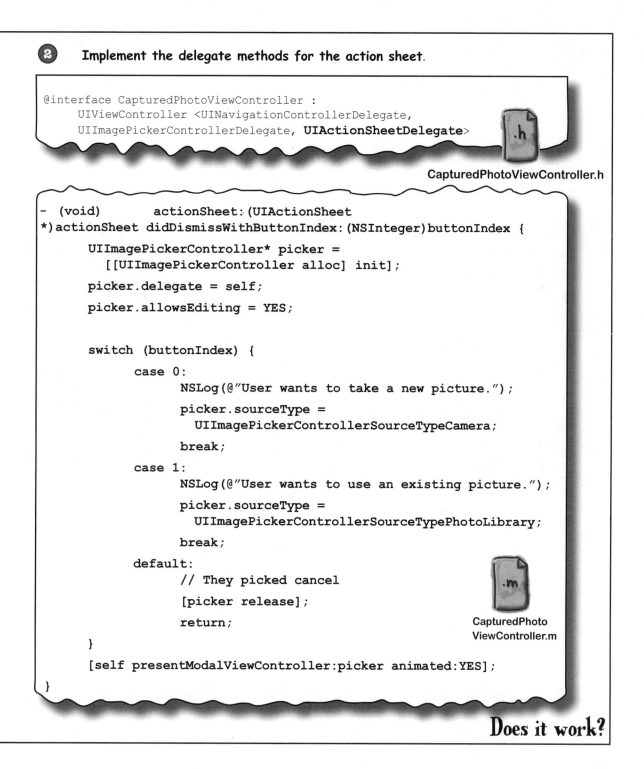

```
@interface CapturedPhotoViewController :
    UIViewController <UINavigationControllerDelegate,
    UIImagePickerControllerDelegate, UIActionSheetDelegate>
```

CapturedPhotoViewController.h

```
- (void)          actionSheet:(UIActionSheet
*)actionSheet didDismissWithButtonIndex:(NSInteger)buttonIndex {

    UIImagePickerController* picker =
        [[UIImagePickerController alloc] init];

    picker.delegate = self;

    picker.allowsEditing = YES;


    switch (buttonIndex) {
        case 0:
            NSLog(@"User wants to take a new picture.");

            picker.sourceType =
                UIImagePickerControllerSourceTypeCamera;

            break;
        case 1:
            NSLog(@"User wants to use an existing picture.");

            picker.sourceType =
                UIImagePickerControllerSourceTypePhotoLibrary;

            break;
        default:
            // They picked cancel
            [picker release];

            return;
    }

    [self presentModalViewController:picker animated:YES];

}
```

CapturedPhoto
ViewController.m

Does it work?

TEST DRIVE

Fire up iBountyHunter and drill down through a fugitive to the point of taking a picture. If you've used the `SourceTypePhotoLibrary` in the `takePictureButton` code, you'll get everything to work and see the action sheet.

The action sheet pops up, and once you select choose the existing photo...

...you get launched into the photo library and you can select a photo.

Geek Bits

It might be time to register with Apple's Developer Program. If you do, you can install the app on your actual iPhone and test it yourself. Check out the appendix at the end of the book to help you walk through the provisioning process to make it work.

Dumb Questions

Q: **Doesn't iPhone 3GS support video now? How do I get to that?**

A: It's another media type you can access when you use the UIImagePickerController. By default, it uses still images, which is what we want for iBountyHunter.

Q: **What about the whole augmented reality thing with the camera? Can I do something like that?**

A: Yes. You can give the UIImagePickerController a custom overlay view to use if it invokes the camera. There are still limitations on what you can actually do in the camera view, but you can overlay it with your own information if you want.

Q: **What's with the allowEditing thing we turned on in the UIImagePickerController?**

A: The picker controller has built-in support for cropping and zooming images

if you want to use it. The allowEditing flag controls whether or not the users get a chance to move and resize their image before it's sent to the delegate. If you enable it, and the user tweaks the image, you'll be given editing information in the callback.

Q: **Do we really have to worry about the iPod Touch?**

A: Yes. When you submit your application to Apple for inclusion in the iTunes App Store, you specify the devices your application works with. If you say it works, Apple will test it on both types of devices. They also run tests where your application cannot get network access to ensure you handle that properly as well. Think defensively. Apple is going to test your application in a variety of scenarios.

Q: **Is there any way to test the camera in the simulator?**

A: No. What we've done is about as close as you can get, which is to implement

the code for the camera and test it with the photo library. You've learned a lot so far, and lots of the functionality that you're moving into has outgrown the simulator. GPS functionality, the accelerometer, speaker capabilities, all of these things can't be tested at the simulator, and to really test them, you'll need to install them on your iPhone.

Q: **What's the deal with Apple's Developer Program again?**

A: In order to install an app on your device or to submit an app to the App Store, you need to be a registered iPhone developer with Apple. The fee currently is $99. Even if you want to just install an app for your own personal use, you'll need to be registered.

Look at the appendix for more detailed directions of how installing an app on your phone actually works.

Let's show it to Bob...

Bob needs the where, in addition to the when

You've given Bob a way to record the proof he captured someone with a photo, and an easy way to note when it happened, but what about the where?

Cool—I love the pictures—but I need location info about the grab, too.

Bob has a jurisdiction problem.

There are rules about where Bob can nab criminals, so he needs to keep track of where the capture occurred.

The easiest way for Bob to keep track of these things is by recording the latitude and longitude of the capture.

Sharpen your pencil

How are two new fields going to affect the app? Use this space to show where, and on what view, the latitude and longitude info will end up.

Sketch here →

What needs to happen to the data model and the data itself?

....
....
....
....
....
....

Sharpen your pencil
Solution

Here's what we came up with for the new view and the data changes:

This will just be a label.

Since we're running low on space in the view, we're going to list the latitude and longitude together.

Location: Lat., Long.

What needs to happen to the data model and the data itself?

The database needs to be updated: we're going to be getting a latitude and longitude value in degrees. To hold them in the database, they'll need to be broken up into two new attributes for the Fugitive class: latitude and longitude.

LOCATION CONSTRUCTION

Get into it and get the app ready for the capture coordinates:

 Implement the new fields in the view for the location label and the latitude and longitude fields.

 Migrate the database again and produce the new `Fugitive` class with the latitude and longitude fields.

↖ We called them capturedlat and capturedlon and made them type "Double".

LOCATION CONSTRUCTION

Get into it and get the app ready for the capture coordinates:

✓ Implement the new fields in the view for the location label and the latitude and longitude fields.

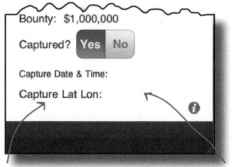

```objc
UILabel *capturedLatLon;

@property (nonatomic, retain)
  IBOutlet UILabel *capturedLatLon;
```

FugitiveDetailViewController.h

```objc
@synthesize capturedLatLon;

capturedLatLon.text = [NSString stringWithFormat:
  @"%.3f, %.3f", [fugitive.capturedLat doubleValue],
                 [fugitive.capturedLon doubleValue]];

[capturedLatLon release];
```

FugitiveDetailViewController.m

Create the outlet for the capturedLatLong label. We'll fill it in soon.

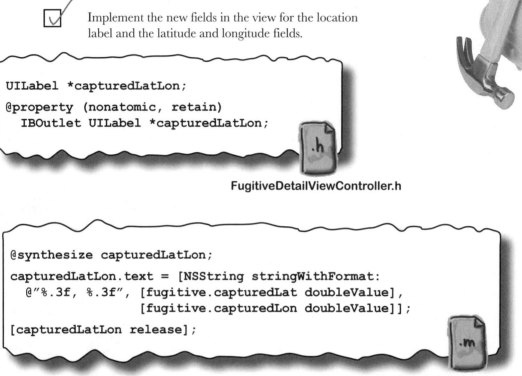

We've added the Lat Lon field here.

The values will be added here when the fugitive is captured.

Migrate the database again and produce the new `Fugitive` class with the latitude and longitude fields.

The new fields, capturedLat and catpuredLon, are both of type "Double".

We're up to iBountyHunter 4.xcdatamodel.

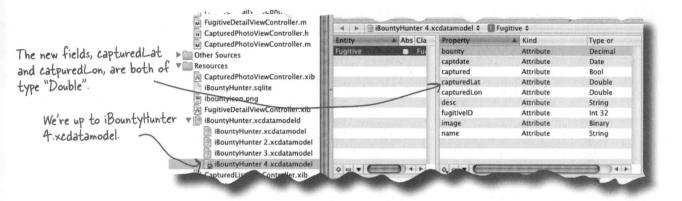

OK so I'd bet you can get that from the GPS on the iPhone, but didn't you just warn us that the iPod Touch doesn't have that?

That's true, but you've got options.

You may remember back in that pool puzzle we said something about the iPod Touch being able to handle limited location. The iPhone (and iPod Touch) have more than one way to get at where you are in the world.

Core Location can find you in a few ways

GPS is the first thought most people come up with, but the first generation iPhone didn't have GPS, and neither does the iPod Touch. That doesn't mean that you're out of options. There area actually three ways available for the iPhone to determine your location: GPS, cell tower triangulation, and Wi-Fi Positioning Service.

GPS is the most accurate, followed by cell towers and Wi-Fi. iPhones can use two or three of these, while the iPod Touch can only use Wi-Fi, but it beats nothing. Core Location actually decides which method to use based on what's available to the device and what kind of accuracy you're after. That means none of that checking for source stuff; the iPhone OS will handle it.

Allocate the CLLocation Manager

You'll need to pass in the accuracy. 10 meters is fine for Bob.

```
self.locationManager = [[CLLocationManager alloc] init];
self.locationManager.desiredAccuracy = kCLLocationAccuracyNearestTenMeters;
self.locationManager.delegate = self;
[self.locationManager startUpdatingLocation];
```

Once the locationManager has the position, it will start sending it back to the delegate for you to use.

Core Location relies on the LocationManager

To use Core Location, you simply need to create a location manager and ask it to start sending updates. It can provide position, altitude, and orientation, depending upon the device's capabilities. In order for it to send you this info, you need to provide it with a delegate as well as your required accuracy. The CLLocationManager will notify you when positions are available or if there's an error. You'll want to make sure you're also properly handing when you don't get a position from the location manager. Even if the device supports it, the users get asked before you collect location information, and can say "No" to having their position recorded (either intentionally or by accident).

BRAIN POWER

Where should we implement this code in our app?

I guess we're going to need a new header file for those Core Location constants?

Yes, and a new framework.

To keep the size of your app small, Apple breaks apart functionality into libraries. As you start adding new functionality, like Core Location, you'll need to start adding frameworks. Since the Core Location framework isn't included by default, we need to go add it.

Add a new framework

So far we've been spoiled and have used default frameworks, or they've been imported with the template. Now that we're branching out, it's time to add the Core Location framework to the app.

Highlight the frameworks folder and right-click to navigate to the **Add** → **Existing Frameworks...** option. Then select "Core Location" and **Add**.

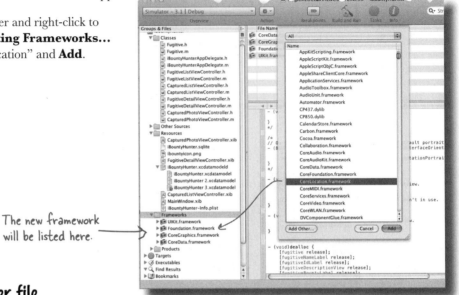

Then update the header file

We still need to declare ourselves as conforming to the CLLocationManagerDelegate protocol and add our property.

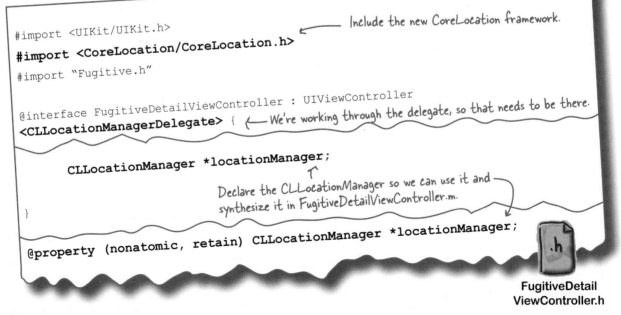

```
#import <UIKit/UIKit.h>              ← Include the new CoreLocation framework.
#import <CoreLocation/CoreLocation.h>
#import "Fugitive.h"


@interface FugitiveDetailViewController : UIViewController
<CLLocationManagerDelegate> {   ← We're working through the delegate, so that needs to be there.


      CLLocationManager *locationManager;
                              ↑
               Declare the CLLocationManager so we can use it and
               synthesize it in FugitiveDetailViewController.m.

}

@property (nonatomic, retain) CLLocationManager *locationManager;
```

**FugitiveDetail
ViewController.h**

BE the developer

Your job is to be the developer and figure out where you're going to implement Core Location into our user flow. Assume that Bob needs the location and date and time to mark a capture.

1 What method will be used to kick off Core Location in the detail view?

....

2 What happens when the location is returned to the view controller?

....

....

3 What happens if Core Location can't get anything or the user disables it?

....

....

4 When will you shut down Core Location?

....

....

5 What about other devices?

....

....

Watch it!

Core Location inhales batteries.

Making frequent calls from your app to find locations will quickly drain batteries, since it turns on the GPS/cellular/Wi-Fi receiver. That'll lead to upset users and cranky iTunes reviews. Keep it to a minimum!

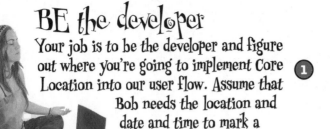

BE the developer

Your job is to be the developer and figure out where you're going to implement Core Location into our user flow. Assume that Bob needs the location and date and time to mark a capture.

1 What method will be used to kick off Core Location in the detail view?

Put the code to initialize Core Location in the viewWillAppear for the detail view.

2 What happens when the location is returned to the view controller?

We'll know the location manager can get the current position. If the user marks the fugitive as captured, we need to get the current position from the location manager and update the fugitive.

```
- (IBAction) capturedToggleChanged: (id) sender {
    NSLog(@"Toggling the captured toggle.");
    if (capturedToggle.selectedSegmentIndex == 0) {
        NSLog(@"Dude got captured.");
        NSDate *now = [NSDate date];
        fugitive.captdate = now;
        fugitive.captured = [NSNumber numberWithBool:YES];
        CLLocation *curPos = self.locationManager.location;
        fugitive.capturedLat =
          [NSNumber numberWithDouble:curPos.coordinate.latitude];
        fugitive.capturedLon =
          [NSNumber numberWithDouble:curPos.coordinate.longitude];
    }
    else {
        fugitive.captdate = nil;
        fugitive.captured = [NSNumber numberWithBool:NO];
        fugitive.capturedLat = nil;
        fugitive.capturedLon = nil;
    }
    capturedDateLabel.text = [fugitive.captdate description];
    capturedLatLon.text = [NSString stringWithFormat:@"%.3f, %.3f",
        [fugitive.capturedLat doubleValue],
        [fugitive.capturedLon doubleValue]];
}
```

We don't need the continually updating locations, so we'll ask the location manager for its last location when the user toggles the captured control.

Remember, since Core Data uses objects for everything, we're actually storing NSNumbers in the fugitive. We need to get the double value, then format it for the label.

FugitiveDetailViewController.m

3 What happens if Core Location can't get anything or the user disables it?

Since Bob needs the location info when he marks a fugitive as captured, we'll need to disable the captured switch if we can't get anything.

```objc
- (void)locationManager: (CLLocationManager *)manager
    didUpdateToLocation: (CLLocation *)newLocation
           fromLocation: (CLLocation *)oldLocation {
   NSLog(@"Core location claims to have a position.");
   capturedToggle.enabled = YES;
}

- (void)locationManager: (CLLocationManager *)manager
        didFailWithError: (NSError *)error {
   NSLog(@"Core location says no-go on the position info.");
   capturedToggle.enabled = NO;
}
```

Since the segmented controller really doesn't have a nice disabled look, you might want to consider using a UIAlertView to warn the user that they can't mark anyone as captured.

FugitiveDetailViewController.m

4 When will you shut down Core Location?

We'll shut it down when we leave the detail view.

```objc
- (void) viewWillDisappear: (BOOL) animated {
    [super viewWillDisappear:animated];

    NSLog(@"Shutting down core location...");
    [self.locationManager stopUpdatingLocation];
    self.locationManager = nil;
}
```

FugitiveDetailViewController.m

5 What about other devices?

We're good. All we do is tell Core Location the accuracy we want and it deals with the rest. So, the iPod Touch can get just the best data it can, and we'll get that.

Implement all this code and then take it for a spin...

Do this!

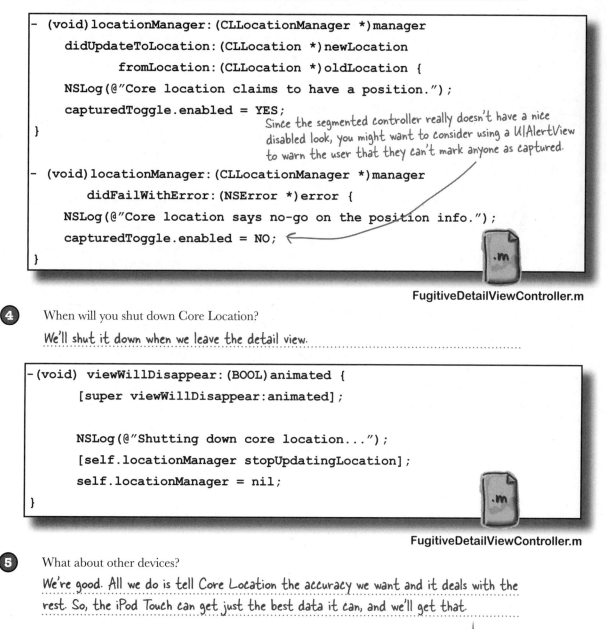

there are no
Dumb Questions

Q: We start and stop Core Location in viewWillAppear and viewWillDisappear. Is that normal?

A: It's normal to start and stop Core Location as you need it. It uses a fair amount of power while it's running, so it's best to shut it down if you don't need it. This gets a little tricky because Core Location can require some time to get its initial position information. To try and make that a little smoother for the user, we enable it as soon as the view appears to give it a head start before the user needs the location.

Q: Is there any way to speed up that initial position?

A: Core Location will try to cache previous position information so it can give you something as quickly as possible. Because of this, if you're really concerned about accuracy, you should check the timestamp sent along with the position information to make sure the position is recent enough for your needs.

Q: Does location accuracy impact things like startup time or battery usage?

A: Absolutely. The more accurate a position you ask for, the more battery Core Location will consume and it will potentially take longer to figure out. Lower fidelity information tends to come to you faster. Use whatever accuracy you need for your application, but be aware of the implications of high resolution information.

Q: Is there a way to just wait for Core Location to have a position rather than having it call back to the delegate like that?

A: No. Core Location, like a lot of other frameworks in iPhone OS, calls back asynchronously as data is available. Network access generally works this way as well. You need to make sure you keep your users informed of what's going on in the application and what they can and can't do at the moment. For example, we disable the Captured button if there's no position information available. Other options display a wait indicator (like a spinning gear) or display position status with a disabled indicator like an icon, button, or label.

Test Drive

Implementing Core Location really wasn't that hard, but making it work in the user flow required a bit more work. Now that it's all done, you should be up and running...

To operate the app here, Bob will navigate into the detail view, which will kick off the Core Location manager.

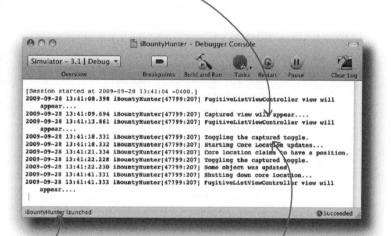

If you add capturedToggle.enabled = NO; to the viewWillAppear, then the user can't engage the control before Core Location starts returning updates.

Once a position is returned, the captured button is enabled and the fields are populated.

It's working! Bob should be psyched...

Just latitude and longitude won't work for Bob

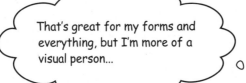

That's great for my forms and everything, but I'm more of a visual person...

It's an iPhone. A map would really be more appropriate.

What's the point of all the network connectivity and fancy graphics if we just show a text field? With just a little bit of code and the iPhone OS Map Kit, we've got something a lot more appealing in the works.

Map Kit is new with iPhone 3.0

With the latest major iPhone update, Apple opened up the API for the maps that are used on the iPhone. The data for the maps comes from Google maps, including satellite imagery.

There's lots of customization that you can do with the maps, such as how wide an area they show, what view they start with, and pins and annotations.

Logistically, using Map Kit is a lot like Core Location: you'll need a new framework and will have to `#import <MapKit/MapKit.h>` in the header file.

MKMapView is a control that pulls map information from Google Maps. You can configure it for the normal road display, satellite imagery, or a hybrid, like you see here.

Depending on the information you want to show on the map, you can create your own Views for annotations and show anything you want, like pictures, formatted text, etc.

Map Kit comes with built-in support for pushpins at specified locations, called annotations.

Watch it!

Map Kit requires a network connection.

Since Map Kit pulls imagery information from Google, you'll need to have a network connection for it to be useful. That's not a problem for the simulator (assuming your Mac is online) but it could be an issue for the iPod Touch and even the iPhone, depending on the location. Map Kit handles this gracefully, but it's something to be aware of.

How can we put that to work?

A little custom setup for the map

Like Core Location, it's not a lot of work to get basic Map Kit
support going in iBountyHunter. We'll update viewWillAppear in
the CapturedPhotoViewController to display the capture location
on a hybrid (satellite plus road information) map.

```objc
- (void) viewWillAppear:(BOOL)animated {
    [super viewWillAppear:animated];
    self.fugitiveImage.image =
        [[[UIImage alloc] initWithData:fugitive.image] autorelease];


    if ([fugitive.captured boolValue] == YES) {
        CLLocationCoordinate2D mapCenter;
        mapCenter.latitude = [fugitive.capturedLat doubleValue];
        mapCenter.longitude = [fugitive.capturedLon doubleValue];

        MKCoordinateSpan mapSpan;
        mapSpan.latitudeDelta = 0.005;
        mapSpan.longitudeDelta = 0.005;

        MKCoordinateRegion mapRegion;
        mapRegion.center = mapCenter;
        mapRegion.span = mapSpan;

        self.fugitiveMapView.region = mapRegion;
        self.fugitiveMapView.mapType = MKMapTypeHybrid;

    }
}
```

Here we'll pass in the value of the lat and lon where the fugitive was captured.

These values allow us to configure the size of the default map shown.

The size of the map is in degrees. We want the map to be pretty zoomed in.

We pull all of this information together to initialize the map.

There are a few map types; hybrid is both satellite and road information.

Here we're setting the map to our view.

CapturedPhotoViewController.m

there are no
Dumb Questions

Q: What's the difference between Core Location and Map Kit?

A: Map Kit is about displaying a map, position-sensitive information, and, user interface. Core Location is about getting you information about where **you** are. You can drag and drop a map onto your view in Interface Builder; you pass it some values and it just works.

Core Location, on the other hand, returns values to the delegate and you need to decide what to do with them. We're going to take that information from Core Location and give it to Map Kit to show us a map of the capture location, for example.

Q: Where do all these frameworks come from? What if I want one that's not on the list?

A: The frameworks are included as part of the SDK. The actual path to the frameworks varies by version and what platform you're developing for. For example, the Map Kit framework we're using is here: /Developer/Platforms/iPhoneOS.platform/Developer/SDKs/ iPhoneOS3.1.sdk/System/Library/Frameworks/MapKit.framework. In general, you should be able to add frameworks using the "Add Existing Framework" and not need to worry about a specific location, but if a framework isn't listed or you're adding a custom one, you can point Xcode to the actual path.

Exercise

Implement the map to show the area where the fugitive was captured.

 1 **Add the Map Kit framework and the #import.**
Add the framework just like we did with Core Location. While you're at it, make sure that you do the #import in the detail view to include the Map Kit header.

 2 **Configure the photo view to show the map.**
Rather than adding a whole new view, go ahead and add the map to the `CapturedPhotoView` with the image. Resize the image and the button then drag an MKMapView to the bottom half of the view.

Resize the image and the button...

...and use the bottom of the view for the MKMapView.

 3 **Add the outlets and code for the MKMapView.**
Now that you have all the support stuff in place, go ahead and add the outlets and the actual Map Kit code we gave you to make the map work. Make sure you wire up the outlet in Interface Builder.

Implement the map to show the area where the fugitive was captured.

Exercise Solution

1 **Add the Map Kit framework and the #import.**

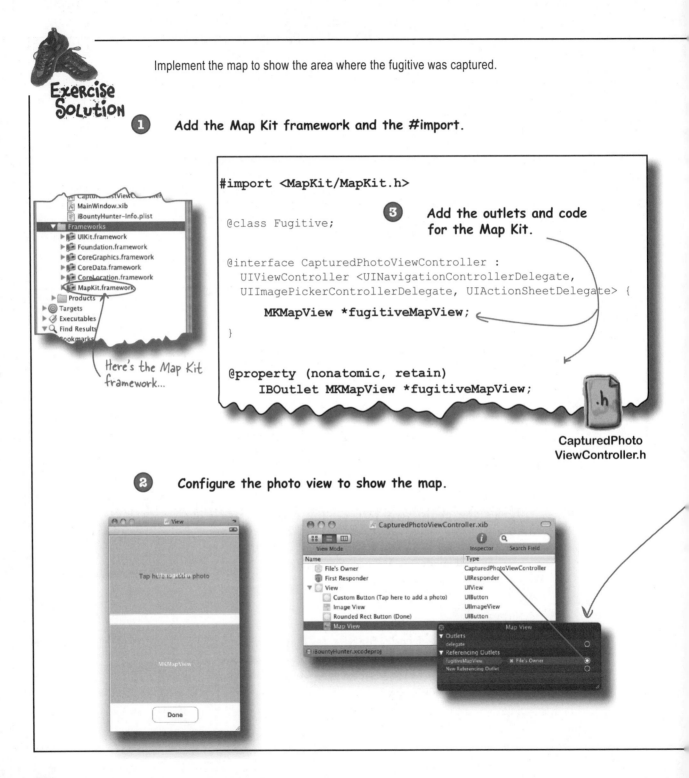

Here's the Map Kit framework...

```
#import <MapKit/MapKit.h>

@class Fugitive;

@interface CapturedPhotoViewController :
  UIViewController <UINavigationControllerDelegate,
  UIImagePickerControllerDelegate, UIActionSheetDelegate> {

    MKMapView *fugitiveMapView;

}

@property (nonatomic, retain)
    IBOutlet MKMapView *fugitiveMapView;
```

3 **Add the outlets and code for the Map Kit.**

.h

CapturedPhoto
ViewController.h

2 **Configure the photo view to show the map.**

3 Add the outlets and code for the MKMapView.

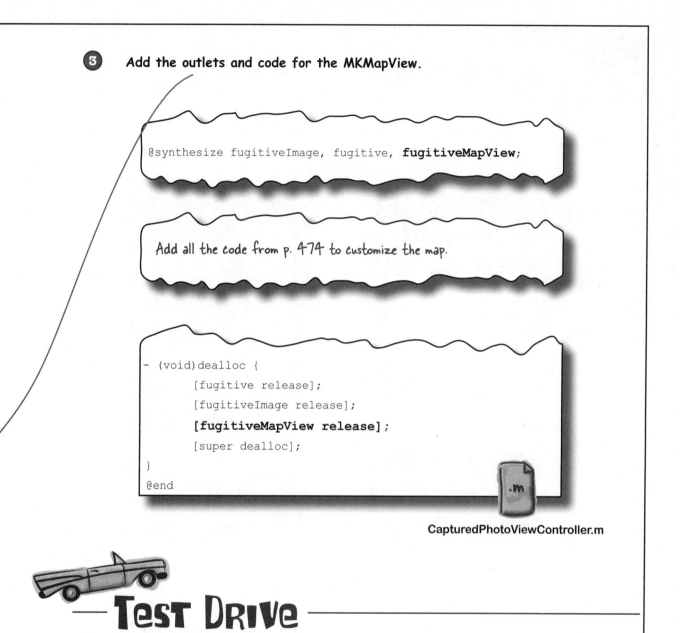

```
@synthesize fugitiveImage, fugitive, fugitiveMapView;
```

Add all the code from p. 474 to customize the map.

```
- (void)dealloc {
    [fugitive release];
    [fugitiveImage release];
    [fugitiveMapView release];
    [super dealloc];
}
@end
```

CapturedPhotoViewController.m

TEST DRIVE

Go ahead and build and run the app. You'll need to make sure that you mark a fugitive as captured, and that the lat/lon field fills in, then flip over the view to look at the map. To try out the zooming on the map you'd use the "pinching" motion on a real device. In the simulator, hold down option and then click.

Test Drive

To try out the zooming on the map, the "pinching" motion in
real life, in the simulator, hold down option and then click.

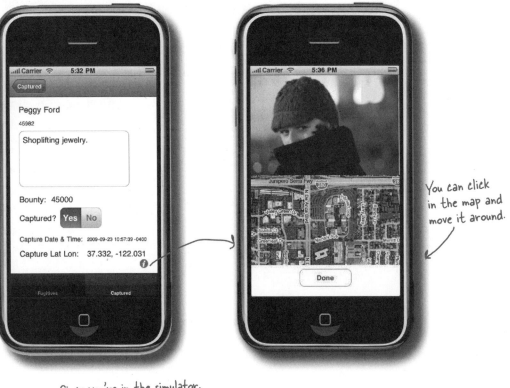

You can click
in the map and
move it around.

Since you're in the simulator,
the location will be Cupertino,
CA, no matter where you are.

**Excellent! Now all we need
is a pin to show where the
capture happened.**

Annotations require a little more ~~work~~ finesse

Annotations are the little flags that come up when you see a point of interest, represented by a pin. The catch? Incorporating annotations means conforming to the Map Kit annotation protocol. Map Kit uses an annotation protocol so that you can use your existing classes and provide them directly to Map Kit. The downside is that means we need to add code to our Fugitive class.

For an application that you expect to have to do more data migration, you should implement a separate class conforming to the protocol that has a reference to its Fugitive (composition) rather than adding code to the Fugitive class directly.

.h
Fugitive.h

```
#import <MapKit/MapKit.h>
@interface Fugitive : NSManagedObject <MKAnnotation>
{
}
#pragma mark -
#pragma mark MapKit Annotation Protocol

@property (nonatomic, readonly)
CLLocationCoordinate2D coordinate;
- (NSString *) title;
- (NSString *) subtitle;
@end
```

```
(CLLocationCoordinate2D) coordinate {
        CLLocationCoordinate2D captureCoord;
        captureCoord.latitude =
            [self.capturedLat doubleValue];
        captureCoord.longitude =
            [self.capturedLon doubleValue];

        return captureCoord;
}
- (NSString *) title {
        return self.name;
}
- (NSString *) subtitle {
        return self.desc;
}
@end
```

.m
Fugitive.m

⟡ Do this! ⟡

The protocol requires us to have a coordinate property, a title, and a subtitle. Instead of synthesizing that coordinate property, we'll implement it ourselves and just return the fugitive's position, name, etc.

Add this at the end of the viewWillAppear in CapturedPhotoViewController.m.

```
[self.fugitiveMapView addAnnotation:fugitive];
```

iBountyHunter

Test Drive

That's it! Everything should be working now. You may not have noticed as you've been working through all this code, but this app is huge and awesome!

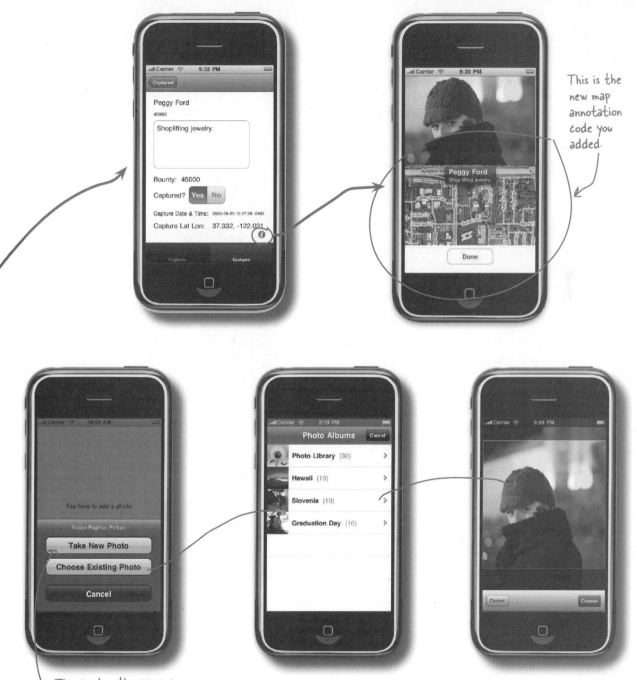

This is the
new map
annotation
code you
added.

This invokes the camera,
which you can see on your
phone, not the simulator.

Justice prevails!

AddingFunctionalitycross

One last time to flex the right side of your brain...

Across

2. UIImagePickerController gets images from the _____ and the library.
4. The _____ animation comes with UIKit.
6. The info circle is just a configured _____.
7. Additional _____ are needed for MapKit and Core Location.
9. Your app must be able to work on the _____ , too.
10. _____ sheets are a good way to get a user to pick an option.

Down

1. The camera cannot be tested in the _____.
3. The iPhone isn't the only _____ that uses apps.
5. Besides GPS and cell towers, _____ can be used to determine location.
8. _____ doesn't work without a Net connection.

AddingFunctionalitycross solution

One last time to flex the right side of your brain...

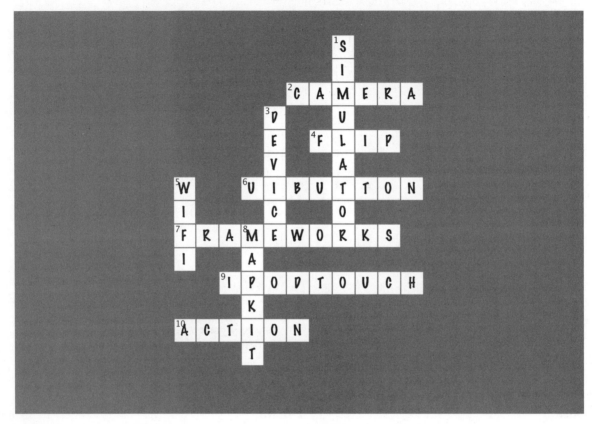

Across

2. UIImagePickerController gets images from the _____ and the library. [CAMERA]
4. The _____ animation comes with UIKit. [FLIP]
6. The info circle is just a configured _____. [UIBUTTON]
7. Additional _____ are needed for MapKit and Core Location. [FRAMEWORKS]
9. Your app must be able to work on the _____ , too. [IPODTOUCH]
10. _____ sheets are a good way to get a user to pick an option. [ACTION]

Down

1. The camera cannot be tested in the _____. [SIMULATOR]
3. The iPhone isn't the only _____ that uses apps. [DEVICE]
5. Besides GPS and cell towers, _____ can be used to determine location. [WIFI]
8. _____ doesn't work without a Net connection. [MAPKIT]

Your extras Toolbox

You've got Chapter 9 under your belt and now you've added the camera, Core Location, and Map Kit to your toolbox. For a complete list of tooltips in the book, go to http://www.headfirstlabs. com/iphonedev.

Camera

Is accessed through the UIImagePickerController.

Is not on all devices and you need to handle that.

Allows you to select and edit an image for use in your app directly from your library.

Flip Animation

Comes with UIKit.

Is the typical interface for utility apps on iPhone.

Is usually implemented as a modal view.

It's been great having you here!

We're sad to see you leave, but there's nothing like taking what you've just learned and putting it to use. You're just beginning your iPhone journey, and we've put the control in your hands. Check out the Appendix after this to find out how to get your brilliant iPhone app up and running in the iTunes App Store. We're dying to hear how things go, so ***drop us a line*** at the Head First Labs site, **http://www.headfirstlabs.com/iphonedev**, and let us know how iPhone development is paying off for **YOU!**

i leftovers

The top 6 things
(we didn't cover)

Ever feel like something's missing? We know what you mean…

Just when you thought you were done, there's more. We couldn't leave you without a few extra details, things we just couldn't fit into the rest of the book. At least, not if you want to be able to carry this book around without a metallic case and castor wheels on the bottom. So take a peek and see what you (still) might be missing out on.

#1. Internationalization and Localization

The iPhone and iPod Touch are sold in over 80 countries and support 30 languages out of the box. Depending on your application, you should consider supporting multiple languages and cultures. Internationalization is the process of identifying the parts of your application that are culture or language-specific and building your app in a way that supports multiple locales. Some of the things you should look at are:

 Nib files (views, labels, button text, etc.)

 Location or culture-specific icons and images such as flags or text

○ Included or online help and documentation

○ Static text in your application

You can change your language and locale on iPhone by going into Settings→General→ International.

Once you've identified the culture or language-specific parts of your application, the next step is to localize them. The iPhone OS has strong support for localizing resources and separates the localizable resources from the rest of the application so you can easily use a localization team or outsource the effort all together.

Up until now our resources have been included in our application in the .app directory. Once you start localizing resources, Xcode creates an lproj directory for each localization (locale) you add and moves the locale specific resources there. For example, if you provide both English and French translations of your nibs, then you will have an en.lproj (or English.lproj) and fr.lproj directories in your application.

Localizing nibs

Xcode and Interface Builder have built-in support for localizing nibs. Before you start translating anything, you need to ask Xcode to create the locale-specific directories.

Right-click on the nib you want to localize and click "Get Info".

Next click on "Make File Localizable." Xcode will turn your nib entry in the project list into a group with each localization listed beneath it. Xcode copies your original nib into your default localization.

Click on the "Make File Localizable" to ask Xcode to create the locale-based directory structure that organizes your resources.

This is the "Get Info" dialog for a nib, but use this approach to localize any generic resource like icons or images.

The next dialog you'll see allows you to add additional localizations. Select the **General** tab and click "Add Localization." In the dialog that appears, you should enter the country code of the localization you wish to add. In our example, we're adding fr for French.

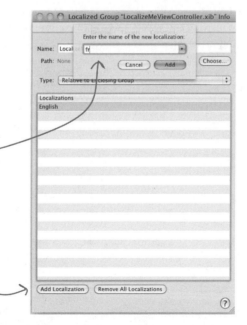

The Add Localization button asks you for the new localization name. Use two or three character country codes found in Apple's documentation. Do not use the values in the drop down list.

Now all you need to do to localize the nib is to double-click on the language you want to localize and translate any text. Remember that depending on the language, you may need to adjust layout as well.

For large projects, there is a command-line tool you can use called `ibtool` that you can use to extract all string values from a nib into an external file, then merge translations back into the nib later. This allows for bulk extraction and translation, but you need to be particularly careful about layout issues as you're not visually inspecting each nib. Once a nib has been translated, you can have Interface Builder mark it as locked to prevent any accidental changes to the text or layout that could impact your translations. See Apple's documentation on bundles and nib localization for more information.

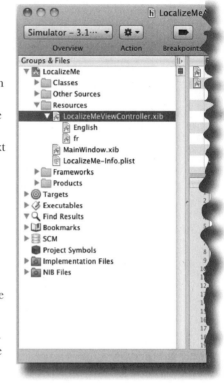

Localizing string resources

In addition to nib text, text in your application that you intend on showing the user needs to be localized as well. For example, the Action Sheet used in iBountyHunter offers the user the option to take a photo, choose an existing one, or cancel. That button text is generated programmatically and needs to be translated appropriately.

For this type of text, called string resources, the iPhone OS uses **strings files**. You'll generally have one of these files for each language you support. Each file contains a description of what the string is trying to communicate, the default language version of the string, and the translated version. Like this:

```
/* Confirms a really bad decision. */
"All In" = "All In";

/* Cancels the dialog */
"Cancel" = "Cancel";

/* Title for the important alert view */
"This is important!" = "This is important!";

/* Warns the user about impending badness. */
"This will empty your bank account. Are you sure?" = "This will empty
your bank account. Are you sure?";
```

Each string resource can have a description that helps the translators understand the context of the string.

Then each string has the original string and its translation.

Generating your strings file

You could create your strings file by hand, but a much simpler way is to have Xcode generate it for you. Xcode does this by looking for the localization macros that load the translated text. To support localized strings, you should use one of the NSLocalizedString macros, like this:

The first argument to NSLocalizedString is used as a key into the translations file. This is usually the default language for the string.

The second argument is the comment to be shown with the string in the strings file.

```
- (IBAction) pushMePressed: (id) sender {
    UIAlertView *alertView = [[UIAlertView alloc]
       initWithTitle:NSLocalizedString(@"This is important!",
                            @"Title for the important alert view")
       message:NSLocalizedString(@"This will empty your bank account.  Are you sure?",
                       @"Warns the user about impending badness.")
       delegate:nil
       cancelButtonTitle:NSLocalizedString(@"Cancel", @"Cancels the dialog")
       otherButtonTitles:NSLocalizedString(@"All In",
                                @"Confirms a really bad decision."),
       nil];
    [alertView show];
}
```

If you've used the NSLocalizedString macros in your code, you can generate your strings file by simply running the `genstrings` command at the command line, like this:

```
genstrings -o English.lproj *.m */*.m
```

You'll want to run this for each translation you support. This will create a file named Localized.strings in the specified locale directory that you can give out to translators. You'll need to add that strings file to your Xcode project like any other resource, but once it's there, the iPhone OS will look in the appropriate strings file at runtime based on the language the users select for their device.

The iPhone OS provides robust localization capabilities, including currency, time, and date presentation support; we've just scratched the surface. Apple provides several documents on internationalization and localization, including the **Introduction to Internationalization Programming Topics** document in the Xcode documentation, to help you with more complex scenarios.

Watch it!

The iPhone OS caches resources!

If you've installed your app before doing translations, it's likely that the iPhone OS has cached resources so that even after adding translations, you won't see them until you uninstall and reinstall your app!

#2. UIWebView

The iPhone OS comes with a powerful control called UIWebView that uses Web Kit to handle web content. It's basically the Safari browser in a box. You can use this control to load external URLs like a normal browser or to load local content for displaying documentation written in HTML. Despite how powerful it is, it's one of the simplest controls to use.

To create a UIWebView, simply drop one onto your view in Interface Builder and set up an outlet for it in the view controller.

Simply drag the UIWebView control onto your view to get access to a powerful browser component.

Using UIWebView

UIWebView is extremely easy to work with. To load a URL, you simply send it the loadRequest: message with the URL you want it to load, like this:

```
NSURL *url = [NSURL URLWithString:@"http://www.headfirstlabs.com"];
NSURLRequest *request = [NSURLRequest requestWithURL:url];
webView.scalesPageToFit = YES;
[webView loadRequest:request];
```

Initialize an NSURL with the actual URL we want.

We want the whole page shown initially, so we enable scalesPageToFit.

UIWebView properties

Once you've loaded a URL, you can then use the `loading` property to find out if UIWebView is currently trying to load a URL. To stop it, simply send it the `stopLoading` message. To control how the page is shown, you have a few options. You can turn off the `detectsPhoneNumbers` property to tell it to ignore phone numbers in the page its displaying (otherwise it turns them into hyperlinks to the phone application). By default, UIWebView will render the page full size. However, you can enable the `scalesPageToFit` property to have it scale the URL's content to fit the screen. If this property is enabled, users can use the usual pinch gesture to zoom and pan around the contents.

UIWebView has built-in support for navigation history as well. It will set its canGoBack and canGoForward properties based on whether there are pages in its forward or back history. Typically you use those to enable or disable forward and back buttons if you want navigation support. UIWebView knows what the history looks like, so you can simply send it the goBack: or goFoward: mesages and it will handle the rest.

Loading generated content

You can also use UIWebView to load locally generated content (such as displaying HTML help files or reports) by asking it to load an HTML string, like this:

```
NSString *html = @"<html><body><h1>Look what I can do!</h1></body></html>";
[webView loadHTMLString:html baseURL:[NSURL URLWithString:@"file:///."]];
```

The UIWebView supports a delegate, too

If you want to know more about what's going on with the UIWebView, you can conform to the UIWebViewDelegate protocol and set the delegate on your web view. The delegate protocol lets you get notified when loading starts and stops as well as gives you an opportunity to inspect links before they are followed. If a UIWebView has a delegate, it will send the delegate the `webView:should StartLoadWithRequest:navigationType:` message when the user taps on a link before actually following it. You can return NO if the web view shouldn't follow the URL.

#3. Device orientation and view rotation

On the surface, the iPhone OS makes handling screen rotation simple. The iPhone and iPod Touch each contain an accelerometer that lets the device detect orientation. When you build an application using UIKit, the iPhone OS asks the active view controller if it can handle rotating. The iPhone OS supports the following orientations:

Interface Orientation Constant	Description
UIInterfaceOrientationPortrait	The typical orientation with the home button at the bottom. By default this is the only orientation view controllers support.
UIInterfaceOrientationPortraitUpsideDown	Like the portrait orientation but with the home button at the top of the device.
UIInterfaceOrientationLandscapeLeft	The device is held on its side with the home button on the right.
UIInterfaceOrientationLandscapeRight	The device is held on its side with the home button on the left.

The view controller tells the iPhone OS what orientations it supports

When the iPhone OS detects that the device has rotated to one of those views, it calls `shouldAutorotateToInterfaceOrientation:` on the active view controller and passes in the new orientation. If your view can handle the given orientation, it simply returns YES. If not, it returns NO. If you don't explicitly implement this method, the default implementation returns NO for all rotations except `UIInterfaceOrientationPortrait`.

When the iPhone OS needs to rotate to a new orientation, it will notify the view controller by sending it the willRotateToInterfaceOrientation: message with the duration that it will animate the transition. You can use this method to disable buttons or timers or anything else that could cause a problem while the view is changing. Once the animation is complete, you'll receive the didRotateFromInterfaceOrientation: message, where you can reenable everything.

The iPhone simulator supports rotations so you can test your application in each orientation. To rotate the simulator you can either use Hardware→Rotate Right (or Left) or ⌘→ (or Left).

Handling view rotations

The easiest way to handle view rotations is to take advantage of UIKit's ability to autosize your controls. To do this, select a control then bring up the inspector on the Ruler page (⌘3). From here, you can select autosizing anchors, basically edges of the control that will be anchored in place. By configuring the autosizing information, you can have UIKit automatically resize the control when the view size changes.

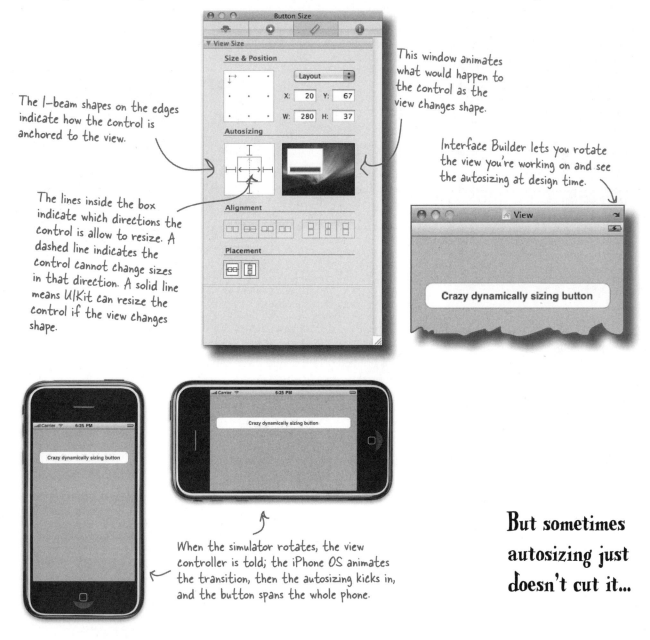

The I-beam shapes on the edges indicate how the control is anchored to the view.

This window animates what would happen to the control as the view changes shape.

Interface Builder lets you rotate the view you're working on and see the autosizing at design time.

The lines inside the box indicate which directions the control is allow to resize. A dashed line indicates the control cannot change sizes in that direction. A solid line means UIKit can resize the control if the view changes shape.

When the simulator rotates, the view controller is told; the iPhone OS animates the transition, then the autosizing kicks in, and the button spans the whole phone.

But sometimes autosizing just doesn't cut it...

Handling rotation with two different views

Depending on your application, your view may be sufficiently complex that autosizing just doesn't get you what you want for the rotated view. Alternatively, some applications present a totally different perspective to the user in landscape mode than in portrait mode.

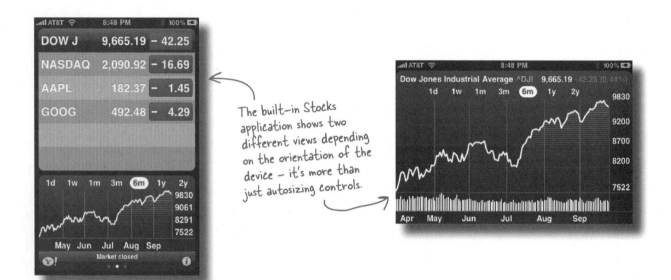

The built-in Stocks application shows two different views depending on the orientation of the device — it's more than just autosizing controls.

To support multiple views, you'll need to either define multiple UIViews in your nib or create separate nibs. Then, when your view controller is notified of the rotation, you can change your `self.view` to the appropriate view depending on the target orientation.

Watch it!

You can only have one object for any given IBOutlet!

If you have similar controls (but in different positions or altered styles) in your views, you'll need separate outlets for each control.

#4. View animations

If you've spent any time with an iPhone or iPod Touch you know that smooth transitions and graceful animations define the user experience. In the applications we've built so far, we've only touched on a few basic animations (like the flip animation used in iBountyHunter). However, everything from adding and removing table rows to sliding controls around the screen can be animated.

Animating table view updates

If you're going to add or remove multiple rows in a table view, you can ask it to provide a smooth animation (as well as a more efficient handling of updating the table view itself) by sending it the beginUpdates message before you start manipulating the data, then an endUpdates when you're finished, like this:

```
[self.tableView beginUpdates];
[self.tableView insertRowsAtIndexPaths:insertIndexPaths
    withRowAnimation:UITableViewRowAnimationRight];

[self.tableView deleteRowsAtIndexPaths:deleteIndexPaths
    withRowAnimation:UITableViewRowAnimationFade];

[self.tableView endUpdates];
```

When inserting multiple rows you can use the insertRowsAtIndexPaths to tell the tableView the new indexPaths you want to add. The tableView will immediately ask the datasource and delegate for cell information for those new rows and, if you specify the animation information, they'll smoothly slide in to the table.

The beginUpdates and endUpdates tell the tableView that you're about to make multiple changes so it won't actually animate anything until it gets the endUpdates call; then everything (the insertions and deletions) will be animated at once.

Animating view and control changes

Similar to table views, UIViews have built-in support for smoothly animating changes to several of their properties. You simply need to tell the view that you want it to animate a change by sending it the beginAnimations message, describe the end point of the change, then ask it to start the transition by sending it the commitAnimations message. The following UIView properties can be animated automatically:

UIView property	Description
frame	The physical rectangle that describes the view – the view's origin and size – in the superview's coordinate system.
bounds	The origin and size of the view in local coordinates.
centerpoint	The center of the view in the superview's coordinates.
transform	Any transformations (rotations, translations, etc.) applied to the view.
alpha	The transparency of the view.

#5. Accelerometer

One of the most versatile pieces of hardware in the iPhone and iPod Touch is the accelerometer. The accelerometer allows the device to detect acceleration and the pull of gravity along three axes. With just a few lines of code, you can tell whether the device is right-side up, upside down, laying flat on a table, etc. You can even detect how quickly the device is changing direction.

All you need is the UIAccelerometer

Getting orientation information from your device is straightforward. There's a shared UIAccelerometer instance you can access. Like many other iPhone OS classes, the UAccelerometer has a delegate protocol, UIAccelerometerDelegate, that declares a single method for receiving acceleration information. The class you want to receive that acceleration information should conform to the UIAccelerometerDelegate protocol and implement didAccelerate: method:

```
- (void)accelerometer:(UIAccelerometer *)accelerometer
didAccelerate:(UIAcceleration *)acceleration;
```

You'll receive a reference to the accelerometer along with an instance of a UIAcceleration class, which contains the actual acceleration information.

To receive acceleration information you simply need to tell the accelerometer about the delegate and how frequently to send acceleration information, like this:

```
self.accelerometer = [UIAccelerometer sharedAccelerometer];
self.accelerometer.delegate = self;
self.accelerometer.updateInterval = 0.5f;
```

Get the shared accelerometer...

...then configure the delegate and an update rate in seconds. We're asking for two updates a second.

Each UIAcceleration object contains acceleration information along the x, y, and z axes and a timestamp that the data was collected. In a simple example, you can update labels with the acceleration information, like this:

```
- (void)accelerometer:(UIAccelerometer *)accelerometer
didAccelerate:(UIAcceleration *)acceleration {
        self.xOutput.text = [NSString stringWithFormat:@"%.4f", acceleration.x];
        self.yOutput.text = [NSString stringWithFormat:@"%.4f", acceleration.y];
        self.zOutput.text = [NSString stringWithFormat:@"%.4f", acceleration.z];
}
```

Understanding the device acceleration

First, the bad news. The simulator doesn't simulate the accelerometer at all. You'll get no information back, regardless of how much you shake your Mac. You'll need to install the application on a real device to get actual accelerometer information back. But once you do...

+Y

The accelerometer returns acceleration along a particular axis. If the device is held still, the pull of gravity is defined as 1.0 along some axis.

If you shake the phone you can get an acceleration value greater than 1. To detect a shake (to clear the screen for example) you can watch for an acceleration value greater than "normal". It's not hard to get an acceleration value above 1, but above, say, 1.5 requires some effort.

-X   +X

+Z

The Z axis runs through the display of the phone, with positive Z pointing out of the front of the display. Place the device face up on the table and your Z axis value will be -1.

Hold the device in landscape orientation with the home button to the left and you'll get an x value of +1.

Held upright, you'll get nearly -1.0 along the Y axis (the acceleration.y value will be just about -1).

-Y

If you're building a typical view-based application, UIKit hides a lot of the need for the accelerometer by letting you know about orientation changes and automatically providing undo/redo when the user shakes the phone. The accelerometer is most useful for custom-drawn applications like games (steering or balance) and utility applications (levels).

#6. A word or two about gaming...

iPhone games are a huge market and get played a lot, but they are also pretty advanced applications. It's outside of the scope of our book to get into those applications—which can use multitouch interactions, Quartz and OpenGL graphics, and peer to peer networking—but here we'll give you a quick pass at the technologies that you can use and where to find more information about them.

Multitouch

You probably noticed that we only used one of the possible events that can be triggered for a button in our apps, the **touch up inside** event. The iPhone is capable of detecting up to five finger touches at a time and can interpret how each of those fingers are interacting with the screen with several different types of events.

In addition to touches, the iPhone can detect swipes and gestures that can be configured as well. By defining the length and direction of a swipe, you can create lots of different ways to interact with your application.

Pinching is a custom gesture that Apple uses in many of its default applications, most notably Safari, to zoom in and out of a view. It is just registering for a two-finger touch and keeping track of the change in the distance between them: if it increases, zoom out, if it decreases, zoom in.

Using these events means that you can create custom interfaces, not just touching buttons, for your user. Working with multitouch means that your view needs to be configured to be a multitouch view, and then you need code to work with each different type of event that you're interested in leveraging.

Working with these events requires working with the responder chain (see the `UIResponder` class reference) and the `UIEvents` class reference.

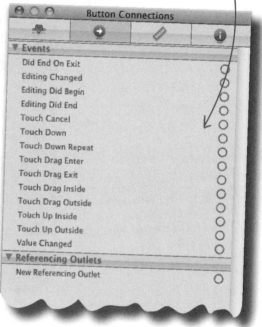

These are all of the button events than can be triggered.

Quartz and OpenGL

Quartz and OpenGL are the two ways to create graphics on the iPhone and they are both big enough to be books on their own, but here's a small sample of what you'd be dealing with.

Quartz

Ed note: Now there's a fine idea...

Quartz is the simpler of the two, allowing you to draw in two dimensions directly into the view. The drawing code uses the `Core Graphics Framework` and renders directly into the view. It follows a **painter's model**, which means that the order of commands is important. The first thing drawn will be covered up with a subsequent drawing in the same location. Quartz can handle shading, color, and interfacing with other image and video types.

The **Quartz 2D Programming Guide** in the developer documentation has a lot of information to help get you started.

OpenGL

OpenGL can work in two or three-dimensional graphics and is significantly more complex, but that means that you have more flexibility to work with. It is a well-established, cross platform library that has been implemented for mobile devices with OpenGL ES, and is used through the `OpenGL ES Framework.`

You can use it to draw lines, polygons, and objects, and animate them as well. A good place to get started is with the **OpenGL ES Programming Guide for iPhone OS** in the developer documentation.

Game Kit

New with the iPhone OS 3, the `GameKit` framework allows you to use both peer to peer networking and voice over bluetooth to facilitate interaction with other devices within game play. This functionality does not exist for the first generation iPhone, iPod Touch, or the simulator alone.

Similar to the image picker, there is a `GKPeerPickerController` that provides a standard interface for finding other devices running your application and establishing a connection. After that connection is established, you can transmit data or voice between devices.

A good place to get started is with the **GameKit Programming Guide** to leverage this new functionality in your app.

ii preparing an app for distribution

Get ready for the App Store

It's time to take this thing out for a spin, don't you think?

You want to get your app in the App Store, right?

So far, we've basically worked with apps in the simulator, which is fine. But to get things to the next level, you'll need to install an app on an actual iPhone or iPod Touch before applying to get it in the App Store. And the only way to do that is to register with Apple as a developer. Even then, it's not just a matter of clicking a button in Xcode to get an app you wrote on your personal device. To do that, it's time to talk with Apple.

Apple has rules

We've talked about the HIG, and how stringent Apple can be through the approval process—they're protecting their platform. Part of that is keeping track of what goes on your own iPhone, even when it's stuff you've written yourself.

Here we're going to give you an overview of how you can get an app onto your device, and then, in turn, ready for submission. We can't get into the nitty gritty of the full process—for that you need to be a member of the iPhone Development Program and pay the $99 fee.

The iPhone Development Guide in the Xcode documentation has some more good information that you can look at before you join the Development Program.

Start at the Apple Developer Portal

The Developer Portal, where you first downloaded the SDK, is also your hub for managing all the parts of electronic signatures that you'll need to get an app up and running on your iPhone.

First get your Development Certificate

Getting through the process to go from having your app in Xcode to installing it on an iPhone or iPod Touch for testing means that you need a Development Certificate and a Provisioning Profile. This certificate is signed by you and Apple to register you as a developer. It creates a public and a private key, and the private key is stored on the keychain app on your Mac. Here's how getting that certificate works.

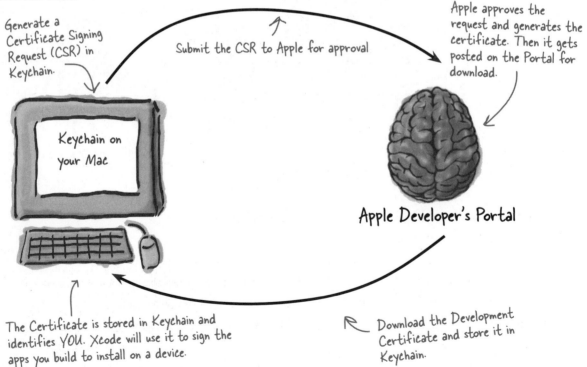

Generate a Certificate Signing Request (CSR) in Keychain.

Submit the CSR to Apple for approval

Apple approves the request and generates the certificate. Then it gets posted on the Portal for download.

Keychain on your Mac

Apple Developer's Portal

The Certificate is stored in Keychain and identifies YOU. Xcode will use it to sign the apps you build to install on a device.

Download the Development Certificate and store it in Keychain.

The Provisioning Profile pulls it all together

Now that you have a Development Certificate in place, to complete the process you need a Provisioning Profile. That electronic document ties the app (through an iPhone application ID), the developer, and the certificate together for installation onto the device.

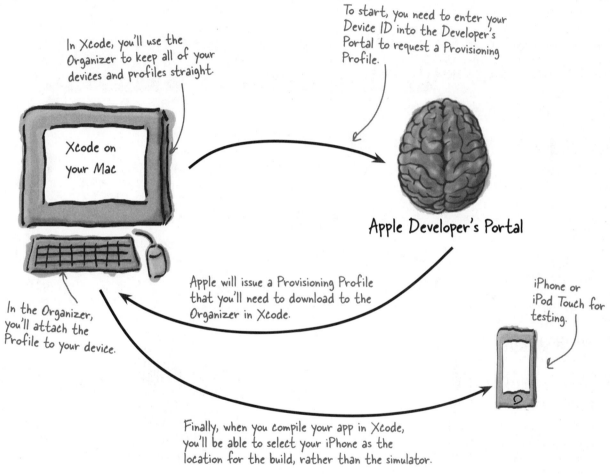

In Xcode, you'll use the Organizer to keep all of your devices and profiles straight.

To start, you need to enter your Device ID into the Developer's Portal to request a Provisioning Profile.

Xcode on your Mac

Apple Developer's Portal

In the Organizer, you'll attach the Profile to your device.

Apple will issue a Provisioning Profile that you'll need to download to the Organizer in Xcode.

iPhone or iPod Touch for testing.

Finally, when you compile your app in Xcode, you'll be able to select your iPhone as the location for the build, rather than the simulator.

Watch it!

You can't get a Provisioning Profile without a Development Certificate.

Keep track in the Organizer

The Organizer is a tool that comes with Xcode that we haven't been able to talk much about, but it is key for keeping all of this electronic paperwork straight. In Xcode, go to the **Window** → **Organizer** menu option.

If you have your iPhone plugged in, you'll get a similar display.

This Identifier is required for a Provisioning Profile and is unique to each device.

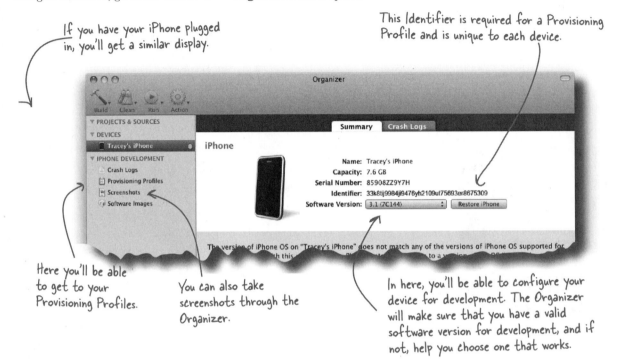

Here you'll be able to get to your Provisioning Profiles.

You can also take screenshots through the Organizer.

In here, you'll be able to configure your device for development. The Organizer will make sure that you have a valid software version for development, and if not, help you choose one that works.

A few final tips...

This quick overview gives you an idea of how the process works, but you need to get into the Developer Program to learn all the details. Our goal here was just to help you see the big picture of the process.

A couple of things to be aware of. First, when you're developing as part of a team, the team admin has to be involved in many of these steps. Second, you need to go through this process to install *anything* on your device, regardless of whether you plan to release it to the world or not.

And finally, what about the app store? Once you've joined the Developer Program, and the application has been tested, then you can submit it for approval.

More Information

After you've joined the Developer Program, get into the Developer's Portal and look for the iPhone Development Program User Guide.

It has a lot of good information to get you through the process.

Index

Symbols

& (ampersand), indicating address reference, 405

<> (angle brackets), enclosing protocols, 94

* (asterisk), preceding pointer types, 94

@ (at-sign) symbol, for NSStrings, 30, 147

: (colon), in named arguments, 117

- (minus sign), preceding instance methods, 95, 116

+ (plus sign), preceding static or class methods, 95, 116

[] (square brackets), enclosing message passing, 115

A

accelerometer, 17, 498–499

accessors
  auto-generated, 95, 96, 99–100, 109
  multithread safety and, 98

action methods
  connecting events to, 24–25
  writing code for, 18–20

action sheets, 452–455

aesthetics, importance of, 43. *See also* iPhone apps, designing

ampersand (&), indicating address reference, 405

angle brackets (<>), enclosing protocols, 94

animations
  flip animations, 434–438, 485
  view animations, 497

API documentation, 56

app layout, sketching, 40–43
  for DrinkMixer app example, 135
  for iBountyHunter app example, 306–307, 309–311, 363, 434, 460
  for iDecide app example, 7
  for InstaTwit app example, 41–43

App Store, submitting apps to, 2, 199–200, 237, 504–506

app templates. *See* templates

Apple Developer's Program, registering with, 456, 457, 504

Application Programming Guide, 44

application resources, 5, 11, 12, 35, 159

apps. *See* desktop apps; iPhone apps; mobile apps

arrays, 64
  of dictionaries, 171–172, 189–192, 194–197
  mutable, 110, 144–145, 147
  of strings, 149–153

assign property attribute, 98, 100, 129

asterisk (*), preceding pointer types, 94

atomic keyword, 98

at-sign (@) symbol, for NSStrings, 30, 147

autorelease pool, 101

B

bartending app example. *See* DrinkMixer app example

Boolean data type, 332

borders, using buttons as, 368

bounty hunter app example. *See* iBountyHunter app example

D

datasource, 58–59, 63–67, 87. *See also* Core Data; datasource under specific example apps

Date data type, 332

debugging, 175–181, 183, 237
- breakpoints for, 178–181, 187
- call stack, viewing, 188
- commands for, 177
- console for, 176
- continue command, 187
- DrinkMixer app example, 175–181, 183, 187–190, 273–274
- next command, 187
- walking through code, 187

Decimal data type, 332

decision app example. *See* iDecide app example

delegate, 58–59, 63–64, 68–69, 87

desktop apps, differences from mobile apps, 3–4

Detail View, Xcode, 12

detail views
- for DrinkMixer app example, 155–164, 169, 198, 215–222
- for iBountyHunter app example, 362–371, 394–402, 434–438, 460–470, 472–477, 479

developer, registering with Apple as, 456, 457, 504

Development Certificate, 504

device orientation, 494–496

dictionaries, 237
- arrays of, 171–172, 189–192, 194–197
- key names in separate file for, 198
- saving, 286
- valueForKey compared to objectForKey, 198

disclosure indicators, 200–203

display. *See* screen

Documents directory, 358–359, 361

DrinkMixer app example
- Add button, 209–213
- Cancel button, 229, 232–233, 235, 279
- datasource
  - creating, 147
  - users adding data to, 207–226, 265–269
- debugging, 175–181, 183, 187–190, 273–274
- delegate, 147
- detail view, 155–164, 169, 198, 215–222
- disclosure indicators, 200–203
- Edit button, 288, 291, 292, 299
- keyboard for adding data, 227, 240–243, 248–264
- modal view, 224–226, 230–233
- navigation controller
  - adding Add button to, 209–213
  - back button in, 138, 173
  - creating, 136–137
  - for modal view, 230–233
  - switching between views, 167–168
- notifications
  - for app quitting, 282–284, 286
  - for keyboard displaying, 250–264
- plist of dictionaries for detail view data, 171–172, 189–192, 194–197
- plist of strings for table view data, 149–153
- plists, saving when app quits, 282–284
- project, creating, 136–137
- requirements for, 132–135
- Save button, 229, 232–233, 235
- scroll view for adding data, 242–247, 257–263, 265–269
- sketch for, 135
- submitting to App Store, 199–200, 205
- switching between views, 165–169
- table view, 140–143, 187
  - cell labels for, 147
  - code for, customizing, 141–145
  - created by navigation template, 137, 139
  - disclosure indicators in, 200–203
  - notifying of new data, 276, 279
  - resorting, 280

Q

Quartz, 501

R

read and write permissions for data, 358

readonly property attribute, 98, 129

readwrite property attribute, 96, 98, 129

reference counting, 99, 101, 102, 109

references, listing for items in views, 23, 24

release method?, 99, 101, 106, 110

reloadData message, 276

reservations mystery, 270, 275

resources, caching of, 491

Resources files, 5, 11, 12, 35, 159

retain count. *See* reference counting

retain method?, 99, 110

retain property attribute, 98, 99, 129

root view, 11, 52–53

rotation of view, 494–496

S

screen
    capabilities of, 4
    resolution of, 7
    rotation of, 494–496

scroll views, 242–247, 257–263, 265–269

SDK, 8. *See also* Instruments; Interface Builder; Simulator; Xcode

segmented controls, 396, 398–402

selectors, 120

setter methods. *See* accessors

Settings page, 43

Simulator, 30
    app crashing on real iPhone but not in Simulator, 110
    differences from real iPhone, 17
    limitations of, 17, 457
    testing apps in, 13, 16–17

sketching app layout, 40–43
    for DrinkMixer app example, 135
    for iBountyHunter app example, 306–307, 309–311, 363, 434, 460
    for iDecide app example, 7
    for InstaTwit app example, 41–43

SQLLite database, 337

square brackets ([]), enclosing message passing, 115

stack, debugger. *See* call stack

static methods, plus sign (+) indicating, 95

status bar, 7

String data type, 332

strings, 30, 124–126, 332
    arrays of, 149–153
    localizing, 490–491
    mutable, 110

switches, 400

@synthesize keyword, 77, 96, 98

T

tab bar controller, 307, 312, 375
    creating, 313–315, 320–321
    embedding in UIWindow, 324
    icons for, 321
    notifications for changing tabs, 321
    number of views in, 321

U

Get even more for your money.

Join the O'Reilly Community, and register the O'Reilly books you own.It's free, and you'll get:

- 40% upgrade offer on O'Reilly books
- Membership discounts on books and events
- Free lifetime updates to electronic formats of books
- Multiple ebook formats, DRM FREE
- Participation in the O'Reilly community
- Newsletters
- Account management
- 100% Satisfaction Guarantee

Signing up is easy:

1. **Go to: oreilly.com/go/register**
2. **Create an O'Reilly login.**
3. **Provide your address.**
4. **Register your books.**

Note: English-language books only

To order books online:

oreilly.com/order_new

For questions about products or an order:

orders@oreilly.com

To sign up to get topic-specific email announcements and/or news about upcoming books, conferences, special offers, and new technologies:

elists@oreilly.com

For technical questions about book content:

booktech@oreilly.com

To submit new book proposals to our editors:

proposals@oreilly.com

Many O'Reilly books are available in PDF and several ebook formats. For more information:

oreilly.com/ebooks

O'REILLY®

Spreading the knowledge of innovators   www.oreilly.com

Buy this book and get access to the online edition for 45 days—for free!

Head First iPhone Development

By Dan Pilone & Tracey Pilone
October 2009, $44.99
ISBN 9780596803544

With Safari Books Online, you can:

Access the contents of thousands of technology and business books

- Quickly search over 7000 books and certification guides
- Download whole books or chapters in PDF format, at no extra cost, to print or read on the go
- Copy and paste code
- Save up to 35% on O'Reilly print books
- **New!** Access mobile-friendly books directly from cell phones and mobile devices

Stay up-to-date on emerging topics before the books are published

- Get on-demand access to evolving manuscripts.
- Interact directly with authors of upcoming books

Explore thousands of hours of video on technology and design topics

- Learn from expert video tutorials
- Watch and replay recorded conference sessions

To try out Safari and the online edition of this book FREE for 45 days,
go to *www.oreilly.com/go/safarienabled* and enter the coupon code APIUREH.
To see the complete Safari Library, visit safari.oreilly.com.

Spreading the knowledge of innovators   safari.oreilly.com